The
Regime
in World War I

ALSO BY MICHAEL A. EGGLESTON
AND FROM MCFARLAND

*Exiting Vietnam: The Era of Vietnamization
and American Withdrawal
Revealed in First-Person Accounts* (2014)

*President Lincoln's Recruiter:
General Lorenzo Thomas and the United States
Colored Troops in the Civil War* (2013)

*The Tenth Minnesota Volunteers, 1862–1865:
A History of Action in the Sioux Uprising and the Civil War,
with a Regimental Roster* (2012)

The 5th Marine Regiment Devil Dogs in World War I

A History and Roster

MICHAEL A. EGGLESTON

McFarland & Company, Inc., Publishers
Jefferson, North Carolina

LIBRARY OF CONGRESS CATALOGUING-IN-PUBLICATION DATA

Names: Eggleston, Michael A., 1937–
Title: The 5th Marine Regiment Devil Dogs in World War I :
a history and roster / Michael A. Eggleston.
Other titles: Fifth Marine Regiment Devil Dogs in World War I |
5th Marine Regiment Devil Dogs in World War One |
5th Marine Regiment Devil Dogs in World War 1
Description: Jefferson, North Carolina : McFarland & Company, Inc.,
Publishers, 2016. | Includes bibliographical references and index.
Identifiers: LCCN 2016007439 | ISBN 9780786497492
(softcover : alkaline paper) ∞
Subjects: LCSH: United States. Marine Corps. Marine
Regiment, 5th. | World War, 1914–1918—Regimental histories—
United States. | World War, 1914–1918—Campaigns—Germany. |
World War, 1914–1918—Registers. | United States. Marine Corps—
Registers. | Marines—United States—Registers. | World War,
1914–1918—Personal narratives, American. | Marines—
United States—Biography. | Veterans—United States—Biography.
Classification: LCC D570.348 5th .E33 2016 | DDC 940.4/5973—dc23
LC record available at https://lccn.loc.gov/2016007439

BRITISH LIBRARY CATALOGUING DATA ARE AVAILABLE

ISBN (print) 978-0-7864-9749-2
ISBN (ebook) 978-1-4766-2261-3

© 2016 Michael A. Eggleston. All rights reserved

*No part of this book may be reproduced or transmitted in any form
or by any means, electronic or mechanical, including photocopying
or recording, or by any information storage and retrieval system,
without permission in writing from the publisher.*

On the cover: World War I U.S. Marine lithograph,
First in France, The U.S. Marines in World War I,
1917, John A. Coughlin (Library of Congress)

Printed in the United States of America

*McFarland & Company, Inc., Publishers
Box 611, Jefferson, North Carolina 28640
www.mcfarlandpub.com*

In remembrance of
Raymond P. Rogers, U.S.M.C., 1899–1976,
Marine Veteran of World War I

Table of Contents

Acknowledgments

I would like to thank my wife, Margaret, for her endless patience and efforts to comment on and edit this book. Without her help, this book would not have been possible. I would also like to express my gratitude to all who contributed to this book or helped in its preparation: Forrest Ashcraft, Marty Ganderson, Bill Garbett, Mary Gilchrist, Jack Harrigan, Danté Puccetti, Mitch Ryder of the 2nd Division Association, Frances Rogers, Professor Robert Wilensky, and the USMC History Division, Quantico, Virginia.

I would also like to express my appreciation to historian George B. Clark, who edited this history as he did the following books that contributed significantly to this history:

Jackson, Warren R. *His Time in Hell, a Texas Marine in France: The World War I Memoir of Warren R. Jackson.* Edited by G.B Clark. Novato, CA: Presidio, 2001.

Mackin, Elton E. *Suddenly We Didn't Want to Die.* Edited by G.B. Clark. Novato, CA: Presidio, 1993.

Thomason, John W. *The United States Army Second Division Northwest of Chateau Thierry in World War I.* Edited by G.B. Clark. Jefferson, NC: McFarland, 2006.

Preface

In a *60 Minutes* interview on 4 November 2012, historian David McCullough provided his insight:

> The only way to teach history, to write history, to bring people into the magic of transforming yourself into other times is through the vehicle of the story. ***It isn't just the chronology; it's about people. History is human.*** Jefferson said "when in the course of human events ..." "Human" is the operative word here.

This book tells the human story of the members of the U.S. 5th Marine Regiment and others involved in World War I and its aftermath. This book was written for people who want to learn more about World War I. For this reason, I summarize some of the background and history of the war beyond the time frame and context indicated in the title. That way, a common frame of reference is established before I launch into specific events. Similarly, I address two topics in depth that affected all servicemen and civilians, not just the Marines. One topic is the influenza pandemic that had a profound effect on the war in 1918, and the other is the Bonus March in 1932 that affected all veterans after World War I. This history is organized chronologically by the battles and other events in which the 5th Regiment served. Frequently, the history and memoirs of the 6th Marine Regiment are included, because the two regiments served together. I have avoided specific details about generals and units in favor of broad summaries needed as an introduction to the activities of the 5th and 6th Marine Regiments that composed the 4th Marine Brigade. I am indebted to those who provided the recollections incorporated in this book.

Many times the relevance of accounts depends upon who is talking and when. At the risk of being tedious, I have taken pains to insert date, time, and name of individual relating what he saw. Without that, it is difficult to figure out what was occurring. This history is different from others since it weaves the reflections of individual Marines with the official accounts of the battles. Many of the extracts from unpublished memoirs and letters are seen in print for the first time. These are from family records and of documents that I was fortunate to purchase for this history at auctions at estate sales. Letters home from France all had to pass the censor, so this restricted the author in what he could write. An example of letters purchased is the following one from Sergeant Richard Cleveland to his friend Helen Ericson. Both had contracted influenza but survived. While the influenza pandemic was a frequent topic in letters from both sides of the Atlantic, this letter avoids mention of the pandemic in favor of war news. Occasionally, letters provide new information about the war that got past the censor. In August 1918 Cleveland wrote that German artillery, the "Big Bertha"[1] German heavy siege gun, was still hitting Paris after most histories indicate that it had been shipped back to Germany:

Aug 12, 1918

Paris, France

Dearest Little Girl O' Mine—

Am sort of "fatigue" to-night. There were many "things" coming in to-day and had much to do. Things are moving very fast here. You have no idea. Simply marvelous—and believe me the fellows are giving all that's in them ... "Bertha" has been busy lately–Just paying her regular visits. She doesn't cause much excitement.... Would love to have you with me in Paris—someday. I know you would like it—nearly everyone does -

Good-night my dearest—
Best love and kisses—
Dick[2]

Raymond P. Rogers in France, 1918 (author's collection).

I have also quoted memoirs of others who served in World War I. Among the best are the memoirs of Raymond Rogers, 2nd Battalion, 5th Marines, and Elton Mackin, 1st Battalion, 5th Marines, published twenty years after his death. Rogers related his recollections to his family years after the events of World War I. Mackin was a highly decorated Marine who received the Navy Cross and other valor awards for his service in World War I. Mackin spent years refining his memoir that was published in 1993. Many of his quotes are contained within this book.

The story of this war is told through the recollections of Mackin, Rogers, and many others. The reader will find many names of World War I Marines in this book. Most are contained in the roster in Appendix D. The names of all 5th Marines and many others who served in World War I are found in this book.

As a career army officer I served two tours of duty in Vietnam during the periods 1965–1966 and 1970–1971, so I have combat experience. I was also familiar with the details of World War I since at one point in my career I taught military history at West Point. My father-in-law, Raymond P. Rogers, was a veteran of World War I, having served in the 5th Marine Regiment. He was wounded twice and shared his experiences with members of his family. These, in turn, were related to me long after Raymond P. had died. The photo of Raymond Rogers shown here is from 1918.[3]

Introduction

As the centennial of U.S. involvement in World War I approaches, it is timely to look back on this conflict, the people involved in it and its effect upon us. The last U.S. veteran, Frank Buckles, died in 2011 and the last veteran from all nations, Florence Green of Great Britain, died a year later. Over 65 million people served in that war and over 7 million were killed in it.[1] This does not include civilian casualties. They are now all gone, so historians tell the veterans' story through their own words recorded over the last century. Wherever possible, I tried to provide photos of these faces from the past.

It was a war to end all wars and was different from any other war before or since. It was a long war. By the time the United States became involved, the British, the French and the other warring nations had been fighting for three years and millions of dead were stacked on the battlefields. While the United States entered the war in 1917, it took nearly a year before U.S. troops in large numbers could be recruited, trained, and shipped to France. By the time U.S. troops were fully engaged in combat (June 1918) all of the combatants were war weary. In 1917 the French army had mutinied and it took weeks to restore order. All recognized that the entry of the United States could be the decisive factor to end the war. For the Germans, it became a U-boat campaign to sink U.S. ships before they could supply men and material to fight the war. For the Allies, it was a contest to see who would control the U.S. troops when they arrived. The French wanted to assign U.S. units to French armies, but the United States insisted that the units would remain independent under U.S. command separate from the British and the French. In a very short amount of time (little more than a year) between the arrival of U.S. troops and the Armistice in November 1918 hundreds of thousands of U.S. troops were killed or wounded or died of disease. The battles described in this book may have been the deciding factor in determining the outcome of the war. The Marines were among the first to serve and sustained higher casualty rates than other U.S. units.

The 5th and 6th Marine Regiments were unique. They composed the 4th Marine Brigade in the 2d U.S. Army Division. The organization of the 4th Marine Brigade of the 2nd Infantry Division (called the Indianhead Division) is provided in Appendix C. Appendix D provides the 5th Regiment roster. Over eight thousand Marines served in the 5th during the war and through the occupation of Germany.[2] The roster is a listing of Marines by company and it is more than a list of names: It has notes about many of those listed.[3] Before the 5th was fully engaged in combat, many notes list: drunk and disorderly, disrespect, fighting, absent without leave and other minor offenses. By October 1918, the notes were different. Many indicate killed, wounded, missing in action or sick. The minor offenses had disappeared for obvious reasons: The troops were busy with war. The intensity of the battles is reflected in the rosters that note those killed and wounded. The greatest number killed were on 6 June (Belleau Wood) followed by 4 October (Blanc Mont).

The reader will find that this history covers the background of the war and the introduction of U.S. forces before addressing the battles of the 5th Marine Regiment. The great influenza epidemic that raged during and after the war had an impact on all nations and this is also covered. No history of the World War I experience of the 5th Marine Regiment would be complete without addressing occupation duty in Germany after the war.

August 1914

Background

As with many wars, most people today would agree that World War I was an unnecessary conflict. It happened by accident. It was based upon old grievances between the Europeans such as the loss by France in the Franco-Prussian War of 1870. Disputes over colonies and the desire to expand influence in other continents added to the fuel. The more immediate cause for the war was tensions over territory in the Balkans. Austria-Hungary competed with Serbia and Russia for territory and influence in the region, and they pulled other nations into the conflict through their various alliances and treaties. Alliances formed among the belligerents and were comprised of an immense list of nations, over fifty-seven on six continents. The Allies (also called the Entente Powers) included France, Great Britain, Russia, Italy (1915), Romania, Canada, Australia, and Serbia. Colonies were included. This led to interesting problems. The French colonies in Asia contributed to the war effort. The Cantonese truck drivers (who appeared to enjoy hitting every pothole in the road) who ferried U.S. troops could not speak English and perhaps could speak no French, either. Finding destinations was a problem.

The United States was not included in the initial Allied nations but was called an Associated Power when it entered the war in 1917. The Central Powers included Germany, Austria-Hungry, Bulgaria, and the Ottoman Empire. Their colonies were also included. Some nations such as Italy were neutral at the start but later took sides. Others such as Spain remained neutral. The situation was summarized by historian George B. Clark:

The massive conflict, the Great War, or the World War, as it later became known, was triggered by Bosnian nationalists when they assassinated the Austro-Hungarian archduke Franz Ferdinand, heir to the Austrian throne, and his wife, at Sarajevo, Bosnia, on June 28, 1914. The background is complicated but the real trouble originated with Serbian members of the Black Hand Society who armed the assassins. There seemed to be no question in anyone's mind that the Serbian government, or its employees, sponsored it. Control of Bosnia had been "awarded" to Austria-Hungary at the 1878 Treaty of San Stefano, which angered the Bosnian nationalists who fought for independence but lost. Serbia, a newly independent nation, was anxious to attach Bosnia and Herzegovina to itself and consequently brooded over the treaty settlement.

Within a few weeks of the assassination, Austria-Hungary demanded that the Serbian government obey a set of rules established by the former, or else. Serbia agreed to obey all but one; that one was tantamount toward eliminating their national independence and they, at

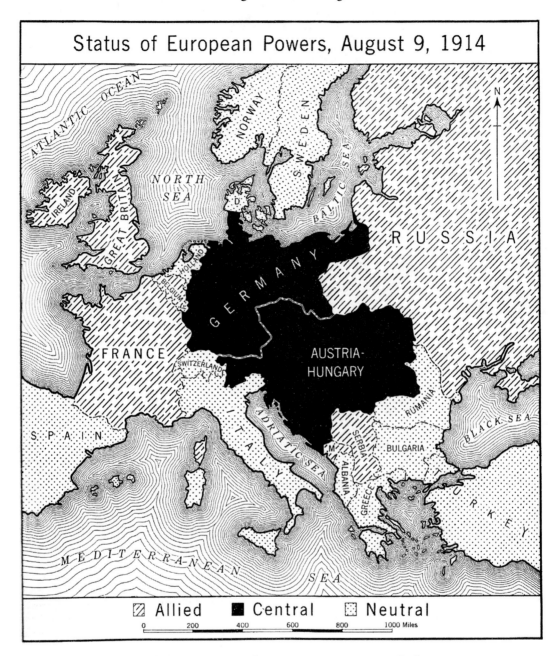

Status of European Powers, August 9, 1914

Allied   ■ Central   Neutral

0   200   400   600   800   1000 Miles

The alliances in 1914 (U.S. Government Printing Office).

the urging of Russia, refused to accept it. Russia had long threatened to intervene should Austria-Hungary attack Serbia.

The background alliances and involvement of the several important nations were quite confused. Russia and Germany had treaties that terminated in 1887 after Chancellor Otto von Bismarck refused to allow Berlin banks to loan Russia money, whereas French banks would and did loan them money. That resulted in treaties between France and Russia to come to the other nations' aid if attacked by a third party (Germany). Not long after, Bismarck was unseated and the very young Kaiser Wilhelm II, who desired to control the destiny of a recently united Germany himself, assumed almost complete control. In fact, he was not a bad fellow as he has been portrayed, but leaving a powerful growing nation's affairs in his hands was a calamity of huge proportions.[1]

The Leaders

Woodrow Wilson was in his second term as president and had reluctantly committed the United States to this war in Europe. Indeed, he was reelected in 1916 with the campaign slogan "He kept us out of war."

David Lloyd George was prime minister of Great Britain and would be a major player in the Paris Peace Conference that followed the war.

Czar Nicholas II was Russia's head of state.

President Woodrow Wilson (Library of Congress).

Czar Nicholas II (Library of Congress).

David Lloyd George (Library of Congress).

He was deposed by the Bolsheviks on 2 March 1917 before the United States entered the war. He and his entire family were executed by the Bolsheviks on 17 July 1918.

Wilhelm II was emperor of Germany, commonly referred to as the Kaiser. At the end of the war the monarchy was abolished and he faded into obscurity.

Georges Clemenceau was prime minister of France. His long career included authoring a journal in New York City, where he also practiced medicine. Following World War I he argued for major reparations against Germany.

August 1914

For years, both sides had been building up their armed forces, expecting that a conflict would erupt. In the United States, the people and its government were wary of the Europeans and intended to avoid involvement in any conflict following Washington's advice at his Farewell Address to avoid foreign influences. Among other things, he said:

> The great rule of conduct for us in regard to foreign nations is in extending our commercial relations, to have with them as little political connection as possible. So far as we have already formed engagements, let them be fulfilled with perfect good faith. Here let us stop. Europe has a set of primary interests which to us have none; or a very remote relation. Hence she must be engaged in frequent controversies, the causes of which are essentially foreign to our concerns. Hence, therefore, it must be unwise in us to implicate ourselves by artificial ties in the ordinary vicissitudes of her politics, or the ordinary combinations and collisions of her friendships or enmities.[2]

Those who shared this view were called isolationists, but in Europe the nations were closer and could not embrace this point of view. All it would take was a spark to set off a war. On 28 June 1914, Archduke Franz Fer-

Kaiser Wilhelm II (Library of Congress).

Georges Clemenceau of France (Library of Congress).

Archduke Franz Ferdinand with his wife, Sophie, and children (from left: Ernst, Maximillian and Sophia) in 1910 (Library of Congress).

dinand, heir to the throne of the Austro-Hungarian Empire, and his wife, Sophie, were assassinated in the Austrian province of Bosnia. Their killer was Gavrilo Princip, a nineteen-year-old Bosnian with close ties to a Serbian terrorist organization.

A month later, Austria-Hungary declared war on Serbia. Soon millions of men in the uniforms of many nations were on the march. Two quick shots had set in motion one of the bloodiest wars in history. The interlocking alliances brought in nations on one side or the other and the key to the tragedy was mobilization. Once started, it could not be undone without causing chaos and vulnerability for the affected nation. Russia came to the aid of its ally Serbia, declaring war on Austria-Hungry, and millions of men were brought under arms as allies on both sides mobilized. The Great War had started and would last over four years. The death toll from all causes, both military and civilians, was 17 million. First blood occurred in Belgium when the Germans invaded neutral Belgium on their way to France, where most of the heavy fighting of the war would occur. It was here that propaganda became a mainstay of the war, influencing people like those of the United States to fight and others to fight harder. Grisly posters depicting German atrocities in Belgium became popular and the point was not lost in America, where the isolationists were still the majority.

"The Rape of Belgium" invoked in a poster advertising war bonds (Library of Congress).

The United States Goes to War

Turning from Isolationism

The United States remained neutral for nearly three years before entering the war for the Allies and was ill equipped to do so. Many factors influenced the U.S. entry in the war in spite of a very sizable population of first-generation German-Americans who would be expected to support Germany (they didn't). Allied propaganda took its toll on both sides of the Atlantic.

With the start of the war, British propaganda bombarded the United States in order to get it to enter the war. Stories of the atrocities of the barbaric Huns circulated in the United States. These included the murders of Belgium civilians and other atrocities. Some of these were imagined; some were real.[1]

One of the greatest blunders of the Germans was their decision to practice unrestricted submarine warfare in an effort to limit the flow of supplies to the Allies. This meant that any German U-boat or surface ship could sink any ship, military or civilian, from any nation. The United States felt the sting of unrestricted submarine warfare six months after the start of the

Propaganda reached new heights after the sinking of the *Lusitania* (Library of Congress).

war when a U-boat sank the U.S. oil tanker *Gulflight*. A short time later, the British civilian luxury line *Lusitania* was sunk off the coast of Ireland by a German U-boat on 7 May 1915. On board were 1,959 passengers and crew, including 159 U.S. citizens. A single torpedo struck the *Lusitania*, followed by an internal explosion on board the ship. The *Lusitania* went down in eighteen minutes, carrying 1,198 passengers and crew to their deaths. Ernest C. Cowper was one of the few survivors and later wrote to the family members of two who did not,

12 March 1916

Dear Mr. Hubbard:

I should have written what I have written to you a long while ago—but I don't know, it seems as if the Lusitania left its seal on every one who was in it, and even now, almost a year later, I am afraid all the survivors are thinking more seriously of May 7, than they are of their business or the other things they should attend to. I know that *is* the case with me. If you have been informed that there was a man on board who was in the company of your father and Mrs. Hubbard on many occasions, I guess they have me in mind , for we really did spend a lot of time together.... On finishing mine [lunch] I went to the top deck, and was smoking ... when I saw the torpedo coming toward us.... Mrs. Hubbard smiled and said, "There does not seem anything to do." The expression seemed to produce action on the part of your father, for then he did one of the most dramatic I ever saw done. He simply turned with Mrs. Hubbard and entered a room on the top deck, the door of which was open, and closed it behind him. It was apparent that it was his idea that they should die together, and not risk being parted on going into the water. The blow to yourself and your sister must have been terrible, and yet, had you seen what I have seen, you would be greatly consoled, for never in history, I am sure, did two people look the Reaper so squarely in the eye at his approach as did your father and Mrs. Hubbard....

Yours very faithfully,
Ernest C. Cowper[2]

Outrage over the destruction of a civilian passenger ship did not trigger the entry of the United States into the war in Europe, much to the disappointment of the British, who circulated untrue rumors that German schoolchildren were given a holiday to celebrate the sinking of the *Lusitania*. Much was made of the fact that the *Lusitania* carried ammunition on board, but this was no secret and the ammunition was listed on the ship's manifest. The question was: Did that fact warrant the murder of over a thousand civilians? Most thought not. President Wilson demanded an apology and reparations from the Germans and by September Germany abandoned unrestricted submarine warfare. War fever subsided in the United States.

Two years later the situation was changing. Stalemate continued on the western front and Russia was collapsing. Soon a Russian revolution would end Russia's involvement in the war. In January of 1917, British cryptographers deciphered a telegram that became known as the Zimmermann Telegram from German foreign minister Arthur Zimmermann to the German minister to Mexico, von Eckhardt, offering U.S. territory to Mexico in return for joining the German cause. The British provided the telegram to President Wilson on 24 February 1917 and it was released to the press on 1 April:

We intend to begin on the first of February unrestricted submarine warfare. We shall endeavor in spite of this to keep the United States of America neutral. In the event of this not succeeding, we make Mexico a proposal or alliance on the following basis: make war together, make peace together, generous financial support and an understanding on our part that Mexico is to reconquer the lost territory in Texas, New Mexico, and Arizona. The settlement in detail is left to you. You will inform the President of the above most secretly as soon as the outbreak of war with the United States of America is certain and add the suggestion that he should, on his own initiative, invite Japan to immediate adherence and at the same time mediate between Japan and ourselves. Please call the President's attention to the fact that the ruthless employment of our submarines now offers the prospect of compelling England in a few months to make peace.

Signed, ZIMMERMANN.[3]

Rumors that the telegram was a fake were soon dashed when Zimmerman himself admitted it was authentic weeks after it was published. The Zimmermann Telegram and Germany's return to unrestricted submarine warfare were the immediate causes of the U.S. entry into World War I. On 6 April 1917 the U.S. Congress declared war on Germany.

Going to War

The day after war was declared, I left high school where I would have graduated in two months. I went from Newburgh, New York to New York City to enlist, lying about my age. I was 17 years old. The recruiting officer told me that I did not weigh enough and should eat as many bananas as I could, drink a whole lot of water and come back. I did that, passed and I was now a member of the U.S. Marine Corps.[4] I haven't had a banana since. I trained in Philadelphia as a part of the 5th Marine Regiment. I always claimed that I was on the first ship to sail for France. We departed on the *St. Louis* for New York where we boarded the *Henderson* bound for France. On board, we were sick most of the time and tried to stay on deck where we could easily vomit over the rail.[5]

Private Raymond P. Rogers,
5th Marine Regiment

In 1917 the U.S. Army and National Guard combined totaled 200,000, a number less than the casualties of a single major battle in France. For example, over a million men were killed or wounded at the Battle of the Somme. The Marines were a small force. The day after war was declared, thousands of patriotic young men volunteered, but it would not be enough.

The day the United States entered the war found many who would serve in World War I at a variety of different tasks. Their recollections are recorded within and information on their lives after the war are found in the "Biographical Dictionary" later in this book.

Those Who Served

Albert Preston (Bert) Baston was born on 3 December 1894 in Saint Louis Park, Minnesota. He entered the University of Minnesota to study law and played football for three seasons. He was named to Walter Camp's All-American team in 1915 and 1916. When the

United States entered the war, Bert enlisted in the Marine Corps and was assigned to the 17th Company, 5th Marine Regiment.

Carl Andrew Brannen was a cadet at Texas A&M University when the United States entered the war. He was impressed by the Marine "First to Fight" poster and resigned from Texas A&M on 27 January 1918 to join the Marine Corps at age eighteen. He would be assigned to the 6th Marine Regiment.[6]

Smedley Darlington Butler was a career officer commissioned in the Marine Corps on 8 April 1899. He had received two Medals of Honor in the Banana Wars before the United States entered World War I. He was ordered to France to take command of the 13th Marine Regiment.

William Edward Campbell was born on 18 September 1893 in Florida. He was raised in Mobile, Alabama, the eldest son of eleven children. He studied law but ran out of money and moved to New York City to work for a law firm. After the war started he enlisted in the Marines and was assigned to the 17th Company, 5th Regiment. He arrived in France in March 1918.

Clifton Bledsoe Cates was born in Tipton, Tennessee, on 31 August 1893. He attended the Missouri Military Academy and received a law degree from the University of Tennessee in 1916. He was commissioned as a reserve officer following his graduation from the University of Tennessee and reported for active duty as a second lieutenant on 13 June 1917 at the Marine Barracks, Port Royal, South Carolina He sailed for France the following month and became a member of the 96th Company, 6th Regiment.

Albertus W. Catlin was born on 1 December 1868 in Rome, New York, and was commissioned in the Marine Corps on 1 July 1892. He was commanding the Marine detachment aboard the USS *Maine* when it was destroyed in Havana Harbor in 1898 and served in the Spanish-American War. He received the Medal of Honor for his actions while commanding a battalion of the 3rd Marine Regiment at Veracruz in 1914. After the United States entered World War I he was placed in command of Marine training at Quantico, Virginia, and then sailed for France, where he would take command of the 6th Marine Regiment.

William O. Corbin enlisted in the Marines on 27 May 1913. He was stationed in Philadelphia and would later be assigned to the 51st Company, 5th Regiment, in France.

Louis Cukela was born on 1 May 1888 in Split (Spalato), Croatia (then part of the Austro-Hungarian Empire and later of Yugoslavia). He immigrated to the United States in 1913 and enlisted a year later in the U.S. Army from the state of Minnesota, reaching the rank of corporal before being honorably discharged in 1916. He enlisted in the U.S. Marine Corps in January 1917 and, after the United States entered World War I later in the year, was sent to France with the 66th Company, 5th Marine Regiment.

Samuel C. Cumming was born in Kobe, Japan, on 14 October 1895. He attended the Virginia Military Institute, graduating with the Class of 1917. He was commissioned a second lieutenant in the Marines and shipped to France, where he would ultimately be assigned to command the 51st Company of the 5th Marine Regiment.

Daniel Joseph Daly enlisted in the Marine Corps on 10 January 1899. He had been awarded two Medals of Honor before the U.S. entry into World War I. His awards were for action in China in 1900 and in Haiti in 1915. In France Gunnery Sergeant Daly was assigned to the 73rd Machine Gun Company.

Charles Augustus Doyen was born on 3 September 1859 in Concord, New Hampshire. He attended the U.S. Naval Academy and graduated with the Class of 1881. He was later commissioned as a second lieutenant in the Marine Corps. At the start of World War I, he organized the 5th Marine Regiment and took it to France.

Charley Dunbeck was born in Ohio on 26 March 1885. He enlisted in the Marine Corps on 13 March 1903. When he was sent to France, he was assigned to the 43rd Company, 5th Regiment.

Frank Edgar Evans was born on 19 November 1876 in Franklin, Pennsylvania. He served as an infantryman in the Spanish-American War and was commissioned in the Marine Corps 15 February 1900. He served in the Philippines and in the United States prior to World War I and would join the 6th Regiment.

Logan Feland was born in Hopkinsville, Kentucky, on 11 August 1869. He served in the army infantry during the Spanish-American War and because of that was directly appointed as a first lieutenant in the Marine Corps in 1899. He went to France with the 5th Marine Regiment and commanded the regiment from 17 July 1918 to 21 March 1919.

Ferdinand Foch was born in Tarbes, France, on 2 October 1851. He was a soldier, military theorist and ultimately commander in chief of the Allied Armies during World War I.

Verner S. Gaggin was born in Pittsburgh, Pennsylvania, in 1870. He was a physician who left his practice in Pittsburgh to serve in World War I.

Joseph Addison Hagan was born in Richmond, Virginia, on 26 October 1895. He graduated from the Virginia Military Institute with the Class of 1916 and was commissioned in the Marine Corps. He was assigned to the 51st Company, 5th Marines.

Douglas Haig was born on 19 June 1861 in Edinburgh, Scotland. He would command the British Expeditionary Force in France during World War I.

George Wallis Hamilton was born on 5 July 1892 in Washington, D.C., and graduated from Central High School in 1912. He enrolled in Georgetown University but dropped out and became a bank teller in 1912. He was commissioned in the Marine Corps in 1913 and spent several years at sea duty before reporting for duty at Quantico, Virginia, in May 1917. At age twenty-five he joined the 1st Battalion, 5th Marine Regiment, 49th Company.

James Guthrie Harbord was born on 21 March 1866 in Bloomington, Illinois and graduated from Kansas State Agricultural College in 1886. He spent a short time teaching before enlisting in the army as a private. He received his commission in 1891 and served during the Spanish-American War. He was a career army officer who served with Pershing on the Punitive Expedition into Mexico. Harbord returned to the United States shortly before it declared war on Germany. He would become Pershing's chief of staff of the American Expeditionary Force (AEF).[7] When the commander of the 4th Marine Brigade become ill, Harbord took command of the brigade in 1918.

James E. Hatcher was born in Texas and enlisted at the USMC recruiting station at the Alamo in San Antonio, Texas, on 5 May 1917. He was assigned to the 84th Company, 6th Marine Regiment.

David Ephraim Hayden was born on 2 October 1897 in Florence, Texas. He enlisted in the U.S. Navy from that state and received training at San Diego Naval Base, California, and at Quantico, Virginia. He served in France with the Second Battalion, 6th Marine Regiment, as a hospital apprentice first class.

Levi Hemrick was born in Clarke County, Georgia, on 20 July 1890. At the start of World War I he was principal of a three-teacher school in Georgia and thought it would be nice to see Paris. He hopped aboard a milk truck headed for Atlanta and a recruiting station. He joined the Marines and would spend time at the Paris Island,[8] South Carolina, Marine training base before he would see Paris, France. He was assigned to the 80th Company, 6th Marine Regiment.[9]

Paul von Hindenburg was a German general and statesman. He was born in Posen, Poland, on 2 October 1847. He was appointed Germany's chief of the General Staff in 1916 and with his deputy Erich Ludendorff guided the German war effort.

Charles F. Hoffman was born on 17 August 1878 in Brooklyn, New York. He enlisted in the U.S. Army from that state and served for nearly a decade before enlisting in the U.S. Marine Corps at Bremerton, Washington, in June 1910. Promoted to the rank of corporal in March 1911, he reenlisted in June 1914. Hoffman, who also served under the name Ernest August Janson, sailed for France in June 1917 as a member of the 49th Company, 5th Regiment.

Warren R. Jackson enlisted on 10 June 1917. He was from Texas. After training at Paris Island he shipped to France and served the entire war as a member of the 95th Company, 6th Regiment.

Joseph Jacques Césaire Joffre was born in Rivesaltes, France, on 12 January 1852. He attended the École Polytechnique and became a career army officer. He served in the Franco-Prussian War in 1870. Joffre was appointed commander in chief of the French army in 1911 although he had never served as commander of an army and had no experience with general staff work.

John Joseph Kelly from Chicago's South Side was born on 24 June 1898, the youngest of four sons. He ran off to join the circus at age sixteen and returned two years later when the United States declared war. He was five feet, five inches tall and weighed 112 pounds and was tough. He had an irrepressible sense of humor and a quick temper. When he returned from the circus he found that his older brothers were already in the army, so he joined the Marines.[10] He was assigned to the 78th Company, 6th Marine Regiment, and would earn the Medal of Honor in France.

Matej Kocak was born on 31 December 1882 in Gbely, Slovakia (then part of the Austro-Hungarian Empire). Immigrating to the United States in 1906, he enlisted from New York in the U.S. Marine Corps a year later. From mid–1916 until the end of that year, he participated in the Dominican Campaign. Kocak served with the 66th Company, 5th Marine Regiment, in France during World War I.

Melvin L. Krulewitch graduated from Columbia University in 1916. He had wrestled, rowed and thrown the shot put. He enlisted in New York City and joined the 6th Marine Regiment.[11]

John Archer Lejeune was born in Pointe Coupee, Louisiana, on 10 January 1867. He graduated from the U.S. Naval Academy with the Class of 1888 and served two years in the navy before he was commissioned in the Marine Corps. He served in the Spanish-American War in the Marine detachment aboard the USS *Cincinnati*. With the start of the war he was assigned to command the newly constructed Marine barracks at Quantico, Virginia. He then sailed to France, where he would command a brigade of the 32nd Division, the 4th Marine Brigade, and finally the 2nd Infantry Division.

Louis Carlesle Linn was born in Laurel, Maryland, on 19 March 1895 the son of William Edgar Linn and Agnes Maud Watkins. Louis attended McKinley High School in McLean, Virginia, and took evening art classes at the Corcoran in Washington. He also worked as a page in Congress. After high school he worked on the last Geodetic Survey of the Rocky

Mountains, and when the United States entered the war he enlisted in the Marine Corps and was sworn in on 5 June 1917. He was sent to Norfolk, Virginia, for basic training.[12] Louis Linn would serve with the 77th Company of the 6th Machine Gun Battalion in France.

Erich Ludendorff was born on 9 April 1865 in Posen, Prussia. He was commissioned a subaltern into the German 57th Infantry Regiment in 1885. By 1911 he was a full colonel. At the outbreak of World War I he was a brigade commander stationed in Strasburg, Germany. Barbara W. Tuchman, author of *The Guns of August*, described him as a man of granite character and a glutton for work.[13] He would become the chief manager of the German war effort.

Douglas MacArthur was born on 26 January 1880 in Little Rock, Arkansas. He was a graduate of the U.S. Military Academy in 1903 and served in the 42nd Infantry Division during World War I.

Elton E. Mackin was born on 22 February 1898 in New York. He was sixteen years old when World War I started in 1914 and he attempted to join the Third Canadian Contingent with several of his friends. However, he never went through the enlistment process and instead left school to begin working full-time. In April of 1917, at the age of nineteen, he enlisted in the Marines and completed basic training at Paris Island, South Carolina. Ultimately, he was assigned to the 67th Company, 1st Battalion, of the 5th Marine Regiment.

Wendell C. Neville was born in Portsmouth, Virginia, on 12 May 1870. After graduating from the U.S. Naval Academy with the Class of 1890, he was commissioned as a lieutenant in the Marine Corps. His service included Veracruz, Mexico, where he was awarded the Medal of Honor for the action on 21 April 1914. Colonel Neville was assigned to the 5th Marine Regiment after the start of World War I.

Don V. Paradis was a big man working at the Detroit City Gas Company and at age twenty-one had a bright future with the company. The "First to Fight" Marine slogan appealed to Paradis and he joined. He enlisted on 19 May 1917 and would be assigned to the 80th Company, 6th Regiment. The "First to Fight" and "First in France" poster campaigns became the most successful in U.S. history.[14]

John J. Pershing had commanded the Punitive Expedition into Mexico in 1916 to apprehend Pancho Villa, a Mexican bandit who had crossed the U.S. border and raided Columbus, New Mexico. While Pershing was in Mexico, his wife and children died in a fire at the Presidio in San Francisco. Only his son, Warren, survived. Pershing returned from the unsuccessful Mexican expedition in February 1917 and did the undiplomatic thing of telling correspondents that there would be war with Germany and he wanted to command the troops sent to Europe: This was two months before the president and Congress declared war.[15] Nevertheless, in spite of failure in Mexico and diplomatic fumbles, Pershing would command the American Expeditionary Force in Europe.

Orlando Henderson Perry was born in Cadiz, Ohio, on 20 February 1874. He graduated from Jefferson Medical College in Philadelphia in 1904, married Marcia P. Mellersh in 1908 and joined the U.S. Naval Reserve Force as a Lieutenant, Junior Grade, in December 1916. He served in the Medical Corps, was sent to France, and was attached to the 5th Marine Regiment during the Battle of Belleau Wood.

Philippe Pétain (the Lion of Verdun) was born on 24 April 1856 in Cauchy-à-la-Tour, France. His father was a farmer. Pétain joined the French army in 1876 and entered St. Cyr Military Academy in 1887. He served in infantry assignments in mainland France and at the start of World War I was a colonel. He led a brigade at the Battle of Guise in August 1914. He was quickly promoted to general and commanded the French 2nd Army at the Battle of Verdun in February 1916. He believed in the use of field artillery rather than massive frontal attacks by infantry: artillery kills; infantry occupies. The heavy losses by the French army caused mutiny. By the time that the United States entered the war, Pétain was commander in chief of the French army and had successfully quelled the mutiny. He restored the morale of the French army.

John Henry Pruitt was born on 4 October 1896 in Fayetteville, Arkansas. He enlisted in the U.S. Marine Corps from Arizona in May 1917, less than a month after the United States entered World War I. He served with 78th Company, 6th Marine Regiment.

Corporal Joseph Edward Rendinell was born on 12 January 1894 in Youngstown, Ohio. After he enlisted, he was trained at Paris Island, South Carolina, and was assigned to the 97th Company, 6th Marine Regiment. He sailed for France on 31 October 1917. He kept a diary that would be published years after the war. He recalled the start of the war:

> In the spring of 1917 I was working in the steel mills as an electrician…. We were eating dinner when we got word the U.S. had declared war with Germany. I went to the Navy Recruiting Station. The sergeant in charge was being bombarded with questions as to how soon U.S. would send troops over. We signed up and was told to wait until we were called for examination…. Next morning I went to Cleveland and stayed for three days to get away from home until Mother stopped her crying. I got back home and told Mother & Dad that I had enlisted and nobody was going to stop me. It was like a funeral around home. That night I went to say goodbye to my friends.[16]

Raymond P. Rogers was born on August 4, 1899, in Newburgh, New York. At the time that the United States declared war on Germany he was a high school senior with two months left before graduation from the Newburgh Free Academy in northern New York. The day after war was declared he went to New York City to enlist. He was 17 years old. He was assigned to the 51st Company, 5th Marine Regiment, 4th Marine Brigade, 2nd Division, and was on the first ship to land Marines in France.

James Russell Scarbrough was born in Tennessee on 12 May 1898. He was living in Cincinnati, Ohio, when the United States entered the war and was working in the Procter & Gamble Crisco plant filling the cans. He read about the terrible things that the Germans were doing in Belgium and joined the Marines on 16 May 1917. He would join the 83rd Company of the 6th Marines.[17]

Lemuel Cornick Shepherd, Jr., was born in Norfolk, Virginia, on 10 February 1896. He was enrolled in the Virginia Military Institute and graduated a year early in order to join the Marine Corps. He was commissioned in the Marine Corps on 11 April 1917, less than a week after the United States entered World War I. His initial assignment was at Marine Barracks, Port Royal, South Carolina, on 19 May 1917. Less than a month later he left for France as a member of the 5th Marine Regiment.

Merwin Hancock Silverthorn was born in Minneapolis, Minnesota, on 22 September 1896. During World War I he served in 20th Company, 5th Marine Regiment.

Lawrence Tucker Stallings was born on 25 November 1894 in Macon, Georgia. He entered Wake Forest University in North Carolina in 1912, graduating in 1916. He enlisted in the Marines and was assigned to the 47th Company, 5th Regiment.

Gunnery Sergeant Fred W. Stockham was born in Detroit, Michigan, on 16 March 1881. He enlisted in the Marine Corps on 16 July 1903 and was honorably discharged at New York

City on 15 July 1907. Four years later, on 31 May 1912, he reenlisted in the Marine Corps. By the time he was again discharged, on 30 May 1916, he had risen to the rank of sergeant. Within a week, he had returned to New York City, where on 7 June he reenlisted. By 8 February 1918, Sergeant Stockham was in France and heading for the trenches.

John W. Thomason, Jr., was born in Huntsville, Texas, on 28 February 1893. He was from a prominent Texas family. His maternal grandfather, Major Tom Goree, had served on Confederate general Longstreet's staff during the Civil War. John W. Thomason, Jr., was the first of nine children. He attended Southwestern University in Georgetown, Texas. He was working as a reporter for the *Chronicle* in Houston, Texas, when the United States declared war on Germany. He excelled as both an artist and a writer. He had read Marine Corps Commandant George Barnett's article that stated applications were being accepted for young men to obtain commissions in the Marine Corps. The day war was declared Thomason collected his last paycheck from the *Chronicle* and enlisted in the Marines.

Lloyd William Williams was born in Berryville, Virginia, on 5 January 1887. He graduated in 1907 from Virginia Polytechnic Institute and was a member of the Cadet Corps. Williams served in the Banana Wars before shipping to France as a member of the 5th Marines.

Frederic May Wise joined the Marine Corps in 1899 at age twenty-one. He was a newly appointed lieutenant colonel in Philadelphia when the war started and was given command of the 2nd Battalion, 5th Marines.[18]

Michael "The Polish Warhorse" Wodarezyk was born in Poland and immigrated to the United States. He enlisted in the Marines and was assigned to the 43rd Company, 5th Regiment.

The Draft

To bolster the army, which included few regiments, Congress passed the Selective Service Act on 19 May 1917. Men of ages twenty-one to thirty-one were required to register. By the end of the war, 24 million men had registered and 2.8 million were inducted.[19] The Selective Service Act was a courageous decision given the dismal performance of the draft in the Civil War that included riots and corruption. To organize, equip and train what would become an army of millions, the army had a tiny general staff of fifty-five people.[20]

The Training

Organization, training and seemingly endless inoculations were accomplished at locations including Paris Island, South Carolina, and Quantico, Virginia. One recruit wrote home to his mother,

The first day I was at camp I was afraid that I was going to die. The next two weeks my sole fear was that I wasn't going to die. And after that I knew I'd never die because I'd become so hard that nothing could kill me.[21]

The training continued in France and was summarized by one of the Marines:

It was this period that made us tough. In my battalion we had one case of sickness in two months—a man evacuated for appendicitis. We had no colds—nothing. We got tough, we stayed tough. When we went to the trench we were so mean that we would have fought our own grandmothers.[22]

The Weapons of War and Medical Treatment

Great strides were made in improving weapons between the U.S. Civil War and World War I. The airplane, tanks and trucks were made possible by the internal combustion engine. Horrible weapons such as poison gas and flamethrowers were introduced. The machine gun and rapid-firing breech-loading artillery weapons were also introduced. All of these were designed to more efficiently kill or maim people in larger numbers. The reaction to this was a reliance on trench warfare, since the mobility seen in earlier wars had become too costly. The cavalry charge was disappearing. Jim Scarbrough remembered,

> The idea of taking horses directly onto the battlefield seemed so risky that it just wasn't smart. But there they were, about 60 men [French] on horses, rifles slung across their backs…. They were about: I'd say 100 or 200 yards into that ravine when artillery started to hail down on them.

Thank God the artillery reports drowned out the horses' screams but it was quite a sight. You'd see the shells hit and then you'd see these large forms thrown high into the air, sometimes 100 feet high. These were horses. You didn't really see men thrown like that. Artillery has a devastating effect on a man's body: it will tear you like a sheet of paper. But there wasn't a single man or horse that came out of that ravine.[23]

The Wartime Industries Board was established to manage the wartime economy and production. While the board did an exceptional job, there were anomalies. Small arms such as the pistols (M1911), rifles (M1903) and Browning Automatic Rifles (BARs) (M1918) were available in quantity except for the BAR, which had limited production during World War I. Other weapons of war such as the tanks, airplanes and machine guns were supplied by the French and other allies and were not available from U.S. industry. The United States had no machine gun of its own.[24] The U.S. Browning Machine Gun (M1917) was not available until the end of the war due to production delays. For example, the Marine 6th Machine Gun Battalion did not exchange their French machine gun for a Browning until after the war. No U.S. tanks, flamethrowers or military aircraft saw service during the war. U.S. artillery support was augmented by the use of the French 75(mm) gun and other Allied artillery pieces. Upon entry into the armed forces, troops were issued blank identification tags or dog tags, as they were called. These were stamped with name and serial number. If a soldier was killed, the tag hung around his neck would identify him. Unfortunately, in some cases the stamping was not done and dead troops were found on the battlefield with blank dog tags. Raymond Rogers had his dog tags stamped and they were passed on to his grandson nearly one hundred years after they were issued.

Author Mark Mortensen summarized:

> New to this war was motorized transportation. Trucks, referred to as camions in Europe, were the best means to rush reserve battalions to the front lines, and more than 30,000 trucks were sent to France from America. Five- and ten-ton tractors were used to haul large guns across rough terrain. Motorized ambulances provided a quicker response time, transporting wounded men away from the front lines with added comfort. Basic autos were accessible to certain high commanders, and motorcycles could traverse the crowded roads and varying landscape for special errands.
>
> Aviation was still in its infancy, but technology and pilot flying skills were improving every day. There were many different production models of biplanes; some were agile and could maneuver easily, while others had increased speed and horsepower. Naturally, quality and reliability were important factors. Many young pilots often found that the type of plane that they had been trained to fly was different from the one they were assigned to fly during the war. A critical factor was how quickly the pilot adapted and became comfortable in handling his new warplane.
>
> General Pershing determined in the beginning that aviation was to be a support group and not the focal part of the action. The plane's biggest contribution to the cause was its use as a means for important observation and surveillance of enemy ground troops. Fighter planes were generally called upon to protect the observation planes. Additionally planes were used for bombing raids, searching over land for prime targets, such as storage ammunition and rail cars, and over water for submarines and their home-bases. The planes carried mounted machine guns, and the pilots were fully trained in their use.
>
> Balloons were an integral part of observation, and pilots were also cross-trained for this job. The balloonist was placed in a basket below the large inflated object, which was attached to a winch cable and commonly secured to the rear of a flatbed three-ton truck. Using a telescope along with radio or telephone communication, the observer provided detailed intelligence to the

Opposite: **The French 75 in action (USMC History Division).**

men in the truck below. The information was relayed to assist heavy ground artillery with focal points to fine tune their accuracy as well as to assist Allied troops with enemy troop movement. If weather conditions were favorable, the balloons were deployed at sunrise to a height of 2,000 feet along both sides of the Western Front. For added safety they were placed at least two miles behind the front lines and spaced about 15 miles apart. With common dimensions of 200 feet in length and a diameter of 50 feet, they were noticeable targets for enemy planes and served as featured backdrop scenery for ground troops throughout their adventure.

With planes and balloons in the air there came along another new weapon known as anti-aircraft guns to be used against enemy planes. The weapons were also strategically placed to protect the defenseless balloon pilots.

Radio and telephone communication on the battlefield was a new concept. When war was declared the Signal Corps of the Regular Army had 55 officers and 1,570 men. The Signal Corps expanded quickly, taking talented men from leading companies like American Telephone and Telegraph and Western Union Telegraph. Over time in France, they installed over 100,000 miles of telephone and telegraph lines. Having temporary telephone lines strung was one thing, but having a secure private conversation was another. One report mentioned "party lines," and therefore basic human "runners" were the most common reliable method of communication for fast moving troops along the Western Front. The war brought about another new motorized vehicle, the tank. The armored equipment was used for a variety of purposes, but the main use was to search and destroy machine guns in heavily fortified positions. Tanks were not an abundant commodity, and the French and British generally kept the larger tanks to support their own troops. There were not a lot of small tanks either, but those which were available to the American Forces were generally deployed in groups.

Chemical warfare was one of the most feared weapons, consisting of a variety of chemical mixtures to form a poisonous gas. This new type of warfare was used extensively by the Germans and to a limited extent by the French and English, but not by Americans. Although gas attacks did not kill men in large numbers, it caused many casualties and created panic which ultimately disengaged troops for a period of time. It was therefore considered a psychological weapon as well. Some gasses were chlorine based, some phosgene, and others were combinations. Canisters of gas were sent towards the enemy via exploding shells, with the hope that a light prevailing wind would carry the mixture throughout the opposing troops. Mustard gas (dichlorodiethyl-sulfide) used by the Germans was the most feared and essentially not a true gas, but more of an agent that caused skin blisters, or even worse, internal blisters on lungs. As the gasses were attracted to moisture through the nose or mouth, one often started sneezing and soon realized that his lungs were full of the toxic poison, followed by vomiting. In such cases the gas caused lingering, increasing pain over a period of days to weeks followed by potential death. The heavy mustard gas also differed from other gasses in that it did not take effect right away, but rather lasted for longer periods of time in areas lower to the ground around fox holes. To overcome the colorless gasses troops would immediately put on their personal gas masks and evacuate the low areas, where they had sought shelter. The uncomfortable mask severely hampered visibility and communication, but it was essential equipment.

The machine gun was definitely one of the most lethal weapons. It was, by itself, not a new invention, but the latest technology made it an advanced piece of equipment. Hiram Maxim came up with a simple design, and the Germans took his concept, producing the feared Maxim machine gun. Although small, the Maxim, which weighed about 135 pounds, usually remained in one spot as a major defensive weapon. In a losing scenario men usually kept the machine gun operational, firing up to 600 bullets per minute until their death.

The Americans liked their own Lewis Gun, which was capable of firing over 500 rounds of ammunition a minute and was highly mobile, weighing only about 26 pounds. Manufacturing conditions in the United States limited the production of these preferred lightweight guns, which soon found their way to the Air Corps. The AEF ground troops ended up with the less favorable lightweight French Chauchat and the heavier Hotchkiss. The Chauchat automatic rifle, which the men called "sho-sho," was the most mass produced automatic weapon of the war. Due to its specifications and raw material components, it was not a high quality gun, and many comments were

Lewis Gun training at Quantico, Virginia—training included disassembly and assembly of the gun while blindfolded in order to simulate night operations (USMC History Division).

made concerning the guns [*sic*] comprehensive reliability under constant use. The French supplied the Americans with much of the heavy artillery equipment, including the reliable workhorse French 75 model. It fired a shell weighing 13 pounds a little more than five miles, while the 155mm howitzer shot a projectile weighing 117 pounds roughly seven miles. Although not abundant, the French had a huge gun dubbed the "Mosquito," which, supported by a railway truck, was capable of handling an 1,800-pound bomb.[25]

Improvements in medical treatment reduced the death rate. Blood transfusions became routine. Innovations developed in the First World War such as the Thomas splint that secured a broken leg had a massive impact on survival rates. Rapid movement of the wounded helped reduce mortality, as did improved sanitation, but standing in trenches for long periods meant that a leg wound included an almost instant infection. Little could be done for those with the flu and a vast number of soldiers on both sides died.

Organization

In the nineteenth century the Marine Corps was a small force of men guarding facilities, enforcing U.S. policy abroad, and maintaining discipline and fighting on board sailing ships in sea battles. It expanded to 13,725 when the United States entered the war in 1917.[26] A steady increase in the strength of the Marine Corps continued throughout the war and the strength of the Marine Corps reached a peak of 75,101 in December 1918.[27] In spite of the desperate need for manpower, nearly three-quarters of Marine Corps applicants were rejected during the war. As would be expected, most of these rejections were by medical officers, but there were other categories, such as men whose parents refused consent.[28]

Marines relied on the navy to provide chaplains, medics, surgeons, and hospital staff. Marines and army units were equipped with many different weapons by the Allies, such as mortars and some machine guns. Even some food was provided by the French, such as the dreaded canned rations that the troops called monkey meat.

The 5th Marine Regiment was the first organized from detachments scattered around the world and especially the Caribbean. Many of these were old-timers who had fought in the Banana Wars and elsewhere. In this way, experienced Marines were brought into the 5th Regiment while the 6th Marines and other units that followed relied on recruiting after the U.S. entry into the war.[29] Some of Marines had served in other conflicts and were highly decorated with valor awards including the Medal of Honor.[30]

Valor awards were slightly different in World War I from those seen today. The Silver Star Medal was authorized by Congress in 1942. Prior to that servicemen were awarded the Silver Star Citation, a small silver star affixed to the World War I Victory Medal. The Navy Cross (NC) approved in 1919 is the equivalent to the Army Distinguished Service Cross (DSC). In some cases, a Marine was awarded the DSC and the NC for the same act. Also, in

Marines depart for France, 1917 (USMC History Division).

some cases an individual received both the Army and Navy Medal of Honor for the same act (the two medals are slightly different in design) and other valor awards. There was no consistent policy on this. Added to this was a vast array of foreign awards such as the French Croix de Guerre. Some authors claim that Pershing had a policy to deny recommendations for the Medal of Honor to Marine officers. If so, he made up for it in Medal of Honor awards to enlisted Marines. Six Marines in the 4th Marine Brigade received the Medal of Honor while only two army soldiers in other brigades of the 2nd Division (Bart and Van Iersel) received the same award. Suffice to say that troops entering World War I would have ample opportunity for recognition.

In spite of equipment shortages, lack of men and inadequate time for organization and training, two months

General John J. Pershing (Library of Congress).

after the United States entered the war General John J. Pershing landed in Great Britain to start the monumental task of organizing the U.S. forces

The 5th Marines landed in France later in June. The Marines had earned the title "First in France." At the time it landed, the 5th Regiment numbered 70 officers and 2,689 enlisted men who comprised one-fifth of the total enlisted strength of the Marine Corps.[31] Being the First in France had disadvantages. The Marines were short of essential items such as crew-served weapons.

General John J. Pershing commanded the American Expeditionary Force in France throughout the war. He successfully pushed to maintain an independent American command rather than piecemeal U.S. troops in French and British units. There was also a fundamental difference in philosophy between Pershing, who stressed the use of breakthrough and maneuver to win, and the Allies, who favored trench warfare. Erich Luden-

Fourth Brigade shoulder patch (author's collection).

General Charles A. Doyen, the first 4th Brigade commander (USMC History Division).

dorff took control of the German war effort in July 1917. He was the mastermind of German offensive efforts such as Operation Blücher. Ferdinand Foch commanded French forces and was a marshal of France. He was appointed supreme commander of the Allied armies in order to improve coordination among the allies. General Douglas Haig commanded the British Expeditionary Force.

The U.S. Army 2nd Infantry Division that served in World War I was a hybrid. It was composed of a Marine brigade (the 4th) as well as army brigades. The 4th Brigade included the 5th and 6th Marine Regiments as well as the 6th Machine Gun Battalion. The Marines wore a modified 2nd Division shoulder patch.

At various times the division was commanded by an army general or a Marine general. This may seem odd, but it worked well. Effective people were promoted in rank and command regardless of their branch of service. U.S. divisions were about twice the size of Allied divisions, numbering between 25 and 26 thousand men. Details of organization are provided in Appendix C.

3

The Pandemic

Some say it began in the spring of 1918, when soldiers at Fort Riley, Kansas, burned tons of manure. A gale kicked up. A choking dust storm swept out over the land—a stinging, stinking yellow haze. The sun went dead black in Kansas. Two days later—on March 11th, 1918—an Army private reported to the camp hospital before breakfast. He had a fever, sore throat, headache... nothing serious. One minute later, another soldier showed up. By noon, the hospital had over a hundred cases; in a week, 500. That spring, 48 soldiers—all in the prime of life—died at Fort Riley. The cause of death was listed as pneumonia. The sickness then seemed to disappear, leaving as quickly as it had come.[1]

It was called many things. Historians call it the Pandemic, U.S. troops called it the Three-Day Fever. Germans called it Flanders Fever; the French: La Grippe. The most common name was the Spanish Flu, but it had little to do with Spain. Something happened early in 1918. What appeared to be pneumonia in Kansas mutated to become a deadly flu as it moved east and infected millions of people in the United States. It would later return to Kansas in a more deadly form. By 1919 it had become a worldwide pandemic that killed between 50 and 100 million people: more than the plague in Europe centuries earlier.[2] It affected everyone, rich and poor; even President Wilson was felled by the flu during his attendance at the Paris Peace Conference in 1919, but he survived. "People didn't want to believe that they could be healthy in the morning and dead by nightfall, they didn't want to believe that."[3] A history of the pandemic written nearly a century later summarized:

> This particular strain of influenza defied all previous understandings of the disease. It struck quickly and without warning, felling people in their homes, in schools, in stores and businesses, and in the streets. The nature and scope of the flu compelled medical authorities to abandon their ordinarily clinical accounts and describe the situation in highly charged, graphic language.[4]

It affected the young people of soldier's ages, but the very young and older people were largely spared. It attacked the lungs and people died drowning in their own fluids. When it arrived on the East Coast, the number of cases exploded from a few thousand to millions. This occurred at a time when the United States was at war with Germany and thousands of young recruits died before they could be trained. It was immediately understood that close quarters in military barracks caused the contagion to spread as it did in large cities such as Boston, Philadelphia, New York City, and even smaller cities such as Seattle. There were no vaccines and those that were tried or invented did not work. People wore masks in public that may have helped prevent the spread, but this was not a universal conclusion:

Police lining up in Seattle—December 1918 (National Archives).

Dr. W.H. Kellogg of the State Board of Health spent most of one of that institution's bulletins declaring masks ineffective. Masks, he declared, had not prevented 78 percent of the nurses at San Francisco Hospital from contracting flu in the fall, though it was probably the best-run hospital with the most highly disciplined staff in the state. San Franciscans, he noted, habitually wore their masks on the streets in the open air, where they needed them least, and took them off in their offices and homes, where conditions were most favorable for infection. He pointed out that Stockton, the only city in California where masks had been worn consistently and faithfully in the fall, had had a death rate no better than that of Boston, which had staggered through its epidemic with a minimum of preventatives or remedies of any kind.[5]

In large cities events that caused people to assemble such as bond drives were canceled. It did very little good. Quarantine was not effective because the flu was highly contagious, transmitted through the air, and had an incubation period of only a couple of days. The flu would strike one out of four soldiers in army camps.[6] It struck in three waves. In March 1918, the army surgeon general received reports from Kansas of the initial outbreaks. Symptoms were high fever, headache, pain in the bones, rash and nausea. Treatment was bed rest, aspirin for fever, light diet and keeping the patient warm. Recovery time (or death) was in four days.

The flu subsided from July through early September. It seemed to abate for reasons never understood. The mortality rate dropped from double digits in the U.S. stateside camps to 2.1 percent in July and 2.3 percent in early September 1918.[7] It returned with a vengeance later in September. Public health officials realized the return when a Norwegian steamer from Europe docked in New York City with two hundred flu patients on board. The return of the pandemic was also reported in France.

The second wave of the flu struck first at Camp Devens outside Boston on 8 September. It was a surprise. On 14 September, more than five hundred soldiers were admitted to the hospital with the flu. For the next three days over a thousand soldiers were admitted each day into the two-thousand-bed facility.[8] The flu made the rounds of the camps, returning to Fort Riley, where it had started. One of the last places where it hit was at Camp Greenleaf in Georgia on 11 October 1918. There were all sorts of measures taken, such as suspension of transfers from the camps and additional medical personnel being brought in, but they seemed to have little effect. People came to realize that the epidemic simply needed to run its course; i.e., everyone who could be exposed was exposed and they either survived or died. At Camp Devens, over a quarter of the camp population became victims of the flu: fourteen thousand cases and 757 deaths.[9]

The outbreak at Camp Devens formed a pattern repeated in army camps, hospital wards, and morgues across the country. When the flu hit a camp, it exploded in a day or two, sending thousands to their beds. Hospital admissions would crest in two or three weeks, but pneumonia cases continued to increase for at least a week as the sicker patients developed complications. Camp Upton on Long Island, for example, hospitalized more than one hundred men every day for three weeks, from 15 September to 9 October. Admissions peaked at 483 admissions on 4 October. More than five hundred patients died at Camp Upton.[10]

Thousands of autopsies were completed that found little except that the soldier was dead and lungs were devastated. Nearly a century later the influenza strain H1N1 was identified as the cause based upon specimens taken and preserved during the 1918–1920 Pandemic.

Captain Verner S. Gaggin was an army doctor stationed at Camp Greenleaf, Georgia, before he shipped to France late in the war. Camp Greenleaf was a new training camp for medical officers established in May 1917 at Camp Oglethorpe at Chickamauga Park, Georgia.[11] It would also become a treatment facility for soldiers with the flu. Camp Greenleaf was a horrible place established on swampland that took time to drain *after* the first officers arrived at the new camp. Poor housing, overcrowding and lack of adequate heating made it a breeding ground for the flu. A U.S. Army Medical Department history of the camp summarized the situation:

> The influenza epidemic made its first appearance at Camp Greenleaf September 25, 1918, 26 cases being reported that day. During the month of October, the epidemic reached its height and disappeared completely by the 26th of the month. During this time there were 2,353 cases of influenza and 1,200 cases of pneumonia admitted to the hospital. Most of the latter entered as influenza cases. The deaths numbered 325. Approximately 25 per cent of the pneumonia cases terminated fatally. The epidemic greatly interfered with the activities of the camp; few men were received during the period and few organizations departed.[12]

In a series of letters to his wife, Nell, in Pittsburgh, Pennsylvania, Dr. Gaggin related the course of the flu at Camp Greenleaf. Most of his letters discussed the situation as the second wave began to subside:

19 October 1918

My Dearest Nell,

I had a good, long sleep last night at my barracks after five nights at Hospital. I asked for a night off which they granted, and I am feeling all right for my work tonight. I am to show my cases to the man in charge of the next Ward and he will take both of them hereafter: and I hope that I can then get work. The epidemic is subsiding almost as fast as it began and the wards will soon be consolidated. Hardly any new cases today reported of either Influenza or Pneumonia while a week ago there were hundreds of pneumonia alone every day. I am glad you have escaped. Keep away from people until it is over. The disease is contracted directly from another case, and the latter may not be very sick and be about in stores etc....

Lots & lots of love
Verner[13]

24 October 1918

My Dearest Nell,

No letter today and I am worried over Vinn. If no letter tomorrow I'll telegraph. Mail is very much congested on account the Influenza. The Epidemic here is over and believe me I am glad. Someday I'll tell you all about it and it will make your hair stand on end. I don't mean danger to me but the severity of the disease and the way those poor young fellows died. The disease attacks mostly the young adults. I do not have to work tonight but will have about two more nights, then my ward will be cleared out. No more cases coming in. We are having good weather....

Lots & lots of love
Verner[14]

Fighting Germans and the Germs

The flu wreaked its havoc on military and civilian populations throughout the world.... Arising first, we think, in the American Midwest in the late winter and early spring of 1918, it appears to have spread from Camp Funston outside Fort Riley, Kansas, to Camp Oglethorpe in Georgia, thence rapidly to Europe on board the troopships transporting U.S. forces to the western front. Contemporaries called it the "Spanish flu," mistakenly believing that it had originated in Spain. It had not, but Spain was one of the few countries in Europe that had not imposed an embargo on information emanating from its borders and allowed news reports of illness there to disseminate. Other European countries, engaged in a bloody, brutal, horrific war of attrition, censored what news could be put out and were quick to jump on Spain as the source of what would prove to be a terrible killer. An exhausted, emotionally and physically stressed European population proved no match for the illness, which marched through the continent, made its way to Asia and Africa, and arrived in Australasia in July 1918.[15]

That summer and fall [1918], over 1.5 million Americans crossed the Atlantic for war. But some of those doughboys came from Kansas. And they'd brought something with them: a tiny, silent companion. Almost immediately, the Kansas sickness resurfaced in Europe. American soldiers got sick. English soldiers. French. German. As it spread, the microbe mutated—day by day becoming more and more deadly. By the time the silent traveler came back to America, it had become a relentless killer.[16]

The situation was upside down and backwards, a disease that's supposed to be a mild disease is killing people, the people it's killing are the strongest members, the most robust, members of our society.... For example: soldiers. In Europe, the flu was devastating both sides. 70,000 American soldiers were sick; in some units, the flu killed 80 percent of the men. General John Pershing made a desperate plea for reinforcements. But that would mean sending soldiers across the Atlantic on troop ships.... There's nothing more crowded than a troop ship, it's just being jammed in there like sardines and if somebody has a respiratory disease, everybody's going to get it.[17]

While the flu started in the United States in March 1918, it first appeared in Europe in April. It coincided with the arrival of the first Americans at Bordeaux, one of the chief disembarkation ports for U.S. troops. It may be that the United States sent more than troops to Europe. The flu moved from army to army with great ease. It appeared in the British Expeditionary Force in April and was widespread in the French army in May. It also appeared in the German army in April among the troops who were closest to Allied lines. The AEF found that the troops in the rear areas suffered the most, apparently because they were packed tightly into billets while the front-line troops enjoyed the fresh air of the trenches. The flu was incredibly contagious: 90 percent of the troops in the 168th Infantry regiment at Dunkirk had the flu.[18]

Shortly after the initial outbreak in the States, the flu entered the AEF. While the 4th Marine Brigade prepared to attack at Belleau Wood, Louis C. Duncan, with the Second Division, reported on the flu during the military operations at Château-Thierry in late May:

> "Influenza was epidemic," he wrote, and "when the troops started on the march many developed that disease and were unable to march." Captain Samuel Bradbury, with the Eleventh Engineers, reported an influenza epidemic from 19 May to 3 July, during which 613 men were sick. He confined most to their quarters for an average of about four days, but he had to hospitalize twenty-two soldiers, one of whom died from pneumonia. Bradbury considered the incident worth writing an article about because of the "explosive nature of the epidemic, the comparative mildness of the disease and short duration of illness in each case, the absence of complications and yet the extraordinary manner in which the disease cut down the number of effectives." This wave of the flu spread with surprising suddenness, weakened but did not yet kill its victims, and was therefore remarkable to only a few medical officers.[19]

After a summer lull the second wave of the flu pandemic hit the AEF. In August troopships heading for Europe were savaged by an outbreak of flu with 425 cases on board among two transports that landed. From there the flu quickly spread to the troop units. It began to affect combat operations during the St.-Mihiel offensive, 12–16 September. At Blanc Mont the Marines as well as the U.S. Army were fighting two enemies: the flu and the German army. General Pershing cabled Washington:

> Cable Number 1744, To Adjutant General, Washington, D.C., 3 Oct. 1918. Influenza exists in epidemic form among our troops in many localities in France accompanied by many serious cases of pneumonia.... Request 1500 members of Army Nurse Corps, item M 1181 W, be sent to France as an emergency requirement.
>
> Cable Number 1785, To Adjutant General, Washington, D.C., 12 Oct. 1918.... It is absolutely imperative that one base hospital and 31 evacuation hospitals due September 30, and 14 base hospitals, due in October, should be sent immediately and that their nurses and equipment should be sent with them, or, when possible, in advance.

Many times the sick soldiers remained with their units and were not included in the statistics. In some cases, no transportation could get them back to an aid station. In other cases, they would not leave their unit because buddies relied on them. In many cases, they were afraid of what overburdened medics at the aid station would do to them.

Sometime after I arrived in France, it was winter and I came down with the flu. There were so many people that were sick that we were housed in an old barn. I lay in a loft with one blanket. There was an opening in the roof. I remember waking in the morning and realizing that it had snowed through the night. The snow had filtered through cracks in the roof of the barn and I was covered with a mound of snow on top of my blanket. I was so weak and sick I couldn't even muster the energy to shake the snow off my blanket.

Private Raymond P. Rogers, 5th
Marine Regiment [20]

The Germans in the trenches were hit harder because they were less well fed and not as healthy as the Allies in the opposing trenches. The British blockade was blamed for the fall in the diet of the Germans down to one and a half pounds of potatoes (a staple) per week.[21] They called the flu Flanders Fever, while the Allies called it Three-Day Fever (even though it usually lasted four days). By June 1918, nearly half a million German soldiers were sick with the flu. Over 580,000 German soldiers and civilians perished. This hampered the ability of Germany to mount an offensive or defend its terrain.[22]

> The German high command was struggling to find replacements for the more than 900,000 casualties their army had sustained during their offensive drive, and, as the *Times* had reported, the flu was putting even more German soldiers out of commission. "Our army suffered. Influenza was rampant," wrote German commander Erich Ludendorf after the war. In his memoir he complained, "It was a grievous business having to listen every morning to the chiefs of staffs' recital of the number of influenza cases, and their complaints about the weakness of their troops if the English attacked again!"[23]
> On October 17 Ludendorff acknowledged that influenza was again raging in the German front lines. He attributed its especially lethal nature to the absolute weariness of his army: "A tired man succumbs to contagion more easily than a vigorous man."[24]

By late October 1918, the flu pandemic was waning. By 2 November, only seventy-two troops out of 25,000 who landed in France had the flu. In spite of combat casualties and the flu, the Allies won when the war ended on 11 November 1918 with the Armistice. The Pandemic continued after the war. The third wave of the Pandemic struck in early 1919. In the last week of January 1919, over one thousand people died in New York City from the flu and pneumonia. The Third Wave, also called the winter wave, crested in Paris in the week ending 22 February. The flu would run its course and appeared to be influenced by cold weather, possibly because fewer people congregated. The Pandemic died out by 1920. It is thought that it burned itself out: Everyone who could be infected had already been exposed. Medical authorities downplayed its importance since they were powerless to do anything.[25] The AEF suffered 50,280 deaths in combat and 57,460 deaths of disease: Over 90 percent of these were from the flu.[26] The percent of deaths from disease was far less than during the Civil War, but advances in medicine led some to conclude that the medical profession should have done better. The problem was that they were dealing with a virus: hard to stop, hard to treat. By then, between 50 and 100 million people had died worldwide of the flu ... all because of cow dung in Kansas.

Nearly seventy years after the Pandemic, people recalled their experiences:

My father, being the health officer, was very concerned about the Indians who were our neighbors, they were only six miles away. So Dad and the city marshal rode up there one day to see how things were going at the Indian camps and they were horrified at what they saw. After an Indian died, his family and friends would sit around chanting him to the Happy Hunting Grounds and they'd spend all night there. And, by that time, they were all exposed, everybody had the flu. Ultimately, it killed about half the Indians.

Lee Reay[27]

I had camphor balls in a little sack around my neck. I know I couldn't stand myself, let alone somebody coming near me. I smelled so bad, I guess, in those days.... And then when we got out again and went back to school, I was shocked to see that my friends were not around, they weren't home. I would knock on their door and they would open the door just a little bit and say, "No, Jimmy's not here" or "Frankie's not here" and when I asked "Where is he?" "Let your mother tell you." They wouldn't tell me. "Let your mother tell you." I was a pretty lonely kid at the time because these were my friends that I played with all those years, and went to school with and when I lost them, why, my whole world changed.

John de Lano[28]

As a young girl, my mother had survived the pandemic and told me that pneumonia was the old people's friend because it ended their agony. They had many health problems and in the end, their lungs filled and they died drowning in their own fluids. As a child, I recall seeing my eighty-year old grandmother die gasping for breath. This was over thirty years after the pandemic. The question that lodged in my mind since then is: why did soldiers and other young people die in the same way from the flu? It appears that in some cases, the virus demonstrated extreme violence toward its young victims. The culprit was not the flu itself but the very massive immune system response of healthy young people that overreacted to the virus. Their immune system filled the lungs to kill the virus and in doing so killed the patient.

Mike Eggleston, 2014[29]

A history of the pandemic attempted to quantify the loss of life, which was difficult since many of the nations involved in the war suppressed the number of deaths, fearing the reaction of a public that already had too much bad war news. Of all of the world's nations, the United States appears to have been the hardest hit:

The mortality figures for the flu pandemic beggar the imagination. Where influenza epidemics in the past produced death rates of about 0.1 percent of those infected, this one killed 2.5 percent of those infected. Britain lost 250,000 people to the disease, as did France and Germany. In the Russian empire, 450,000 inhabitants died, as disease combined with revolution and civil war to decimate the population; 50,000 died in Canada. In the United States, 675,000 Americans died, and *life expectancy dropped by some twelve years in 1918 as a consequence of the huge numbers of deaths recorded that year* [Italics added by the author]. Indigenous peoples in North and Latin America and in Australia and New Zealand suffered disproportionate mortality rates; some communities lost upwards of 80 percent of their members.[30]

We always like to think that actions follow a disaster, like a law passed or more money put into research, but nothing happened after the Pandemic. The influenza pandemic of 1918–

1920 became a forgotten chapter even though there were encores. The history of the Pandemic is full of contradictions, failures, lack of knowledge, and confusion and was obscured by the war that caused it to flourish.

> Common soldiers, our kind, never get to know the way of things. We have only the pictures from our memories, and what the politicians tell us—afterward.
>
> Elton Mackin, 5th Marine
> Regiment [31]

4

First in France

By the time that the United States entered the war in 1917, the warring nations in Europe had been engaged for nearly three years. On the western front the war had subsided into trench warfare along a line from the Channel to the Alps and south. In the East, Russia fought and lost on a colossal scale against the Germans and other members of the Central Powers. Europe was mired in a blood bath with millions of people already dead. It was at this point that U.S. troops sailed for Europe, and among the first was the 5th Marine Regiment.

General Pershing and his party reached Liverpool aboard the British steamship *Baltic* on 7 June 1917 after a ten-day crossing. On the same day, the 5th Marines were officially organized at Quantico and moved by train to embark for France.[1] The 5th Marine Regiment was a part of the 4th Marine Brigade (see Appendix D):

> In simplistic numbers the Fourth Brigade was composed of the following: each company contained 250 Marines, and a battalion consisted of four companies and therefore at least 1,000 men. A regiment was three battalions or well over 3,000 Marines, and a brigade was made up of two regiments plus the machine gun battalion and other support personnel. Specifically, the total composition of the Fourth Brigade at full strength was 258 officers and 8,211 enlisted men. The First Battalion, Fifth Regiment, was commonly identified as 1/5 and correspondingly the Third Battalion, Sixth Regiment, was classified as 3/6. During World War I each Marine company was identified by a alphabetical letter number, but later in the war numbers replaced the alphabetical letters.[2]

While Pershing was being hosted by royalty, the 5th Marine Regiment was at sea on board the *Henderson, Hancock* and *De Kalb*. The *Henderson* was a recently commissioned troopship, which made the crossing more tolerable than other ships.

By 17 June, Pershing and his party had landed in France while the 5th landed at St.-Nazaire on the Bay of Biscay ten days later. This led to the Marine Corps motto "First in France." On arrival, the Marines spent time unloading and setting up at the port. Due to lack of stevedores at the port, Marines did that job, which got old very fast, since they were eager to get on with the business of fighting the Germans. Merwin Silverthorn was an enlisted Marine in 1917 and recalled: "We didn't have little hand trucks [or] cargo hooks ... we didn't even have gloves."[3] Silverthorn would later rise to the rank of lieutenant general before he retired. It was nearly a month before the Marines broke camp and headed for their training areas.

On 15 July, the 5th moved to training areas:

Left to Right: Major Holland (Staff), General Doyen (4th Brigade commander) and Colonel Wise (USMC History Division).

Maj. "Fritz" Wise's 2d Battalion drew the village of Menancourt as its billeting area. The townspeople turned out to greet them, children presented bouquets of flowers, and the band of the Chasseurs Alpins played the "Star-Spangled Banner": The Marines were billeted in houses, stables, haylofts, or almost anything with a roof. Wise and his headquarters officers had a house and their own mess. Wise's reputation as an officer who dined often and well had preceded him. His personal orderly, Pvt. John McKeown, who had been with him since Santo Domingo, was in charge of Wise's mess, which soon became famous throughout the 1st Division [later the Marines would be assigned to the 2nd Infantry Division], particularly after Wise acquired a French chef. Enlisted messing was more Spartan. The company galleys were set up in stable yards, and the troops ate in the open. Boiled and baked beans figured large in the enlisted menu. Luckily, there was splendid summer weather.[4]

The battalions of the 5th moved to Gondrecourt except for the 3rd Battalion, which remained at St.-Nazaire.

Training

It seemed a luxury at the time because the arriving U.S. units were allowed three months of training while the war hung in the balance a few miles away. The time spent training would pay handsome dividends later when the U.S. units were committed to battle, but training was cut short because of the unexpected German offensive.[5] A pairing arrangement was developed that assigned British or French regiments to train the Americans in trench warfare while tactical training was accomplished by the 5th Regiment officers. The 2nd Battalion of the 5th was paired with the French 115th Chasseurs Alpins. Major Wise, the commander of the 2nd Battalion, recalled:

> The British at that time were crazy about the bayonet. They knew it was going to win the war. The French were equally obsessed with the grenade. They knew it was going to win the war. So we also got a full dose of training in hand grenade throwing…. Hour after hour we threw those grenades into the "enemy trenches" ducked, and waited for the explosions.[6]

As summer faded into fall in 1917, time was consumed in training and reorganization. The Marines were assigned as the 4th Brigade of the newly formed 2nd Infantry Division. The French and the British were bogged down in the concept of trench warfare while Pershing promoted the more aggressive concept of open warfare, a successful concept learned during the Civil War. Training under the French and British focused on trench warfare. Training was needed, so the new concept was to assign American battalions to "quiet" sectors of the front under French command.

In mid–March 1918, the entire 2nd Division moved to a quiet sector southeast of Verdun to gain experience in trench warfare. Getting to their assigned position in the quiet sector had its problems:

Marines en route to the front lines in March 1918 (USMC History Division).

Grenade training included a French demonstration—Yanks wanted to throw the grenade like a baseball, while the French wanted a stiff-arm throw to get more loft. Either works (USMC History Division).

Walking on we passed several places where the track had been entirely blown away by shells, further on we came to a trench. Two French soldiers with bayoneted rifles sprang up out of it before us and barred our way. Roper ignored whatever it was that they were trying to whisper to him and insisted we must pass. He didn't know any French, only gestures.

We passed through the trench and then waited while two Frogs took out sections of barbed wire. These, I noticed, they very carefully replaced after us. Again we were arching forward. Roper whispered, "I believe I have gotten lost. There shouldn't be any trench there.

"Crawl over and find out where we are. If we all go they might take us for Germans and fire on *us*." We certainly had gotten turned around. The first thing I ran into was the barbed wire again. I squirmed and wriggled through it and crawled up the embankment of the trench and peered in.

I think it took me a minute to comprehend what I saw. I was looking at a trench full of German soldiers. Some were lounging at the firing step talking, others were busily filling sacks with earth that still others were digging with nothing but a pen knife. I stared, too scared to move. Outside the French wire we all met up again. We stood a fine chance now of being shot by the French before they could recognize *us*.

Both lines were quiet. Occasionally a star shell would shoot up into the sky, burn for a while and fall back to earth. We waited and waited and still Roper did not return. Had the fool forgotten *us*? We knew positively that this was the French line. You could trace both lines from here when the star shells were up. There had been no shot so we knew that he had not been killed. Why didn't he come back or send someone for *us*? Finally Rats and I decided to look for him before we froze. Rats said, "If that fool doesn't get us shot tonight it'll be pure miracle." The man from headquarters did not say anything, neither did his horse. We promised to come back and get him as soon as we found the lieutenant. This private's conversation seemed entirely reserved for the horse, whose mistakes he had meticulously pointed out along with directions for future improvement. To our proposal he merely nodded.

Going through the wire some tangled strands squeaked and the machine gun response was instantaneous. We went up the face of the trench on our hands and knees and dived into it. In seconds we were face down in the mud with our hands tied behind *us*. I had been prepared for some such reception. I was laughing at Rats and the job we made of getting on our feet.

Louis Linn, 77th Company [7]

I recall that our unit found a huge supply of canned peaches on a farm. We all fell on this gourmet delight and ate all of the peaches. Shortly after as the unit was being trucked forward toward the action, we all suffered from stomach issues. The image I recall was the men of the unit taking turns sitting on the back of the trucks, pants down, leaving their "fertilizer" on the road. When we finally arrived, life in the trenches was awful. The trenches were full of mud and rats. When it rained, the water would not run off. I tried to keep up my appearance in the trenches using some coffee that I had saved to polish my boots. I was teased by the other troops. I was a young red-headed teenager. I was a Marine and determined to keep up my appearance.

Private Raymond P. Rogers,
2nd Battalion, 5th Marine
Regiment [8]

Everything became twice as hard to do because of the mud…. Now we were constantly cold and wet. and hungry. A lot of us got trench foot, myself included from not being able to get our feet dry for days on end. My feet were already bad from the ice and cold, but now they were swollen up like bear's feet. I had frozen my lower legs that winter and I had almost no skin on my shins at all. It wasn't until sometime in the 1920s when a doctor had me keep my legs in potato poultices that I was able to grow skin back on my shins. At that time of the war, I couldn't lace my boots up tight because of the pain. It was becoming a war with the mud as much as a war with the Germans.

Jim Scarbrough, 6th Marines [9]

Operations bogged down during the winter of 1917–1918 and Marines became acquainted with new friends. Corporal Adel Storey of the 6th Marines had thoughts on this:

We nearly always have time to sleep in the daytime, but at night we either have to stay up all the time, or, if we lie down, we have to lie with cartridge belts and gas masks on, and rifle and bayonet by our sides.

To that was added the body lice that infested everyone. They were called "arithmetic bugs" because, according to one Marine, "they added to our troubles, subtracted from our pleasures, divided our attention, and multiplied like hell. [10]

Jim Scarbrough remembered,

A lot of the time around the camp, we just tried to keep clean. We were getting lousy; lice were everywhere. They'd bite at you and cause a kind of a rash if you didn't keep after them. Some

Opposite: Life in the trenches (USMC History Division).

guys would pass the time with a lice race. You'd take a frying pan and make a two chalk marks in it, a starting line and a finish line. Then you'd pick two lice from your body and bet on which one would win. If you got the pan too hot they wouldn't run and they'd just pop. They didn't run so much as hopped anyway. We spent long hours picking lice and throwing them in a hot pan.[11]

The rats were incredible. After feeding on corpses, they were huge and unafraid of anything.[12] Sergeant Johnson wrote home,

The trenches alive with them. Jamey Johnson, my bunkmate, and I used to plug every hole we could find in our dugout. They still got in and crawled over our blankets at night. I was never bitten. Some men probably were but I don't believe anyone was seriously ill from it. I guess we were as tough as the rats.[13]

In a letter home Corporal Storey noted,

Never in my life have I seen rats of such size as these are here. They don't run from us, either, like any ordinary rat does. They will fight like a good fellow when you fool with them.[14]

Louis Linn wrote of his revenge,

I froze. From right behind my head came that miserable each-each-each. In spite of the racket that night, my rat was coughing as usual. For a minute I saw red. I was more infuriated at that rat than at the whole German army.

I reached my bayonet and softly rolled back my blankets. Then for a long time I remained with the bayonet poised, moving its point from hole to hole until I should be sure I was directly over that rat. Then I drove with fury.

On the instant there issued from beneath my bed a scream of anguish, then squeal on squeal. I was startled myself and would have jerked the bayonet free, only it was embedded in some timber so far I could not release it. Then I realized what had happened. I had stuck the rat through a foot or some fold of skin, hurting but not killing him. Loosening the point very carefully, I tried to make another jab before he got away, but I missed and he was gone. In the silence, I became aware of a commotion at the end of the cellar. I heard Norton say, "Throw a hand grenade."[15]

Other maladies entered the scene. The first casualties from shell shock appeared among the U.S. troops. The major cause was heavy bombardments that had major effects on the nervous systems of the troops. James E. Hatcher, 84th Company, 6th Marines, described what happened to his buddy:

The next day Private Markham and I started back to our quarters from the "Y" [YMCA facility] and had about reached the center of the village when suddenly a salvo of shells came tearing down.... As soon as the stones and timbers stopped falling about us I raised my head and looked back at Markham and saw at once that something was wrong with him. He lay flat on the ground with his head raised and rocking from side to side. His jaw was set firmly and his breath was hissing through his teeth.[16]

Markham was returned to his unit after a few days at the dressing station, but as soon as the next barrage arrived his nerves gave way and while he begged to remain at his post, he was returned to the hospital. In Hatcher's words, "But when a man is once shell shocked, he is through for that war no matter how high his individual courage may be."[17]

Modern Weapons Took Their Toll

The flamethrowers were a fearsome thing. It was a unit of two tanks a man carried on his back, one of compressed air and the other of gasoline. They were ignited at the end of a nozzle the man held and would shoot a line of fuel and fire about 30 feet. In trenches, it was very effective and it caused a horrible death. I think its power was more psychological. I mean the fear of being burned was the main thing that made men retreat from it. But you'd feel the heat from a hundred yards away when somebody was using a flamethrower. They were terrible, The smell of men burning with that gasoline vapor stays with you.

Jim Scarbrough, 6th Marines [18]

Operation Blücher (27 May–16 June 1918)

When Russia quit the war in December 1917, fifty German divisions were free to move to the western front and engage the Allies in France. This enabled the Germans to launch a series of attacks against the Allies. These were called the German 1918 Spring Offensives. The second to the last of the five offensives was aimed at Paris in May of 1918.[19] The goal was to defeat France and Britain before U.S. forces could be deployed in strength. At that time, U.S. forces were arriving in France at a rate of a quarter of a million men per month.[20] In addition, famine and political upheaval in Germany made a near-term victory essential.[21] While the Americans were training, Ludendorff, the German commander, was planning Operation Blücher. This German offensive was designed to attack the French and draw off French reserves in preparation for an attack on the British. Ludendorff concluded,

> The army all called for an attack that would bring about an early decision. This was possible only on the western front. All that had gone before was merely a means to the one end of creating a situation that would make it a feasible operation…. All that mattered was to get together enough troops for an attack in the west.[22]

Ludendorff intended to put an end to years of trench warfare by adopting new tactics and mobility to break through Allied defenses. Small combat groups that quickly moved their machine guns swiftly to the front were among the innovations. Also, gas shells were used more extensively than before. These shells used the agent dichlorodiethyl-sulfide. It was a yellowish liquid and the drops settled into low areas such as the trenches of defenders. It caused blisters and attacked the lungs and eyes, causing at least temporary blindness. It was called mustard gas because it smelled like mustard.

On the western front, in mid–March 1918, the Allies were organized along a line with twelve Belgian divisions in the extreme north on an eighteen-mile front. Next Britain had four armies holding a 125-mile front and on the British right were the French (including Americans), with eight army groups holding a line of 312 miles. In all, 173 Allied divisions faced 194 German divisions.[23] The German attack struck hard on a twenty-two-mile front in the early morning of 27 May along the Chemin des Dames highway northwest of Rheims. The French were horribly unprepared and unaware of the German buildup. One of Pétain's staff officers, Jean de Pierrefeu later, wrote,

> The staff of the Sixth Army which was holding the Chemin des Dames had not the least idea of the preparations which the enemy had been making for a month on this front. It was declared at G.Q.G. that there was nothing surprising in this, that if General Duchene had not unfortunately been in command in this sector, any sort of a staff, especially after the lesson of March 21st, should have been able to find out something of what was going on; that at least it should have made some effort in that direction; that in any case no other major general [Anthoine] not related

Colonel Catlin (right) with General Omar Bundy, 2nd Division commander (USMC History Division).

to him could have had so blind a confidence in the commander of the Sixth Army, or could have neglected to inquire what was happening in this sector, which was obviously badly watched.[24]

Nearly four thousand German artillery guns supported the attack of 17 divisions.[25] The objective was to reach a line between Soissons and Rheims.[26] It became known as the Third Battle of the Aisne and the Germans reached the northern bank of the Marne at Château-Thierry, 59 miles from Paris. The French mood was abysmal. Jean de Pierrefeu summarized:

> In truth we found ourselves confronted by a new condition. The rapidity of maneuver of the enemy was amazing; not only the speed with which the German command shifted the battle area and the assault against the spots they considered least protected, but also the efficiency of their method, the short and savage artillery preparation which paralyzed the defenders, and the skill of their units in making their way always to the point of junction of French and British corps. The Allied troops seemed ill adapted to these unexpected methods, and had no defensive parry corresponding to the offensive thrust…. For the future the brains of the Chiefs must find a method capable of counter-balancing that of our adversaries. Up till now the indomitable will of the joint command not to give way, transmitted to the troops, was merely a makeshift. Things could no longer remain in this state. The moment when the infantryman would weary of being one against six must be foreseen…. All General Pétain's cares were directed to the solution of the problem.[27]

Tense Marines of the 77th Company, 6th Machine Gun Battalion, dug in to stop the German advance (USMC History Division).

The German attack destroyed two French divisions, the 21st and 22nd of Duchene's 6th Army.[28] It tore open the French front and the French commanders panicked. Realizing that the path was open to seize Paris, the Germans pursued the attack against the French.[29] The U.S. 2nd and 3rd Divisions were committed to stop the German advance.

Friday, 31 May 1918

The German 231st Division moved toward Château-Thierry, a town built on both sides of the Marne River. The German 231st Division started a crossing of the Marne as elements of the U.S. 3rd Infantry Division followed by the 2nd Division arrived. The 7th Machine Gun Battalion, 3rd Infantry Division, commanded by Major James Taylor rushed forward to stem the German tide arriving in early afternoon on 31 May.[30] The Germans attempted to cross the river but were driven back.[31] Albertus Catlin, 6th Marine Regiment commander, summarized:

> Never have men fought with greater heroism, dash, and gallantry under the American flag than did those machine gunners of the lone battalion at Château-Thierry. They fell, dead and wounded, many of them, but not one was taken prisoner, though they captured a number of Germans as well as machine guns. The Germans held the northern part of the town until the Allied offensive of July 18th and 19th, when they withdrew before Franco-American pressure, but they never once gained a foothold in the part of the city lying south of the Marne.[32]

Saturday, 1 June

A short distance northeast of Château-Thierry the Marines would make a stand against the Germans at Belleau Wood. On 1 June, German troops entered Belleau Wood, which was near the river Marne. The 2nd Division, including the Marines, moved forward to stop the Germans who were moving through Belleau Wood to cross the Marne and threaten Paris.

On 1 June, the 2nd Division moved forward toward Belleau Wood. The Germans would learn that the 2nd Division was between them and the direct road to Paris.[33]

5

Belleau Wood—1–26 June 1918

Château-Thierry Sector—Paris Is Saved

Gyrenes, gyrenes, you—you goddamn leathernecks, go take 'em! You're needed up there, bad. The outfit is all shot to hell—go get 'em, Marines.[1]

Belleau Wood (in French: Bois de Belleau) was an old hunting preserve covering about a square mile of terrain, a mile long and 1000 to 2000 yards wide of irregular shape. The battle

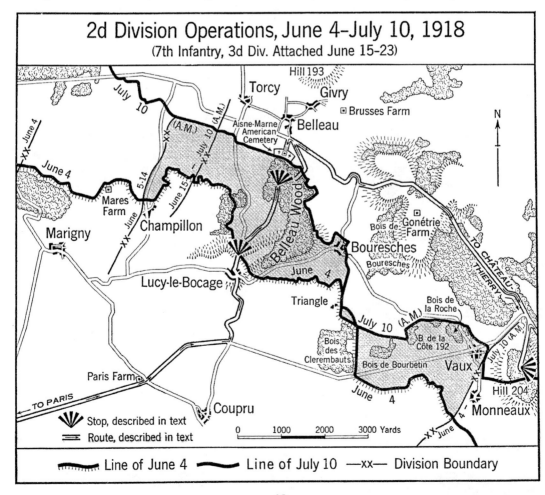

fought here took on a significance beyond the military impact that it had on the war. It was a small engagement fought by a few thousand in opposing armies of millions. Its importance was that it demonstrated the effectiveness of the Americans in their first major engagement. The Germans were stopped and it had a positive effect on the French, who were recovering from a major army mutiny the previous year that could have ended the war. Pershing would later recall:

> As a result of the German successes against the French, something akin to a panic prevailed in Paris. Probably a million people left during the spring and there was grave apprehension among the officials lest the city be taken. Plans were made to remove the French government offices to Bordeaux and we were prepared to move those of our own that were in Paris. At the request of General Bliss, trucks were placed at his disposal for the removal, in case of necessity, of his offices and those of his British colleagues on the Supreme War Council. It was a matter of considerable satisfaction to feel that our base ports, lines of communication and supply areas were outside of the zone of the British armies and south of Paris, and hence comparatively safe.[2]

Belleau Wood was heavily overgrown and in some places nearly impenetrable. It was half a kilometer south of the village Belleau and was also heavily fortified by the Germans, including nearly two hundred machine guns. Jim Scarbrough of the 6th Regiment described the scene:

The Belleau Wood Hunting Lodge after the battle. It was used as a command post and observation post during the fighting (USMC History Division).

Opposite: Belleau Wood (U.S. Government Printing Office).

One of the things that became apparent at Belleau Wood was that the Germans had had some time to make preparations. Their defenses were tough and we paid a heavy price to take many areas that would have seemed routine at first glance. For example, the Germans had erected big pieces of steel pipe and disguised them as trees. This allowed them to make elevated observation points by climbing up the inside of the pipe. From there they could direct artillery fire and machine gun fire on us and keep us pinned down.[3]

The Germans had significant forces surrounding Belleau Wood and were bringing up more. The German forces at Belleau Wood included the Royal Prussian 237th Infantry Division, the 10th and the 197th Divisions; parts of the 87th and the 5th Prussian Guards Division as well as the 460th, 461st, and 462nd Regiments.[4] There was also an abundant amount of supporting artillery. The Germans for the most part held the high ground at Belleau Wood.[5] The Allies attacked:

> The plan was for the Fourth [Marine] Brigade to take the area north of the Paris-Metz highway, which included Hill 142, about two-thirds of a mile southwest of Torcy, along with Belleau Wood and the rail junction and village of Bouresches. The hill contained several slopes, ridges and many Germans. Hamilton [commanding officer of the 49th Company, 5th Regiment] was used to hills from his fun loving days at the Conesus Lake house, but he soon found out that the hills he faced in France were all too often occupied by the enemy and these elevated works of nature were not friendly places.[6]

Hamilton's company would play a key role in the attack:

> At noon on 1 June, all three battalions of the 9th [the 9th Regiment was part of the 3rd Infantry Brigade of the 2nd Division] were up, and the first two were deployed between Le Thiolet and Bonneil. The 5th Marines and the 23rd Infantry [3rd Infantry Brigade] were on the road from May-en-Multien, marching down through Crouy-sur-Ourcq, Venderest and Cocherel, to Montreuil. The 5th Marines were ahead and while the Marines continued to march the 23rd Infantry had been delayed by conflicting orders and by the authorization of the Division commander. In the meantime, Division headquarters were set up in Montreuil: the supply trains were up, the infantry Brigadiers, Generals Harbord and Lewis, had moved ahead through Montreuil and examined the terrain they were to occupy and Colonel Chamberlaine, had received orders from the Division commander in Meaux at 8:30 a.m. to march his artillery units from their detraining points to Cocherel for assembly. But no more troops arrived in the battle area until mid-afternoon.[7]
>
> In the meantime, the Marines of the 4th Brigade had completely arrived and were taking up their assigned positions. Colonel Wendell Neville and his 5th Marines moved north off the well-traveled Paris-Metz highway and moved about a mile up the Marigny-en-Orxois road. There Neville established his first headquarters at what was then known as Pyramide Farm. The regiment set up camp in the open field opposite. There, "we all did it shipshape and by the numbers," according to 1st Lt. Elliott D. Cooke, USA, of the 18th Company who wound up becoming a genuine Marine before the war was over. He soon began talking the slang and when he wrote his memoir, many years after, it was leavened with the salty talk of the regular marine. He was one of sixty, perhaps more, U.S. Army officers loaned to the 4th Brigade when the personnel expansion took place and the Corps was deficient in 2d lieutenants but the army wasn't. All in all, they each served the Marine Brigade exceptionally well during the earliest battles. The 6th Marines were spread out covering a large area. They were even opposite the Bois de Belleau, which would loom very large for the Marines in the ensuing days. French troops, making a last stand along this line as the Germans weighed heavily on them, came through the American lines as they fell back under the pressure. One reported that a bruised and battered Poilu "showed me his rifle…. The butt had been shot away and he had been hit in the shoulder. 'Beaucoup d'allermands' [Many Germans] and he hurried away."[8]

Private Onnie J. Coders, 1st Battalion of the 5th, recalled the scene as the Marines moved forward to Belleau Wood:

About 4:00 a.m. [1 June 1918] we started to hike to where we later caught the French trucks which were to take us to the point from which the English and French were retreating. At this time the Germans changed plans and started a big drive near Château Thierry. Well, we rode all day and in the afternoon saw the first signs of actual war. The heartbreaking sights in and near Meaux were enough to set anyone's blood boiling. We saw many children poorly clad running from the town with men and women who merely had a handful of their worldly belongings hastily snatched together some with a basket on their heads, some with bread in their arms. Others who were more thoughtful had packed some clothes into wagons which were pulled by horses, cows or oxen.... The sky was fiery red from the large fires caused by the Germans burning those poor French peasants' homes ... we got into a reserve position at about 7:00 p.m. God, but we were tired! Here we camped for the balance of the night.[9]

Sergeant Don V. Paradis in the 80th Company of the 6th Regiment recalled the move forward and setup near Triangle Farm:

When the companies deployed from trucks Major Holcomb sent details to pick up ammunition nearby. Just before dark these details were returning with bandoleers of ammunition strung on poles, when about a half a mile from Triangle Farm, in plain sight of us and the Germans also, the German artillery opened up. This was really our first sight of our own men being wounded. One of my own buddies, who enlisted from Detroit, Charlie Munn, was wounded and never returned to active duty. The detail staggered across the field, with heavy loads of ammunition. Shells dropping around and among them and we could see those who were wounded or killed lying amidst the smoke of the shells. As the smoke would clear, after each round of shell burst we could see but were powerless to help them or retaliate in any way. Hospital corpsmen, always too few, and too slow, and extra details were sent to rescue the men and ammunition. The major's post of command was the main living quarters of the farm while we runners were quartered in the horse barn in the center of the courtyard in front of his post.[10]

Sunday, 2 June

Neville [5th Regiment commander] decided to move his PC northward to a quarry at Carrieres which was less susceptible to German artillery fire. While these changes were taking place Lt. Col. Frederick "Fritz" Wise received orders to take 2/5 and defend Les Mares Farm just north of Champillon. He was to also tie up with Marines on Hill 142 and thinly spread himself westward to the Bois de Veuilly. This was an area much greater than one battalion should have been required to fill. But 2/5 went to it and was soon situated around and about the farm. They never seemed to make contact, nor did Shearer with Wise, who was still near but not on Hill 142. The Les Mares Farm location was clocked at thirty miles from Paris and would be the closest the Germans would get to Paris until 1940. Their voyage, however, was stopped at this farm and its environs on 3–5 June. Someone later called it the "Bloody Angle of the AEF," in a magazine article. It was one of the most important victories of the 2d Division northwest of Château Thierry. Had the Germans punched through 2/5 they would have been well within and behind the 2d Division, which would then have been cut off. Needless to add, the road to Paris would then have been wide open.[11]

On 2 June, the French lost the villages of Belleau and Torcy. This loss was a disaster for the Allies, especially the French 43rd Division.[12]

Monday, 3 June

Early on 3 June, such elements of the 43rd [French Division] as could be gotten together delivered a series of ineffective counter thrusts in front of the 4th Brigade of Marines, around Hill 142 and Hill 165, mainly against the German 197th Division. They were easily stopped, and regained no ground: it was nothing more than a gallant gesture. But it had the result of slowing up the German advance: the 197th could not understand why the exhausted French attempted anything in the nature of a counter-stroke, and they proceeded during the rest of the day with elaborate caution.[13]

On 3 June ... the French on the front of the 2/5 Marines, in line west of Hill 142, covering Les Mares Farm, fell back during the afternoon. Passing through the Marines, a French Major ordered Captain [William O.] Corbin of 2/5 to fall back with them. This order was passed quickly to Captain Lloyd W. Williams, the 51st Company, and the senior officer present. He sent the following message to Lieutenant Colonel Wise, commanding 2/5.

3:10 p.m.

To: Battalion Commander- Second Battalion

The French Major gave Capt. Corbin written orders to fall back—I have countermanded the order—kindly see that the French do not shorten their artillery range—82nd and 84th Companies are on their way to fill gap on the right of this company—

Lloyd W. Williams,
Captain, U.S.M.C.[14]

On 3 June the Germans attacked.[15] It was here that the Marines demonstrated the result of their training. While the French training stressed use of the grenade and the British emphasized the bayonet, rifle marksmanship training was the focus for Marines.

The Marines could squeeze off round after round, hitting the German targets at ranges to five hundred meters and beyond. It was terrifying for the Germans. They had never faced a threat like this before and the attack ground to a halt while the German troops took cover.[16]

Lieutenant Lemuel Shepherd of the 55th would command a fourteen-man outpost in front of the line. He could clearly observe the German advance. Shepherd would later become the commandant of the Marine Corps and recalled the scene years later:

> Our orders were basic: "Form as skirmishers to withstand attacks." And that's what we did. We had to spread ourselves pretty thin because we didn't know just where they'd hit us. I'd suggested we put a dozen or so men on this commanding piece of land about two or three hundred

General Lemuel Shepherd later as Commandant, USMC (USMC History Division).

yards in front of our lines, with explicit orders to retreat if the pressure got too hot. Just about the time the attack started I'd decided to go out and see how they were doing. Actually, when I'd cleared it with our Captain [Blanchfield of the 55th Company], I'd really been asking more or less as a form of bravado. But he'd O.K.'d it, and I was off. Well, after I'd covered about a hundred yards or so, this huge German shell landed about six feet to my right; for one horribly tantalizing instant I saw it coming in at me. It covered me with dirt, but that's all. It was a dud. But it sure scared the hell out of me—I can still see it coming down today. In the meantime, the Germans are attacking, and we're knocking the hell out of them with rifle fire, which was something they obviously didn't expect. The French, you see, were great on the attack and with their grenades but not much with the rifle. I guess the Germans didn't realize they were coming against Americans. we could actually hear them yelling about it. After my dud episode I tried to find a spot where I wouldn't be too exposed but could still see what was going on. I was leaning against this tree when all of a sudden something struck me in the neck and spun me around. Well, 1 didn't know what the hell had hit me or how bad it was. The first thing I did was spit to see if blood was coming out that way. When there wasn't any, 1 knew I'd picked up an ugly wound but nothing fatal. I went back to a field hospital, had it patched up, and returned to my company.[17]

Shepherd was awarded the Navy Cross for his actions at Belleau Wood. He declined medical treatment while leading his men.[18]

Catlin (6th Regiment commander) had a good view of the German attack:

The rifle and machine gun fire were incessant and overhead the shrapnel was bursting. Then the shrapnel came on the target at each shot. It broke just over and just ahead of those columns and then the next bursts sprayed over the very green in which we could see the columns moving. It seemed for all the world that the green field had burst out in patches of white daisies where those columns were doggedly moving. And it did again and again; no barrage, but with the skill and accuracy of a cat playing with two brown mice that she could reach and mutilate at will and without any hurry. The white patches would roll away, and we could see that some of the columns were still there, slowed up, and it seemed perfect suicide from them to try. You couldn't begrudge a tribute to their pluck at that! Then, under that deadly fire and the barrage of rifle and machine gun fire, the Boches [*sic*] stopped. It was too much for any men. They burrowed in or broke to the cover of the woods.[19]

The Marines had ideal positions firing from behind the farm's stone walls. They held their fire until the Germans were within three hundred meters before opening fire with devastating consequences, mowing down waves of German infantry. A young Marine machine gunner finally got the word to fire:

Rat-tat-tat-tat full into them, and low down, oh! But it was good to jam down on the trigger, to feel her kick, to look out ahead, hand on the controlling wheel, and see the Heinies fall like wheat under the mower. They were brave enough, but they didn't stand a chance.[20]

Nearby, the French line collapsed and the French troops fled. Blanchfield refused his line (rotated back his exposed flank) and 2nd Division artillery rained down on the advancing Germans stopping the attack. The last action at Les Mares Farm occurred when the Germans tried to creep back to a field opposite the farm. They were discovered and only five escaped with their lives. The Germans fell back and dug in on Hill 204 near the Paris-Metz Highway. This was as close as the Germans would get to Paris after the United States entered the war. The battle at Les Mares Farm stopped the great Château-Thierry drive.[21] A German staff officer observed:

Though we told ourselves and our men, "On to Paris," we knew this was not to be.... Our casualties were increasingly alarming; ammunition was running short and the problem of supply, in

Marksmanship practice in France (USMC History Division).

view of the large demands, became more and more difficult. It became all too clear that actions so stubbornly contested and involving us in such formidable losses would never enable us to capture Paris. In truth the brilliant offensive had petered out.[22]

The French 43rd Infantry Division (DI) was torn apart by the German offense and streamed away from the front to escape the Germans. The sudden collapse of the French left a four-kilometer-wide gap in the front. The French government started to evacuate Paris.[23] Jean Degoutte of the French staff asked Colonel Preston Brown, the U.S. 2d Division chief of staff, if the Americans could be counted on. Brown's reply was one for the history books: "General, these are American regulars. In a hundred and fifty years they have never been beaten. They will hold."[24] The Marine Brigade was ordered to move east up the Paris-Metz Highway to stem the German tide:

> The French ordered Captain Lloyd Williams [of the 51st Company, 5th Marine Regiment] to fall back. William's response became a Marine Corps battle cry: "Retreat? Hell! We just got here!"[25] He then ordered his platoon leaders to take up firing positions and "let the 'Frogs' pass through."[26]

Tuesday, 4 June

By 4 June, General Bundy, commander of the 2nd Division had consolidated his line helped by the arrival of 167th French Division. The 2nd Division line now stretched from Monneaux near the base of Hill 204 to Lucy to Hill 142. The Marine brigade held the north of the line and over the next two days the Marines repelled successive German attacks.

The German Attack Stalls

On 4 June, the Germans prepared Belleau Wood for defense. The German 461st Regiment established positions near Bouresches.[27]

That morning, effective at 0800, the 2d Division was ordered to assume command over the entire sector and the French 43d DI withdrew from the Clignon line behind the 2d Division lines. French cavalry in Bois de la Marette, which was temporarily assigned to the 2d Division, remained where they were. Early that morning, before 0500, 1/9 left its place as right flank of division and was replaced by the 30th Infantry, of the nearby 3d Division. The French 10th Colonial DI was on that division's right flank down to the Marne River. The 2d Division area of responsibility was now extensive. No longer could the Americans count upon the French artillery nor any of its other experienced forces before them. The division's right flank began from just above the village of Monneaux, located at the base of Hill 204; to Le Thiolet on the Paris-Metz Road; northwest to Lucy-le-Bocage; continuing on to Hill 142 and finally to Les Mares Farm. Now there was nothing between the Americans and the Germans.[28]

John Thomason later wrote,

The principal event of 4 June was the return of the 23rd Infantry and attached units to the 2nd Division. Colonel Malone had been on the extreme left for 4 days, and although not engaged, his men had suffered losses from shelling and had effected a great deal in the way of organization and patrolling. They were relieved by the French 167th Division during the night 4–5 June, and were extricated from the front without incident. The 1/23 and 2/23 moved at once to the 3rd Brigade, relieving Marines of the 6th Regiment in the line from Le Thiolet to Triangle Farm. The 2/23 went to La Langue Farm as Division Reserve. On this day, 5 June, there occurred a contact with the enemy. The 2/5 Marines, in line on the ridge of Les Mares Farm, noted activity on their front during the afternoon. The wheat was high here, and Marines saw the grain shake, as though men crawled through it. Gunnery Sergeant Buford and eight Marines of the 55th Company went out and came upon a German patrol of twelve men, with a light machine gun. Shooting ensued; ten Germans were killed, and two wounded, together with the light Maxim were captured. They were identified as Saxons of the 26th Jager Battalion of the 7th Regiment, a formation of the 197th Division. They were the first prisoners taken by the 2nd Division in the area northwest of Château Thierry.[29]

Wednesday, 5 June

By 5 June, French reinforcements had arrived and the French wanted to mount an attack against the Germans. The Allies would attack on the sixth with the 167th Division on the left of the American line while the Marines attacked Hill 142 to prevent flanking German fire against the French. French intelligence reported that Belleau Wood was "Boche free" or lightly held.[30] The French were wrong. In addition, bad intelligence was compounded by failure to reconnoiter the ground. James G. Harbord, the commander of the 4th (Marine) Brigade, would later say, "I thought that the French had done all of that."[31]

Harbord recalled:

Little or no reconnaissance or scouting appears to have been done by the companies in front of their positions between June 4th and 6th, the responsibility having been ours since the withdrawal of the French on the 4th. This was probably due to inexperience. Maps were scarce, on any scale, and the hachures[32] gave no real information as to the physical features of the ground.[33]

With the arrival of the 167th DI on the left, the 2d Division's boundary, effective at 0800 that morning, moved back east to the brook at Champillon. This was a day when the infantry units of the division had a rather "soft time." The Germans weren't trying to kill them and the Americans were acting kindly in response. Instead of fighting, the entire division lineup was reorganized.[34]

The 6th Marine Regiment plugged the gap between Triangle Farm and Hill 142 while the 5th Marines set up southwest of Hill 142.

Gunnery Sergeant Michael Wodarezyk of 43rd Company helped repel a German attack

General James G. Harbord wearing his French helmet (USMC History Division).

and was awarded the Silver Star Citation. He was commanding the 4th Platoon and although outnumbered four to one he forced the enemy to retire.[35]

It became a waiting game. Colonel Catlin recalled:

All through June 5th we waited, with nothing of moment occurring save increasing artillery fire on both sides. The sound of it was deafening. To this day I do not know why the Germans did not attempt a sortie ~ whether they felt so secure in their position that they could afford to wait for overwhelming reinforcements, or whether the resistance and then the offensive dash of the Fifth Marines had frightened them into caution. As a matter of history, they never did come out, for on the following day the Marines went in.[36]

Thursday, 6 June

Hill 142—the Bloodiest Day in Marine Corps History (6 June 1918)

Artillery support included six batteries manned by a combination of French and the Marines. There would be no artillery preparation in order to avoid attracting the attention of the Germans.[37] The 1st Battalion of the 5th would attack but only had two companies on line when the troops were ordered forward. Its 17th and 66th Companies had been assigned to support the 2nd Battalion of the 5th. The 49th and 67th companies of the 1st Battalion of the 5th attacked at 3:45 a.m. The plan was that the two companies would sweep down from Hill 176 and hit Hill 142 from the south end. Hill 142 was elongated and the companies could roll across the top of the hill. The attack started.

The line of Marines advanced as planned and came out of the woods. They were hit by artillery and machine-gun fire after they had gotten fifty yards forward. The Marines advanced in waves from wood to wood under heavy fire from the machine guns. Many of the Marines were cut down as they moved across an open wheat field leading to the objective, Hill 142.

For some reason, the companies swept over Hill 142 by a distance of 600 yards and then had to double back. George Hamilton of the 49th Company recalled that he went over the nose of Hill 142 and did not realize it.[38] Hamilton's unit lost heavily. All five of his junior officers had been hit, which may have added to the confusion and the difficulty in identifying the objective. Hamilton remembered the attack:

The open wheat field where 1st Battalion attacked on 6 June. German machine guns in the woods took a heavy toll (USMC History Division).

Artist's rendering of the Marine attack in Belleau Wood (USMC History Division).

I have vague recollections of urging the whole line on, faster, perhaps, than they should have gone—of grouping prisoners and sending them to the rear under *one* man instead of several—of snatching an iron cross ribbon off the first officer I got and of shooting wildly at several rapidly retreating Boches. (I carried a rifle on the whole trip and used it to good advantage.) Farther on, we came to an open field—a wheat-field full of red poppies—and here we caught hell. Again it was a case of rushing across the open and getting into the woods. Afterwards we found why it was they made it so hot for us—three *machine-gun companies* were holding down these woods and the infantry were farther back. Besides several of the heavy Maxims we later found several empty belts and a dead gunner sitting on the seat or lying nearby. It was only because we rushed the positions that we were able to take them, as there were too many guns to take in any other way.

After going through this second wood we were really at our objective, but I was looking for an unimproved road which showed up on the map. We now had the Germans pretty well on the run except a few machine-gun nests. I was anxious to get to that road, so pushed forward with the men I had with me—one platoon (I knew the rest were coming, but thought they were closer). We went right down over the nose of a hill and on across an open field between two hills. What saved me from getting hit I don't know—the Maxims on both sides cut at us unmercifully—but although I lost heavily here I came out unscratched. I was pushing ahead with an automatic rifle team and didn't notice that most of the platoon had swerved off to the left to rout out the machine guns. All I knew was that there was a road ahead and that the bank gave good protection *to the front.*

I realized that I had gone too far—that the nose of the hill I had come over was our objective, and that it was up to me to get back, reorganize, and dig in. It was a case of every man for himself. I crawled back through a drainage ditch filled with cold water and shiny reeds. Machine-gun bullets were just grazing my back and our own artillery was dropping close (I was six hundred yards too far to the front). Finally I got back, and started getting the two companies together.[39]

Gunnery Sergeant Charles F. Hoffman (also called Ernest A. Janson) of the 49th Company was awarded the Medal of Honor for his actions:

For conspicuous gallantry and intrepidity above and beyond the call of duty in action with the enemy near Château-Thierry, France, 6 June 1918. Immediately after the company to which Gunnery Sergeant Janson belonged, had reached its objective on Hill 142, several hostile counterattacks were launched against the line before the new position had been consolidated. Gunnery Sergeant Janson was attempting to organize a position on the north slope of the hill when he saw 12 of the enemy, armed with five light machine guns, crawling toward his group. Giving the alarm, he rushed the hostile detachment, bayoneted the two leaders, and forced the others to flee, abandoning their guns. His quick action, initiative and courage drove the enemy from a position from which they could have swept the hill with machine-gun fire and forced the withdrawal of our troops.[40]

Medal of Honor winner Charles F. Hoffman (Naval History and Heritage Command).

Hamilton provided his account of the action:

Gunnery Sergeant Hoffman had been wounded in the arm. I am sitting talking to him in a little patch of scrub pines and much as I regretted it, had just told him that he must go back to the dressing station. Suddenly Hoffman gave a yell and with a "Come on Captain," dashed past me through the pines to the edge of the hill. I turned just in time to see a German raise his rifle and aim at Hoffman. I fired as quickly as possible and missed. Luckily, however, the German also missed, and Hoffman finished him with his bayonet. Hoffman was now tearing into a group of four or five Germans, slashing, jabbing and firing with lightning-like rapidness. I too found myself in a rather bad fix and bayoneted two men who had closed in on me. The others broke and Hoffman and I shot at them as they ran. All told, I think we got some twelve raiders. We later found that they were in the act of setting up five light machine guns when discovered by Hoffman. His wound was not bothering him so much that I ordered him to the rear. Later upon my recommendation, he was awarded the Medal of Honor.[41]

Elton E. Mackin, 67th Company, 1st Battalion, 5th Marines, recalled:

Zero hour. Dawn of 6 June 1918. Hushed commands brought the chilled, sleepy men to their feet. A skirmish line formed along the edge of the woods.... The entire front was quiet....

First Sergeant "Pop" Hunter ... strode out into the field and, a soldier to the last, threw a competent glance to right and left, noting the dress of his company line.... A single burst of shrapnel came to greet the moving line of men. There was a scream of pain, a plaintive cry of hurt. In some alarm, a soldier yelled, "Hey Pop, there's a man hit over here!" Pop's reply was terse and pungent: "C'mon, goddamnit! He ain't the last man who's gonna be hit today."[42]

Pop Hunter was killed in action on that day. At the burial detail an old-timer stopped and saluted: "Get a blanket, soldier. Wrap him up proper. That's Pop Hunter."[43] When the 67th swept past the hill, German machine gunners fired in their rear as they passed, inflicting many casualties. Joseph Baker of the 67th saw a Maxim firing and attacked, killing the crew. He received the Distinguished Service

Captain John Thomason (USMC History Division).

Cross for his actions that day. The Marines learned that the Germans had many tricks that they played. The troops noticed a German first-aid team carrying what appeared to be a wounded soldier, but the wind blew back the flap from the "wounded" man and revealed his legs were curled up with a Maxim and cases of ammunition below being carried to the German position. The Marines were cut down by massed artillery and machine-gun fire from the "Boche free" area of Belleau Wood. Captain John Thomason was assigned to the 55th Company, 1st Battalion, and wrote,

> The platoons came out of the woods as dawn was getting gray. The light was strong when they advanced into the open wheat, now all starred with dewy poppies, red as blood. To the east the sun appeared, immensely red and round, a hand's breadth above the horizon; a German shell burst black across the face of it, just to the left of the line. Men turned their heads to see, and many looked no more upon the sun forever. "Boys, it's a fine, clear mornin'! Guess we get chow after we get done molestin' these here Heinies, hey?"—One old non-com—was it Jerry Finnegan of the 49th?—had taken out a can of salmon, hoarded somehow against hard times. He haggled it open with his bayonet, and went forward so, eating chunks of goldfish from the point of that wicked knife. "Finnegan"—his platoon commander, a young gentleman inclined to peevishness before he'd had his morning coffee, was annoyed—"when you are quite through with your refreshments, you can-damn well fix that bayonet and get on with the war!" "Aye, aye, sir!" Finnegan was an old Haitian soldier, and had a breezy manner with very young lieutenants—"Th' lootenant want some?"—Two hours later Sergeant Jerry Finnegan lay dead across a Maxim gun with his bayonet in the body of the gunner.[44]

Lieutenant Joseph Hagan of the 51st Company was awarded the Distinguished Service Cross for rescuing a platoon sergeant and carrying him across an open space of two hundred yards through heavy enemy fire to safety.[45]

By the afternoon the Marines had captured and held Hill 142 at a cost of nine officers and most of the 325 men of the battalion. They succeeded because of the great courage of the troops but also their good fortune of striking the Germans at their weakest point, the boundary of two divisions.[46] Hamilton sent a message back by runner. Being a runner was a very hazardous occupation, as seen by some of the posthumous valor awards.

> Elements of this Company and the 67th Company reached their objective, but because very much disorganized were forced to retire to our present position which is on the nose of Hill 142 and about 400 yards northeast of square woods. Our position is not very good because of salient. We are entrenching and have 4 machine guns in place. We have been counter-attacked several times but so far have held this hill. Our casualties are *very* heavy. We need medical aid badly, cannot locate any hospital apprentices and need many. We will need artillery assistance to hold this line tonight. Ammunition of all kinds is needed. The line is being held by detachments from the 49th, 66th and 67th Company and are very much mixed together. No Very pistols. All my officers are gone.[47]

Strange things happened:

> Catlin [commander of the 6th Regiment] came across a German officer seated comfortably with his knees crossed. Before him was spread a little field table on which was cake, jam, cookies and a fine array of food. A knife and fork was in either hand. Beside the officer was seated a large, bulky sergeant who had been knitting socks. The darning needles were still between his fingers. Both their heads had been blown off by a large shell.[48]

Private Smith later told Catlin:

> Every blamed tree must have had a machine gunner. As soon as we spied them we dropped down and picked them off with our rifles. Potting the Germans became great sport. Even the officers

would seize rifles from wounded Marines and go to it. On the second day of our advance my captain and two others besides myself were lying prone and cracking away at 'em. I was second in line. Before I knew what had happened a machine gun got me in the right arm just at the elbow. Five shots hit right in succession. The elbow was torn into shreds but the hits didn't hurt. It seemed just like getting five little stings of electricity. The captain ordered two men to help me back. I said I could make it alone. I picked up the part of the arm that was hanging loose and walked. It was a two mile hike to the dressing station. I got nearly to it when everything began to go black and wobbly. I guess it was loss of blood. But I played in luck, the stretcher bearers were right near when I went down.[49]

Captain Bert Baston of the 17th Company was seriously wounded during the attack. He received the Navy Cross for his actions. He was wounded in both legs while leading his men through the woods and refused treatment until all of his men were safe and in good firing positions.[50]

John Thomason writing years later summarized the action:

The French had been fighting for years and were pretty much spent; however, this did not relieve them of their important support roles that were an integral part of the overall plan. When the H-hour came, as Hamilton described the situation, "We were to have Americans on our right and French on our left, and were to make our getaway at 3:45 A.M.... I was supposed to guide left and keep in "liaison" with the French. I couldn't see them and knew that at 3:45 they had not started. At 3:50 I started things by myself, and we were off."

The new moon for the month of June would fall on the 8th, and the official sunrise for these long summer days was about 0530. Still at 0345 there were hints of light, and any movement or even a shadow in the vast open territory was noticed by well trained eyes, triggering a reaction. Along the Western Front scouts were always watching. There would be no protection crossing the open areas.[51]

The line of Marines, advancing at a foot-pace through the open wheat, and guiding center with great care, came first under fire of the 9th Company of the 460th Regiment [German], and overran it in spite of sharp resistance. At once the 9th Company sent up a red rocket, the barrage call, and the signal was repeated by the 10th and 11th Companies to the east. The 67th Company, on the left, overlapped and swept past the position of [the 9th Company] 9/460, and then came under the fire of the heavy machine gun in the coppice thrust up from the Champillon ravine west of the Hill, losing heavily in officers and men. It penetrated the cover, bayoneted the machine gunners and such infantry as stood, and forced the 2/273rd violently aside. The 49th Company emerged from the woods it had pierced, and the fight streamed, confused—down the north end of the Hill, Marines and Germans mixed together. The [10th Company] 10/462nd was next encountered and, broken up, and 49th Company, passing down the eastern side, took enfilading fire at close range from the 10th and 11th Companies in the wood across the ravine. There was further disorganized combat on the brushy north end of the hill; here Gunnery Sergeant [Charles F.] Hoffman of the 49th Company bayoneted the crew of a heavy Maxim [machine gun] had the Congressional Medal of Honor for it. The Germans in the woods to the east record that very little was taken of them, the Marines, whom they believed, to be English soldiers, passing straight through their fire and pressing north after the fugitives, so that the 10th and 11th Companies were presently isolated. They lay in cover, holding the edge of the wood, and attempting no movement. The Marines reached the objective, without recognizing it, for most of their officers were down. They climbed the slope of Hill 126, towards Torcy, and some of them followed the Germans into the town. A Corporal sent back word by a wounded man that he had taken the place and wanted reinforcements and ammunition. He, and the man with him, never came out. Just south of the first house in Torcy, by the Bussiares road, there was a deep, dry hole from which rock had been taken.": In 1927 the French farmer who owned the land cleared away a tangle of weeds and brush that had grown up around the hole, and found in the bottom of it the weathered corpses of 2 Marines of its 5th Regiment and 2 German soldiers, their arms and equipment lying undisturbed upon them. Since on this occasion only the Marines approached Torcy; they must have fallen in the close and savage fighting of the 6th of June.[52]

The reports received by the French XXI Corps during the morning were encouraging. By noon, the French 167th Division had made good progress towards Veuilly, across Hill 165, and towards Bussiares, and the left of the Marine Brigade had advanced 1100 meters, throwing the enemy off of Hill 142. The Bussiares depression leading to the Clignon line, which was the objective for the combined attack, was now denied to the Germans, and the 167th Division would push on to the stream. Corps saw no reason to delay the next step. About noon, General Degoutte ordered the 2nd Division to proceed with the second part of its operation, the reduction of the Bois de Belleau, and the seizure of the dominating ridge above Torcy, to the west of the Wood. At 2:05 p.m. Headquarters, 4th Brigade, issued Field Order 2, the general plan of which had already been communicated verbally to the regimental commanders concerned. Field Order 2 announced that this Brigade attacks on the general line Bouresches-Torcy. The attack would be in two phases: first, to take the Bois de Belleau; and second, to take the railroad station of Bouresches, the town of Bouresches, the brook crossing 173.9–264.1, Hill 126, and Hill 133. The final designated objectives would place the line of the Marine Brigade on the south heights of the Clignon.[53]

TAKING BOURESCHES

The Germans now held a salient with its apex pointed at Lucy-Le-Bocage southeast of Belleau. Harbord's original plan was to conduct an attack in two phases: first clear Belleau Wood and then establish a line to Bouresches, a town just east of Belleau Wood.[54] The French urged caution and use of infiltration to take the woods, but Harbord wanted the woods taken by storm, which was a major error, since the Germans were dug in.[55] While the Marines were struggling to hold Hill 142, artillery preparation of Belleau Wood started before 1700 hours and was largely ineffective. There were still over three hours of daylight left. Colonel Catlin observed:

> We now stood facing the dark, sullen mystery of Belleau Wood. That the wood was strongly held we knew, and so we waited. That something was going on within those threatening woods we knew, for our intelligence men were not idle.... The report on this morning [6 June] was to the effect that the Germans were organizing in the woods and were consolidating their machine gun positions, so that a sortie in force seemed not unlikely. As a matter of fact, we had been prepared for something of the sort for nearly two days. On the night of the 4th Lieutenant Eddy, the intelligence officer of the Sixth [Marine Regiment], with two men stole through the German lines and penetrated the enemy country almost as far as Torcy. They lay in a clover field near the road and watched the Germans filing past them. They listened to the talk and observed what was going into the woods.[56]

The 1st Battalion of the 5th was decimated taking Hill 142; the 2nd Battalion was tied up at Saint-Martin Wood, so the 3rd Battalion would lead the attack against Belleau Wood. The battalion was without Stokes mortars or hand grenades to use against the German Maxims.[57] To make matters worse, Harbord did not know the condition of the troops. Like many senior officers of the day, he did not go forward to check.[58] The 3rd Battalion attacked east with the 6th Marine Regiment on their right and were stopped. Catlin, the 6th Regimental commander, had never been in Belleau Wood and assumed that it was a nicely manicured hunting preserve. Nothing could be further from the truth. Due to heavy undergrowth, visibility was limited to fifteen to twenty feet.[59] The fog of war settled in. Due to poor communications between the 3rd Battalion, 5th Marines, and the 6th Regiment attacking Belleau Wood from the south, the unit attacks were independent rather than a coordinated attack. The 6th Marines were moving through an open wheat field and the Germans would later say that they could clearly see the Marines advancing.

Lieutenant Clifford Cates, 96th Company, described the scene in a letter to his mother:

We moved across an open field and stopped in a small woods and my platoon was in a wheat field. The Boche machine guns and artillery opened up on us and it was some party. At a certain time and signal we got up and swept over a ground literally covered with machine gun bullets— it was my first charge, and mother it was a wonderful thrill to be out there in front of a bunch of men that will follow you to death.... Just a little note on some paper that was torn up by some shrapnel.... We charge across an open field for eight hundred yards and there were eleven machine guns playing on us—honest, the bullets hitting the ground were as thick as rain drops—one hit me solid on the helmet[60]—denting a dent in the size of a hen egg—it knocked me cold for a minute; another bullet went through the brim of my helmet, clipping my ear; another hit my shoulder bar, bending it, and went thru the shoulder of my coat—skimming my shoulder— pretty close, eh?[61]

Seeing that the line faltered, Gunnery Sergeant Dan Daly, 73rd Machine Gun Company, shouted, "For Christ's sake, men, come on! Do you want to live forever?"[62] The 3rd Battalion lost 400 men. Before the war Daly had been awarded two Medals of Honor, one in China and a second in Haiti. He received the Distinguished Service Cross for his actions in June 1918. He brought wounded men in while under fire and captured a machine gun emplacement single-handedly.[63]

Lieutenant Timmerman was with the 83rd Company, 6th Regiment. His diary describes the scene:

I again advanced out to the mound. The machine gun fire from the town opened up all around. I halted the platoon behind the mound. Immediately a terrible fire from the left flank was opened up from a little rise of ground about fifty yards away, also from our left rear by machine guns. I faced around and saw Swenson lying dead with a bullet hole through his forehead. At the same time I shouted to "Open fire to the right" pointing toward the hillock where a terrific fire was coming from. At this moment we had only been at the mound a minute or so while all this happened. I was hit in the left side of the face and fell forward thinking, "I've got mine," as I thought a bullet had ripped through under my eye. It knocked me out for a minute and then I felt better and although I was covered with blood I realized I had not been dangerously hit. My men were dropping around there so I told them to follow me and we ran back for the shelter of the woods.[64]

Harbord had already sent an order to Wise by runner:

Take three companies of reserve north on road to Torcy and go into the line on right of Feland between him and the 3d Battalion, 5th Marines [Berry]. Feland's

Medal of Honor two-time winner Dan Daly (USMC History Division).

right is supposed to be about one kilometer south of Hill 126. Berry's left near Hill 133. When you arrive approximately in position report by runner to Feland who is on road Champillon Torcy. Orders will be sent to Feland.[65]

In Wise's words:

That was the damndest order I ever got in my life—or anyone else ever got. It went on the calm assumption that all the objectives of the First and Third Battalion had been secured. Starting at two A.M. I was to go along the Lucy-Torcy road, find Colonel Feland, second in command of the Fifth Marines, whose P.C. was supposed to be somewhere near Champillon, and get orders from him what to do. I was between the devil and the deep sea. If I didn't move, I knew I'd catch hell. If I did move, I knew I was going right down into Germany.

It was dark as pitch. Finding Feland would be a miracle. Getting the men together after that blasting we'd just had was no easy job. I started to do it, after sending runners out to try and find Feland, inform him of my orders, and tell him I would get under way as near two A.M. as possible. That might have been a fine order to have sent out on a maneuver field. I didn't see exactly how it was going to work in war. But, being disciplined, we started. I had received no word from Feland. Evidently my runners hadn't been able to find him.[66]

Lieutenant Graves B. Erskine, later wrote,

We jumped off after about ten minutes of very light artillery concentration in and around the area of Bouresches and were met with murderous fire, mainly automatic weapons, some artillery and some mortar. My platoon consisted of fifty-eight men in addition to myself when we jumped off. About forty minutes later, five of us were left. A wounded Marine passed my platoon P.C. with a wound in his nose. I asked him to tell my captain, some distance in the rear, that we were

Fifth Marine Regiment gun crew in action (USMC History Division).

pinned down and could advance no further. About an hour later this poor kid crawled back to report the captain's words: "Goddamnit, continue the advance." This was at early night fall. We continued the advance.[67]

It was a slaughter and the attack was called off at 2115 hours. The sixth of June 1918 was the "Longest Day" for the Marines. The Marine brigade lost a total of 31 officers and 1,056 men, exceeding the collective losses suffered by the Marine Corps in its prior history.[68]

Lawrence Stallings was there and was awarded the Silver Star Citation for his valor that day for leading his men in the capture of a machine-gun position.[69] He was badly wounded and would become a famous author after the war.

In spite of losses, the 3rd Battalion entered Bouresches and held on while the fighting continued for over two weeks. Lieutenant Cates of the 2nd Battalion, 6th Regiment, occupied Bouresches with a total of twenty-one effective troops.[70] Jim Hatcher was there:

> A leading American magazine printed a story asserting that we found the bodies of three French women in the streets who had been outraged and killed by the Germans. As a matter of fact only one civilian remained in Bouresches when the enemy occupied it and that was an old man. He informed us that he had been treated with courtesy by the Germans and when our barrage fell on the town as we attacked, an officer had sent him to the most sheltered dugout available.[71]

The Marines mounted attacks six times before the Germans were expelled from Belleau Wood. One German private wrote home after his company had 30 out of 120 soldiers left: "We have Americans opposite us who are terribly reckless fellows."[72]

> This would be the big day for the 4th Brigade. At 0300 Wise and 2/5, less the 51st Co, and the two companies from 1/5, 17th and 66th, were relieved by the French and the latter began their trek homeward. In the meantime, Turrill with his orders, sent and received after midnight from brigade headquarters, was struggling with his two companies to make the deadline imposed for 1/5's assault upon Hill 142. He had at least two miles over broken ground, unreconnoitered in daylight, to get to his jumping-off post. When he arrived he had barely minutes to launch his attack over territory heavily defended by well-entrenched Germans with a multitude of Maxim machine guns, and with half of his battalion missing.[73]

Late in the afternoon, a single German eight-inch shell killed Captain Duncan, commander of the 96th Company, his first sergeant Joseph A. Sissler, a medic, and Lieutenant (jg) Weeden E. Osborne, a dentist, attached to the 4th Marine Brigade, who was attempting to treat Duncan for an earlier wound. Osborne received the Medal of Honor for attempting to treat the wounded while under fire:

> For extraordinary heroism while attached to the Fifth Regiment, United States Marines, in actual conflict with the enemy

Lieutenant (jg) Weeden E. Osborne (U.S. Navy)*

Captain Williams, 51st Company commander (center), and his company officers (author's collection).

and under fire during the advance on Bouresche, France, on 6 June 1918. In the hottest of the fighting when the Marines made their famous advance on Bouresche at the southern edge of Belleau Wood, Lieutenant, Junior Grade, Osborne threw himself zealously into the work of rescuing the wounded. Extremely courageous in the performance of this perilous task, he was killed while carrying a wounded officer to a place of safety.[74]

The Marines of the 2nd Division dug in near Les Mares Farm just west of Belleau Wood. The 55th Company's left flank was anchored on the farm and tied into the 51st Company on the right. There was a gap of 450 meters on the 55th Company's left and to where the 43rd Company picked up the line. Some French soldiers were used as gap fillers, but they would flee when the fighting started. The French were concerned about the color of the Marine uniform, which was different from U.S. Army brown. The Marines wore green and the shade was nearly the same as the Germans', so the French asked for a Marine to visit to check the uniforms since they did not want to shoot the wrong troops. All agreed it was the same color as the Germans', but there was nothing that could be done about it, so in French fashion all had a drink, and at least one Marine returned to his lines drunk.[75]

Friday, 7 June

Harbord reported his positions to General Bundy early on 7 June. The line ran starting on the right from Triangle Farm north to Bouresches and then northwest to the edge of the Belleau Wood two kilometers north of Lucy. The dressing stations and field hospitals were overloaded with wounded. It was an enormous task. On 6 June the 4th Brigade had lost thirty-one officers and 1,056 men, and of these six officers and 222 men were killed or died of wounds.[76]

> According to the division history, "June 7th was quiet," and "the 4th Brigade was preparing a resumption of its attacks on Belleau Woods," while several German divisions were pretty much used up and being replaced or retired. Factually, the 4th Brigade was in no condition to do anything except save itself. However, at 0200, 2/5 was moved forward into the St. Martin's Wood and placed to the right of 1/5 and the left of 3/5. A couple of hours later they repulsed a vigorous German attack and in early afternoon replaced 3/5 in line. Men and guns of the 23d Co., 6th MG Bn, helped to repel this dangerous attack from Torcy. At some time on this day a platoon of engineers from B Co., had been provided to Capt. Roswell Winans of the 17th Co. to prepare trenches in the first line. The 2d Engineers also had a busy day. Their personnel officer, lst Lt Alexander Kennedy, reported casualties of five killed and nineteen wounded.[77]

Saturday, 8 June

At midnight Bouresches came under attack, but machine guns had arrived and the line held. The Americans counterattacked on the morning of 8 June. After refitting, reinforcing and artillery preparation, the attack in Belleau Wood resumed. The 6th Regiment attacked the southern edges of Belleau Wood at 0540 hours. Reports were negative, as the advance was checked by more German machine guns than had been expected. Bouresches remained a key position for the 2nd Division and such forces as could be spared were sent to reinforce Bouresches.

Sunday, 9 June

On 9 June, an enormous Allied artillery barrage leveled Belleau Wood. What had been a beautiful hunting preserve was now a landscape of twisted downed trees and undergrowth. The Germans countered with artillery fire into Lucy and Bouresches and reorganized their defenses.

Monday, 10 June

On the morning of 10 June, elements of the 6th Marine Regiment and 6th Machine Gun Battalion attacked north into Belleau Wood. The commander of the 6th Machine Gun Battalion, Major Cole, was mortally wounded and was replaced by Captain Harlan Major. Initial reports were overly optimistic, indicating that the southern half of the wood had been taken. In fact, the 6th was only on the fringe of the Belleau Wood. German machine guns were holding up the advance. In addition, the density of the woods and confusion caused the Allied attack to stop without any gains.

Village of Bouresches after the battle (USMC History Division).

Tuesday, 11 June

Field Order 4 issued at the end of the day on 10 June called for the 2/5 supported by the 1/6 Battalion to attack the southeastern edge of the wood. The objective was the northeastern edge of the Belleau Wood. Wise, 2/5, was upset "[Harbord's order] meant needless death of most of my battalion.... Now instead of hitting the Germans from the rear, I had to take that battalion to a frontal attack against a prepared position."[78]

Gunnery Sergeant Don Paradis in 80th Company, 6th Regiment, later wrote,

> On June 11th Major Hughes' 1st Battalion (of the 6th Marines) Major Wise's (2nd Battalion of the) 5th Marines combined to make an attack on the center of Belleau Wood. The Germans plastered the entire area with artillery of all sizes. Added to the horror of mustard gas was the inclusion in their high explosives of a vomiting gas that made it almost impossible to keep a mask on and made eyes water to obstruct vision. That day the Germans showed clearly that their ammunition supply had caught up to the advance on Paris. Their observation system and communication were well coordinated for the immediate destruction of any sized detail we could advance. The enemy's observation was accurate so it could not have accidental that our medics and evacuation vehicles were hit indiscriminately. Captain Duncan of the 96th Company had been wounded. As the stretcher was being carried to the rear accompanied by the battalion doctor a German shell had made a direct hit, killing all four men [Duncan's death occurred on 6 June].[79]

The 2nd Battalion, 5th Regiment, commanded by Wise, was to attack east against the southern part of Belleau Wood. His objective was the northeastern edge of the wood including

Hill 133. Attack time was 0430 hours. As the troops moved forward, Wise quickly lost control of his companies. Among the companies, platoons lost contact with one another due to the heavy undergrowth and morning mist. Good news started to arrive indicating success, but the truth was that the companies were not sure where they were. Only Headquarters Company under Lieutenant de Carre was on track and had reached the area around Hill 169. He also cautioned Wise that the 2nd Battalion left flank was open. The companies were also uncertain where they were. Other commanders, including Neville, who were remote from the action echoed the success story. Nothing could have been further from the truth. Lieutenant William Mathews went forward with his intelligence section:

> With my men I went up through the big clearing, but when we came near the woods we ran on to scores of wounded who were lying unattended calling for help. We started giving first aid as best we could. A few minutes afterward [Marine Gunner] Mike Wodarezyk came marching out of the woods with a large group of prisoners of the 40th German regiment…. We could find no one in the north part of the woods and when I asked Mike what was over there he said nothing. I went back into the woods with Mike and he directed me to the point where I found Dunbeck, Wass, and Lieutenant Cooke standing together…. I said to them: "Are you sure you have reached your objectives?" All of them spoke up and said yes, and I distinctly remember that one of them, I believe it was Dunbeck, said: "We are at the north end of the woods, because there is Torcy (pointing to Belleau) and there is Belleau (pointing to Bouresches)." When I asked them or rather told them that a great mass of the woods was totally unoccupied they insisted that it was all behind them and therefore safe.[80]

Line after line of Marines were mowed down by the entrenched German machine guns as they moved forward and achieved nothing. Lloyd Williams, 51st Company, was fatally wounded during the fight on 11 June. He was posthumously awarded the Distinguished Service Cross for his actions during the Battle of Belleau Wood. With over 50 percent of his men casualties and only one officer remaining, he continued fighting until wounded by machine-gun fire. Lieutenant Orlando Perry, the navy surgeon assigned to the 5th Regiment, located his dressing station at Lucy-Le-Bocage. When the dressing station was destroyed by artillery, he carried Lloyd Williams to safety while under fire and was awarded the Medal of Honor for his actions to save the wounded.[81]

Wise, who had no clue where his companies were located, passed false reports of success to Harbord, who sent them to Division, and so on. On 11 June the *New York Times* published the following headline: "OUR MEN TAKE BELLEAU WOOD, 300 CAPTIVES," and continued:

Dr. Orlando Perry (U.S. Navy).

Paris, June 11

The official statement of the War Office tonight says: South of the Ourcq River the American troops this morning brilliantly captured Belleau Wood and took 300 prisoners.[82]

In the following days as reality set in attacks to seize terrain already reported as seized continued. By mid–June, the effects of gas attacks were taking their toll.

Wednesday, 12 June

Wise received 150 badly needed replacements who were distributed among the companies. The 51st Company had been virtually wiped out and the survivors would constitute a reserve. The plan was for a renewed attack against the southeastern wood by the three surviving companies of the 2/5 moving abreast. They met the Germans within fifty feet of the jump-off line and overran the enemy positions.

Captain William O. Corbin took command of the 51st Company when Williams died. Captain Samuel C. Cumming followed Corbin as company commander. Cumming received the Silver Star Citation for his actions. Cumming was severely wounded while leading his platoon under fire and later at Blanc Mont he fearlessly led his troops in disregard for his own safety.[83]

Thursday, 13 June

On 13 June, the Americans and Germans were equally exhausted, but the Germans started early at 0130 with a counterattack that was repulsed. On this day and the days that followed German artillery and gas attacks took their toll.

Gunnery Sergeant Fred W. Stockham, 96th Company, was awarded the Medal of Honor for his actions during a gas attack on the 13th of June:

> During an intense enemy bombardment with high explosive and gas shells which wounded or killed many members of the company, G/Sgt. Stockham, upon noticing that the gas mask of a wounded comrade was shot away, without hesitation, removed his own gas mask and insisted upon giving it to the wounded man, well knowing that the effects of the gas would be fatal to himself. He continued with undaunted courage and valor to direct and assist in the evacuation of the wounded, until he himself collapsed from the effects of gas, dying as a result thereof a few days later. His courageous conduct undoubtedly saved the lives of many of his wounded comrades and his conspicuous gallantry and spirit of self-sacrifice were a source of great inspiration to all who served with him.[84]

In his memoir, Wise recalled one of his last meetings with Harbord:

> I met with Brigadier General Harbord behind the lines. He was sore because I hadn't cleared out the Germans in the woods on the left of our line in Bois de Belleau. I was sore at that last-minute change of orders that had thrown my battalion into that suicidal frontal attack on a prepared position after I had completed the plans for taking it from the rear; after Harbord himself had given me a free hand. It wasn't a pleasant interview. "Twice you reported to me that those woods were clear of Germans when they weren't," he said. "I did," I told him, "but the minute I found out my error by personal inspection, you were notified about it." Then I learned what was irking him. He himself had reported the woods clear, and had had to back-fire on it!… I blew up. "If you had so much doubt about those woods being clear, why the hell didn't somebody from Brigade come out and take a look?" I asked him. I don't remember exactly what I did say after that. It must have been plenty. General Harbord wasn't pleased. He departed. I knew then my goose was cooked as far as he was concerned.[85]

By 23 June, Major Ralph S. Keyser replaced Wise as commander of the 2nd Battalion, 5th Marines. Wise paid the price for the bad reports of success that he had sent forward to Harbord but would later return to the 5th.[86]

The Battle of Belleau Wood dragged on for weeks and is summarized by Elton E. Mackin, 67th Company, 1st Battalion, 5th Marines:

> We took Belleau Wood over a period of weeks, a bit at a time. Our method of attack was a departure from orthodox warfare as practiced by Europe folks. We didn't confine our time of attack to the hour of early dawn, but were liable to go forward without warning at any hour of the day or night. These attacks were an aggravation to the enemy in that they were always unexpected and not planned to be extensive, instead being gauged only on the ability of the men concerned for themselves a bit more, ever a bit more, of enemy-held territory…. The enemy found this very disconcerting.[87]

The carnage had the effect of causing people to do what they normally would not:

> I can't explain the man's motivations. With the rest of us standing around on guard. Steiny drove his bayonet through each of those fifteen German prisoners [we had taken]. Nobody tried to stop him. Nobody much questioned it. The reality was that we couldn't take the prisoners with us and they were going to get away in the darkness. We didn't have any men to spare to guard them. It was done and nobody said a thing. We picked up our gear and moved out going single file through the weeds along a trench line. I had a case of German hand grenades in each hand.
>
> Jim Scarbrough, 6th Marines[88]

Major Maurice Shearer now commanded the 3rd Battalion of the 5th Marines and his battalion was ordered in to Belleau Wood. On 26 June 1918, Major Shearer was able to truthfully report: "Woods entirely U.S. Marine Corps."[89] The French soon learned of the victory.

> On June 30, General Degoutte, commanding the French Sixth Army, sent the following message: In view of the brilliant conduct of the 4th Brigade of the 2nd U.S. Division, which, in a spirited fight, took Bouresches and the important strong point of Bois de Belleau, stubbornly defended by a large enemy force, the General Commanding the Sixth Army orders that henceforth, in all official papers the "Bois de Belleau" shall be named, "Bois de la Brigade des Marines."[90]

As word spread of the Allied victories, Ludendorff was losing touch with reality:

> In spite of a few unavoidable temporary crises, our troops remained masters of the situation, both in attack and in defense. They proved themselves superior to both the English and the French, even when their opponents were assisted by tanks. At Château Thierry [sic], Americans who had been a long time in France bravely attacked our thinly held fronts. but they were unskillfully led, attacked in dense masses, and failed. Here, too, our men felt themselves superior. Our tactics had proved sound in every way, our losses, compared with those of the enemy and the large number of prisoners, though in themselves distressing, had been very slight.[91]

General Pershing summarized the Battle of Belleau Wood:

The attacks begun on June 6th by the 2d Division culminated in the capture of the last German positions in Belleau Wood by its Marine Brigade and of Vaux by its Regular Infantry Brigade. The fighting during most of this period was intense. The German lines were favorably located on commanding ground and were made more formidable by the extensive use of machine guns, especially in Belleau Wood. The success of this division against an enemy determined to crush it was obtained with but little assistance from the tired French divisions on its flanks. In the initial advance, the Marine Brigade (Harbord) captured Bouresches, and the Infantry Brigade (Lewis) made substantial gains. The progress during the next few days was slow but steady. On the 15th, the 7th Infantry, 3d Division, was attached to the 2d Division, relieving the Marines in the Wood, and holding the front there for a few days. The Marines then reentered the line beginning on the night of the 21st, After an all-day artillery preparation on the 25th, they drove the enemy from his last position in Belleau Wood during the late afternoon and night. Meanwhile, the Infantry Brigade continued its attacks, and on

German prisoners after Belleau Wood—they looked tough, but that was not enough (Library of Congress).

July 1st, in a brilliantly executed operation, captured the village of Vaux. The division made no further advance. By July 9th, when it was relieved by the 26th Division, its lines had been consolidated on high ground captured from the enemy.[92]

Aftermath

Belleau Wood did not win the war, but it was a good start. It demonstrated that the Allies were better than just planning retreats. The Germans had been stopped and withdrew. Paris was saved, but before the battle was over Harbord had developed his own set of lessons learned that he distributed to the battalions on 8 June. Had he waited, a bit, he could have added more, but it is a fairly good set applicable to any war:

> The following suggestions occur from consideration of the week's fighting and are published for the information and action of company, battalion and regimental commanders:
>
> 1. Reports that do not show the time of sending are worthless.
> 2. "Losses are heavy" may mean anything. Percentages or numbers are desired.
> 3. Figures or conditions that are only estimated should be so stated.
> 4. Flanks of positions and any important peculiarities such as re-entrants, salient's and refusals, should be described by [map] coordinates as far as practicable. Artillery cannot be called for with safety unless position of our Infantry is accurately known.
> 5. The number of machine guns and prisoners captured to hour of writing reports is information that ought to be included in them.

After the Armistice: visiting the graves of Belleau Wood (USMC History Division).

6. Dispersion of troops is the fault of beginners as pointed out by all military authorities, and has in our Brigade, with the length of our line, deprived us of the necessary echelons in depth.

7. Officers given a task must plan to execute it with forces at their own command, and not count on reinforcements which may not be available. Only a grave emergency not apparent when the task is begun will justify requests for help. Supports have been thrown in during this first week at a rate not to be expected hereafter.

8. The enemy have been told that Americans do not take prisoners, which makes their men fight to the death rather than surrender when they think they will be given no quarters. This idea that we do not take prisoners undoubtedly costs us many lives.

9. The heavy losses of officers compared to those among the men are most eloquent as to the gallantry of our officers, and correspond nearly to the propor-

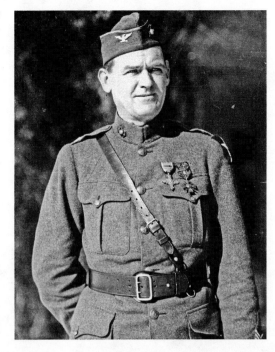

Colonel Logan Feland after the war (USMC History Division).

Village of Belleau after the battle (USMC History Division).

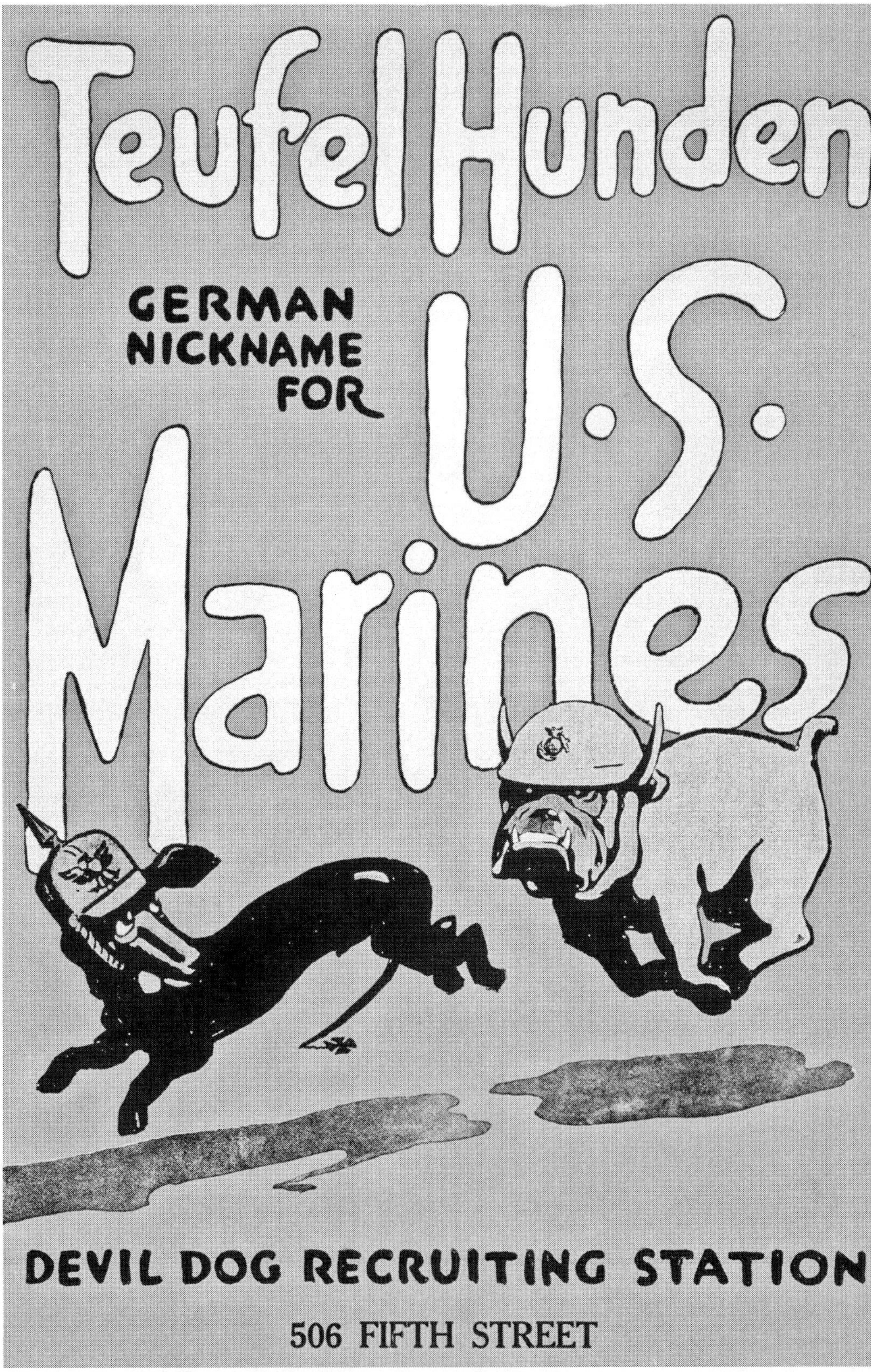
Teufel Hunden
GERMAN NICKNAME FOR
U.S. Marines
DEVIL DOG RECRUITING STATION
506 FIFTH STREET

The Marine Corps mascot (USMC History Division).

tions suffered by both the Allies and the enemy in 1914–15. Officers of experience are a most valuable asset and must not be wasted.

10. Recommendations for decorations should be made with discretion but as promptly as possible. The "extraordinary heroism" which calls for the D.S.C. [Distinguished Service Cross] must be liberally interpreted in cases of officers and men who have met death or suffered the loss of a leg, an arm, or an eye in action. The French Corps Commander has asked for recommendations for awards of the Croix de Guerre. This should be submitted promptly and in good faith.[93]

The secret of the success at Belleau Wood was due largely to the superior marksmanship of the American Marines and soldiers. No doubt the German soldier was the best trained in the world, and a soldier's training marks the upward stride towards victory over defeat. He is no coward, as he demonstrated over and again, especially when amply supported by his comrades and officers. He did lack quick perception, resource, and beyond all he was a poor marksman. General Albertus Catlin, in his report of the Battle of Belleau Wood, declared: "The enemy remained in force to the north of the town [Bouresches], his machine guns were still thick in the greater part of the wood, and his big guns thundered from back of Torcy. He was daunted by our first rush, but he came back. It took the Marines many days to finish the job, but finish it they did."[94]

U.S. forces suffered 9,777 casualties, included 1,811 killed. Many are buried in the nearby Aisne-Marne American Cemetery.

Opposite: **The Devil Dog (Library of Congress).**

After I experienced the incredible fighting at Belleau Wood and had not been injured, I honestly thought I was immortal. Shortly afterwards, I was wounded at Soissons. I was also gassed and for the rest of my life when I had to have chest x-rays, technicians would claim that I had TB because of the scarring on my lungs. In 1963 I visited Château Thierry where there is a U.S. cemetery for Americans lost in the battle. The land for the cemetery was given to the U.S. and is no longer French territory. I walked among the graves seeing crosses for friends who had died there 45 years before.

Raymond P. Rogers,
51st Company[95]

Many personnel changes occurred. General Harbord took over the 2nd Division while newly promoted General Buck Neville replaced Harbord as commander of the Marine brigade. Colonel Feland took command of the 5th Regiment when Neville departed.

Nearly all of the original company and platoon commanders had been lost. Companies had only one or two officers remaining, so General Pershing decided to promote enlisted soldiers and fill the officer ranks with these rather than bringing in new officers.

One of the greatest tributes to the Marines was provided by the Germans. It was rumored that a captured German dispatch reported that the Marines fought like *Teufelhunden,* the mythical canine guardians of the underworld. From this, the Marines adopted the name "Devil Dogs," a name still used today.[96]

There were rumors among the troops that they would get a two-week liberty in Paris for a 4th of July parade, but this would not happen for most Marines. A few were selected,[97] but fate intervened for most at a place called Soissons.

Fourth of July 1918, parade in Paris (USMC History Division).

Soissons—18–22 July 1918

The Germans had gained ground during their offensives during May through June 1918. A German salient or bulge in the Allied line aimed at Paris remained in spite of the Allied victories at Belleau Wood and Château-Thierry. At home the Germans were faced with famine

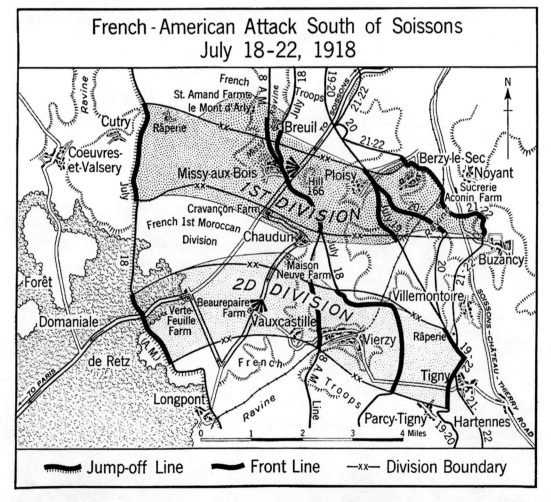

Attack at Soissons (U.S. Government Printing Office).

and political upheaval. Although the collapse of Russia allowed the Germans to move divisions to the western front, they were threatened by the continuing arrival of new U.S. units from the States. In spite of unrestricted submarine warfare by the Germans, not a single life was lost by the United States in moving troops to Europe. In the end, the United States would raise an army of 4 million men and by 1918 the troops were arriving in increasing numbers. The Germans would need to act now, before it was too late.[1]

The Germans planned a continuation of their series of offensives to start on 15 July, in another thrust toward Paris. This, the fifth and last German offensive, was called Frieden-sturm. They hoped the attack would force the Allies to commit their reserves and cripple any planned Allied offense. The Allies planned a counteroffensive to eliminate the German salient and its supply and communications hub at Soissons. The Allied attack would commence on Bastille Day,[2] 14 July 1918. While the Allied attack was delayed, the German attack went forward as planned at 1310 hours on 15 July. It crossed the Marne River but then ground to a halt. The Germans were informed by a traitor on the French general staff of the planned Allied attack. Also, there were other indications that the Allies were on the move. As a result, it was apparent that any further German penetration would increase danger to their forces in the salient.[3] The German offensive stopped and they moved to the defense. The Allied plan was

French Renault light tank (USMC History Division).

to attack the rail junction at Soissons, cutting the German supply line and reducing the German salient that bulged as far as the Marne River. This would trap thousands of Germans and force the rest to withdraw to the German border.[4]

The Battle of Soissons was fought from 18 to 22 July 1918. It was an Allied offense that sought to eliminate a German salient aimed at Paris. The Allies under Foch included 345,000 troops of French, British and U.S. units (mostly the 1st and 2nd Divisions). The Germans under Ludendorff fielded 234,000 troops. The battle involved significant use of tanks, including 350 Allied and 230 German.

Thursday, 18 July

The 1st and 2nd U.S. Divisions were a part of the French XX Corps. The attack against the German salient started on 18 July. The 1st Division was in the north, with the 2nd Division farther south, the two U.S. divisions separated by the French 1st Moroccan Division. The 2nd Division had an eight-mile sector with the Marine brigade on the left flank. The battle would be fought on a plateau with some deep ravines. Gone were the trenches that had dominated the World War I landscape to that point. This was mobile warfare.[5]

The 5th Regiment along with other 2nd Division units had moved south after Belleau Wood for rest and relaxation (R & R). Rumors abounded that the division would move to Paris for more R & R. This would not happen. The 5th Regiment would lead the attack with the 6th Regiment in reserve. The objective was the town of Tigny, which dominated the Château-Thierry road. Significant resources were available to support the attack. In addition to massed artillery, many French tanks and aircraft were available. The Marines moved forward to their attack positions on the night of 17–18 July in a driving rainstorm. This led to delays and confusion. To make matters worse, the French trucks called camions,[6] after finding every pothole in the road, had dropped off the regiment twelve miles short of its destination.[7]

A disabled German tank (Library of Congress).

The 5th Regiment preparing to board camions (USMC History Division).

They now proceeded to hike through a dense forest known as Bois de Retz. The humid day brought forth an abundance of dark clouds, followed by rain, and in short order the trail was a muddy mess and getting worse. When evening approached, the increasing clouds created a thunderstorm full of wild lightning, wind gusts and constant loud thunder that masked the sound of bombs bursting in the distance. France does not have a lot of electric storms, so these weather conditions were quite uncharacteristic. Any enemy observation planes that were scouring the area were now taking protective cover. The black clouds remained through the night, but even without the clouds, the forest was so dense there would be total darkness everywhere. Occasionally a large cloud burst really opened up fully drenching everything, making the continuous deep ruts in the road sloshing mud pits.

Hiking in total darkness is not easy, but when combined with a lack of sleep, wet slushy conditions and soaked backpacks, which increased the overall load, the venture was now extremely difficult. Along their path was a constant procession of horses pulling pieces of artillery. There was not supposed to be any movement in the opposite direction, but at times there was a row heading back, away from the front lines, containing mules, wagons and equipment, making the trail very narrow. Rolling equipment often sank in the mud up to its axles and needed pushing to continue on.

It was so dark that one could not see the man in front of him, and when the line movement slowed, one's face usually hit the backpack or trenching tool of the man in front, and a domino effect soon started down the line. One considered himself lucky if he stayed on his feet. To avoid falling down, most men tried to hold onto the shoulder of the man in front to keep pace. At other times they tried to grab hold of anything they could but often didn't have much strength to hold on to maintain balance.

With the grueling march and sleep deprivation, some men literally passed out and were left by the wayside, while others fell off the side of the slightly elevated road into ditches and swamps breaking an arm or leg.[8]

Louis Linn's 77th Company of the Machine Gun Battalion was to support the attack:

We were dumped from a line of trucks on the roadside. We had been riding all night (16th and 17th) and up until then—about three o'clock in the afternoon—the trucks had been full of men and equipment and that ride had been more of an ordeal than a respite. There had not been space for us all to sit down at one time and we had been jounced and banged about unmercifully on the rough roads. Yet we had managed to catch some sleep in short, interrupted naps. From the roadside we climbed a wall into a meadow field, crossed it and the brook at its border, and arrived at the base of a great forest-clad hill. This forest teemed with life and soldiers of all nations. There were French batteries, limbered and ready to go forward; English tanks and tank corps; Italian engineers; Polish and Belgian infantry; and Bengalese and Sengalese and Chinese, all milling through these trees, intent upon their own affairs and going up or coming down that enormous hillside. It took the better part of an hour to gain the summit. The day was blazing hot and we breathed a sigh of pleasure when we got there. We were told to prepare our suppers and rest; at midnight we were to go in.[9]

The 5th Regiment, slipping and sliding, moved forward to their attack position well back from the edge of a forest. Some had legs broken when they skidded off of the trail. Later they would recall that the move forward was worse than the battle. Nevertheless, the attack kicked off at 0435.[10] French tanks clanked forward and this reduced German resistance, which was far less than that encountered at Belleau Wood. The long war and the fatigue had taken their toll on the Germans. The attack proceeded on schedule until the tanks pulled back to rearm and refuel. This was followed by a heavy German artillery barrage that caused many casualties, and dusk found the Marines in an old trench line two kilometers short of the objective. Sergeant (later Lieutenant) Louis Cukela received the Medal of Honor for his actions on that day:

> For extraordinary heroism while serving with the Sixty-sixth Company, Fifth Regiment, during action in the Forest de Retz, near Viller-Cottertes, France, 18 July 1918. Sergeant Cukela advanced alone against an enemy strong point that was holding up his line. Disregarding the warnings of his comrades, he crawled out from the flank in the face of heavy fire and worked his way to the rear of the enemy position. Rushing a machine-gun emplacement, he killed or drove off the crew with his bayonet, bombed out the remaining part of the strong point with German hand grenades and captured two machine guns and four men.[11]

Sergeant Matej Kocak of the 66th Company was also awarded the Medal of Honor for his actions at that time. He was later killed at Blanc Mont:

> For extraordinary heroism while serving with the Sixty-sixth Company, Fifth Regiment, Second Division, in action in the Viller-Cottertes section, south of Soissons, France, 18 July 1918. When a hidden machine-gun nest halted the advance of his battalion, Sergeant Kocak went forward alone unprotected by covering fire and worked his way in between the German positions in the face of heavy enemy fire. Rushing the enemy positions with his bayonet, he drove off his crew. Later the same day, Sergeant Kocak organized French colonial soldiers who had become separated from their company and led them in an attack on another machine-gun nest which was also put out of action.[12]

John Thomason was recommended for the Medal of Honor for his actions on 18 July, but that was downgraded to the Navy Cross. With seven other Marines he destroyed a German machine-gun nest, killed thirteen Germans and captured two machine guns.[13]

The 5th Marines was exhausted by the day's fighting and in the morning the 6th Marines took over leading the attack. The 5th had taken four miles of German territory as well as many prisoners and weapons.[14]

Friday, 19 July

At dawn on 19 July, the 6th Marines led the attack against strong German resistance and withstood German counterattacks. As a result the German forces were forced to withdraw. Casualties were heavy.

Louis Cukela (left) with other officers after the battle (USMC History Division).

Louis Linn's 77th Company was supporting the 6th Marines and he recalled the attack:

Behind the crest of a hill we lay as tight to the ground as we could stick. We were in a nasty box, caught in a crossfire of our own and the enemy's artillery. The air above hissed with flying bullets from the German maxim, that plugged into the ground or our bodies, as the case might be. We had outrun our schedule as usual, and our own artillery, instead of lifting to clear away before us, was drilling the hillside on which we lay, with holes, and our bodies with metal. How many of our own men at that spot were killed by our own shells, I would not like to say. [Linn was mistaken. It was actually German and not friendly fire.] So we lay praying that at least our own fire would raise; the German fire was heavy enough. While shells came screaming in from front and back, tearing up the ground and rolling over the men like inanimate bundles of rags, we lay with our faces thrust hard into the dirt, slightly contracting our features as each shell scream ended in a roar and cloud of blown up earth and smoke. Then forward. From the crest of the hill, all hope of descending that shell-beaten, exposed slope alive looked impossible. The earth fairly danced beneath a hail of exploding "eight-eights." We ran straight into that fire. In no order at all, we ran down that hill. Who fell in that run, we neither saw nor cared. Throwing ourselves into the ditch that edged it, we thrust our rifles through the hedge, on its bank, and began to fire. We were in action again and that was some relief.[15]

The Allies lost 125,000 troops while the Germans lost 168,000. The 5th Marines lost five officers and 38 enlisted killed and eighteen officers and 360 enlisted wounded. Thirty-four enlisted were missing. These were heavy casualties coming on the heels of Belleau Wood. At Soissons, company commanders were hard hit, with one killed and four wounded and evacuated.[16] When the battle ended, the Allies had recaptured most of the ground lost in May and had forced a general withdrawal by the Germans. Some historians conclude that this battle was the turning point of the war.[17]

The battlefield of Soissons (USMC History Division).

After I was wounded in Soissons I was sent to a hospital in Paris to recover. At some point prior to being re-assigned to a unit, I was tapped to serve as a bodyguard for General Pershing. I stood guard outside the box occupied by General Pershing at the famous *Follies Bergere*. When the show was over and General Pershing was departing, he turned to me and said: "Well, I see we still have a few good Marines." What he didn't know was that I was too young and skinny to be a Marine, but I had worked hard to be in the Corps and eventually succeeded. Forty five years later, I sat in a box directly across the theater from where Pershing had viewed the show. Also during that visit in 1963 I liked to talk about the women of Paris. Claimed they would walk up to you on the street and offer their services. My wife told me that had been during the war but was not true, today. Following our attendance at the *Follies*, we were outside the theater waiting for a cab when a woman approached me, chatted me up and asked if I was alone. I quickly pointed out my wife and daughters and she moved on. No visit to France would have been complete without a visit to the Aisne-Marne Cemetery where some of my buddies were buried. We visited the cemetery and it was well cared for.

Private Raymond P. Rogers,
51st Company[18]

7

St.-Mihiel—September 1918

We looked like army men. Our forest greens had gone at Belleau Wood because we looked too much like Germans at a distance—and suffered casualties from our own troops because of it. We wore the army uniform, and only an occasional insignia here and there on pistol holsters, caps, and such identified us as Marine Corps—until you heard us talk. We were proud of many things, not least of all the fact that we were the outcasts of the

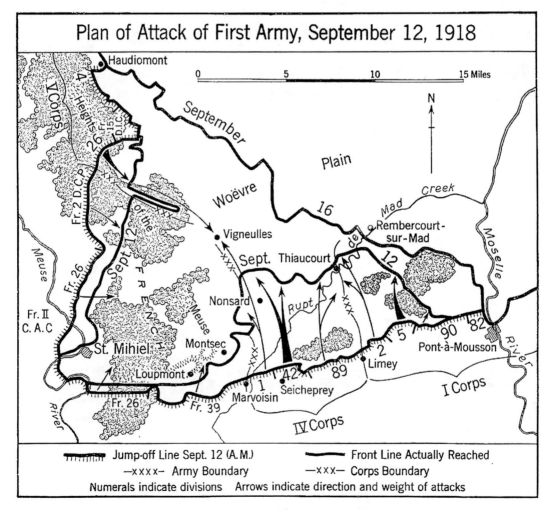

Plan of Attack of First Army, September 12, 1918

Jump-off Line Sept. 12 (A.M.) — Front Line Actually Reached
—xxxx— Army Boundary — xxx— Corps Boundary
Numerals indicate divisions   Arrows indicate direction and weight of attacks

Fourth Brigade Commander General Lejeune (center) and staff planning the St.-Mihiel operation (USMC History Division).

> AEF—the leathernecks. We kept our fierce self-conceit and pride…. [The new Marine arrivals assumed that the 5th was an army regiment because of the brown uniform.] The cocky kid? If his service record said he was more than seventeen years, he had sure lied to the recruiting sergeant. "You're goddam right we're leathernecks, you sons of bitches, you! Yah! Look us over, army—you drafted bastards."
>
> Elton Mackin, 5th Marines[1]

Following the Battle of Soissons, the 5th Regiment moved to reserve and took a two-day train journey to the Marbache Sector near Nancy. The move was also intended to deceive the Germans and divert their attention from St.-Mihiel, where the next Allied offensive was planned.

General Lejeune moved from command of the 4th Brigade on 28 July to command of the 2nd Division. Nancy was a quiet sector and the troops got much-needed rest and liberty. On 5 August, the secretary of the navy and future president of the United States, Franklin D. Roosevelt, inspected the regiment. While Marbache was a quiet sector, casualties occurred.

Opposite: **The Battle of St.-Mihiel (U.S. Government Printing Office).**

Two men of the 5th were killed and seven were wounded. Most were lost when an ammunition dump exploded. On 14 August the 5th Regiment was relieved of responsibilities in the Marbache sector and moved to a nearby training area.[2]

Then, in early September, the 5th Regiment moved to the St.-Mihiel sector in preparation for the Allied offensive. The Germans had developed a salient at St.-Mihiel early in the war and the French had failed to dislodge the Germans. The salient was shaped like a triangle measuring twenty-five miles wide and sixteen miles deep. Its value to the Germans was that it protected the strategic centers of Metz and Briery. It also cut Allied traffic from Paris to Nancy as well as between Verdun and Toul. Its reduction was essential to future Allied operations.[3] The St.-Mihiel offensive would start on 12 September to reduce the salient as a part of a more decisive operation in the same area. This was the first independent AEF operation and was designed to give front-line experience to the U.S. divisions.

> On September 12, in the first major action of the war under American command, ten divisions (216,000 men) of the First American Army under General Pershing, supported by four French divisions (48,000 men), launches an attack on the Saint Mihiel salient against 75,000 German troops under Lt. Gen. von Fuchs. The Allies advance five miles along a twelve-mile front in heavy rain.... The assigned objective of the Second Division is to take the towns of Thiaucourt and Jaulny and continue to the northwest another six miles or so, until their line is straightened out. The Third Brigade of the Second Division leads the attack, with the Twenty-third Infantry on the left and the Ninth Infantry on the right. The Fourth Brigade of Marines follows in support, with Seventy-seventh Company joining the Third Battalion, Fifth Marines on the Ninth Infantry's right flank.[4]
>
> The Germans were in the process of retreating from areas they had held since 1914. The bulk of the upcoming battle would not take place in the town itself [Thiacourt] but in the neighboring vicinity. The Allied Forces wished to reconnect with Saint-Mihiel for several reasons, one of which was to open up several of the railroad lines for movement of supplies further into the region. Therefore the current overall objective was to push the Germans back further and capture control of the double and four track railways. Additionally, the Allied Force wished to recapture coal fields and the all important Briey iron fields, which were essential to steel production for the German aggression. The iron basin was believed to contain roughly 80 percent of all the iron in continental Europe.[5]
>
> ...the Germans had been preparing a withdrawal.... However, they didn't seriously begin planning or moving until they observed the American development opposite them during the previous few weeks So when the advance began, the enemy was not standing and fighting fiercely as they would a few days later on. Therefore, the advance by the 1st Army on the southern face was comparatively easy, meaning that for once the 2d Division had a relatively easy time of it.[6]

Thursday, 12 September

Louis Linn described the Allied artillery preparation. It started at 0100 and lasted four hours, followed by the attack:

> We were to be the first over. We were, therefore, of course, the last to arrive. In a deluge of rain we came to the end of the communicating trench, holding to one another's coats to keep from getting lost in the blackness. Occasionally a cannon spoke from the German lines. Otherwise the rattle of the falling water and the slosh of our feet in the mud made up the only sounds to be heard.
>
> We were stopped for a time at the entrance to the trenches and as we stood looking gloomily into the rainy night, a roar like the end of the world burst suddenly upon our

ears. Our whole side of the horizon suddenly leaped into a flashing stupendous uproar. A wavering, vibrating light, like the aurora borealis, crept up across the sky and as battery after battery added its crash to the prevailing din, the whole universe seemed shaken to one mad crash of explosion.

Although we were prepared for this, its arrival was so much more than we had expected, we instinctively tensed our bodies expecting a blow. The sound was so great, to be heard it was necessary to shout in the face of your listener, and even then it was doubtful he would understand.

The weird and ghostly light had now brought everything into visibility and through it the pouring rain looked like stripes of metal tinsel or some unreal effect of artificial scenery. We were now in a great hurry and floundered through the churned up mud of the trenches, tripping and falling in a wild scramble to get to our places. To add to our difficulty, the trenches were banked with men who had to flatten themselves against the sides to give us passage. But we got there at last, covered with mud and panting from our exertions.... At the point where we crossed, without the least opposition, the first line of enemy trenches, I don't think a man had been left alive in them. The trench had literally been torn open from end to end, its sides blown in, its emplacements shattered. Only maimed inanimate bodies mixed with the debris lay across our path.

At this point our tank foundered. These trenches were enormously deep and wide, regular tank traps, and further increased by the shell craters in them. The little whippet failed to bridge it and went down on its tail with its nose cocked up in the air. The more it squirmed and twisted the lower it sank. Finally its driver and gunner climbed out to look the situation over. The driver made a gesture so significant no words were needed. Only a Frenchman could have done it, a little shrug, a cant of the head, and an elevation of the palms, and he had written his "finis" to his career. This gesture, on a field of battle.

> Louis Linn,
> 5th Regiment[7]

The 2nd Division was part of I Corps and had the area around Thiaucourt as its objective. The exhausted Germans were facing a rested, trained and experienced army of determined fighters. Problems developed early on. The 3rd Brigade of army troops took off at 0500 hours, followed by the Marines. The Marines jumped off at 0540 hours on 12 September. The 3rd Battalion, 6th, led the Marines. Because of the delay, the Marines had trouble keeping up with the advance of the 3rd Brigade. In addition, the French light tanks were a problem. They had trouble keeping up with the fast-moving infantry and were constantly out of position. As a consequence, they were largely ignored by the battalion commanders. As the day wore on the Marines started to catch up with the 3rd Brigade and by 1700 hours the 3rd Brigade, passed through Thiaucourt. It was nearly to the army objective. Elton Mackin relates the tale of the wounded soldier who was passing through the 5th Marine lines headed back for "repairs," when an earnest young Marine replacement yelled, "Hey, buddy, how's things goin' up there?" His response sent a laugh through the Marines who heard: "Aw, hell, son, goin' fine. We're goin' through them like a dose of salts through a tall, thin woman."[8] Intermediate objectives fell quickly and Thiaucourt was seized. The attack covered over nine kilometers in less than a day, a distance unheard of in the earlier days of the war, when progress was measured in meters. One German counterattack was easily repelled.

Friday, 13 September

By now, the Germans knew that they had a problem and were streaming away from the battle area. Hospitals were evacuated and ammunition dumps were moved, but at the same time three German divisions were moved forward as a reserve to counter a continuation of the U.S. attack. Lejeune ordered the 4th Brigade to take over the attack and the 3rd Brigade took over the positions vacated by the Marines. The move was completed without incident by 0400 the following morning.

Saturday, 14 September

Early in the morning the Marines sent out patrols from their new positions vacated by the army. German artillery was firing on the Marine lines, but there were few casualties. The Marines established contact with the U.S. 89th Division on the left and the 5th Division on the right. It was a quiet day of patrolling, with light enemy resistance.

Sunday, 15 September

German resistance stiffened and their artillery increased. The 2nd Battalion was leading the 6th Regiment and was encountering heavy machine-gun fire. Casualties were mounting when a group of retreating Germans were pursued by Gunnery Sergeant William Ulrich of the 80th Company. He yelled at them to surrender:

> Most of them stopped and appeared to be responding to his direction. Just then, unfortunately, a nervous young Marine private opened up on them. This caused panic among those with their hands up and again they ran. Catching up with them Ulrich, again using his native German tongue, soon convinced the remaining group, all fifty one of them, to surrender to him. They did and he brought them back through the jittery Marines without further incident.[9]

Ulrich was awarded the Navy Cross for his actions that day. David E. Hayden was awarded the Medal of Honor for his work during the advance on Thiaucourt:

> For gallantry and intrepidity at the risk of his life above and beyond the call of duty in action at Thiaucourt, 15 September 1918, with the Second Battalion, Sixth Regiment, United States Marines. During the advance, when Corporal Creed was mortally wounded while crossing an open field swept by machine-gun fire, HAYDEN unhesitatingly ran to his assistance and, finding him so severely wounded as to require immediate attention, disregarded his own personal safety to dress the wound under intense machine-gun fire, and then carried the wounded man back to a place of safety.[10]
>
> Other men of 2/6 earned fine reputations that afternoon, one being a Chicago lad, Pvt. John Joseph Kelly, who will be later recognized, especially at Blanc Mont, a great battle to come. But at St Mihiel, as at Verdun, Belleau Wood and Soissons, this young man was at the forefront of fighting and leadership, assisting in capturing a machine gun nest. He convinced a senior sergeant, Henry S. Brogan, to pull together his 78th Company after it had been shattered and all officers were down. Kelly had done this same thing before but then he had assumed the leadership role.[11]

The U.S. divisions continued to move forward and the 5th Division took Rembercourt. As night fell, the Germans launched a counterattack at 2000 hours that was beaten back.[12]

The 5th Marines held their position until relieved by the 78th Division on the night of 15–16 September. Total 5th Marine losses during the St.-Mihiel battle were 28 killed and 143 wounded, while the 6th lost 101 killed with 416 wounded. The 6th Machine Gun Battalion lost an additional forty-one wounded. Total losses for the Marines were 132 dead and over

600 wounded. Some Marines thought that the battle was an easy one, a cakewalk. The 3rd Army Brigade thought otherwise with much higher losses. The St.-Mihiel battle occurred at the start of the second wave of the influenza pandemic. The wet weather and strain of battle sent hundreds back for medical treatment for the flu.[13]

Paul Gardner of the 207th Machine Gun Battalion wrote to his parents:

September 16, 1918

Dear Father and Mother,

I am still well and feeling fine. We are having fine times. The Germans go so fast that you can't see them…. I wish I was home to help you [with the planting], but I'm not but hope to be there by next year the way the Germans are making dust, the war will soon be over. I want to get back home and sleep in a good bed or in other words live like a civilized person once more.

Love, Paul[14]

8

Blanc Mont—September–October 1918

The next grinding field was the heights which the French had not been able to retake from the Boche for nearly four years. It was called Blanc Mont Ridge and its occupation allowed the Boche to easily view French territory for nearly fifty miles in every direction. No wonder the French casualties were enormous. Beginning on 3 October 1918 the 2d Division, split in half, was to climb the heights; the 4th Brigade on the west and the 3d Brigade on the east. The 6th Marines led off the 4th Brigade and by the early morning had made it to the ridge and had nearly, but not quite, cleared it of German defenders. The following day it was the turn of the 5th Marines to venture out on the plain against the town of St. Étienne. The plain, with several heights in between, was well covered by enemy artillery and machine guns. Marines at the scene unhappily called their position "The Box."[1]

Blanc Mont had been churned up by years of shelling to the point that the topsoil was gone and only the white chalk was visible. It was against this backdrop that the Allies advanced against the Germans who had held Blanc Mont since 1914. The Germans had been refining their defensive network at Blanc Mont for years. It was an important objective for the Allies since it would crack the German Hindenburg Line thought to be impenetrable.

In early September the French asked Pershing for the loan of a U.S. division to form a combined attack on the German-held high ground, Blanc Mont Ridge. Pershing obliged and the 2nd Division entrained on 25 September to move to Blanc Mont. The 4th Brigade was positioned on the left of the 2nd Division and the French were on the 4th Brigade's left flank.[2]

Thursday, 3 October

Most important were a series of trenches that faced the Marines. The Marine objective was Hill 210, with the French attacking at the same time on their left. The Essen Hook in the French sector was a strongpoint consisting of concrete bunkers and pillboxes. The 2nd Division attack was split around a known German strongpoint called Viper Woods. The main attack kicked off on 3 October at 0550 hours. The 6th Marines led off, followed by the 5th. Hill 210 was soon captured. By 0830 the 3rd Brigade objective was taken, which was the road leading to the Medeah Farm.[3] This was in spite of the fact that the attack ran into trouble early on when the French failed to take the Essen Hook but the 17th Company under Captain Hunt was diverted to protect the Marine left flank:

> The Marines also had a tough climb and suffered heavily on their left flank from German fire. At times the various platoons and even entire companies ventured over into the territory of where the 21st French DI should have been and killed, or drove out, the Maxims and gunners. Along this route "Johnny" Kelly, a runner for Capt. James McB. Sellers, skipper of the 78th Co., advanced

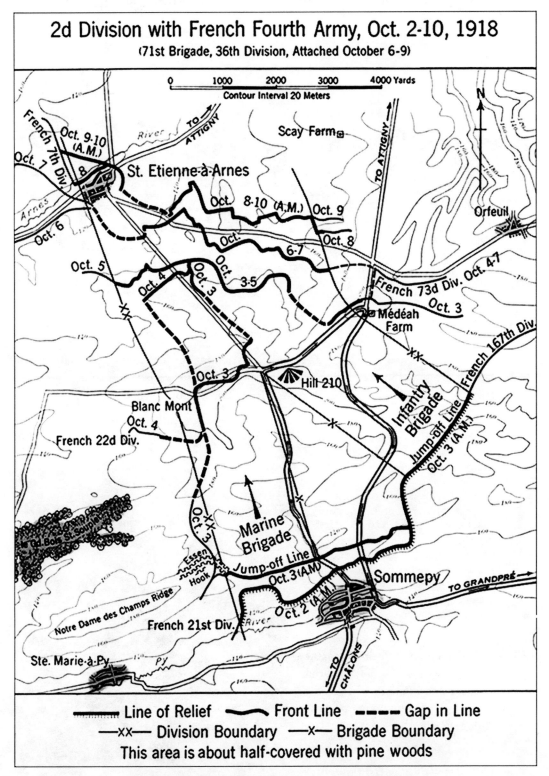

The Battle of Blanc Mont (U.S. Government Printing Office).

The chalk of Blanc Mont (USMC History Division).

before his company and the division's rolling barrage by at least 100 yards and took out a Maxim gunner and his assistant and then captured another eight Germans, making them prisoners. Marching them back to his company through the barrage he yelled "See! I told ya I'd do it."[4]

Kelly was awarded the Medal of Honor for his actions and survived the war, although he had a rocky career in the Marine Corps. His heroism occurred between court-martials. He later said that his fourth court-martial was for telling his company commander what he could do with his orders.[5]

For conspicuous gallantry and intrepidity above and beyond the call of duty while serving with the Seventy-eighth Company, Sixth Regiment, Second Division, in action with the enemy at Blanc Mont Ridge, France, 3 October 1918. Private Kelly ran through our own barrage a hundred yards in advance of the front line and attacked an enemy machine-gun nest, killing the gunner with a grenade, shooting another member of the crew with his pistol, and returning through the barrage with eight prisoners.[6]

Corporal John H. Pruitt also of the 78th Company, 6th Marines, took out two Maxims and would be awarded the Medal of Honor posthumously, since he was killed shortly after:

John J. Kelly wearing the French Croix de Guerre (with Palm) (USMC History Division).

For extraordinary gallantry and intrepidity above and beyond the call of duty while serving with the Seventy-eighth Company, Sixth Regiment, Second Division, in action with the enemy at Blanc Mont Ridge, France, 3 October 1918. Corporal Pruitt, single-handed, attacked two machine guns, capturing them and killing two of the enemy. He then captured 40 prisoners in a dugout nearby. This gallant soldier was killed soon afterward by shellfire while he was sniping the enemy.[7]

By 1100 the Marines were on the lower slopes of Blanc Mont, but the French had not moved forward, so a widening gap had developed on the Marines' left flank. To make matters worse, the Germans counterattacked and retook the ground covered by the 6th:

Corporal John H. Pruitt (USMC History Division).

The French 22nd Division was no better than the 21st Division they replaced, as they were nowhere in sight and the void of flank coverage was now an extremely serious issue. The Sixth Regiment in reserve was not able to advance and relieve the pressure, as they were caught up with fighting similar to what the Fifth Regiment faced on the prior day. Without backup the Fifth Regiment now had to handle on their own whatever came their way. There was now a constant procession of wounded Marines filling the makeshift dressing station, and Division Surgeon Derby decided to query one individual about his injury and what was transpiring on the front lines. Like a true Marine the wounded warrior knew exactly what the problem was, and he further enjoyed answering the officer's direct question without mincing words. He bluntly replied: "I got mine, sir, because those d——d 'Frogs' [French] never came up on our left, and we ran into cross fire. It's a habit with 'em. They're never there when you need their support."[8]

Friday, 4 October

The 5th Marines attacked at 0400 hours on 4 October but were stopped taking fire from three sides. It was a German trap. Portions of the attacking force (Major Larsen's 3rd Battalion) were cut off, but relief in the form of the 1st Battalion arrived and the 2nd Battalion was also engaged. They assembled in a small rectangle of woods called the Box. They continued taking heavy casualties until night fell.[9] The 6th Marine Regiment was ordered to take over the attack.

Lieutenant Merwin Silverthorne of the 20th Company earned the Navy Cross that day. He carried important messages to his battalion commander under heavy fire and was wounded.[10]

In addition, portions of the 6th Regiment arrived and a line was stabilized. Casualties had been heavy. Nearly half of the men of the 5th had been hit. Sergeant William E. Campbell received the Navy Cross for his actions. Although wounded twice, he assisted in giving first aid to the wounded and helped in defense of his position when the Germans advanced to within three hundred yards of the dressing station.[11]

Captain Macon Overton of the 76th Company was awarded the Navy Cross for his actions at Blanc Mont on 4 October. His battalion was held up by a machine gun he attacked and destroyed the position and then captured a field piece that was firing on his company.[12] He would not survive the war.

The 5th Regiment was ordered to pass through the 6th and move forward to seize Saint-Étienne-a-Arnes but was tied up defending their left flank since the French still had not moved. Casualties among the Marines were mounting.

As a consequence, the attack on Saint-Étienne was delayed until the following day:

Guarding the prisoners (while watching the card game) (USMC History Division).

The skipper made it a practice to travel well supplied with good cigars, and when things were hot we'd see him with a strong cheroot clamped in the comer of his mouth, barking orders like the noncom he had been in other days. Walking but a few steps away, I was with him when he first was hit. He had just finished saying, "Bring a Hotchkiss over here." The bullet caught him in the muscles of his neck and scarcely made him stagger. I swear he didn't even stop puffing on that big old black cigar. He stood there flat-footed and serene, as though it were a matter of everyday occurrence, while the rest of us sought shelter. He reached up to unsnap the collar of his blouse, opened his shirt, and turned the collar down, thrusting an exploratory finger into the wound along the side of his neck. After a little prodding he flipped the blood from his fingertips and gingerly took apart his

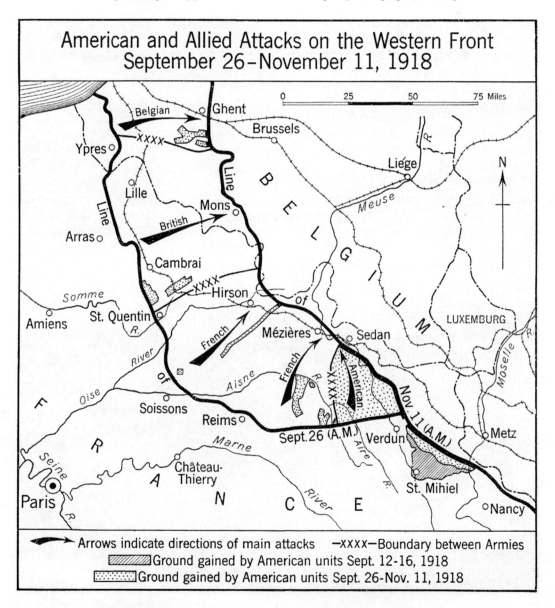

The western front as the war ended (U.S. Government Printing Office).

first-aid kit, then wrapped the bandage in it 'round and 'round his throat, reminding me of a man having difficulty with his necktie. Finishing that, he buttoned up his blouse again and went on being the skipper.

Elton Mackin, 1918[13]

Mackin was awarded the Navy Cross for his valor that day.[14]

George Hamilton of the 1st Battalion received the Silver Star Citation. He led his battalion and overwhelmed the Germans even though his unit's casualties were 85 percent.[15]

All of the company commanders of the 3rd Battalion were down. Late that night, a German counterattack was stopped.[16] All across the front, casualties were heavy. The bloodiest day of the war for the 2nd Division was 4 October 1918.[17]

> By the end of the day, the 5th Marines was in worse shape than the 6th had been in on 19 July at Soissons. It was the worse one-day loss the Marines had yet suffered in this or any war. Conditions were such that the 5th was pulled out of the battle and placed in reserve, not to be called upon except in dire emergency.[18]

The Marines moved to defensive positions on Blanc Mont Ridge and then were withdrawn to a rest area, relieved by the U.S. 36th Division. The 4th Brigade had lost 726 killed and 3,500 wounded between 2 and 10 October.[19]

> The Allied victories throughout the Argonne were decisive blows to Germany and the Central Powers. On the night of October 4, following the bloody full day at Blanc Mont, Germany's new chancellor, Prince Maximilian of Baden, offered a proposal for an armistice. The statement was first issued to leaders of Switzerland as mediators and upon translation the wording was forwarded to President Wilson on October 6. It read:

> The German Government requests the President of the United States of America to take steps for the restoration of peace, to notify all belligerents of this request, and to invite them to delegate plenipotentiaries for the purpose of taking up negotiations. The German Government accepts, as a basis for the peace negotiations, the program laid down by the President of the United States in his message to Congress of January 8, 1918, and in his subsequent announcements, particularly in his address of September 27, 1918. In order to avoid further bloodshed, the German Government requests to bring about the immediate conclusion of a general armistice on land, on water, and in the air."[20]

The Allies were preparing for the final push that would end the war.

9

Crossing the Meuse River—November 1918

The 4th Brigade rested, received replacements and refitted in preparation for what was to be their last offensive of the war. The brigade would be the spearhead of an attack against the German V Corps, which had been forced back across the Meuse River.

The 89th Infantry Division was on the left of the 2nd Division. The Meuse wound around and in front of the attacking force, including a run across the 89th and 2nd Divisions' boundary. Cold-water swimming was common, but not for recreation. Three members of the U.S. Army 89th Division were awarded the Medal of Honor for swimming the Meuse:

> During the operations near Pouilly, Sergeant M. Waldo Hartler, Private First Class Harold I. Johnston and Private David B. Barkeley, all of the 89th Division, volunteered to make reconnaissance of the hostile position on this bank of the river, although there were no means of crossing except by swimming. In carrying out their dangerous missions, Private Barkeley while returning to the American lines with the desired information which he had obtained, was drowned. The others succeeded after the greatest difficulty in securing and taking back valuable information concerning the enemy forces. For these daring acts the three were awarded Medals of Honor.[1]

As seen in the following extract, Raymond Rogers performed the same act and was charged with being AWOL because he had trouble finding his way back. "C'est la guerre!"

> The commanding officer [51st Company, 5th Marines] asked for volunteers to carry a message across the Meuse to the adjacent army division [the 89th]. I swam across with my buddy and it was icy cold water. My buddy later got pneumonia, but we got through okay and delivered the message [coordinating the move of the 5th Marines to the right flank of the 89th]. Our return was delayed. The problem was that we had great difficulty getting back because much of the journey was through terrain held by the Germans. As a result, I was declared AWOL and this held up the award of the Purple Heart for previous actions. Things settled out and the charge of AWOL was later dismissed.
>
> Private Raymond P. Rogers,
> 5th Marine Regiment[2]

Friday, 1 November

The Marine attack started from Buzancy on 1 November and at first met light resistance. Heavy fighting occurred at Landreville, but the advance toward the Meuse continued:

> November 7 was yet another rainy, bone-chilling day. Captain John W. Thomason Jr. of the 49th Company had been alongside Hamilton since the early days of Belleau Wood and survived

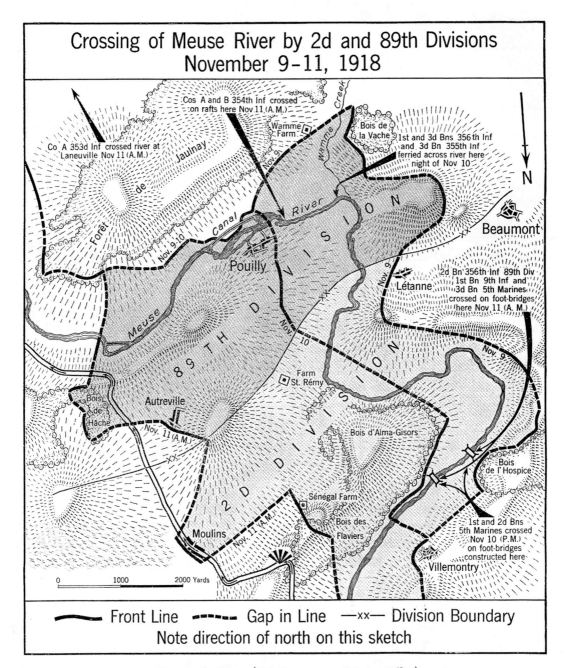

Crossing of Meuse River by 2d and 89th Divisions
November 9-11, 1918

Cos A and B 354th Inf crossed on rafts here Nov 11 (A.M.)

Co A 353d Inf crossed river at Laneuville Nov 11 (A.M.)

Wamme Farm

Bois de la Vache

1st and 3d Bns 356th Inf and 3d Bn 355th Inf ferried across river here night of Nov 10

N

Beaumont

Pouilly

Létanne

2d Bn 356th Inf 89th Div
1st Bn 9th Inf and
3d Bn 5th Marines
crossed on foot-bridges
here Nov 11 (A.M.)

Farm St. Rémy

Autreville

Bois d'Alma-Gisors

Bois de Hâche

Bois de l' Hospice

Sénégal Farm

Bois des Flaviers

1st and 2d Bns 5th Marines crossed Nov 10 (P.M.) on foot-bridges constructed here

Moulins

Villemontry

0   1000   2000 Yards

⸺ Front Line ▬▬▬ Gap in Line ⸺xx⸺ Division Boundary
Note direction of north on this sketch

Crossing the Meuse (U.S. Government Printing Office).

"The Box" at Blanc Mont. It was reassuring to Hamilton knowing that the officer was still along fighting and sketching as he went. The incessant cold rain however had taken its toll on Thomason's immune system, and with a 104 degree temperature, he had to temporarily fall out and receive medical assistance.

There was a constant trail of others like Thomason, who became weak with severe cold symptoms. During this week, the Second Division, which was already less than full strength, was losing about 500 men a day, 100 of which were battle casualties and 400 due to illness. Each battalion

The Meuse River where the Marines crossed (USMC History Division).

in the Fourth Brigade was now drastically reduced in size and losing more men each day. Most of these illnesses did not display symptoms of the Spanish Flu epidemic, which was killing many in Europe and America. It was exceptionally rare for the men in the open outdoors on the Western Front to get the flu. Military personnel who contracted the flu were usually well behind the front lines and indoors. Bronchitis and other cold symptoms were more common side effects from constant exposure to dampness and temperature fluctuations.[3]

Monday, 11 November

The plan to cross the Meuse on the night of 9–10 November was delayed due to lack of building materials, but on 11 November the Marines crossed on two bridges that had been constructed. They were to seize Bois de Flaviers and establish a bridgehead. The Marines crossed and heavy fighting occurred as they moved toward Bois de Flaviers.

Captain Cumming of the 51st was now the senior officer on the west side of the river and personally took out a machine-gun position as he attempted to link up with the 6th Marine Regiment. At this point, early in the morning of 11 November, rumors of an impending cease-fire were circulating among the troops. By 0845, the rumor was now fact and word was sent forward that the cease-fire would go into effect in two hours. This was difficult because the lead element command post, Major Hamilton's 1st Battalion, 5th Marines, was now on the far side of the river and the rickety footbridges were not holding well and occasionally collapsed. They were nothing more than empty drums with duckboards on top:

> As the width of the footbridge was only three feet, the Marines, as representatives of the "Indian Head" Division, went single file, Indian style. The path ahead on the flimsy bridge was reminiscent of past individual and team skill obstacle-course relay drills from their basic training days at Quantico and Paris Island. Now they were involved with the real deal. If the over-anxious men got too close to each other and bunched up, the bridge started to sink, so they quickly learned to space themselves 15 to 20 feet apart, leaving them only ankle deep in water. At the halfway point the

eastern bank was still not visible, although through the fog one could see the muted hot yellow flashes of the machine guns ahead.

Under the extreme conditions many casualties occurred during the crossing. Men later recalled hearing a "sock" noise that meant only one thing, the sound of a bullet hitting the flesh of a man in front or behind. Some wounded men ended up drowning in the river, while a few jumped into the river, believing it was safer, only to find that the strong current along with their weighted equipment was a lot to handle.[4]

Hamilton received an additional Silver Star Citations for his actions:

Then he received an SS and (2)CdG-P. at the Meuse River crossing, on the night of 10–11, when he again led his battalion forward and was again successful in crossing a pontoon bridge under heavy enemy fire, taking up positions on the east bank.[5]

Nov. 11, 1918.–9:10 a.m.

To Major Hamilton:

All firing will cease at 11 a.m. today. Hold every inch of ground that you have gained, including that gained by patrols. Send in as soon as possible a sketch showing positions of all until 11 a.m.

[Signed] Feland

Although the fighting stopped at 1100, Major Hamilton was properly holding his territory and following orders until official notification arrived. His dash had taken his men forward to such a distant and remote location over rugged terrain that inevitably a courier would have difficulty making contact with him. Most assuredly the major was in his proper location, as noted by his strong record of always ending up where he was supposed to be. The eight small Marine companies and the battalion of the 89th under his ultimate command were scattered around the surrounding vicinity. One noted historian stated, "It appears as though the 66th Company had penetrated farthest eastward."[6]

Word of the cease-fire reached Hamilton at 1145, but Cumming was isolated and got the word from the Germans three hours later. Everyone on both sides dug in to see if the cease-fire would hold. It did. Fortunately, no one was killed after the cease-fire, but on the last night of the war the 5th Marines lost 31 killed and 148 wounded. General Lejeune, the division commander, would write to his wife: "We fought our last battle ... it was pitiful for men to go to their death on the eve of Peace."[7]

On the eve of peace, Sergeant Melvin L. Krulewitch of the 78th Company was positioned near the bridges across the Muse:

Suddenly there came a new note in the approach of a whiz-bang and every marine froze to the spot. Each knew from experience that this particular high explosive had his name on it. Even if cover had been available, none could have been reached in time. Fascinated, immobile, they could only await the end. The shell landed squarely in the middle of the company. And in that fraction of a second between hit and explosion, there was no thought as to past and future. Each soldier braced himself for the terrific impact of the next moment when the fuse would detonate the charge. Nothing happened. For that little group of men came the war's greatest thrill—and my best birthday present. The fuse was a dud.[8]

On the eleventh hour of the eleventh day of the eleventh month in 1918 the guns fell silent: Armistice. As with so many fateful events, people recalled what they were doing at that time. Eugene Lee from Syracuse, New York, in the 51st Company, 5th Marines, remembered over eighty years after the event,

> At exactly 11:00 a.m. on the morning of November 11, 1918, somewhere in the Meuse-Argonne sector a German soldier come out waving a white flag, and he started walking down, and our officer went out to meet him. When they got there, all of a sudden, all the German soldiers come running down, and our fellows—well, we got up, and they got mixed up talking to—some could speak our language, and a lot of our fellows could speak German, so we had a great time changing, trying to talk. And they showed us pictures of their family, you know, and we had a great time to celebrate ... swapping souvenirs.[9]

Elton Mackin recalled,

> Rifles lay in readiness atop the little mounds of earth; a row of firing pits, a battle line. The bayonets, like sentinels, winked dully now and then, reflecting the light of distant fires along the front. Machine guns stood out starkly, tripods braced, muzzles peering ahead like eager, watchful dogs against the dark. The men were restless, wakeful, gathering about in little groups on blankets spread against the damp. They talked in quiet tones among themselves. Habit hid their cigarettes against their breasts, still fearful that an enemy would spot the glow. Lone fellows took their ease in quiet, staring thoughtfulness. Why did they, like their bayonets, peer toward the front? Was something gone? Why did no single one of them look toward the rear? There was a nervous tension in the air. It shattered when a fellow struck a match or laughed or raised his voice or moved too suddenly. At such time one saw men's heads snap up in quick alarm, in instant, wary watchfulness, and saw them search the shadows near at hand, then heard the hearty breath of quick relief as they remembered, trying to talk in a normal tone of voice, like normal men. Was there ever in the history of our race a night like that? So queer, so still, so full of listening? Silence laid a pall on everything that first night after the Armistice. The guns of four long years were still at last.[10]

Jim Scarbrough remembered,

> On the morning of the 11th of November we were fighting in an area south of the city of Sedan. The fighting kind of just died off. The Germans stopped shooting at us and we stopped shooting at them, gradually. The word got around that they had an armistice signed. Well, a holler went up among all men You never saw such a celebration. I shot all my ammunition up firing through a train rail just to put holes in it.[11]

Louis Linn had been wounded a second time at St.-Mihiel. He was now in a hospital at Orléans:

> One morning an atmosphere of excitement pervaded the ward. It was known that an armistice had been agreed upon and would be proclaimed at noon. Then noon struck and immediately all the bells in town began to ring. The boats on the river and all the factories blew their whistles and the great organ of the cathedral by the hospital began to play. Four years of bloodshed and carnage was to come to an end at last. From the streets below came one mighty roar from the combined voices of humanity mixed with the barking of dogs and blowing of automobile horns. Whether the people sang or just yelled or did both, it was impossible to tell. It all blended into one great roar, mixing with the ceaselessly chiming bells and the thunderous chant of the great organ. One mighty surge of sound, proclaiming victory.[12]

Levi Hemrick of the 80th Company was in a hospital on a sightseeing tour of Paris while recovering from wounds when he heard that an armistice would be signed on 11 November. He doubted that, and on return to the hospital everyone watched the clock as the hand hit the eleven o'clock hour. By his watch it was eleven seconds after eleven o'clock when they heard the boom of an artillery gun signaling the end of the war. He and friends got a pass to go into the heart of Paris to see the crowd:

> Yes, it was a kissing crowd, a dancing crowd, a singing crowd, a war shackled people suddenly free from their bonds. A sad people made happy and whose deadened spirit had suddenly blossomed back to life by that magic word PEACE. It was a wonderful crowd, a wonderful celebration and it was great to be in "Gay Paree" on the night of November eleventh of the year 1918.
>
> Levi Hemrick, 80th Company[13]

Warren R. Jackson of the 95th Company wrote,

> We of course knew that the war could not last always. In the days and months before, there had been talk among the bunch that the war might end anytime. However, when I was waked on that morning of 11 November 1918, to be told that the war would cease that day, the thought was inconceivable. To be told that someone was flying to the moon would have been easier to believe. Impossible. I spoke roughly to the fellow who waked me and went back to sleep—or tried to sleep. Before eleven all were awake and talking, wondering. Was it a trick of the Germans? Could it be that the war was actually going to end? With baited breath we waited until eleven. Would the guns cease firing? Eleven came. Officers assured us the war was over, but silence did not reign along the front. An explosion here and yonder in the distance—what could that be but that the war was still on! That uneasiness, that vague uncertainty! I learned long afterward that at eleven o'clock there were Americans still advancing, due to the fact that the line of communication had been broken and word of the Armistice had not reached them. Other disturbing noises that came to our ears that day were occasioned by the Germans in their preparation to evacuate. According to the terms of the Armistice the Germans were to leave behind them no mines. Some of the Germans were in too big a hurry and too thoughtless of destruction to remove the explosives. Instead, mines under railroad stations and bridges were touched off. We heard these explosions, and they sounded very like war to us.[14]

Carl A. Brannen in the 80th Company, 6th Marine Regiment, recalled,

> At 11 o'clock [on] November 11 we were told that an armistice was in effect and were ordered not to fire another shot. These orders were easily obeyed. That night you could see fires up and down the front where the men were warming and sleeping. This would have been unthinkable before.[15]

> I will start in on the eleventh of this month…. It was the eleventh hour of the eleventh day of the eleventh month that the last boche shell came whistling into our lines and exploded with a terrific crash. Luckily, it did not get anyone. Then there was death-like stillness along the whole front. Could it be that it was all over? We could not believe it possible. Each man would look at the others in doubt. Finally, word came that the armistice had been signed. Not a cheer did I hear, but there was not a man in the regiment that did not thank God that rainy, muddy, cold morning that it was all over and that he was safe…. The night of the eleventh was spent in thawing out and getting. dry; there must have been a million bonfires along the front. It was a beautiful sight to look at. The woods on both sides looked as if they were all afire. This was one time that a person could light an open fire and not get shelled.
>
> Clifton Cates, 96th Company[16]

Occupation Duty and the Russian Adventure

The bridgehead into Germany (U.S. Government Printing Office).

We had thought that with the end of the war, we would all go home immediately, but that was not to be. My outfit [51st Company, 5th Marines] got split up. Some of us went to Germany for occupation duty while others went to Russia to fight the Bolsheviks. It was not until late in 1919 that all of us got home.[1]

The Watch on the Rhine[2]—November 1918

When the Armistice was signed on 11 November 1918, the AEF had nearly 2,000,000 men under arms in France. It was a cease-fire, not a surrender or peace treaty. The war could resume at any time and the Allies wanted to assure that they were positioned *in* Germany should hostilities resume. The desire to return to the United States was universal, but there were a limited number of ships to support such an enormous undertaking. Further, the French wanted a token U.S. force to remain behind "to keep the American flag on the Rhine." After much haggling between the Allies it was agreed that a significant U.S. force would remain. This force would be known as the American Forces in Germany. This six-division force included the 2nd Division and was organized as the American 3rd Army, composed of two corps, the III and IV: a total of a quarter of a million men.[3] The Marines not included in the American Forces in Germany and other committed units such as those in Russia had their embarkation orders to sail for the United States by 19 May 1919. The last U.S. forces left Germany on 24 January 1923.[4]

On 17 November 1918, the 3rd Army moved forward as German forces withdrew to Germany. It was largely uneventful. The French troops were on the right and the British were on the left. A respectful distance was maintained between the Allies and Germans to avoid any resumption of hostilities. The 5th Regiment was relieved of its duties defending the Meuse on 14 November and moved out toward the Rhine at 0500 hours on 17 November:

> Based upon the articles of the armistice, the German army had begun their withdrawal from the occupied zones at once. The allies and Americans allowed a couple of days in order to provide a semblance of a neutral zone between them. For the 2d Division, it was just as well. The weather and enemy action had produced a Division far less ready for additional trouble than some of the lesser tried units. Influenza, then rampant in the world, was, and had been, causing nearly as many casualties as enemy shells. The actual American occupation force was composed of six divisions in a newly formed Third Army (Maj. Gen. Joseph T. Dickman). The 2d Division was selected for this additional honor and was assigned to III Corps (Maj. Gen. John L. Hines). Six days were allotted for the trip with one day for rest. After receiving much new clothing and especially new shoes, which didn't fit, making the march a bit difficult, some of the Marines were back into their uniforms, which made them happy.

The march was through recently enemy occupied territory and the residents of each country were along the route to warmly receive their deliverers. Scenery in these lands, not torn apart as was France, was a pleasant change. The weather was cold but dry and the roads free from snow or other impediments, which helped make the march less difficult than it might have been.

The occupying forces were to cross the border no sooner than 1 December and for a few days, especially around Thanksgiving (28 November), they just sat and waited.[5]

As the 3rd Army advanced, its Intelligence and Situation Reports focused on the morale and conduct of the Germans as they moved through Luxembourg on their return to Germany:

The watch on the Rhine (USMC History Division).

20 November 1918

IV. ENEMY MORALE: Enemy morale may be summarized: The relations between officers and the men have in many cases been bad: insubordination is frequent: troops at the rear going farther to the rear discarded much of their equipment. Troops coming from the front. however were on the whole better disciplined, and retreated armed, and in good order. The bearing of troops varied in different regions. Troops from the region of METZ were contaminated by Bolshevism, and were often out of control, though not extremely disorderly. Inhabitants of BRIEY report that the troops marching through there all carried red flags [This is unexplained, but evidently indicated support for Bolshevism], but on the whole were orderly and in good spirits. In LUXEMBURG the report in general that troops passing through in good marching order and apparently under control. Many of them carried the red flags, but on the 18th and 19th German flags were brought by them in large quantities in the city of LUXEMBURG and appeared in the columns. Especially on the entry of LUXEMBURG and of GERMANY a conscious effort was made to keep up the morale. Bands played, flags were flying, and the troops though fatigued, were on the whole happy that the war was over. German reports say that the withdrawal in the Rhineland is orderly. In BADEN and WURTEMBURG, however, the food supply service has broken down and there are conflicts between the troops and their own people.... VI. CONDUCT OF THE ENEMY: Even in regiments where decisions were made entirely by the soldiers council and where only red flags were accepted, the retreat order does not appear on the whole to have been bad. Pillage in general has been limited to German supply depots, and in the last weeks has not affected the civil populations. This is especially true of Luxembourg, the Mayor of which declares that in the last three weeks the attitude of the German forces abruptly changed for the better. He has no complaints of violation of international law other than the conventional one which his country has constantly made against the compulsory billeting of troops on the population. Livestock, however, has been taken in large quantities from Northern FRANCE. Withdrawing troops refused to distinguish between their own cattle and those of the farmer where theirs were grazing. The civil authorities in both LONGWY and Southern LUXEMBURG region welcome American occupation to check looting by stragglers in connection with unruly elements of the civil population.[6]

German looting of civilians continued:

Some of the prisoners belonging to and attached to the 80th Reserve Division stated that a divisional order had been issued a few days ago in which it was stated they would be demobilized immediately, and that the orders for same were en route to the division.

Interrogation of some civilians at OLINGEN elicited the fact that the Germans had taken a considerable quantity of foodstuffs without remuneration, excusing their action by "The Americans, who are biggest robbers in the world. will take it anyway when they come."[7]

Discipline returned as the Germans got closer to home:

21 November 1918

ENEMY MORALE: Further evidence has been received that the greatest demoralization came just before and just after the signing of the Armistice. Since then the officers have recovered their control over the men to such an extent, at least, that good road discipline is maintained. On the other hand, deserters are coming into our lines with permits to return to their homes in ALSACE, which permits are said to have been signed by the soldiers' committee. Whether the apparent improved morale is due to the fact that some of the best German divisions form the rearguard or because greater discipline has been restored throughout the German army is a question.[8]

25 November 1918

A German soldier of the 4th Battery, 280th Field Artillery, states that all German soldiers are being discharged except the classes of 1898 and 1899, who are being held in service until General von Hindenburg sees fit to discharge them. That von Hindenburg is commander of all the German armies at present. That there are at present no civilian police in Germany, only military police and as yet no stable form of government has been organized. That conditions in Germany are good. people being at work and all is quiet. That there is enough to eat but it is not distributed as it should be, and part of the food spoils.

Statement from a reliable source that for several days after the Armistice was signed. all railroad trains leading from the French front were packed with German soldiers who had deserted their commands and were returning home. All passenger and freight trains were loaded with them and in some cases they had taken entire possession of the train, including the engine. and were directing its movements. The stations and particularly the one in the city of LUXEMBOURG, were the scenes of much disorder. Officers had no control over their men. Those who were on the trains or at the stations being treated with gross disrespect. While he had heard of cases of assault made upon the officers, but had no knowledge of specific cases. He had, however, knowledge that officers had been compelled to remove their insignia of rank and were openly disrespected by their soldiers. Pillaging of military stores was open. It was estimated that there passed through LUXEMBURG in this demoralized condition at least 100.000 of the enemy.

Immediately the general retreat began, the troops that marched through on the roads were not at all disorganized, but on the contrary, showed very good discipline and were well under the control of their officers. The condition of the animals and equipment and the state of the men was normal. There was a shortage of forage for the horses and some shortage of animals for transports. He judged that many of the officers had left their commands and were returning home. From the statement of a discharged German soldier who entered our lines we learned that on November l0, the day before the signing of the Armistice, street riots took place in BERLIN, and his battalion, with a number of similar battalions was called out. They occupied the SCHOENEBERGER railroad station. He said that Marine troops agitated most of the riots. and that members of a railroad regiment advised him and his comrades to throw away their rifles, which they did. He saw none of the riots himself. but was told that the Marines and other troops had besieged the Imperial Palace for several days and finally succeeded in driving out the officers and soldier garrison which occupied the place. He said the houses and stores which line the Unter den Linden were all occupied by machine guns. He. as well as other prisoners. travelled by train through the greater part of GERMANY and they declare that a reaction has now set in and the rioting has ceased, at least for the present. This man further states that his own officers. as well as those of other units, were disarmed by their own men and that a soldiers' council is now in charge of the situation. This body is composed mostly of enlisted men and only a few subaltern officers are members.[9]

On 1 December, the Allied advance crossed the Rhine River and established bridgeheads, the largest of which was at Koblenz. John W. Thomason, Jr., recalled:

The rain fell, the road grew heavier. The battalion, soaked and miserable, plodded on. They passed through many villages, all alike; all ugly and without character. The houses were closed and shuttered. You saw few people, but you always had the feeling of eyes behind the shutters. One thick-bodied Boche, in uniform—an artilleryman, by his leather breeches—stood in the doorway of a house, smoking a porcelain pipe that hung to his knee. His face was set in a cast of hate. He stood and stared, and the battalion, passing, looked him over with respect…. These kids were different. They did not point or talk or cry out, after the manner of children. They stood in stolid groups, wooden-faced, with unwinking pale-blue eyes. The boys were nearly all in field-gray uniform cloth—cut down, perhaps, from the cast-off clothes of an elder. Some of them wore boots and round soldier-caps. They carried books and lunch-boxes, knapsack fashion, on their shoulders.—"Look, will you—that kid there ain't more'n a yearlin,' and they've got him in heavy marchin' order a'ready" "Yeh, -they start 'em early that's how come they're the way they are these Boche." There were round-faced little girls with straw-colored braids, in cloaks. They did not look poorly fed, like the waxen-faced children the battalion remembered in France. And at every corner there were more of them. The battalion was impressed. -" Say—you see all those kids—all those little square-heads! Hundreds of 'em, I'll swear! Something's got to be done about these people. I tell you, these Boche are dangerous! They have too many children—"[10]

Also, a letter home from Lieutenant Matt Eggr on duty in Germany tells that many officers thought that they should stay much longer in Germany or Russia to prevent the start of another war:

On Active Service
AMERICAN RED CROSS

With the   Feb. 15, 1919
American Expeditionary Force

Dear Dad,

Rec'd a letter from you yesterday dated Chic Jan 26th. Mother writes that she did not receive a couple of letters I wrote about Xmas since telling how I spent the holidays. As I remember they were rather lengthy epistles and surely hope she got them later. I received a letter from Carl Weitzel from Brest. He is still in that mud hole, sleeping in tents. He arrived the same day I did at Brest. Our boat overtook his convoy the day we hit Brest and the Geo. Washington was the first boat to steam into the harbor.

Not much of any news here. Had some snails the other day. They are served in the shell and seasoned with garlic, which lingers on your breath for ages. Well, my stomach was thrown out of joint about as badly as it was in N.Y. last summer so I don't think I'll eat snails very soon again. I received a nice letter from Margaret Trimble. She is still in Washington in the Construction Division of the Army. She is living at the Kappa Kappa Gamma House 1413 Mass. Ave. N.W. You ought to look her up sometime.

The "Stars & Stripes" reports 300,000 have sailed for America. There are many officers over here that believe the troops are being returned too soon. And they look for further trouble with Germany or Russia. I wish this mess was settled and I can't see how it is going to end myself.

We are not at all busy in the lab and it is very difficult to find something to do. I have not rec'd any commentation since I came to Dijin, Nov. 21st but I have taken the matter up with the adj. and he is trying to get my orders changed to read "duty & station." As they now read "for duty" the Q.M. here will not pay commentation on that. If I ever get the money I plan to take a leave in March or April and go down to Nice or Italy. I think it would be a wonderful opportunity & I probably would never have the opportunity again. Can you imagine me at Monte Carlo, Monaco, Rome & Naples? I can't either. Will write you a few lines again soon.

Love, Matt.

C.M.DL.
A.P.O. 721.[11]

Trouble occurred during occupation duty. There were thousands of criminal offenses by the Germans and also Allied military personnel. Nearly all of these were minor offenses. Security was tight at American bases since it was rumored that disgruntled Germans would attempt to penetrate perimeters to assassinate U.S. leaders. This was a rare occurrence. When captured these Germans were dealt with as would be expected. Records from the occupation reveal that three German civilians were convicted by military commissions of murder of members of the American army. The hanging shown in the photograph may be one of the three, but details were not provided.[12]

As the soldiers settled in at Koblenz, relations with German civilians were good. The soldiers were billeted in German homes:

The American soldiers were, of course, beginning with their first night on German soil, billeted in the houses of the civil population, who, inspired partly by fear and partly

Not all offenses were minor; some Germans were hanged (author's collection).

by orders they had received from the Buergermister and other officials. did everything in their power to placate them. The soldiers, for the first time in months, slept in beds. The peasant women prepared a supper on the family stoves. probably believing; that they were required to furnish food to the invading soldiers. as they had been to their own. After supper, the soldiers probably sat in the warm kitchen surrounded by the family, which is a luxury which can be appreciated only by those who have spent long, cold nights in the field. Soldiers and children almost always strike up a strong friendship, and the American soldier and the German boy or girl were no exception to the rule.

Soldiers of German extraction who could understand the language. of course got promptly on friendly terms with the civilians with whom they were billeted, despite the rigors of the anti-fraternization order. By the time the troops reached their permanent stations. their mental attitude towards the inhabitants had entirely changed. Though by no means friendly to them, they no longer regarded them with the nervous hatred engendered by fear of sudden treachery. Furthermore, they saw that a great deal of what they had read about the innate viciousness of all Germans was not true, and their war memories in consequence began to fade. A soldier was even occasionally heard to grudgingly admit that the Germans were "pretty good fighters," which remark foreshadowed the eventual revolution of sentiment.[13]

Following the Armistice I was assigned to Koblenz, Germany as part of the American Expeditionary Force. I lived over a candy store in Koblenz and the owners of the store had a little four year old girl. Whenever I had some money, I would buy candy from the store and give it to this little girl. I also shared chocolate that I got with my rations. We never received supplies in a timely manner. We went all winter with summer uniforms and as soon as the warmer weather arrived, the winter clothes did too. Following the war, my unit paraded down the Champs Elysée in Paris on a victory march with the Allies. I also paraded in NYC upon our return to the States. I recall that one of my buddies from the hospital in France saw me and wanted to give me his Purple Heart. I refused and would later receive my own Purple Heart for the wounds that I had received. I then went to Quantico, Virginia where I was discharged in 1919.

Private Raymond P. Rogers, 5th
Marine Regiment[14]

The 100,000-mark note in 1923 (author's collection).

Many times small things speak volumes. A 100,000-mark bank note found among the personal effects of Raymond Rogers gives us an understanding of the depreciation of marks in Germany after World War I in 1918–1919. This was followed by hyperinflation from 1921 through 1924 after most Americans had departed. This fueled the rise of Hitler and the Second World War. Hyperinflation rose in Germany to the point that housewives burned marks to stay warm. Marks were also used as wallpaper.[15] One hundred thousand marks may have been enough to buy a beer.

The following report on the occupation of Germany summarized the situation in 1918–1919:

Marines in Koblenz, 1919, Medal of Honor winner John J. Kelly on the right (USMC History Division).

Curiously enough. instead of injuring the commercial prosperity of the Rhineland, the American occupation greatly benefited it. The American soldier nominally received his pay in dollars. but as it was given him in the equivalent value in marks, and as the marks had greatly depreciated, the pay even of privates was prodigious. For instance, in the month of October 1919, the rate of exchange being about 28 marks to $1.00, the private, who normally received $30.00 per month. was paid 840 marks, or about 50 percent more than the best paid skilled German laborer. From the point of view of the Germans, the American army seemed an army of millionaires. Soldiers proverbially spend money like water, and the American soldiers in Germany were no exception. A good 70 percent of their pay must have found its way into the pockets of eager German merchants and tavern keepers.[16]

The 5th Regiment's stay in Koblenz was for the most part uneventful. Sports and training consumed time while the troops waited to go home.

When the Germans refused to accept the Allied terms of surrender at the peace conference in Versailles, a show of force was necessary and the 2nd Division prepared to march farther east into Germany. The 3rd Army Operations Report provided details on 17 June 1919:

ESTIMATE OF THE SITUATION: The Armistice having been provisionally renounced by the Allied and Associated Powers contingent only upon the non-acceptance by GERMANY of the proposed Treaty of Peace before June 23, 1919, it has become necessary to concentrate and prepare our forces for the anticipated resumption of the advance into GERMANY. As no great resistance to our forward movement is expected. we may, by a rapid movement of our advance troops, seize important centers and lines of supply and communication far to the east of the present limit of the bridgehead, thus providing for an extensive forward movement upon further orders from the Allied Commander-in-Chief. Consequently F.O. No. 9. as amended by F.O. No. 10. becomes effective and troops must be assembled prepared to advance on June 20, 1919.[17]

Concentration of units and preparation for the advance east into Germany continued until 28 June, when the 3rd Army announced to its units that the signing of the treaty of

Wounded Marines watching the 1919 Victory Parade in New York City (USMC History Division).

peace terminated the necessity for forward movement and units were returned to normal areas.[18] The Treaty of Versailles signed on 28 June 1919 was bitter humiliation for the German people. The treaty provided that Germany would accept responsibility for starting the war, give up some its possessions to other nations, and drastically reduce its armed forces. Most serious, the Germans were required to pay the Allies $33 billion in war reparations.[19] This would lead to hyperinflation after the war. The mood in the German army was that it had been betrayed by politicians and other civilians at home. It had not been decisively defeated on the battlefield. The stage was set for the rise of Hitler and the Second World War twenty years later.

The 5th Regiment returned to the United States in July and was disbanded at Quantico, Virginia, in August 1919.[20]

Summary of Operations of the 4th Marine Brigade

The history of the American Army in Europe provides the following summary of Marine actions during World War I:

A summary of the operations of the Fourth Brigade of Marines is set forth below: The Fourth Brigade of Marines as a unit of the Second Division participated in actual battle in France in the following sectors between the inclusive dates set down (as published in General Orders No. 37, Second Division, April 25, 1919); Toulon sector, Verdun: From March 15 to May 13, 1918. Aisne defensive, in the Château-Thierry sector: From May 31 to June 5, 1918. Château-Thierry sector (capture of Hill 142, Bouresches, Belleau Wood): From June 6 to July 9 1918. Aisne-Marne (Soissons) offensive: From July 18 to July 19, 1918. Marbache sector, near Pont-a-Moueson on the Moselle River: From August 9 to August 16, 1918. St. Mihiel Offensive, in the vicinity of Thiaucourt, Xammes, and Jaulny: From September 12 to September 16, 1918. Meuse-Argonne (Champagne) including the capture of Blanc Mont Ridge and St. Étienne: From October 1 to October 10, 1918. Meuse-Argonne (including crossing of the Meuse River): From November 1 to November 11, 1918.

SILVER BANDS FOR COLORS.

Under the rulings of General Headquarters, American Expeditionary Forces, the Marine Corps units serving with the Second Division are entitled to silver bands on the staffs of their colors for battle participation in the above mentioned Engagements.

MAJOR OPERATIONS.

General Headquarters, American Expeditionary Forces, ruled that the Second Division, including the Fourth Brigade of Marines, participated in only four major operations, the Aisne defensive (May 31 to June 5, 1918); the Aisne-Marne offensive (July 18 and 19, 1918); the St. Mime) offensive (Sept. 12 to 16, 1918); and the Meuse-Argonne Offensive (Oct. 1 to 10, 1918, and Nov. 1 to 10, 1918). The operations which resulted in the capture of Blanc Mont and St. Étienne were construed to be included in the Meuse-Argonne offensive despite the fact that the operations were a part of the operations of the Fourth French Army, far to the west of the western limit of the American' Meuse-Argonne sector and further that the work of the Second Division was continued by another American division. The operation which resulted in the capture of Hill 142, Bouresches, Bois de la Brigade de Marine, by the Marine brigade, assisted by Artillery, Engineers, etc., of the Second Division, and the capture of Vaux by the Third Brigade, Engineers and Artillery of the Second Division, were held to be local engagements rather than a major operation. The Second Division suffered about 9,000 casualties in the Château-Thierry sector. In addition to

Arkhangelsk, 2006 (photograph by Schekinov Alexey Victorovich).

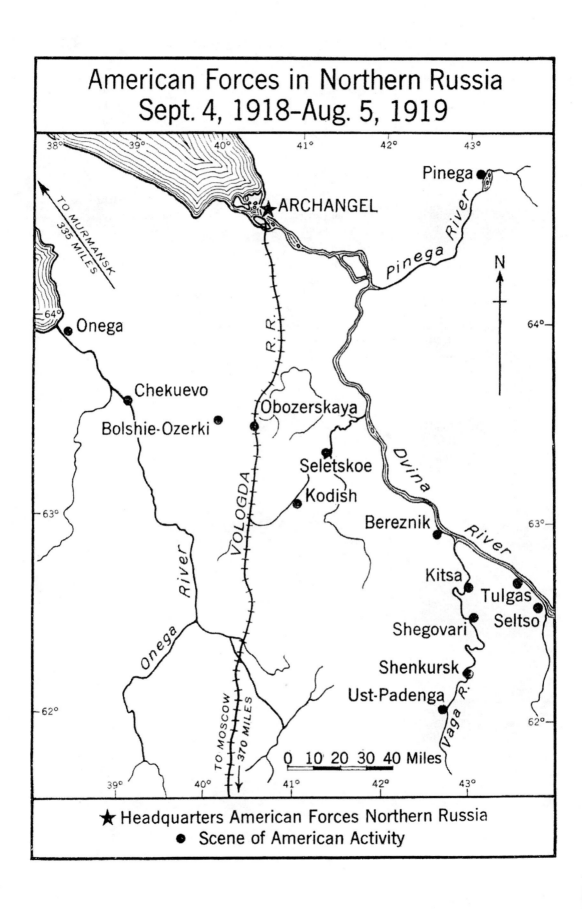

American Forces in Northern Russia
Sept. 4, 1918–Aug. 5, 1919

Pinega

ARCHANGEL

TO MURMANSK 335 MILES

Pinega River

N

Onega

Chekuevo

Obozerskaya

Bolshie-Ozerki

Seletskoe

Kodish

Dvina

Bereznik

River

Kitsa

Tulgas

Shegovari

Seltso

Shenkursk

Ust-Padenga

Onega River

VOLOGDA R.R.

TO MOSCOW 370 MILES

Vaga R.

0 10 20 30 40 Miles

★ Headquarters American Forces Northern Russia
● Scene of American Activity

Guard duty in Russia (USMC History Division).

Opposite: The Russian campaign (U.S. Government Printing Office).

the above major operations, Marine Corps personnel, other than that of the Fourth Brigade and Second Division, participated in the Champagne-Marne defensive, the Oise-Aisne offensive, and the Ypres-Lys Offensive.[21]

Total U.S. Marine deaths in World War I, including disease, were 3,284.[22] Most of these occurred in the 4th Brigade, 2nd Infantry Division. The U.S. Marine Corps achieved its maximum active-duty strength of 75,101 on 11 December 1918.[23] This was the worldwide strength, but most were in the AEF. The active-duty strength at the start of the war was 13,725.[24]

The Russian Adventure

Today, in Arkhangelsk, northern Russia, a British Mark V tank sits on a concrete pad. The huge monster was captured by the Russians during the Allied stay in Russia in the period of 1918–1920. The Allied intervention in Russia was a multinational military expedition launched during the Russian Civil War in 1918. The U.S. contribution to this ill-fated effort was small. Wilson agreed to the limited participation of 5,000 U.S. Army troops in the campaign. This force, which become known as the "American North Russia Expeditionary Force" (aka the Polar Bear Expedition), was sent to Arkhangelsk while another 8,000 soldiers, organized as the American Expeditionary Force Siberia, were shipped to Vladivostok from the Philippines and from Camp Fremont in California. The initial goals were to help the Czechoslovak Legions secure supplies of munitions and armaments in Russian ports and reestablish the eastern front. There was great concern that the large amount of Allied supplies sent to Russia to help fight the Germans might fall into German hands after Russia withdrew from the war. After winning World War I, the Allies militarily backed the anti–Bolshevik White forces in Russia. The Marine participation in the ill-fated Allied intervention in Russia was minimal, as described in McClellan's summary of Marine involvement in World War I. Raymond Rogers recalled that members of the 51st Company of the 5th Marines went to Russia in November 1918. If so, they went as members of ships deployed as a part of the Asiatic Fleet. McClellan summarized:

> The Marines of the *Brooklyn,* flagship of the Asiatic Fleet, participated in the activities around Vladivostok, Siberia, in 1918. In June 1918, Vladivostok, and practically all of Siberia, was under the control of the Bolsheviks. The Bolsheviks, assisted by German and Austrian prisoners of war, were resisting the advance of the Czecho-Slovaks, who were trying to reach Vladivostok. In that city on June 29, 1918, there were approximately 12,000 well-organized Czecho-Slovaks, only about 2,500 of whom were armed or equipped. On the foregoing date the Czecho-Slovaks in the city took it over from the Bolsheviks after a three hour battle near its center, and on the afternoon of that day Rear Admiral Austin M. Knight, commander in chief of the Asiatic Fleet, ordered a detachment of American Marines ashore to guard the American consulate and to act as part of an Allied force composed of British, Japanese, Chinese, and Czecho-Slovaks, to patrol the city.
> In July, 1918, Marines from the *Brooklyn* acted as guards over German and Austrian prisoners of war on Russian Island, about 5 miles from Vladivostok, while Marines from the same vessel constituted part of an Allied military force of American and British Marines, Japanese and Chinese bluejackets, and Czecho-Slovak soldiers, which was organized to prevent a threatened strike and disorder among the workmen in the Russian navy yard at Vladivostok. The *Albany* was at Vladivostok from April 2, 1919, until relieved by the *New Orleans* on July 25, 1919. Each of these ships, while they were anchored off Vladivostok, kept a small guard of Marines at the United States Naval radio station on Russian Island.
> Col. Carl Gamborg-Andresen was fleet Marine officer of the Asiatic Fleet from August 25, 1915

to July 17, 1917; Col. Louis McC. Little from July 18, 1917 to April 25, 1918; and Col. Eli T. Fryer from that date until after the armistice.[25]

The Russian Civil War ended in November 1920 with the victory of the Red Army over the anti–Bolshevik White forces. That same year marked the withdrawal of the last Allied forces from Russia, but Japan would stay on for several more years. U.S. casualties were low, less than three hundred.[26]

Biographical Dictionary

This section provides a summary of the lives of the participants mentioned in this book.

Bert Baston survived the war and was awarded the Navy Cross for "extraordinary heroism" at Belleau Wood. He was hospitalized for a year due to leg wounds sustained on 6 June 1918. He would later say that he could have shoved a broom handle through the hole in one leg. He also served in World War II as a Marine colonel in North Africa. As a former University of Minnesota football player he was elected to the National Football Hall of Fame in 1954. Bert Baston died in St. Cloud, Minnesota, on November 15, 1979, and is buried at Lakewood Cemetery in Minneapolis.

Carl Andrew Brannen, although wounded, survived the war and obtained two degrees in history. He had a long career as a schoolmaster and administrator. He died at age 76. His wartime recollections, *Over There: A Marine in the Great War,* were published by his son, J.P. Brannen, in 1996.

Smedley Darlington Butler, "Ol' Gimlet Eye," was the most decorated Marine in the history of the Marine Corps. He is one of two Marines who were awarded two Medals of Honor. (The other is Sergeant Major Daly, as seen later.) Butler was born in West Chester, Pennsylvania, on 30 July 1881. He was the son of Thomas S. Butler, a Pennsylvania representative to the U.S. Congress and longtime chairman of the House Naval Affairs Committee. When Smedley Butler was in his teens he was appointed a lieutenant in the Marine Corps on 20 May 1898. His first Medal of Honor was for action at Veracruz, Mexico, 21–22 April 1914, when he commanded and led a Marine regiment that occupied the city. His second award was for action in Haiti on 17 April 1915. During World War I he commanded the 13th Marine Regiment in France. Upon return from France in 1919 he was appointed commanding general of Marine Barracks, Quantico, Virginia. He retired on 1 October 1931. He was a vocal supporter of the veteran's pension and the Bonus March. He died at the Naval Hospital in Philadelphia on 21 June 1940 after a short illness.

William Edward Campbell, the hero of Blanc Mont, survived the war and like several other members of 5th Marines pursued a writing career, under the pen name William March. Two books stand out: *Company K* and *The Bad Seed,* a best seller that also became a play and a film. Campbell appears to have suffered from PTSD and had difficulty in his writing differentiating between fact and fiction. William Campbell died on 15 May 1954 from a heart attack and is buried in Tuscaloosa, Alabama, with his parents.

Clifton Bledsoe Cates as a lieutenant in the 6th Marine Regiment received many valor awards during World War I, including the Navy Cross, Army Distinguished Service Cross, and Silver Star Citations. He was wounded twice during the war and returned to the United States in 1919 after serving with the occupation forces in Germany. His post-war service included White House aide, aide-de-camp to the commandant of the Marine Corps and War Plans Section, Marine Corps Headquarters. By World War II Cates had achieved general officer rank and served in the Pacific theater. Following the war he was appointed commandant of the Marine Corps in 1948. Cates retired in 1954 and died in Annapolis, Maryland, on 4 June 1970. He was buried in Arlington National Cemetery.

Albertus W. Catlin commanded the 6th Marine Regiment at Belleau Wood, where he was wounded. He retired in December 1919. He was in ill health as a result of his wound and died in Culpepper, Virginia, on 31 May 1933.

Georges Clemenceau, The Tiger, was the prime minister of France during World War I. Clemenceau was born in France on 28 September 1841. He was a man of many talents. He graduated as a doctor in 1865 and also founded several literary magazines. As a political activist in France, Clemenceau was jailed and released, and he eventually left for the United States in 1865. Clemenceau worked as a reporter in New York City. He also practiced medicine, wrote for a Paris newspaper and taught French in Stamford, Connecticut, where he met his future wife. He later returned to Paris, where he was elected to the Chamber of Deputies in 1876. His political and writing career continued for forty years. After World War I broke out he was appointed prime minister in 1917 (for a second time). He continued as prime minister after the war and was defeated in his attempt for election to the French presidency in 1920. He then retired from political life and died on 24 November 1929.

William O. Corbin assumed command of the 51st Company after the death of Captain Williams. Corbin was a gunnery sergeant before the war, promoted to officer ranks when the war started and reverted to enlisted rank after the war.

Louis Cukela was awarded the Medal of Honor for his actions at Soissons on 18 July 1918. He was called back to active duty before U.S. entry into World War II and served at the Navy Yards at Norfolk, Virginia, and Philadelphia, Pennsylvania. In May 1946, he was placed on the inactive retired list. Major Louis Cukela died on 19 March 1956 and is buried at Arlington National Cemetery, Arlington, Virginia. He is remembered for his quote "The next time I need some damn fool for a mission, I'll go myself."[1]

Samuel C. Cumming commanded the 51st Company and survived the war. He received five Silver Star Citations for bravery, including his actions as a platoon leader at Belleau Wood. He achieved the rank of major general during World War II. He retired in 1946 to Upperville, Virginia, where he hosted annual reunions of his unit. Raymond Rogers always helped with and attended the reunions. At one of the last, Cumming sent a photo showing a dwindling group of Marines at the reunion to Rogers with a thank-you note on the back. Samuel Cumming died on 14 January 1983.

Gunnery Sergeant Daniel Joseph Daly, who inspired his troops at Belleau Wood, had received two Medals of Honor before World War I. His first was in China in 1900 and in 1915 he received his second Medal of Honor in Haiti. He inspired his Marines with his battle cry at Belleau Wood "Come on, you sons of bitches, do you want to live forever?"[2] His comment was made famous when *Chicago Tribune* reporter Floyd Gibbons heard the remark and passed it around. Daly survived the war and retired from the Marine Corps in 1920. He then served as a bank guard on Wall Street for seventeen years. He died on 28 April 1937.[3]

Charles A. Doyen was the 5th Regiment's first commanding officer and would later command the 4th Marine Brigade and the 2nd Infantry Division. He became ill with the flu and returned to the United States, where he died on 6 October 1918. He was posthumously awarded the Navy Distinguished Service Medal, the first award of this decoration.

Charley Dunbeck of the 43rd Company, 5th Regiment, commanded a company at Belleau Wood and a battalion at the Meuse River. He was awarded the Navy Cross for extraordinary heroism at Blanc Mont. Although wounded four times and medically retired because of a bad heart, he was recalled to duty and served during World War II. He died in San Diego, California, on 15 July 1978. So much for the bad heart.

Frank Edgar Evans won the Navy Cross and other awards for the distinction of his service as adjutant of the 6th Marine Regiment during the Battle of Belleau Wood and after. He published a book titled *Daddy Pat of the Marines* that was composed of letters that he wrote home to his six-year-old son. He retired on 1 December 1940 and made his home in Honolulu, where he died 25 November 1941.

Logan Feland served at Headquarters, Marine Corps, in Washington and in Nicaragua after the war. Feland was promoted to major general. He retired on 1 September 1933 and died in Columbus, Ohio, on 17 July 1936. He is buried in Arlington National Cemetery.

Ferdinand Foch At the start of the war he commanded the French XX Corps and invaded Germany but withdrew in the face of the German counterattack. Later he commanded the French 9th Army and still later the Army Group North. He was credited with halting the German advance on Paris and the victory at the Second Battle of the Marne. After the war he pressed for peace terms that would make Germany unable to wage war but was unsuccessful in this regard. He died in Paris on 20 March 1929.

Verner S. Gaggin survived World War I and returned to his medical practice in Pittsburgh after the war. His son, Verner, would serve in World War II and survived that war.

Joseph Addison Hagan was born in Richmond, Virginia, and received the Distinguished Service Cross for heroism at Belleau Wood while a member of the 5th Regiment, 51st Company. First Lieutenant Hagan rescued a sergeant while exposed to enemy fire 200 yards away. Hagan was badly wounded and was retired for disability. After the war, he was elected to the Virginia House of Delegates and served 1947–1949. Hagan died in Norfolk, Virginia, 25 August 1978.

Douglas Haig represented the concept of a class-based incompetent commander unable to grasp tactics and technology. Some called him Butcher Haig because of the 2 million casualties that occurred while he was commander of British forces in France. The troops paid for his inadequacies. Haig died in London on 29 January 1928.

George Wallis Hamilton was recommended for the award of the Medal of Honor for bravery at Belleau Wood on 6 June 1918, but the award was downgraded to the Navy Cross. He resigned after the war but reentered in 1921 as an aviation cadet. He died the following year in an aircraft accident at Gettysburg, Pennsylvania.

James Guthrie Harbord was Pershing's chief of staff of the AEF and later commanded the 4th Brigade of the 2nd Division. After the war he attained the rank of major general, retiring in 1922. He served as president of the Radio Corporation of America and later as its chairman of the board until his death. He died in Rye, New York, on 20 August 1947.

James E. Hatcher served with the 84th Company, 6th Regiment, during World War I. His decorations include two Silver Stars for valor. In one incident he advanced beyond the line of battle to destroy enemy machine guns and capture prisoners. After the war he wrote his recollection *A Memoir of Service in World War I as a Private, USMC*, which is available at the Marine Corps Archives, Gray Research Center, Quantico, Virginia. He moved on, enlisting in the army, and served in World War II as a regimental commander fighting over some of the same terrain that he saw in World War I.

David Ephraim Hayden was at St.-Mihiel on 15 September 1918 when a Marine was mortally wounded in the battle and he ran across the open battlefield to administer assistance. Amidst machine-gun fire, he dressed the Marine's severe wounds and carried him to safety. For Hayden's "gallantry and intrepidity" during this action he was awarded the Medal of Honor. Following the war, Hayden was advanced to the rank of pharmacist's mate third class. For the rest of his enlistment, he served on board the troop transport *Princess Matoika* and at the Norfolk Naval Hospital, Virginia. Leaving the navy in the summer of 1920, he later served as a U.S. marshal in California until he retired at the age of seventy. David E. Hayden died on 18 March 1974 and is buried at Arlington National Cemetery.[4]

Levi Hemrick returned home after the war and continued his education, receiving a master's degree from Peabody College for Teachers. He taught agriculture for ten years, but disability from his wounds caused him to abandon that and he was self-employed for the rest of his life. Late in life he wrote his war memoir, *Once a Marine*, which provides many anecdotes about his service. Levi Hemrick died in Athens, Georgia, on 21 October 1976.

Paul von Hindenburg survived the war and was elected president of Germany in 1925. He was pressured by Hitler, who wanted to be named chancellor of Germany. While von Hindenburg viewed Hitler with contempt and referred to him as the "Bohemian Corporal," he eventually gave in to Hitler's demand. Von Hindenburg died in East Prussia on 2 August 1934.

Charles F. Hoffman (also served under the name Ernest August Janson) served on the western front with the 49th Company, 5th Regiment. On 6 June 1918, during fighting near Château-Thierry, France, he attacked and drove off an enemy machine-gun unit that threatened the position recently taken by his unit. For his "conspicuous gallantry and intrepidity" on this occasion, in which he received severe wounds, he was awarded the Medal of Honor by both the U.S. Navy and the U.S. Army. Returning to the United States in November 1918, as World War I's active combat came to an end, Janson reverted to the rank of sergeant and reenlisted in the spring of 1919. He subsequently spent seven years on recruiting duty in New York City. Beginning in July 1926 he briefly served at the Marine Barracks, Quantico, Virginia. Reinstated in the rank of gunnery sergeant, he was promoted to sergeant major in August 1926 and placed on the retired list a month later. Ernest A. Janson died on 14 May 1930 and is buried at Evergreen Cemetery, Brooklyn, New York.[5]

Warren R. Jackson served in the 95th Company, 6th Marine Regiment, throughout the war. He was awarded the Silver Star Citation and other awards for bravery at Blanc Mont. He survived the war and returned to his home in Texas. He wrote his memoir of the events, titled *His Time in Hell, a Texas Marine in France*, which was edited by George B. Clark and published in 2001.

Joseph Jacques Césaire Joffre's greatest achievement as commander of French forces during the war was his defeat of the Germans at the First Battle of the Marne in 1914. He was popular among the troops and was called Papa Joffre. Joffre died in Paris on 3 January 1931.

John Joseph Kelly was at Blanc Mont and on 3 October 1918 ran through the artillery barrage, advanced 100 yards forward of the front line, and attacked an enemy machine-gun nest, killing the gunner and one other crew member. He then returned through the barrage with eight prisoners. For his "conspicuous gallantry and intrepidity" on this occasion, he was awarded the Medal of Honor by both the U.S. Navy and the U.S. Army. On 15 March 1919, General John J. Pershing, USA, commander in chief of the American Expeditionary Force, presented the award to Kelly in Koblenz, Germany. Returning to the United States, he was honorably discharged in August 1919 at the Marine Barracks, Quantico, Virginia. His character rating was excellent. He returned to Chicago and had minor trouble for several years and then went into local politics. He somehow survived alcoholism and tuberculosis. He later claimed he "killed" the latter with the former.[6] John J. Kelly died on 20 November 1957 and is buried at All Saints Cemetery, Des Plaines, Illinois.[7]

Sergeant Matej Kocak was promoted to sergeant in June 1918 while serving with the 66th Company, 5th Regiment. On 18 July, during action in the Viller-Cottertes section, south of Soissons, France, his company was halted by enemy gun fire from a hidden machine-gun nest. While only covered by gunfire, Kocak went forward alone and rushed the enemy position with his bayonet, eventually driving off the enemy. Later on that same day, he organized French colonial soldiers separated from their company and led an attack disabling a second machine-gun nest. For his "extraordinary heroism" on both of these occasions he was posthumously awarded the Medal of Honor by both the U.S. Navy and the U.S. Army. On 4 October 1918 Kocak was killed in action at the Battle of Blanc Mont Ridge in France, and he is buried at Meuse Argonne American Cemetery, Romagne, France.[8]

Melvin L. Krulewitch served with the 78th Company of the 6th Regiment. He survived the war and returned to study law. He worked in New York as a public-utilities attorney. In 1927 he returned to the Marine Corps and was commissioned as a second lieutenant. Krulewitch fought in World War II and the Korean War. He retired as a major general in 1956. He died in New York City on 25 May 1978.

John Archer Lejeune commanded the 4th Marine Brigade from 25 July 1918 to 28 July 1918 and then assumed command of the 2nd Infantry Division, remaining in that position until 1919. Lejeune was appointed commandant of the Marine Corps on 1 July 1920. He was relieved of that position in 1929 and retired in order to assume the position of Superintendent, Virginia Military Institute. Lieutenant General Lejeune died on 20 November 1942 at Union Memorial Hospital, Baltimore, Maryland. He is buried in Arlington National Cemetery.

Louis Linn served in the 77th Company and always carried a sketch pad with him, he said to maintain his sanity. His sketches appear in his memoir *At Belleau Wood with Rifle and Sketchpad*. He was wounded twice during the war, recovered and was discharged at Quantico in 1919. Linn died in Howard, Maryland, on 10 February 1949.

David Lloyd George was the prime minister of Great Britain born in Manchester, England, on 17 January 1863. He was a liberal politician and statesman who led the British coalition government during World War I. He was responsible for the introduction of many reforms that set the foundation for the modern welfare state. After the war he was a key player during the Paris Peace Conference in 1919 that reorganized Europe. His popularity faded after the war and during World War II he was known as a defeatist. He died in Wales on 26 March 1945.

Erich Ludendorff was joint head with von Hindenburg of the German army. Ludendorff was victor of the Battle of Tannenberg, a disastrous defeat for Russia and one of the underlying causes of the Russian Revolution. After the war, Ludendorff became a nationalist leader in

Germany. He participated in coup attempts including Hitler's Beer Hall Putsch in 1923. He ran against von Hindenburg for president in 1925 and lost. Ludendorff died on 20 December 1937.

Douglas MacArthur served in the 42nd Infantry Division during World War I.

Elton E. Mackin's memoir of service in World War I is one of the best because it describes the day-by-day encounters of his regiment, the 5th Marines, during the World War I battles. It tells his personal story of fighting during World War I. He received the Navy Cross and other valor awards for his service. Elton Mackin returned to his hometown of Lewiston, New York, and married Emily Goodsite in 1921. They had three children; Wallace, Marie and Harriet. The family made several moves before settling in Norwalk, Ohio, in 1935. Elton and his son, Wallace, opened an appliance store that remained in business until 1957. In his later years, Mackin worked as a bus driver for handicapped and mentally challenged children. He and his wife also opened their home to numerous foster children. After the war Mackin, who called himself Slim in his memoir (the troops called him Lucky Mackin), held various jobs, including appointment officer in the Veterans Administration. His children recall that he was working on his memoir in the early 1930s and spent years refining it. Mackin died in Norwalk, Ohio, on 21 February 1974.[9]

Wendell C. Neville commanded the 5th Regiment from 1 January to 17 July 1918. He went on to become USMC commandant on 5 March 1929 but died in office on 8 July 1930.

Czar Nicholas II was born on 18 May 1868 in Tsarskoye Selo, Russia. He was the last of the Romanov dynasty and the last emperor of Russia. He was an incompetent leader who presided over many disasters that brought Russia from a leading world power to economic and military collapse. His reign saw the defeat of Russia in the 1905 Russo-Japanese War and many defeats of Russia during World War I. His anti–Semitic pogroms, violent suppression of opposition, and incompetent handling of Russia during World War I led to his overthrow in 1917. Nicholas II and his family were murdered by the Bolsheviks on the night of 16/17 July 1918.

Don V. Paradis was awarded the Silver Star Citation while a member of 80th Company at Belleau Wood for continuously carrying messages while under fire. He was also awarded the Silver Star Citation for his actions at St.-Mihiel. Paradis survived the war and returned to Detroit and the gas company, finding a position in sales. He later said that it was a mistake. He stood around doing nothing and had too much time to think. He was still jittery from his experiences in World War I. He married and he and his wife, Vodra, are shown in the 1940 census. He was unemployed at that time. In 1975 he was invited to accompany Commandant Robert E. Cushman, Jr., back to Belleau Wood, France. Paradis's memoirs were later published, in 2010: *The World War I Memoirs of Don V. Paradis, Gunnery Sergeant, USMC*.

John J. "Black Jack" Pershing commanded the American Expeditionary Forces during World War I. He was born in Laclede, Missouri, on 13 September 1860. He graduated from the U.S. Military Academy with the Class of 1886. Pershing served in the Spanish-American War and commanded the expedition in pursuit of Pancho Villa after Villa crossed the border from Mexico into the United States, raiding Columbus, New Mexico. While the campaign was not successful in capturing Villa, Pershing was the leading candidate to command forces when the United States entered World War I. He was ultimately promoted to the rank of General of the Armies, the highest military rank. He insisted that U.S. forces should remain intact and not be piecemealed into other Allied units.[10] In this way, he improved the effectiveness of the U.S. war effort. He died in Walter Reed General Hospital, Washington, D.C., on 15 July 1948 and is buried at Arlington National Cemetery.

Orlando Henderson Perry returned to Philadelphia after the war to resume teaching at the University of Pennsylvania. He was also personal physician to the Philadelphia mayor Harry Mackey, who appointed Perry to head the city's Health Department. On 2 June 1932 he was found dead in his bedroom from a self-inflicted gunshot wound. He had been in poor health for some time and was buried at Saint Timothy's Episcopal Church Cemetery in Philadelphia.

Philippe Pétain (the Lion of Verdun) was made a marshal of France in December 1918 and was generally regarded as one of France's greatest military heroes. Between the wars, Pétain remained in the army until he retired at age 75 in 1931. He entered government, serving in various positions, including as secretary of war. With the fall of France to Nazi Germany in 1940, Pétain became head of state for what became known as Vichy, France: that part of France not occupied by Nazi Germany. For this he was considered a collaborator and tried for treason after the war. He was convicted and sentenced to death, but the sentence was commuted to a life sentence. Pétain was 89 years old at that time. He died on Ile d'Yeu off of the French coast on 23 July 1951 and is buried there.

John Henry Pruitt fought in France at Bouresches and Belleau Wood and was injured in a German gas attack on 14 June 1918. Following recovery, he participated in more battles and his brave conduct in an action near Thiaucourt on 15 September was officially reported. On 3 October, while in combat at Blanc Mont Ridge, France, Corporal Pruitt conducted a single-handled attack, capturing two machine guns and 40 enemy soldiers before being killed in action later in the day. For his "extraordinary gallantry and intrepidity" on 3 October 1918 John H. Pruitt was posthumously awarded the Medal of Honor by both the U.S. Navy and the U.S. Army. He is buried in Arlington National Cemetery.[11]

Joseph Edward Rendinell was wounded at Belleau Wood (gassed) but recovered. He was wounded, again, at Soissons, on 19 July 1918. Rendinell returned to the States in February 1919 and was discharged in May. He married May Lorraine Delaney and worked as an electrician in Youngstown, Ohio. They had five children. He published his diary of the war, *One Man's War: The Diary of a Leatherneck,* in 1928.

Raymond P. Rogers fought at Belleau Woods and was badly wounded at the Battle of Soissons. During his recovery in Paris, he was assigned to an MP company and guarded General J.J. Pershing at the Follies Bergère. Immediately after the war, he was assigned as

Raymond P. Rogers after the war (author's collection).

Raymond Rogers—the decorations he earned (author's collection).

part of the American Expeditionary Force in Germany and lived in Koblenz. After returning to New York, he was appointed the head of the Veterans Administration in Newburgh as well as the probation officer for the city. When the city—in an effort to save money—did away with the Veterans Administration, he continued to work tirelessly to obtain benefits for veterans of World War I, World War II, Korea and Vietnam and their families. He died in Newburgh on 18 June 1976.

James Russell Scarbrough survived the war and returned home to Ohio, where he became a fireman on the B&O Railroad. During World War II he built Corvette warships at Lorain, Ohio. He died on 6 July 1989 in Elyria, Ohio.

Lemuel Cornick Shepherd, Jr., was awarded the Navy Cross and other decorations for his actions at Belleau Wood. After the war he served with occupation forces in Germany. Four months after the start of World War II he took command of the 9th Marine Regiment, and by the end of the war he had been promoted to major general. He also served in Korea and on 1 January 1952 President Truman appointed him to be the twentieth commandant of the Marine Corps. Shepherd died at his home in La Jolla, California, on 6 August 1990. He is buried at Arlington National Cemetery.

Merwin Hancock Silverthorn was awarded the Navy Cross for his actions at Blanc Mont. He survived the war and served in World War II. He achieved the rank of lieutenant general in 1950. He died in 1985 and is buried in Arlington National Cemetery. All of his children served in the Marine Corps.

Eugene B. "Sledgehammer" Sledge was a member of the 5th Regiment in World War II who wrote a memoir about his experiences, *With the Old Breed*[12] (1st Marine Division) in World War II. It was a best seller and later became a television series (*The Pacific*) after Eugene Sledge died of stomach cancer in 2001.

Lawrence Tucker Stallings was wounded at Belleau Wood and was awarded the Silver Star Citation for valor. He begged the doctors not to amputate his leg after he was hit and they complied. He survived the war but was bedeviled by his leg wound for years and finally had his leg partially amputated in 1922, with another amputation later. He was a literary great and became a famous author. His *What Price Glory* became a Broadway play and a film by the same name. His memoir of World War I was titled *Plumes* and sold well. *Plumes* was an autobiographical novel of the return from World War I of a serviceman and his troubles after the war. Stallings also authored a number of articles with illustrations by a fellow Marine, John Thomason. He was called back for service in World War II as a lieutenant colonel but did not serve overseas. Lawrence Stallings died on 28 February 1968 in Pacific Palisades, California.

Gunnery Sergeant Fred W. Stockham served in the Toulon sector, in the Aisne operation, and at Belleau Wood. During the last-named battle, Gunnery Sergeant Stockham displayed the "conspicuous gallantry and intrepidity above and beyond the call of duty" that later earned him the Medal of Honor by an Act of Congress. Gunnery Sergeant Stockham died in France on June 22, 1918. Thanks to the efforts of his former comrades, one of whom undoubtedly was the man whose life his gas mask saved, Gunnery Sergeant Stockham was belatedly and posthumously awarded the Medal of Honor on December 21, 1939, over 20 years after his sacrifice.

John W. Thomason, Jr., while an officer in the 49th Company of the 5th Regiment, entertained his troops with his sketches made during breaks. He remained on active duty after the war. His friend Lawrence Stallings encouraged him to write and he did. He spent time authoring several books, one of which (*Fix Bayonets!*) is considered a classic and is loaded with his sketches. He was a man of many talents who also served in World War II. He died on 12 March 1944 in San Diego, California.

Wilhelm II was the last German Emperor or Kaiser, as he was called. He ruled the German empire from 15 June 1888 to 9 November 1918. Wilhelm II was born in Berlin on 27 January 1859. Like other monarchs in Europe, he was related to others including Victoria of England and Nicholas II of Russia. Wilhelm attempted to expand the German empire with new colonies and was overbearing and callous in his manner, perhaps a result of his withered arm, a birth defect. He was ineffective as a leader and was largely ignored by von Hindenburg and Ludendorff during the war. At its conclusion Wilhelm abdicated and fled Germany for the Netherlands, where he died in Doorn on 9 June 1941.

Lloyd William Williams was assigned to command the 51st Company of the 2nd Battalion, 5th Regiment. On 2 June 1918 he uttered the famous phrase "retreat, hell, we just got here," when he was ordered to withdraw by the French. On 6 June 1918, he led the attack on the Germans at Belleau Wood, forcing them to withdraw. He was mortally wounded on 11 June 1918. Of the ten officers and 250 enlisted, only one officer and 16 enlisted survived unharmed. After the war, Williams's remains were returned to Virginia and he was buried at the Green Hill Cemetery in Berryville.

Woodrow Wilson, the 28th president of the United States, was born in Staunton, Virginia, on 28 December 1856. As a young boy he experienced the American Civil War firsthand. He served as president of Princeton University and governor of New Jersey. When the Republican Party split, Wilson led his Democratic Party to control Congress and he won the presidency in 1912. This was the first time that a Democrat had won since Grover Cleveland's presidency in 1892. During Wilson's first term, he opposed U.S. entry into the war in Europe and he caused progressive legislation to be passed such as the Clayton Antitrust Act. By 1916 incidents were occurring that caused pressure for the U.S. entry into World War I. The sinking of the ocean liner *Lusitania* by a German U-boat that caused American loss of life is an example. Shortly after his reelection in 1916 on the slogan that he "he kept us out of war" the United States declared war on the Axis Powers. Wilson's second term focused on the war and

Von Hindenburg with Ludendorff on the right during the war (Library of Congress).

subsequent efforts to establish the League of Nations. He suffered a severe stroke in 1919 that left his wife, Edith, in control of the White House until the end of his term in 1921. Wilson died in Washington, D.C., on 3 February 1924.

Frederic May Wise was commissioned as a second lieutenant in the Marine Corps in 1899. He commanded the 2nd Battalion of the 5th Marine Regiment during the Battle of Belleau Wood and received the Distinguished Service Medal for his actions during the battle. After the war his health began to fail and he retired after twenty-seven years' service in 1926. His book, *A Marine Tells It to You*, provides interesting information. He died in Washington, D.C., on 24 July 1940.

Michael "The Polish Warhorse" Wodarezyk was badly wounded at Blanc Mont but survived the war and was medically retired in 1919; however, he was allowed to return to the Corps in 1920, serving in aviation. He became an enlisted Marine aviator. He was then promoted to marine gunner and to chief marine gunner. He was decorated while flying during the second Nicaraguan campaign, earning a Distinguished Flying Cross in February/March 1928. He served during World War II and was promoted to colonel effective 1 June 1946 and retired at that rank on the same date.[13]

Epilogue

The 5th Marine Regiment After World War I

Between the Wars (1919–1933)

After World War I, all of the military services suffered reduction in troop strength to a fraction of what it had been. The Marine Corps was reduced to less than a quarter of its strength and the officer strength dropped to less than a thousand men. Officers promoted from enlisted ranks to temporary grade during the war reverted to enlisted grade while regular (or permanent) officers were reduced in rank. There is nothing new in this. It occurs after every war. For example, Custer, a two-star general in the Civil War, was reduced to lieutenant colonel after the war. More recently, the process to reduce strength has been called a Reduction in Force, or "RIF." The Marine Corps also decided that service in World War I would not be of special weight in determining promotion or retention.[1] This, plus later problems with pensions, created resentment in the ranks and also led to resignations of very talented officers who saw a better career available in the civilian community. The services had no choice in this since service end strength is determined by Congress and after every war Congress is in a budget-cutting mood. Major George Hamilton was one officer who remained in the Marine Corps for nearly two years after the war but would resign in 1920. He would rejoin the Marine Corps later.

With World War I ended the United States continued its series of interventions known as the Banana Wars. These included incursions into Haiti, Santo Domingo and Nicaragua. This continued until President Roosevelt ended the practice in 1934. As manpower strength reductions bottomed out and personnel were added, the 5th Marine Regiment was reactivated at Quantico, Virginia, on 8 July 1920. The Marine Corps commandant, John A. Lejeune, initiated new programs, the most important of which emphasized amphibious warfare. This was in response to the growing threat of Japan that would be countered by the U.S. War Plan Orange, which provided for an island-hopping campaign in the Pacific, a blueprint for the U.S. victory in the Pacific during World War II. The result of War Plan Orange was new tactics, equipment (when it could be afforded) and training. Lejeune's modernization efforts included emphasis on officers' continuing military education. General Smedley Butler[2] assumed command at Quantico and turned it into a showpiece: another innovation ordered by Lejeune.[3]

During the 1920s, the 5th Regiment served in the Caribbean Banana Wars. In 1926 a revolt in Nicaragua backed by the Soviets brought in the 5th Marines when U.S. economic

General Butler at Quantico after the war (USMC History Division).

interests were threatened. A U.S. citizen was later killed and diplomats were threatened. The Marines landed and moved inland to the capital city of Managua to reinforce the legation guard. Continuing unrest required additional forces to be committed. The situation went downhill as rebel forces increased and a pitched battle was fought between Marines and rebel forces (known then and now as the Sandinistas) at Ocotal, a town located in the mountains. The Sandinistas lost over fifty killed while the 5th Marines had one killed and five wounded. Engagements between the Marines and the Sandinistas went on for years. Gradually, Nicaragua's Guardia Nacional replaced the Marines as the Sandinista power dwindled due to desertions and casualties. The 5th Marines were deactivated in 1933 and left Nicaragua for the last time in 1933. Augusto Sandino, the leader of the revolution, was assassinated in 1934, but the Sandinistas carried on until 1990. The Marines lost 136 men in the six-year war in Nicaragua.

Following the Nicaragua affair, the 5th Marines along with the rest of the Marine Corps were focused on the development of an amphibious warfare force. This included a Fleet Marine Force permanently assigned to the U.S. Fleet in 1933. Doctrine, schooling, training and Fleet Landing Exercises continued throughout the 1930s. The army also held exercises to prepare for war. In 1940–1941, the army conducted the Louisiana Maneuvers, which included 400,000 troops divided into "Red" and "Blue" forces. The result was good training for the troops and experience for the officers in commanding large bodies of men. All of the military services were preparing for war in spite of inadequate funding. The result of exercises and training was a combined force better prepared for war than in 1917.

The Bonus March (1932)

The background of the Bonus March started with congressional approval of service certificates for the veterans of World War I that would mature and become payable in 1945. All servicemen were affected and Smedley Butler would play a key role after his retirement from the Marine Corps in 1931.

In 1924, overriding President Calvin Coolidge's veto, Congress legislated compensation for veterans. The Adjusted Compensation Act provided the following benefits for all veterans who had served more than sixty days after 5 April 1917 and before 1 July 1919:

> A bonus of $1.00 was to be paid for every day of home service and $1.25 for every day served overseas. If a veteran had $50 or less due to him, he was to be paid the amount in cash. If the amount or credit earned was over $50 the veteran was to receive a paid-up twenty-year endowment insurance policy with face value equal to the number of days of service plus 25 percent with interest of 4 percent compounded annually. Under the provisions of the act, more than 3,500,000 policies would be issued with a total maturity value in 1945 of more than $3,500,000,000. The first demand for immediate payment of the bonus came in 1931. The Legion's demand for immediate payment met with a hostile reception, so the bonus seekers revised their strategy. They now asked that veterans be granted a 50 percent advance loan on their insurance certificates, the money to be paid immediately. A bill authorizing such loans was passed by Congress, vetoed by President Hoover, and repassed over the President's veto. The money for the loans was to come from the United States Treasury. Actually, the money each veteran was eligible for did not amount to much. While maturity value of certificates averaged around $1,000, each, the face value at the time the loans were authorized averaged only about $500. Not all veterans applied for the loan, and it is estimated that no more than $1,000,000,000 in loans was applied for. While a billion dollars is a lot of money, it does not go far when handed out in amounts of $250 or $300.[4]

As the depression deepened in 1932, a move to obtain immediate payment of the entire bonus started and was opposed by Hoover. With opposition in Congress mounting, the House Ways and Means Committee shelved the bonus bill in early May 1932. This signaled the start of the Bonus March.[5]

Walter W. Waters, a former sergeant of World War I residing in Wenatchee, Washington, concocted the idea of a veterans' march on Washington to obtain support from Congress and the public for early redemption of the certificates.[6] The Bonus Army was born.[7] By word of mouth, telephone, speeches and all other means, the Bonus Army was organized, with Waters named as commander in chief of the Bonus Expeditionary Force (BEF). The march was supported by retired Marine general Smedley Butler, who had won two Medals of Honor during his career. The move to Washington was also by all means: foot, auto, and, in many cases, jumping freights. Nearly 23,000 veterans, including wives and children, marched on Washington in the summer of 1932. They would encamp at Anacostia Flats, including land donated by John Henry Bartlett, and in abandoned buildings in the District.[8]

Herbert Hoover was the first president born west of the Mississippi (Iowa) and remains the only president born in Iowa. He was a former secretary of commerce and a Republican elected to the presidency in 1928. Hoover was a Quaker and humanitarian who presided over the Great Depression. He pursued a balanced budget and higher taxes, the worst possible policies to pursue, as seen in his conflicts with Bernard Baruch, who was both his advisor and critic.[9] FDR described Hoover as follows: "There is nothing inside the man but jelly; maybe there never had been anything." Roosevelt went on to say that he might feel sorry for Hoover if he did not feel sorrier for the people burned out (veterans and their families), eleven thousand of them, according to the *Times*. "They must be camping right now alongside the roads out of Washington."[10]

Due to public revulsion at the horrors of World War I and the economic depression, the U.S. Army at that time was a dwindling force. It ranked behind the Romanian army in total numbers. The USMC numbered less than 20,000. There was little support by the White House, Congress, or the public to adequately fund the U.S. Army. In the words of Eleanor Roosevelt: "The only money the Army needs is to buy Bull Durham [tobacco] for the soldiers."[11] At this point, General Douglas MacArthur was appointed as army chief of staff. Then, as now, the principal duty of the chief of staff was to equip and train the force, not to command troops. This meant many appearances on Capitol Hill in and out of hearings to obtain approval of the army's budget proposal and, if possible, increase it. MacArthur was well suited to the job. His father, Arthur MacArthur, was a Medal of Honor winner from the Civil War and later commanded the U.S. Army troops in the Philippines during the insurrection. Young Douglas graduated from the U.S. Military Academy in 1903, first in his class. He was a brigadier general in World War I, commanding the New York National Guard's "Rainbow" Division. He came out of the war with a good reputation and many decorations leading to continued promotions, finally achieving four stars with his promotion to full general in 1930. As a leader, he delegated authority, did not micromanage and left his subordinates to accomplish the job that he gave them. As a person he was arrogant, abrasive, and possessed an enormous ego: ideal qualities on Capitol Hill.

The Bonus Army encamped at Anacostia Flats, named D.C. Hooverville, and other locations, including abandoned buildings in the District. Their mood is best expressed by a rhyme that went through the camps:

> Mellon [Secretary of Treasury] pulled the whistle,
> Hoover rang the bell,
> Wall Street gave the signal
> —And the country went to Hell![12]

Waters and other veterans met with the press, presented petitions to congressmen and were unsuccessful in achieving approval of the bonus payout. Congress adjourned on 6 July 1932 and this ended any hope for an immediate payment of the bonus. For another ten days, speeches for no purpose, and inactivity, settled in while the Bonus Army ran short of rations. Violence flared and there were confrontations between police and the veterans. On 17 July, Waters issued the following order to the Bonus Army:

> Congress has adjourned. There is nothing more that we can hope to do in Washington at this time until Congress reconvenes in either special or regulated session. Transportation is still available to your homes. To those of you who have homes to go to ... your National Commander suggests that you go.[13]

Hoover was sympathetic to the veterans and had previously supported measures to help them, but he was firmly against the early payout of the bonus for economic reasons. He was also concerned by the presence in the capital of a large number of vagrants, who could include anarchists, Communists and lawless elements. As FDR's biographer states: "The specter of the Bolsheviks storming the [czar's] Winter Palace soon dominated administration [Hoover's] thinking."[14] Hoover did several things. He tried persuasion to get the Bonus Army to depart and he considered use of the army to protect the Capitol. He would later order the attorney general, William D. Mitchell, to investigate and this put J. Edgar Hoover into action and led to an FBI report of several thousand pages on the Bonus Army.

The Communist plan for a march on Washington was described by Felix Morrow (a Bolshevik) in 1932. "The purpose of the [Communist] march on Washington was to put mass pressure on Congress. The date set by the Workers Ex-Serviceman's League [called the Weasels in histories since then], June 8 [1932], for the main body of veterans to arrive in Washington for a monster demonstration before Congress.[15] Morrow explains that the Communist effort was to capture the leadership of the Bonus Army and use the Bonus Army for Communist political purposes. Both Waters and the police attempted to segregate the Weasels from the Bonus Army and to suppress their activities. This effort was largely successful, but the fact remains that the Weasels were an ongoing parallel effort while the Bonus Army was in Washington, and in histories since then their involvement in the Bonus March has always been an issue.

The Military Intelligence Division (MID) of the U.S. Army took the Red Menace as a serious threat and plans were in hand to deal with it.[16] War Plan White was developed to defend Washington against insurrection.[17] War Plan White would be implemented and U.S. Army troops would be deployed when civilian authorities in the Capitol declared that they could no longer maintain law and order. The MID reported Weasel activity to MacArthur and he was convinced that the Bonus Marchers were Bolsheviks masquerading as veterans and that the Capitol was threatened. He prepared for action by alerting army units for deployment to protect the Capitol. Dwight Eisenhower had worked for MacArthur in the Philippines and was now his aide. Eisenhower was a 1915 graduate of USMA who had served as a lieutenant in World War I, although not overseas. He was now a major and very sympathetic to the plight of the veterans. Eisenhower argued against any military involvement in actions against the Bonus Army, but the order was likely to come from the president and the military had little say in the matter.

After the Waters order of 17 July, the strength of the Bonus Army dwindled to 14,925 by 26 July. Everyone knew that the Bonus Army was disbanding, yet on 21 July the Washington, D.C., chief of police, General Glassford, notified Waters that the Bonus Army was going to be evicted from buildings and property in the city. The eviction was to start on the 22nd but was delayed.[18] This seemed quite unnecessary, since the Bonus Army was in fact departing on its own. Nevertheless, the remaining members of the Bonus Army attempted to comply, but the Treasury Department forced the issue by ordering them out before they could move.[19]

> The Bonus March might have ended peacefully if authorities had acted with the same compassion and restraint as the District of Columbia chief of police, Pelham D. Glassford, a former army brigadier general and classmate of MacArthur at West Point. Glassford assisted rather than persecuted the bonus marchers, who might have departed Washington on their own accord before much longer without intervention.[20]

The Metropolitan Police arrived first and cordoned off the area. People from outside of the perimeter tried to break through the line and fighting ensued.[21] Several policemen opened fire, killing two veterans. One of the policemen, Shinault, was later killed, but his assailant was not found. Hoover ordered the army in to clear veterans from abandoned public buildings in the city, on 28 July. Hurley passed the order to MacArthur:

> The President has just informed me that the civil government of the District of Columbia has reported to him that it is unable to maintain law and order in the District. You will have United States troops proceed immediately to the scene of disorder. Co-operate fully with the District of Columbia police force which is now in charge. Surround the affected area and clear it without delay. Turn over all prisoners to civil authorities. *In your orders insist that any women and children who may be in the affected area be accorded every consideration and kindness. Use all humanity consistent with due exercise of this order* [italics are the author's].[22]

This gave MacArthur the authority to execute War Plan White. About six hundred soldiers were committed, with another two thousand in reserve at Fort Myer. Elements of the 12th Infantry, 3rd Cavalry, led by George S. Patton, 16th Brigade, and a platoon of tanks advanced down Pennsylvania Avenue led by MacArthur in Class A uniform. Eisenhower had argued against this as unnecessarily provocative and recalls: "I thought it had the aspect of a riot rather than a big military movement, and so told him that I thought that it was inadvisable, that the Chief of Staff should not dignify the incident by going out himself."[23] To his dismay, Eisenhower was ignored and ordered home to get into his Class A uniform. Eisenhower later said, "Probably no one had tougher fights with a senior than I did with MacArthur. I told him time and time again: "Why the *hell* don't you *fire* me? Goddammit, you do things that I don't agree with and you know damn well I don't'."[24] Eisenhower was more candid after he was in the White House. He privately expressed the opinion that he could not understand how a damn fool like MacArthur could become a general officer. In an interview with historian Stephen Ambrose, Eisenhower said, "I told that dumb son-of-bitch he had no business going down there. I told him it was no place for the Chief of Staff."[25] A military attaché in a Washington embassy remarked: "Sending the Chief of Staff of the United States Army to evict twenty thousand unarmed veterans?" He asked incredulously, 'Great God! Who would Hoover and Hurley [secretary of war] send if a foreign army were rumored to be able to land? The Vice President in Indian costume, I suppose!'"[26] Several reasons were offered for MacArthur's decision to lead the troops, which was clearly outside of his charter, as seen earlier. James M. Gavin, then a Fort Benning lieutenant, opined that it was an act of courage. MacArthur did not want to force this unpleasant duty on a subordinate.[27] Eisenhower said later that MacArthur saw himself as the savior of Washington against a Bolshevik horde.[28] His action could also help the army's budget. The troops cleared the District with bayonets and tear gas. There were civilian injuries. Early that evening, Hoover sent an order to MacArthur to halt at the 11th Street Bridge and not cross to Anacostia Flats, where many of the shacks with women and children were located. MacArthur disobeyed the order, crossed to Anacostia and fired on the shacks. There were civilian casualties. MacArthur later said that he was not going to stop because of a messenger who said he had an order from the president.[29] The job was done and the veterans and their families fled the camp that night. Government damage control started immediately, although the initial public reaction was in favor of Hoover's action.[30]

The nation's press bannered the eviction across its front pages. A few, citing Cleveland's suppression of the Pullman strike in 1895, praised Hoover for acting decisively; most lambasted the administration for excessive force: "What a pitiful spectacle. The mightiest government in the world chasing unarmed men, women and children with Army tanks. If the Army must be called out to make war on unarmed men, women and children, this is no longer America."[31] The *Washington Post* was more favorable in its view toward the administration.

> In their distress, the deluded bonus men have the sympathy of all human citizens. Their constitutional right to peaceably assemble and to petition the Government for redress of grievances is not questioned. But to assume that the right of petition includes the right to disturb public peace and defy lawful authority is absurd. It is not likely that at the start the bonus march was directly organized by communist workers, although it is natural enough that reds should take advantage of it. The Moscow reds are spreading through the world the false statement that the United States is in the throes of revolution and that the government is shooting down defenseless and peaceable citizens who are starving. Americans cannot afford to give aid and comfort to such lying propaganda.[32]

As word seeped out about the casualties, public opinion and the Congress turned against Hoover and MacArthur.[33] The administration realized that reaction to the Bonus Army had gotten out of hand with people injured. The whole episode was avoidable. MacArthur countered, as did Hoover, with public statements and visits to Capitol Hill. MacArthur's statements were numerous and very clear:

> It is my opinion that had the President permitted this thing to go on for 24 hours more, he would have faced a grave situation which would have caused a real battle. Had he let it go for another week, I believe that the institutions of our government would have been seriously threatened.[34]

The government continued its effort to justify its actions, but the nation's conclusion was best stated by FDR when he saw the photos and press accounts: "MacArthur has just prevented Hoover's reelection." Later that day Roosevelt had a discussion with Huey Long. After he hung up, he turned to an aide [Tugwell]: "You know, that's the second most dangerous man in this country." Tugwell could not resist and responded by asking who was first. FDR replied, "Douglas MacArthur. You saw how he strutted down Pennsylvania Avenue. You saw that picture of him in the *Times* after the troops chased all those vets out with tear gas and burned the shelters. Did you ever see anyone more self-satisfied? There's a potential Mussolini for you right here at home."[35]

MacArthur escaped retribution for his insubordination by outmaneuvering Hoover. He appealed to law-and-order Republicans on Capitol Hill by calling a midnight press conference disclaiming responsibility but praising Hoover.[36] There is no evidence that either Hoover or MacArthur ever regretted their actions. The closest MacArthur ever came to regret was a comment recorded by William Manchester, MacArthur's biographer. In responding to the press critical of his actions, he said, "It was a bitter gall and I know that some part of it will always be with me."[37]

In May 1933, a second Bonus March occurred. The veteran leaders met with the newly elected president, FDR.[38] While the second Bonus March was uneventful, it did no better than the first in obtaining early release of the bonus payments. FDR did help the veterans by creating jobs for them. Thousands were employed in Florida on public works projects when disaster struck. On 1 September 1935, a hurricane moved through Florida, killing 259 veterans and many others. The final death toll will never be known. When the details became known, complete with photographs of dead veterans stacked like cordwood, national outrage caused the release of the bonus at last. In June 1936, bonus packets were distributed to 3,518,000 veterans. The cash value was $1.9 billion.[39] FDR did not forget the Bonus Army. Before he died in 1945 he created the G.I. Bill, which has provided benefits to hundreds of thousands of veterans of World War II and beyond. The G.I. Bill is the legacy of the Bonus Army.[40] "Millions of Americans have since peacefully marched on Washington in support of various causes, their way paved by the veterans of 1932."[41] In 1965 construction workers dredging a quarry turned up a rusting automobile with 1935 license plates. Five skeletons were inside.[42] The last of the missing Bonus Marchers were laid to rest.

World War II (1939–1945)

A generation after the "War to End All Wars," Europe saw the start of another conflict, caused by Adolf Hitler, who had taken control of Germany in 1933. His rise to power had been fueled by his vision of a return to greatness, anti–Semitism and promises to regain lands lost in World War I. His 1939 invasion of Poland triggered the war in Europe, but the United States was not involved in the early years of this war. In the Pacific, Japan was building an empire. This included the invasion of China and other lands. Japan viewed the United States as a threat and attacked the U.S. Fleet at Pearl Harbor, Hawaii, on 7 December 1941. The United States was now at war in the Pacific and Hitler would declare war on the United States a few days later. The United States was now faced with a war on two fronts. The U.S. Marine Corps was organized, equipped and trained to fight in the Pacific war, and an island-hopping campaign envisioned years earlier would become the plan to defeat Japan. The Marines would not fight in Europe.

When the war started, the 5th Marines deployed to Wellington, New Zealand, arriving on 14 June 1942.[43] The regiment fought in the island-hopping campaign at Guadalcanal, New Britain, Eastern New Guinea, Peleliu, and Okinawa. War Plan Orange, developed years earlier, now became an execution plan. When the war ended in August 1945, the 5th Marine Regiment moved to Tientsin, China, and participated in the occupation of northern China until May 1947, when it was relocated to Guam. It moved to the Marine Corps base at Camp Pendleton, California, in 1949. Many books have been written about Marines in the Pacific war. One of the best was written by Corporal Eugene Sledge, 3rd Battalion, 5th Marines. His book, *With the Old Breed at Peleliu and Okinawa* was published in 1981 and later became part of the 2010 television series *Pacific*. His book brought home to the reader the horrors of war:

> The men digging in on both sides of me cursed the stench and the mud. I began moving the heavy, sticky clay mud with my entrenching shovel to shape out the extent of the foxhole before digging deeper. Each shovelful had to be knocked off the spade, because it stuck like glue. I was thoroughly exhausted and thought my strength wouldn't last from one sticky shovelful to the next. Kneeling on the mud, I had dug the hole no more than six or eight inches deep when the odor of rotting flesh got worse. There was nothing to do but continue to dig, so I closed up my mouth and inhaled with short shallow breaths. Another spadeful of soil out of the hole released a mass of wriggling maggots that came welling up as though those beneath were pushing them out. I cursed and told the NCO as he came by what a mess I was digging into. "You heard him, he said put the holes five yards apart." In disgust, I drove the spade into the soil, scooped out the insects, and threw them down the front of the ridge. The next stroke of the spade unearthed buttons and scraps of cloth from a Japanese army jacket in the mud—and another mass of maggots. I kept on doggedly. With the next thrust, metal hit the breastbone of a rotting Japanese corpse. I gazed down in horror and disbelief as the metal scraped a clean track through the mud along the dirty whitish bone and cartilage with ribs attached. The shovel skidded into the rotting abdomen with a squishing sound. The odor nearly overwhelmed me as I rocked back on my

heels. I began choking and gagging as I yelled in desperation, "I can't dig in here! There's a dead Nip here!" The NCO came over, looked down at my problem and at me, and growled, "You heard him; he said put the holes five yards apart."[44]

Korean War (1950–1953)

Following World War II, Korea was divided into two nations, North and South, separated by the 38th parallel. Less than five years after the end of World War II, the United States was at war again in June 1950, this time in Korea. Cause of the war was an invasion of South Korea, a U.S. ally, by North Korea, an ally of China and the Soviet Bloc. In this war, the United Nations (UN) agreed to form a command to oppose the invasion, so the United States, while providing the majority of troops, was assisted by the UN. As a result of a treaty, the U.S. 24th Infantry Division had been stationed in South Korea before the North attacked, so there was no doubt that the United States would fight. Our treaty, the UN resolution, and our presence in Korea assured that fact. Over the three years of the war, the UN would be pushed back from the 38th parallel to what became known as the Pusan Perimeter. An amphibious UN landing at Inchon in September 1950 near Seoul, the South Korean capital, threatened to cut off the North Korean army, and it withdrew and was then pushed north to the border with China when the Chinese entered the war in October 1950. The UN withdrew to a line similar to the original border of the 38th parallel, the Demilitarized Zone where a cease-fire ended hostilities on 27 July 1953, three years after they had started.

In June 1950 when the war started (called a Police Action in the United States); the 5th Marines moved from Camp Pendleton to the Pusan Perimeter on 5 August 1950 as a part of the Provisional Marine Brigade. In a very short time after the war had started the UN troops were pushed back to the southeast corner of Korea, where they held as more UN troops arrived. The 5th Marine Regiment participated in the Inchon Landing, the Battle of Chosen Reservoir near the border with China (November–December 1950), and fighting on the east-central front and western front. When the cease-fire occurred in July 1953, the 5th Marines defended the Demilitarized Zone until March 1955, when it returned to Camp Pendleton.

Vietnam (1946–1975)

The Vietnam War started after the end of World War II in 1946 when the French attempted to reclaim their colonial possession, then called Indochina, and were opposed by Nationalists under Ho Chi Minh. The United States supported the French with funding and logistical support, including aircraft resupply missions. After a three-month siege, when the French were defeated at Dien Bien Phu on 7 May 1954 negotiations were conducted in Geneva, Switzerland, to end the war. The result was that the French left Indochina and Vietnam was divided into North and South Vietnam, with the communist North governed by Ho Chi Minh and the South by Ngo Dinh Diem, a U.S. puppet who would rule long after the French left. The United States continued to support the Saigon regime in the South through the 1950s, and as financial assistance increased the U.S. involvement deepened, leading to military advisors, and, by 1965, the first U.S. combat troop units were committed when Marines landed in Vietnam in March.

On 5 March 1966, the 5th Marine Regiment was deployed to South Vietnam. The 5th

Marines served five years in Vietnam in the northern part of the country called I Corps. The regiment fought at the battles of Rung Sat, Phu Loc, Hue, Que Son Valley, An Hoa, Tam Ky and Da Nang. The 5th Marines departed Vietnam in April 1971 as a part of the U.S. withdrawal and effort to hand over the war to the South Vietnamese. The South Vietnamese regime was able to defend itself until 1975, when the country was overrun by the North Vietnamese and collapsed.[45] This ended the longest war fought by the United States until that time. Longer wars have followed.

Post-Vietnam (1975–1991)

The 5th Marine Regiment remained at Camp Pendleton until August 1990, when it participated in the effort to eject Iraq from Kuwait after it invaded that country to seize its oil. Iraq's Saddam Hussein annexed Kuwait after a very short war of less than a week when the Kuwait armed forces were overrun. The United States and its allies responded with military intervention, Operation Desert Shield and Operation Desert Storm, called the Gulf War. Following these campaigns that ended with Iraq's defeat in April 1991, the 5th Marines deployed to participate in a humanitarian effort, Operation Sea Angel, in Bangladesh. This followed a cyclone that cost 138,000 lives in April 1991.

Global War on Terrorism (2001–2014)

The "War on Terror," also known as the "Global War on Terrorism," is a term applied to the international military campaign that started after the 11 September 2001 terrorist attacks on the New York City Twin Towers and other targets in the United States. These have since been called the 9–11 attacks. The campaign led to an international campaign to eliminate al-Qaeda and other militant/terror organizations. The United States and many other NATO and non–NATO countries participated in the campaign. The war included two major campaigns leading to the occupation of Iraq by coalition forces followed by a major buildup of forces in Afghanistan to eliminate terrorists.

The 5th Marine Regiment moved to Kuwait on 5 January 2003 as a part of the force planned for the invasion of Iraq. This was in response to the belief that Iraq played a role in the 9–11 attacks and was also stockpiling weapons of mass destruction. The Coalition Forces, including the 5th Marine Regiment, attacked Iraq on 21 March 2003. The regiment seized the Rumayllah oil fields and moved on to surround the Iraq capital, Baghdad. Rotation back to the United States and other deployments to Iraq continued until the 5th was deployed to Afghanistan in support of Operation Enduring Freedom in August 2011. In Afghanistan the 5th Marine Regiment Served as Regimental Combat Team 5 (RCT-5) with an area of operations in the Marjah, Garmsir and Nawa districts. The mission was to develop local defense forces and expand the police force. The RCT-5 joined the 6th Marine Regiment (RCT-6) in Afghanistan. It was the first time the two Marine regiments had served together since World War I. In August 2012, the RCT-5 returned to Camp Pendleton, where it serves today. The last U.S. Marines left Afghanistan on 26 October 2014 when Camp Leatherneck was handed over to Afghani forces.

Appendix A

World War I Chronology[1]

1914

28 June	Archduke Franz Ferdinand assassinated in Sarajevo.
28 July	Austria-Hungary declares war on Serbia. Russia mobilizes.

1915

4 Feb.	Germany begins unrestricted warfare against merchant ships.
7 May	Sinking of the passenger ship commercial liner *Lusitania* by German submarine.
1 Sept.	Germany suspends unrestricted warfare against merchant ships.

1916

21 Feb.	Battle of Verdun begins. Longest battle of the war (February–December 1916).
1 July	Battle of the Somme begins. First use of tanks.

1917

19 Jan.	Zimmermann Telegram to Mexico.
1 Feb.	Germany resumes unrestricted warfare against merchant ships.
15 March	Russia's Czar Nicholas II abdicates.
6 April	U.S. Congress declares war on Germany.
13 June	General John Pershing and staff leave London for France.
26 June	U.S. 1st Division and 5th Marine Regiment land in France.
7 Nov.	Bolsheviks seize power in Russia.

1918

21 Jan.	Ludendorff decides on Operation Michael, sets offensive to start March 15.
1–12 March	Germany deploys army for Operation Michael. Offensive delayed to March 21.
3 March	Russia signs peace treaty with Central Powers.
16–19 March	Germans move 60 divisions into position for start of offensive.
21 March	Ludendorff begins Operation Michael.
27 May	Operation Blücher drives French from Chemin des Dames.
28 May	First Division attacks and captures village of Cantigny.
31 May	Elements of 3rd Division ordered to Château-Thierry.

1 June	Second Division ordered to defend Paris-Metz road. Germans occupy Belleau Wood and village of Bouresches.
3 June	German drive to Paris is stopped at Les Mares Farm.
4 June	Third Division completes move to Château-Thierry.
6 June	Fifth and 6th Marines capture Hill 142, village of Bouresches, and occupy southern portion of Belleau Wood. Bloodiest day in Marine Corps history.
8 June	Germans and Marines trade attacks in Belleau Wood.
9–13 June	Ludendorff opens Operation Gneiseneu. German army advances 10 miles before being stopped before Compiegne.
10 June	Marines advance into center of Belleau Wood.
12 June	Marines advance into northern portion of Belleau Wood.
15 June	Seventh Infantry Regiment relieves Marines in Belleau Wood.
16–22 June	Seventh Regiment fails to drive Germans from Belleau Wood.
22 June	Marines relieve 7th Regiment.
23 June	Marine attack on northern portion of Belleau Wood fails.
26 June	Marines capture Belleau Wood.
1 July	Ninth Regiment captures village of Vaux.
4 July	Soldiers from 2nd Division march in Paris parade commemorating American Independence Day. Elements of U.S. 131st and 132nd Regiments, 33rd Division, support Australian 4th Division in attack at Hamel.
15–17 July	German Operation Rheims achieves minimal gains. U.S. 3rd, 26th, 28th, and 42nd Divisions participate in stopping German offensive.
18 July–6 Aug.	French/American Aisne-Marne offensive, French XX Corps spearheads attack, U.S. 1st and 2nd Divisions and French Moroccan Division lead main assault near Soissons.
8 Aug.–11 Nov.	British begin Somme offensive. Initial attack includes U.S. 33rd and 80th Divisions as part of British 4th Army.
18 Aug.–11 Nov.	French Oise-Aisne offensive. U.S. 32nd Division captures Juvigny.
19 Aug.–11 Nov.	Pershing responds to Foch's request for reinforcements by sending 37th and 91st Divisions in mid–October 1918.
12–16 Sept.	American St.-Mihiel offensive. Pershing's first major offensive aimed at reducing the St.-Mihiel salient.
October	Battle of Blanc Mont.
26 Sept.–11 Nov.	Meuse-Argonne offensive. Combined Allied offensive includes 1.2 million American troops.
9 Nov.	Kaiser Wilhelm II of Germany abdicates his throne.
11 Nov.	Armistice goes into effect. Hostilities end.
17 Nov.	Fifth Regiment starts its march to the Rhine.
1 Dec.	Fifth Regiment enters Germany.

1919

28 June	Peace treaty ending the war, Treaty of Versailles, signed.
July	Fifth Regiment departs Germany and returns to the United States.

Appendix B

Names, Abbreviations and Terms

ADC—assistant division commander.

AEF—American Expeditionary Force. The organization that included U.S. World War I troops fighting in France.

AKA—also known as.

Allies—see *Entente Powers or Allies*.

Auto rifle—automatic rifle.

AWOL—absent without leave.

Banana Wars—a series of occupations and interventions by the United States in Central America and the Caribbean during the period 1898–1934. The causes were economic in nature and the fighting was usually accomplished by the Marines. The U.S. United Fruit Company had a financial interest in the Caribbean, including bananas, which gave the name to these conflicts.

BandMn—bandsman, musician, in combat often used as runners.

BAR—Browning Automatic Rifle. The weapon issued to small U.S. units to provide automatic fire support.

BCdG—Belgian Croix de Guerre.

Belly wrinkles—if a person has not had food for a while, the stomach muscles contract and wrinkles in the belly appear.

BG–Brigadier General.

Big Bertha—a super heavy German mortar called Dicke Bertha (a literal translation: "Fat or Heavy Bertha)."[1] The Allies applied the name Big Bertha to a range of German weapons that included the *Paris Gun*, which had a 16.5-inch bore and fired a shell weighing over eighteen hundred pounds. Range was eighty-one miles. The Paris Gun was designed to bombard Paris at a very long range to demoralize the French.

Boche—German soldiers.

Bois de Belleau—Belleau Wood.

Bolsheviks—Russians who participated in the revolution against Czar Nicholas II.

Bumped—killed in action.

Camion—French truck.

CdG—Croix de Guerre, French (ranking in order: Palm, Gilt, Silver, Bronze).

Central Powers—the alliance that consisted of the German empire, Austro-Hungarian Empire, Ottoman Empire, and Kingdom of Bulgaria. Other groups also joined, such as Lithuania. The name was derived from the geographic location of the nations: central Europe.

"C'est la guerre!"—translated, it means "it's war!"—a French phrase of resignation for everything that is broken.

CG—commanding general.

Chauchat—a machine gun provided by the French to U.S. forces. It frequently jammed and was replaced by the Browning Automatic Rifle.

Chevaux de Frise—a defensive devise in use since the U.S. Civil War and possibly in earlier wars. It consisted of a frame that could be covered by spikes, barbed or even broken glass. It could be rolled aside to admit friendly forces.

Citation Star (or Silver Star Citation)—established in July 1918 and awarded for heroism. The star was affixed to a service medal. In 1932 the Citation Star was converted to the Silver Star Medal, which is still awarded for bravery to this day.

Cmdr—commander.

CO—commanding officer.

Col—colonel.

Conscription—a military draft.

CoS—chief of staff.

Cossack—an independent post.

CPhM—chief pharmacist mate.

Cpl—corporal.

Cpt—captain.

CWO—chief warrant officer.

DI—French abbreviation for "d'infanterie." In English: infantry division.

doughboy—a slang term for an American soldier. It originated in the U.S. Civil War but did not come into use until World War I. It came from the round buttons on uniforms that resembled flour dumplings or biscuits.

DoW—died of wounds.

DSC—Distinguished Service Cross.

DSM—Distinguished Service Medal.

EM—enlisted man or enlisted Marine—a rank below that of an officer.

Entente Powers or Allies—countries at war with the Central Powers. The Entente Powers included Great Britain (and its colonies), France, Russia and Italy (after 1915). The United States entered the war later with the Entente Powers but was known as an "Associated Power."

EXO—executive officer.

FA—field artillery.

1st lt—first lieutenant.

1st sgt—first sergeant.

Forest green—color of Marine uniforms, which was different from the gray color of the U.S. Army infantry. Unfortunately, the color forest green was close to that of the German uniforms, which led to friendly-fire casualties.

Forty by eights—French boxcars that could accommodate forty troops or eight horses.

Fourragere—a unit award authorized for wear by all members of a unit that was distinguished for service in combat. The troops called these pogey ropes. "Pogey" was a term for candy and was derisively used to refer to Marines who had soft jobs in the rear.

French leave—absent without leave.

French 75—see 75s.

Fritz—a German soldier or civilian.

Frogs—a derogatory U.S. nickname for the French ... then and now. A number of explanations have been offered for this nickname. The most common is that it referred to what they ate: frogs or frogs' legs.

Gyrenes—a slang term used to identify U.S. Marines.

GySgt—gunnery sergeant.

Hachure—a short line on a map used to represent elevation.

Hap—hospital apprentice with a grade added.

Hdqs—headquarters.

Heinie—a German soldier. Also, a reference to the buttocks.

Hooverville—a camp named after President Hoover that was set up near Washington, D.C., to house members of the Bonus Army.

Hotchkiss Gun—a light 42mm cannon first used in the U.S. Indian Wars. It was issued to troops in World War I and could be carried by two mules.

Hun—a negative term for a German soldier that referred to the tribes that ravaged Europe in ancient times.

Indianhead Division—the U.S. 2nd Infantry Division.

Indochina—name for French colonies on the peninsula in Southeast Asia. These included nations established after the breakup of the French empire there: Vietnam, Laos, Cambodia, and Thailand.

Infantry—foot soldiers.

IO—intelligence officer.

IWC—Italian War Cross.

Kamerad! A German call that indicates he wants to surrender.

KIA—killed in action.

Knuckle buster (or duster)—a weapon that was a combination knife and brass knuckles. Many also had a stud at the end of the hilt for cracking skulls. The military nomenclature was "M1918 Trench Knife." Nice weapon, but sometimes hurts the knuckles when used forcefully.

League of Nations—an intercontinental organization founded on 10 January 1920 as a result of the Paris Peace Conference. Its purpose was to maintain world peace. By 1935 it had 58 chartered members. The United States did not join. The League lasted until World War II and was replaced by the United Nations in 1945.

Leatherneck—a U.S. Marine.

Lewis Gun—a machine gun invented in the United States in 1911 and perfected by the British. It was first used in World War I by the British in Belgium. It is said that the Germans called it the Belgium Rattlesnake. It was issued to the British army and the U.S. Army and Marines during World War I.

LH—Legion d'Honneur, French (ranking in order: Cmdr, Off, Ch).

Liberty—a term for vacation or military leave.

Lieut—Lieutenant.

LtCmdr—lieutenant commander.

LtCol or LTC—lieutenant colonel.

Maj—major.

MarGun—Marine gunner.

Maxim—the German machine gun widely used during World War I. It was originally developed in the United States and was adapted by the Germans for their use during World War I.

MG—major general.

MIA—missing in action.

Mills Bomb—a hand grenade developed by the British in 1915. It could also be launched by a rifle with an attachment similar to those used later by the U.S. Army.

Minnenwerfirs—German mortars.

MM—Medaille Militaire, French.

MoH—Medal of Honor, Army or Navy.

Monkey meat—canned meat rations from Madagascar.

Morning Report—a document produced every morning for each unit and signed by the commander. It listed personnel changes and other information about the unit. The 5th Regiment Roster in Appendix D was produced from World War I morning reports.

MPs—U.S. Military Police.

MSMofV—Montenegrin Silver Medal of Valor.

Mustang—an enlisted man who received a direct commission to officer rank.

Mustard gas—the agent dichlorodiethyl-sulfide. It was a yellowish liquid and the drops settled into low areas such as the trenches of defenders. It caused blisters and attacked the lungs and eyes, causing at least temporary blindness. It was called mustard gas because it smelled like mustard.

NC—Navy Cross.

No-man's-land—the unoccupied area between opposing armies.

Oak Leaf Cluster—awarded in place of an additional medal.

Pandemic—the worldwide influenza epidemic that occurred during and after World War I.

P.C.—"poste de commandement," location of a command headquarters.

PFC—private first class.

PhM—pharmacist mate (with grade, e.g., 1 or 2, etc.).

Poilu—French infantry soldier. Literally: "the hairy one."

Potato masher—a German hand grenade. It resembled a potato masher since it had a long handle with a can on top. It was the Model 24 Stielhandgranate (German "stalk hand grenade") and was the standard hand grenade of the German army from World War I until the end of World War II.

Pvt—private.

PWC—Portuguese War Cross.

QM—quartermaster.

QmClk—quartermaster clerk.

Refuse the line—a unit facing either left or right 90 degrees to be in the direction an attack is expected.

Reg'l—regimental.

Runners—men used to carry communications between individuals.

Salient—something that projects outward from its surroundings.

Sausages—observation balloons that were cylindrically shaped.

Sea bags—large artillery projectiles.

2nd lt—second lieutenant.

75s—French 75mm artillery guns used by the United States during World War I. They were very effective and badly needed, since the U.S. had a limited number of artillery guns shipped to France.

Sgt—Sergeant.

SgtMaj or SGM—sergeant major.

Shell shock—a term used to describe trauma caused by stress of battle. It was recognized early in World War I and was most commonly associated with heavy bombardment. Symptoms included loss of self-control; headaches; and inability to reason. It was more than physical. It affected emotions and the brain. The term was replaced in later wars by others such as "combat fatigue" in World War II and "Post Traumatic Stress Disorder" (PTSD) today.

Sick call—a daily lineup of military people needing medical attention.

SS—Silver Star (citation, later a medal).

Stokes mortar—a smooth-bore 3.2-inch British trench mortar designed by Frederick Stokes to counter a similar high-angle-of-fire weapon in use by the Germans. It was issued to British troops in 1915 and was used by armies into World War II.

Storm troopers—German infantry trained to launch a quick attack.

3 in 1—a lubricant oil in a can that was and is used by soldiers and civilians alike to this day.

Top cutter—senior enlisted soldier in a U.S. military unit. Usually the first sergeant in a company.

Tracers—bullets with a chemical in the base that lights when fired. It provides an aid in aiming the weapon, especially at night, when gunners cannot see the strike of the gun's bullets.

Trmptr—trumpeter, bugler, often used as runners.

U–boat—a German submarine. The word is the anglicized version of the German term "Unterseeboot," which means "undersea boat."

United Nations—established in 1945 to promote international cooperation, the successor to the League of Nations. Its objectives include maintaining international peace and security, promoting human rights, fostering social and economic development, protecting the environment, and providing humanitarian aid in cases of famine, natural disaster, and armed conflict.

USA—U.S. Army.

USMA—U.S. Military Academy at West Point, New York.

USMC—U.S. Marine Corps.

USN—U.S. Navy.

USNA—U.S. Naval Academy at Annapolis, Maryland.

Very pistol—flare pistols used to illuminate an area such as a battlefield.

Whippet—the generic name for a tank. The actual tank is the British Medium Mark A Whippet.

Whiz bang—a German 77mm projectile. As a direct-fire weapon, it gave no warning of its approach.

WIA—wounded in action.

Young Men's Christian Association (YMCA)—founded on 6 June 1844 by George Williams in London to put Christian principles into practice by developing a healthy body, mind, and spirit. Unpaid volunteers and paid staff served in the YMCA during the First World War. They operated leave centers, canteens and "huts."

Appendix C

The Organization of the 2nd Infantry Division

The 2nd Division was composed in France of units from the regular army and the USMC during the fall of 1917. Brigadier General Charles A. Doyen, USMC, organized the division and was in command until November 7, 1917, when he was relieved and returned to command the 4th Brigade. One of several senior officers rejected for ill health, Doyen was returned to the United States in May 1918 and died there the following spring. He was succeeded in command of the 4th Brigade by Brigadier General James G. Harbord, U.S. Army. The 2nd Division was commanded by Major General Omar Bundy, who was succeeded by Major General James G. Harbord on July 14, 1918, until July 28, 1918, when Major General John A. Lejeune of the USMC assumed command. The division captured 12,026 men. Its total advance was 60 kilometers. It was quiet 71 days and active 66 days. Its total casualties were 22,230, the largest of any division of the army. It had 4,478 battle deaths and 17,752 wounded. The division received 35,343 replacements.[1]

The 3rd Infantry Brigade

9th Infantry   5th Machine Gun Battalion
23rd Infantry

The 2nd Field Artillery Brigade

12th Field Artillery   17th Field Artillery
15th Field Artillery   2nd Trench Mortar Battery

Divisional Troops

4th Machine Gun Battalion   1st Field Signal Battalion
2nd Engineers   Headquarters Troop

Trains

2nd Train Headquarters   2nd Sanitary Train
2nd Military Police   Ambulance Cos.
2nd Supply Train   Field Hospitals 1, 15, 16, 23

The 4th Brigade of Marines[2]

Commanding Officers[3]

Brigadier General Charles A. Doyen, 23 Oct. 17–6 May 1918
Brigadier General James G. Harbord, 6 May 1899–15 July 1918
Colonel Harry Lee, 15 July 1819–25 July 1819
Major General John A. Lejeune, 28 July 1819–28 July 1819
Brigadier General Wendell C. Neville, 28 July 1819–end
The 4th Brigade of U.S. Marines was composed of the 5th and 6th Regiments of Marines
and the 6th Machine Gun Battalion of Marines. The regimental commanders
and companies forming the battalions were as follows.

5th Regiment

Commanding Officers

Colonel Charles A. Doyen, from time of organization until 1 November 1917
Lieutenant Colonel Hiram I. Bearss, 1 November 1917–1 January 1918
Colonel Wendell C. Neville, 1 January 1917–17 July 1918
Colonel Logan Feland, 17 July–21 March 1919
Colonel Harold O. Snyder, 21 March 1919 to end

Headquarters Company
Supply Company
8th Machine Gun Company
30th Company

First Battalion	Second Battalion	Third Battalion
17th (A) Company	18th (E) Company	16th (I) Company.
49th (B) Company	43rd (F) Company	20th (K) Company
66th (C) Company	51st (G) Company	45th (L) Company
67th (D) Company	55th (H) Company	47th (M) Company

6th Regiment

Commanding Officers

Colonel Albertus W. Catlin, 17 August 1917–6 June 1918, when wounded in Belleau Wood
Lieutenant Colonel Harry Lee, 6 June 1918 to end

First Battalion	Second Battalion	Third Battalion
74th (A) Company	78th (E) Company	82nd (I) Company
75th (B) Company	79th (F) Company	83rd (K) Company
76th (C) Company	80th (G) Company	84th (L) Company
95th (D) Company	96th (H) Company	97th (M) Company

73d Machine Gun Company
Supply Company
Headquarters Company

6th Machine Gun Battalion

Commanding Officers

Major Edward B. Cole, 17 August 1917–10 June 1918
Captain Harlan E. Major, 10–12 June 1918
Captain George H. Osterhout, 12–20 June 1918
Major Littleton W.T. Waller, Jr., 20 June–24 October 1918
Major Matthew H. Kingman, 25 October 1918 to end

15th (A) Company
23rd (B) Company
77th (C) Company
81st (D) Company

Appendix D

The 5th Marine Regiment Roster

During World War I Marine Corps rosters (listings of Marines assigned to each company) were prepared monthly. They contained the name, rank, organization and remarks for each Marine and attached Navy personnel. In 1931–1932, these rosters were typed and stored. Currently the rosters are located at the USMC History Division, Quantico, Virginia. Some of the 5th Marine Regiment rosters are missing. To compensate for this, other sources such as listings of Marines killed in World War I were searched and names of those not found in rosters were added to the compiled listing provided here. The names in each company have been rearranged into alphabetical order except for the officers and first sergeants who lead the listing in each company. The company rosters were designated at various times with either number or alphabetical designations. Both are shown here. For example, the 66th Company was also known as C Company and is shown as 66th (C) Company. Many entries have a remark of "MIA," or missing in action. Most of these Marines became separated from their units during battle but later found their way back. There are many abbreviations, mostly for ranks, and these are defined in Appendix B. The rosters list over eight thousand Marines, navy personnel and an occasional army soldier in the 5th Regiment. Of this number nearly seven hundred were killed or died of wounds while over seven hundred were wounded or died of disease (most from influenza). In some cases Marines were transferred between companies, and in these cases they are listed in both companies. Roster of the headquarters of the 5th Regiment included commanders, staff officers, and enlisted Marines of the three battalion headquarters. Thirtieth Company was a replacement holding and a guard company. As such, it did not take part in combat operations.

Headquarters, Fifth Marine Regiment

(by rank)

NAME (RANK) REMARKS

Doyen, Charles A. (Col) Commanding, 5th Regt'l, from start until 1 Nov 1917.

Bearss, Hiram I. (LTC) Commanding, 5th Regt'l, 1 Nov 17 to 1 Jan 18.

Neville, Wendell C. (Col) Commanding, 5th Regt'l, 1 Jan to 17 Jul 18.

Feland, Logan (Col) Commanding, 5th Regt'l, 17 Jul to 21 Mar 19.

Snyder, Harold O. (Col) Commanding, 5th Regt'l, 21 Mar 19 to end.

Turrill, Julius S. (LTC) Commanding, 1st Bn.

Wise, Frederick M. (LTC) Commanding, 2nd Bn.

Berry, Benjamin S. (Maj) Commanding, 3rd Bn, WIA, 6 June 1918.

Bourne, Louis M. (Maj)

DeCarre, Alphonse (Maj)

Hamilton, George W. (Maj)

Keyser, Ralph S. (Maj)

Larsen, Henry L. (Maj)

Messersmith, Robert E. (Maj)

Murray, Joseph D. (Maj)

Shearer, Maurice E. (Maj)

Fay, John H. (Cpt) Regt'l Adjutant, 5th Regiment.

Gill, Charles G. (Cpt) Liaison Officer.

Keeley, James (Cpt) KIA, 3 October 1918.

McCoy, James (Cpt) Munitions Officer, KIA, 4 June 1918.

Quigley, Thomas F. (Cpt)

Roberts, William T. (Cpt) U.S. Army.
Shuler, George K. (Cpt) Regt'l Adj.
Whitehead, Frank (Cpt) WIA, 4 October 1918.
Willard, Maurice A. (Cpt) Asst. Paymaster.
Winans, Roswell (Cpt)
Wood, Thomas B. (Cpt) Burial Officer.
MacIntosh, Rustin (Lt) USN, gassed 13 June 1918.
Francis, Charles R. (1st Lt)
Godbey, Arnold D. (1st Lt) Regt'l Intelligence Officer.
Hart, John A. (1st Lt) U.S. Army, 1st Signal Battalion.
Jackson, David T. (1st Lt) Adj, 3rd Bn.
Massie, Nathaniel H. (1st Lt) Gas Officer.
Pelander, Arthur J. (1st Lt) Regt'l Liaison Officer.
Talbot, Horace (1st Lt)
Wilcox, Ralph M. (1st Lt) Adjutant, 1st Bn, 5th Regt'l.
Balch, Robert M., Jr. (2nd Lt) Co. "G" 2nd Bn.
Gilmer, William E. (2nd Lt) U.S. Army.
Grohn, Herert C. (2nd Lt) U.S. Army.
Hubert, Richard H. (2nd Lt) U.S. Army.
Kipness, David (2nd Lt) Reserve, Class 4.
Legendre, James H. (2nd Lt) Reserve, Class 4.
McClellan, John M. (2nd Lt) Regt'l. Intelligence Officer, KIA, 18 July 1918.
McClintock, Henry (2nd Lt) Marine Corps Resve, Cl4.
Mueller, Joseph H., Jr. (2nd Lt) Marine Corps Resve, Cl4.
Plambeck, George (2nd Lt) Marine Corps Resve, Cl4.
Rindfleisch, Ray (2nd Lt) WIA, Soissons.
Stevens, Harry (2nd Lt) U.S. Army, KIA, 3 October 1918.
Stockes, George F. (2nd Lt) Adjutant, 2nd Bn, 5th Regt'l.
Swindler, Harold F. (2nd Lt) Marine Corps Resve, Cl4.
Wahlstrom, Frederick (2nd Lt) KIA, 21 August 1917.
White, Errol (2nd Lt) Reserve, Class 4, Interpreter, Regt'l Hq.
Wilson, Claggett (2nd Lt) Marine Corps Reserve Class 4.
Dessez, Paul T. (Regt'l Surgeon)
Lawler, Robert J. (Regt'l Surgeon, Navy)
Lyle, Alexander G. (Dental Surgeon)
Brown, Warrick F. (Asst Surgeon)
Crosby, Paul T. (Asst Surgeon)
Dickinson, Dwight, Jr. (Asst Surgeon)
Gilmere, William P. (Asst Surgeon)
Hook, Frederick R. (Asst Surgeon)
McLandon, Preston A. (Asst Surgeon)
Meggers, Edward C. (Asst Surgeon)
Perry, Orlando H. (Asst Surgeon)
Pratt, Lester L. (Asst Surgeon) WIA, 11 June 1918.
Pratt, Malcolm L. (Asst Surgeon) WIA, 11 June 1918.
Shea, Richard O'B. (Asst Surgeon)
Sims, Harry V. (Asst Surgeon)
Thatcher, Herbert Von H. (Asst Surgeon)
Whitmore, William H. (Asst Surgeon)
Brady, John J. (Chaplain)
Park, Albert N. (Chaplain)

Enlisted

Burns, Francis G. (SGM) Regt'l Sgt Major.
Brennan, James J. (SGM) SGM, 3rd Bn.
Clevenstine, Walter E. (SGM) SGM, 3rd Bn.
Harding, Kenneth W. (SGM) SGM, 2nd Bn.
Jones, Walter G. (SGM)

Norstrand, Carl J. (SGM) SGM, 1st Bn.
O'Sullivan, Thomas M. (SGM) SGM, 1st Bn.
Culpepper, Ralph W. (1st Sgt) Band.
Israel, Frederick (1st Sgt)
Ryan, Michael E. (1st Sgt)
Silva, George B. (1st Sgt) National Naval Volunteer, Band.
Ackerman, John J. (PFC)
Adams, William F.R. (Pvt)
Aitken, Frederick G. (Pvt)
Aldrich, Albert F. (Pvt)
Alexander, Mearl C. (Cpl) Band, KIA, 6 June 1918.
Alrick, Hilman R. (Pvt)
Amerson, Benjamin F. (Pvt) Regt'l Runner.
Ames, Charles E. (Pvt) Munition Detail.
Anderson, Anthony G. (Pvt)
Anderson, Howard E. (Pvt)
Anderson, Roy E. (Pvt) Band.
Anton, Cornelius S. (Cpl) KIA, 4 October 1918.
Apple, Felix (Pvt)
Arata, Emil L. (Cpl) Band.
Armstrong, Harry W. (Cpl)
Arneson, Ludwig O. (Pvt) KIA, 15 September 1918.
Artman, Garrett W. (Pvt)
Ashworth, John D. (Cpl) KIA , 23 June 1918.
Athey, Emmet J. (Pvt)
Atkins, Lonzelle (Pvt) KIA , 6 June 1918.
Atkins, Tyler J. (Pvt)
Babb, Bernard A. (Pvt) Motorcyclist, 1st Bn.
Bagley, Thomas J. (Pvt)
Baier, Ernest H. (Pvt) KIA, 24 June 1918.
Bailey, George W. (PhM3)
Baker, George J. (Pvt)
Baker, John T. (Pvt)
Baldwin, Charles N. (PFC)
Baldwin, Joseph R., Jr. (Sgt)
Ball, Charles W. (Cpl) National Naval Volunteer.
Ball Ernest B. (PhM3)
Balzer, Eugene I. (Pvt) KIA, 1 November 1918.
Barber, Wayne (PhM3) WIA, 4 October 1918.
Barker, Floyd (Sgt) KIA, 15 September 1918.
Barnhart, Frank A. (Sgt)
Batton, Julius E. (Pvt) KIA, 16 January 1918.
Baubie, Edward F. (Pvt)
Bear, Absalom F. (HAp1)
Beausoleil, Frederic E. (Pvt) Regt'l Runner.
Becker, Kenneth H. (Pvt)
Bedosky, Michael T. (Pvt)
Beebe, Stanley G. (PFC)
Beevers, Merle B. (Pvt)
Behary, John G. (Pvt) Band.
Benckert, Charles A. (Pvt)
Bennett, Ellwood A. (Pvt) KIA, 13 June 1918.
Berglund, Raymond R.W. (Pvt)
Best, John S. (GySgt) Band.
Binckley, Herbert J. (Pvt) KIA, 19 July 1918.
Bingham, Robert H. (Pvt)
Bird, Francis M. (PhM1)
Blasco, Samuel (Pvt)
Bleasdale, John L. (Pvt) Band.
Blomgren, Gustaf M. (Pvt)

Boller, John F. (PFC)

Bonner, Guy (PFC) KIA.

Borden, Landrie (Pvt)

Bowen, Robert W. St. C. (Pvt) Band.

Bowman, Alvin L. (PhM2)

Bowman, Paul C. (Pvt)

Bowman, Raymond W. (Pvt)

Boykin, Ralph E. (Pvt)

Bracken, Fay L. (Pvt)

Bradbury, Eben, Jr. (Pvt) KIA, 12 June 1918.

Bradley, Max (Pvt)

Brainerd, Robert L. (Pvt)

Brall, Joshua A. (Cpl)

Brambora, Anton (Pvt) Motorcyclist, 1st Bn.

Brierley, Walter B. (Pvt)

Brodel, Andrew (Cpl) Band.

Bruch, William U. (Cpl) Band.

Buchanan, Fred M. (Pvt) KIA, 23 June 1918.

Bull, Albert N. (Pvt) KIA, 6 November 1918.

Burchadi, Adolph C. (Pvt) Died of Wounds, 7 November 1918.

Burgan, Orrin E. (Cpl) Regt'l Intel Off.

Burke, Chester A. (Pvt) KIA, 9 June 1918.

Burras, Hugh J. (Pvt) National Naval Volunteer, Band.

Burton, Foster J. (Pvt)

Byerrum, Severen S. (Pvt)

Carberry, Leo F. (Pvt)

Caroll, Robert (Pvt)

Carpenter, William F. (Pvt) National Naval Volunteer.

Carr, Lloyd E. (PFC)

Carroll, Benedict R. (Cpl)

Carroll, Robert (Pvt)

Case, Gerald F. (Pvt) Regt'l Intel Off.

Caverly, Leon H. (Sgt) Quartermaster Sgt.

Chaukalian, Aram, R. (Pvt) Motorcyclist, 1st Bn.

Chism, James H. (Pvt) KIA, 18 July 1918.

Clabburn, Frederick (Pvt)

Clark, Harold R. (Sgt)

Clark, Wayne (Cpl) Munition Detail.

Cluney, James E. (Pvt) Regt'l Runner.

Cole, Howard W. (Pvt) Regt'l Runner.

Coleman, Morris V. (Cpl)

Collins, James J. (Pvt)

Collins, John G. (Pvt) Cook, 4th Class.

Connolly, George B. (Sgt)

Conover, Kenneth S. (Pvt) KIA,1 November 1918.

Conroy, Clarence J. (Sgt) Quartermaster Sgt.

Conway, Willis T. (GySgt)

Cook, Charles S. (CPhm)

Copenhaver, Harry A. (Pvt) Regt'l Runner.

Cosgrove, Thomas A. (Pvt)

Cowdrick, Royal R. (Cpl)

Coyle, Joseph C. (Pvt)

Coyne, Martin J. (Pvt)

Craig, Montford N. (Pvt) Messman.

Crosson, Vernon J. (Sgt) KIA, 4 November 1918.

Crow, Arthur J. (Pvt) KIA, 27 July 1918.

Curtis, Harry C. (Cpl)

Custock, Stephen A. (Pvt)

Dalrymple, Sherman H. (Sgt)

Damewood, George W. (Sgt) Auto Driver.

Daurelle, George P. (Sgt)

Davis, Gomer E. (Pvt) Orderly Regt'l Hq.

Decker, George L. (Cpl) Band.

DeHaven, William H. (Cpl)

Demaree, Ralph G. (Pvt) Regt'l Runner.

DeMars, Harold R.J. (Pvt) Cook, 3rd Cl.

Dempsey, Errol L. (Cpl) Regt'l File Clerk.

Detrich, Theodore (Cpl) Band.

Dickerson, Alfred (MarGun)

Dickinson, Howard H. (Pvt) KIA, 6 June 1918.

Dimmick, Howard O. (Pvt) Regt'l Runner.

Divine, Louis S. (Cpl) KIA, 3 June 1918, Asst Police Sgt.

Dixon, Thomas W. (Pvt)

Dobart, Albert E. (Cpl)

Domm, Charles P. (Trumpeter)

Donahue, Charles P. (Cpl) National Naval Volunteer.

Donovan, Raymond D. (Pvt) Regt'l Post Office.

Dorrington, William F. (Cpl) Band.

Dorsek, Stephen J. (Cpl) National Naval Volunteer.

Douglas, Edward Y. (Pvt)

Duberville, Norman A. (Pvt) Mounted Ord Regt'l Hq.

Dudley, George M. (Pvt)

Duke, Jimmie L. (Pvt) KIA, 18 July 1918.

Duricy, Michael (Pvt) Band.

Eastman, Walter D. (Pvt)

Eddy, George G. (Pvt)

Edelstein, Lester (Pvt) Marine Corps Resve, Cl 2.

Edwards, James W. (Sgt) Quartermaster Sgt.

Egerton, Lawrence (Pvt)

Elderson, William F. (Pvt) Died of Wounds, 6 June 1918.

Eldert, Oscar (Pvt)

Elliott, Howard G. (Pvt) Corral.

Ely, Lewis B. (Pvt) Regt'l Runner.

English, William GySgt

Ernst, Earl L. (Pvt)

Evans, Clifford L. (Pvt) Motorcyclist.

Famea, Patsey (Pvt) Band.

Farrow, Roger G. (Pvt) Regt'l Runner.

Feigle, William M. (Sgt) Reserve, Motorcyclist.

Fischer, Terry L. (Pvt) KIA , 27 April 1918.

Fish, Gerald E. (Pvt) KIA, 18 July 1918.

Fletcher, Orion F. (Pvt)

Floyd, Herbert M. (Pvt)

Forrest, Lester M. (Cpl) Band.

Francis, Alfred F. (Pvt) Band.

Francis, Harold R. (Pvt) Orderly.

French, Wayne W. (Pvt)

Fry, Lyman C. (Pvt)

Gardner, James C. (Pvt)

Garis, Earl J. (Cpl)

Gately, John E., Jr. (Pvt)Regt'l Runner.

Gates, Warren F. (Pvt)

Gaudet, Earl E. (Pvt)

Gaume, Victor (Pvt)

Gaw, Herbert W. (GySgt)

George, Walter (Pvt)

Gibb, George W. (Pvt)

Gill, Homer E. (Pvt) Regt'l Runner.

Gill, John J. (Pvt)

Gillespie, William E. (Pvt)

Godfrey, Roland A. (Pvt) Messman.

Golden, John E. (Pvt)
Goldstein, Morris S. (Pvt) Orderly, 3d Bn.
Gosman, Kenneth W. (Pvt)
Graham, Charles D. (Cpl) National Naval Volunteer, KIA, 5 November 1918.
Greelish, John D. (Sgt) Quartermaster Sgt.
Green, Oval H. (Pvt) KIA, 18 July 1918.
Greenberg, Abe (Pvt)
Greenlee, George A. (Cpl) KIA, 20 July 1918.
Greer, William B. PhM3
Griffin, William L. (Cpl) KIA, 6 June 1918.
Griswold, George G. (Cpl)
Groves, Abiel J., Jr. (Pvt)
Groves, John A.A. (Cpl)
Groves, Milton B. (Cpl)
Guame, Victor (Pvt) KIA.
Haggarty, Ira (Pvt)
Hahnke, Bernard (Cpl)
Hale, Herbert R. (Cpl) Regt'l Post Office.
Hamel, Claude C. (Sgt) Regt'l Stat Clerk.
Hamm, Sebastian (Pvt) Motorcyclist, 2nd Bn.
Harbulak, Andrew S. (Pvt)
Harkenrider, Louis H. (Pvt) U.S. Army.
Harnden, Ernest E. (Pvt)
Harney, William F. (Pvt)
Harwell, Malcolm L. (Pvt)
Hastings, Ralph L. (Pvt)
Hathaway, Herschel (Sgt)
Hayes, James E. (Pvt) Band, Reserve Class 2.
Healy, Harold H. (Sgt) Intel Off.
Heinrich, Richard H. (Pvt) KIA, 26 July 1918.
Hellman, Harold J. (PhM1)
Henderson, Edgar A. (Pvt) Regt'l Runner.
Hentschel, Harold I. (Pvt)
Hess, Edwin (Pvt)
Hewitt, Earl D. (Cpl)
Hiatt, Dallas L. (Pvt) Messman.
Hilderbrand, Albert A. (Cpl)
Hill, Charles C. (Pvt)
Hill, Dunk (Cpl) Band.
Hill, Thomas J. (Trumpeter)
Hite, Edward W. (Sgt) Company Clerk.
Hoagland, Herbert A. (Cpl)
Hobbs, Harry G. (Pvt) Orderly Regt'l Hq.
Hobbs, Stafford B. (Pvt) Band.
Hodgen, Grover C. (PFC)
Hodges, Clyde H. (Pvt)
Hoffman, Clarence N. (Pvt) KIA, 15 September 1918.
Hollick, Mikeal M. (Pvt)
Honsermyer, Norman E. (Cpl) Band.
Hooker, Edward E. (Trumpeter)
Hopson, John W. (Pvt)
Horton, Raymond (Sgt) National Naval Volunteer.
Houston, Paul H. (Pvt)
Howard, Clarence L. (Pvt) Gas Officer.
Howarth, Winslow (Pvt)
Howell, John B. (Pvt)
Howell, John D. (Pvt)
Hulburt, Henry L. (MarGun) Asst. Regt'l. Adj.
Hulse, Hezzie R. (Pvt)
Humphrey, Charles (Pvt)

Humphrey, John T. (Sgt) KIA, 1 November 1918.
Huntington, Collis H. (Cpl) Asst. Stat Clerk.
Hurford, Edward P. (Pvt)
Hutchinson, Ulrich M. (Sgt) Band.
Hutchinson, William T. (Sgt) Pay Roll Clerk.
Ineko, Robert L. (Pvt)
Ingram, Thomas E. (Cpl) Orderly.
Irish, Gilbert H. (Pvt)
Irwin, William (Cpl) KIA, 24 June 1918.
Ish, Rex W. (Sgt) KIA, 23 June 1918.
Isler, Samuel G. (Pvt)
Jackson, William C. (Pvt)
Jamison, Roland R. (PhM1)KIA, 4 October 1918.
Jaquess, John R. (Pvt) KIA, 4 October 1918.
Jarvis, Harry W. (CPhM)
Jarvis, Sidney (Pvt)
Jennison Charles S. (PhM2) WIA, 4 October 1918.
John, Frank D. (Pvt)
Johns, Donald F. (Cpl)
Johnson, Fred (Pvt)
Johnson, John O. (Sgt)
Johnson, Joseph S. (HAp1) KIA, 4 October 1918.
Johnson, William K. (Cpl)
Jones, Calvin A. (Pvt)
Jones, Richard M. (Pvt)
Jordon, John H. (Pvt) Died of Wounds, 15 September 1918.
Kaliney, Andrew L. (Pvt)
Kane, Walter T.J. (Pvt)
Kania, Walter J. (Sgt)
Kappeler, John B. (Pvt)
Keffer, Daniel W. (Cpl)
Keggs, Harry W. (Pvt)
Keller, Charles (Cpl)
Kelly, John J. (Sgt) Band.
Kelly, Thomas P. (Pvt)
Kennard, Elmer D. (Pvt)
Kerwin, Oliver M. (Pvt) Regt'l Runner.
Kesler, Edgar H. (Pvt)
Killoran, James L. (Pvt)
Knoles, Philip H. (Sgt)
Knotur, William B. (Pvt)
Knupp, Glenn J. (Cpl)
Koslosky, Percy (Sgt)
Kothman, Frank A. (Pvt)
Kramer, Percy P. (Pvt)
Kretchmar, Charles H. (Cpl) Clerk, Regt'l Hq.
Kroll, Fred W. (Pvt) KIA, 14 September 1918.
Kropacek, Joseph (Cpl)
Kyle, Howard L. (Cpl)
Lalor, James D. (Pvt)
Lathrop, John E. (Pvt) Messman.
Lauerman, Edward G. (Pvt)
Laurentz, Homer G. (Pvt)
Lavelle, John L. (Sgt)
Lawler, Freeman L. (Pvt)
Leenhouts, William G. (Pvt) Messman, KIA, 3 July 1918.
Legg, James H. (Pvt)
Leidemann, Albert J. (Cpl)
Leitner, Aloysius (Pvt) Cook, 2nd Class, Died of Wounds, 11 June 1918.

Lesser, Alfred A. (Cpl) National Naval Volunteer.
Lewis, James C.G. (Sgt) Interpreter.
Lilly, Clarence E. (Sgt) KIA, 25 June 1918.
Linder, Earl S. (Pvt) KIA, 14 June 1918.
Lindsey, Dan K. (Pvt)
Link, Andrew C. (Cpl) Clerk, Regt'l Hq.
Linn, Gilbert C. (Pvt)
Logston, Alvin W. (Pvt) Died, pneumonia.
Long, Alvin E. (Pvt)
Long, Oscar (Pvt) Driver.
Longenecker, Walter D. (Pvt)
Looger, Charles D. (Cpl)
Love, Harry A. (Pvt)
Lowe, Arthur J. (Pvt)
Lubomski, Joseph GySgt
Luchan, Louis (Sgt)
Lutes, Francis E. (Pvt)
Lynch, Carter GySgt
Lynch, Charles O. (Cpl) File Clerk, Regt'l Hq.
Lynch, Daniel J. (Cpl) Marine Corps Reserve Class 4-C.
Lynch, William (Sgt) Police Sgt.
Lyster, Wayne G. (Pvt) Orderly, 2nd Bn.
MacCauley, John L. (Cpl) KIA, 4 October 1918.
MacConnell, Charles F. (Cpl) KIA, 6 June 1918.
Macphee, John D. (GySgt)
Macrae, James (Cpl)
Maher, William J. (Pvt) KIA, 20 July 1918.
Malenfant, Lawrence Y. (Pvt)
Mason, Clyde W. (Cpl)
Mason, John (Pvt)
Matthews, Wilbur N. (Pvt)
Mattingly, Claude (PhM1)
Maxwell, David M. (PhM2) KIA, 16 June 1918.
McCormack, Donald J. (Pvt)
McCormick, James A. (Pvt) KIA, 14 June 1918.
McCormick, James E. (Pvt) Band.
McCoy, Charles T. (Pvt) Orderly, 2nd Bn.
McCutcheon, William A. (PFC)Band.
McDaniel, Lee J. (PhM2)
McDonough, John J. (Pvt)
McElhinney, William A. (Sgt)
McGee, Henry A. (HApl)
McGiffert, Robert D. (Sgt) Regt'l Intel. Off.
McGuigan, John S. (Sgt) Quartermaster Sgt.
McHale, Frank E. (Sgt) Chiropodist.
McKeown, John W. (Pvt) Orderly, 2nd Bn.
McKinery, A.S. (PhM3)
McKinny, Harry W. (Pvt) KIA, 18 July 1918.
McKittrick, William L. (QMSgt)
McPherson, Lewis R. (Pvt) Regt'l Runner.
McQueeney, Joseph J. (Pvt)
Medkirk, Forest T. (CPhM)
Melrose, Jack M. (Cpl) KIA, 14 June 1918.
Menshel, Paul H. (Pvt) KIA, 18 July 1918.
Merry, Bruce R. (Pvt) Orderly Regt'l Hq.
Miles, John P. (Sgt)
Miller, Blair C. (Pvt) Died of Wounds, 24 July 1918.
Miller, Carroll R. (Sgt)
Miller, Fred (Pvt)
Mitchell, Charlie W. (Pvt) Orderly Regt'l Hq.
Moore, Clarence I. (PFC) Regt'l Band.

Moore, Floyd W. (PFC)
Moran, John (Pvt) Band.
Morgan, Edwin L. (Pvt)
Moriarty, John S. (Sgt) Regt'l Mail Orderly.
Morse, Clyde W. (Pvt) KIA, 4 November 1918.
Moynihan, Batt (PFC)
Musbach, Carl F. (Pvt) KIA, 18 July 1918.
Naden Edward (Cpl) KIA, 6 June 1918.
Nash, Earl (Pvt)
Nelson, William (Cpl) Regt'l Post Office.
Neumann, Otto O. (Pvt)
Nilan, M.A. (Pvt) KIA, 19 July 1918.
Ningard, Joseph L. (Pvt)
Nopper, Howard A. (Pvt)
Norris, Paul E. (Cpl)
Nunnally, Edward P. (Sgt)
Nystrom, Elmer L. (Pvt)
O'Connell, Daniel J. (Pvt) KIA, 25 June 1918.
O'Connell, G.S. (Cpl) KIA, 6 June 1918.
Odell, Robert E. (Cpl) Clerk Regt'l Hq.
Olive, George F. (Pvt)
O'Neill, Abraham J. (Sgt) Quartermaster Sgt.
O'Neill, John F. (Pvt)
O'Neill, William F. (PFC)
Osterstock, Lewis W. (Pvt)
Paine, Herbert A. (Sgt) KIA, 1 November 1918.
Palmer, Daniel C. (Pvt)
Parks, Arthur W. (Pvt)
Patterson, Charles H. (PhM3) Died of wounds, 11 December 1918.
Patterson, Merton W. (Pvt)
Pearce, Shem B. (PFC)
Peers, David K. (Cpl) KIA, 25 June 1918.
Pegan, Guy H. (Pvt)
Pelton, Arthur L. (Pvt) Messman.
Peoples, Frederick L. (Pvt)
Peterson, Dutton S. (Cpl) National Naval Volunteer.
Pettigrew, Charles L. (Cpl) Horseshoer.
Pheneger, Joseph R. (Pvt)
Pokorny, Joseph (Pvt) Cook, 1st Class.
Pouchot, Harold E. (Pvt)
Prosser, Fred E. (Cpl) KIA, 24 June 1918.
Pugh, Arthur C. (Cpl) KIA, 14 June 1918.
Purdy, George A. (Cpl) Clerk, Regt'l Hq.
Quinlan, Verne W. (Pvt)
Quinn, Charles S. (Sgt) Regt'l Intel Off.
Rabinowitz, Gdalia (Pvt)
Randle, Walter M. (Cpl) National Naval Volunteer.
Rapport, Burt (Trumpeter)
Rash, Joseph J. (Pvt) KIA, 5 October 1918.
Rathbun, Clarence J. Jr. (Cpl) National Naval Volunteer.
Raume, John (PhM1)
Ream, Lynn (Pvt)
Reamy, Harvey W.W. (Pvt) KIA, 29 November 1917.
Redwine, Mark M. (Sgt)
Reebenacker, Maurice O. (PFC)
Reed, Julian O. (Cpl)
Reed, Rexton K. (Pvt)
Reichie, E.J. (Pvt) Died of Wounds, 12 June 1918.
Reynolds, George W. (PFC)
Reynolds, Leland M. (Pvt) KIA, 24 June 1918.

Richards, Walter (Pvt)
Richey, Guy D. (Pvt)
Riebbeck, William (Pvt)
Riska, John J. (Pvt) KIA, 12 June 1918.
Roberts, Harold C. (PhM3)
Robertson, George (Pvt)
Robins, Howard V. (Sgt) KIA, 25 June 1918.
Robinson, William (Pvt)
Roche, Maurice A. (Pvt)
Rockstrom, Eric A. (Cpl) National Naval Volunteer.
Rodemich, Lorraine F. (PhM3)
Rolfe, Ward A. (Pvt)
Rose, Roger P. (Pvt) Orderly, 2nd Bn.
Ross, William K. (Pvt) KIA, 12 June 1918.
Rowbottom, George V. (Sgt) Chief, Field Music. Died from illness, 8 August 1918.
Rowe, Ellwyn C. (Cpl)
Rowlee, Raymond A. (Sgt) Quartermaster Sgt.
Rugg, Erwin L. (Pvt)
Runge, Edward C. (Cpl)
Runquist, Edwin (Cpl) Orderly, Regt'l Hq.
Rush, Neil J. (Cpl)
Ryder, Francis H. (Pvt)
Safford, Frank L. (Pvt)
St Louis, Roland G. (Sgt) KIA, 19 July 1918.
Salisbury, Ruben W. (Pvt)
Sander, Frederick E. (Sgt) KIA, 19 July 1918.
Sanfilippo, Frank (Pvt)
Schaub, John R. (Cpl) National Naval Volunteer.
Schave, Charles N. (PFC)
Schlageter, M.D. (Cpl) KIA, 6 June 1918.
Schnarr, George B.H. (Pvt) KIA, 20 July 1918.
Schulz, Fred (Pvt) KIA, 6 June 1918.
Schunk, Orie L. (Pvt)
Scott, Thomas M. (Pvt)
Scudder, Albert (Pvt)
Secrist, John W. (Pvt) Regt'l Runner.
Semancik, John (Pvt)
Shannon, James T. (Pvt) Regt'l Runner.
Sharpe, Eugene (Pvt) 3 August 1918.
Shaw, John E. (Pvt)
Shearba, George M. (Pvt)
Shepard, Harold D. (Cpl)
Shimandle, Fred E. (Pvt) Regt'l Runner.
Shoemaker, Clyde F. (Pvt)
Signer, Werner (Cpl)
Skaggs, John E. (Pvt)
Skinner, John T. (Pvt)
Skinner, Lee (PFC)
Slocum, Sanford G. (Cpl)
Smith, Harry D. (Pvt)
Smith, Herbert (Pvt) KIA, 15 September 1918.
Smith, Jay D. (PFC) Intel Dept.
Smith, Ray X. (Sgt) KIA, 23 June 1918.
Smith, Theodore H. (PFC)
Snyder, Curvin A. (Cpl) Band.
Sorber, George (Pvt)
Spire, W.J. (Sgt) KIA, 16 June 1918.
Spottswood, Samuel L. (Cpl) Regt'l Intel Off.
Stach, Walter S. (Pvt) KIA, 18 July 1918.
Steckel, Henry E. (Pvt)

Steckmann, William (Pvt)
Steves, Raymond J. (Pvt) Orderly Captain.
Stewart, William H. (Pvt)
Stiles, Wilbur G. (Pvt)
Stinson, Daniel C. (Pvt) KIA, 16 June 1918.
Stone, Allen W. (Cpl) KIA , 23 April 1918.
Straley, William T. (Sgt) Payroll Clerk.
Straslicka, Andrew (Cpl) Band.
Stuart, Kyle L. (Pvt)
Stuart, Thomas F. (Pvt)
Stuhl, Harry J. (Pvt)
Sturdevant, Edward W. (Maj) National Naval Volunteer.
Swart, McKinley (Pvt) KIA, 6 June 1918.
Sweeney, Edward J. (Pvt) Regt'l Runner.
Sweeney, Miles M. (Sgt) Stable Sgt.
Taggart Frederick P. (Sgt) Died of Wounds, 23 July 1918.
Tallent, John J. (Cpl) Marine Corps Resve, Cl2.
Terwillegar, Earl E. (Pvt)
Thomas, Verl T. (Pvt) KIA, 12 June 1918.
Thompson, William H. (Sgt) Mess Sgt.
Tibbetts, Frank O. (PhM2)
Tomko, John (Cpl)
Tousic, Frank (CPhM)
Towle, Raymond J. (Pvt) Orderly.
Townsend, Edmund M. (Sgt) Driver, Regt'l Hq.
Treadwell, Thomas J. (GySgt)
Tredennick, Charles M. (Cpl) Marine Corps Reserve Class 2.
Truppner, Herbert G. (Sgt) KIA, 15 September 1918.
Tucker, Dan (Pvt) Orderly, Regt'l Hq.
Tyson, Benjamin R. (Pvt) KIA, 25 June 1918.
Vanderpool, Roy E. (Pvt) Band. Reserve Class 2.
Vollmer, Frank D. (Pvt)
Voss, Cleveland A. (Paymaster's Clerk.)
Wagner, Harry, M (Pvt) Died of wounds, 18 October 1918.
Wahl, Arthur A. (Pvt)
Wall, James R. (Pvt) KIA, 15 September 1918.
Wanser, James D. (Cpl) Band.
Ward, John W. (Pvt)
Ward, William F. (Pvt) Messman.
Warner, Nial S. (Pvt)
Warren, Edward G. (GySgt) KIA, 20 April 1918.
Weidemann, Wesley E. (Pvt)
Weidman, Frederick H. (Cpl)
Weis, Edward J. (Pvt)
Weis, Joseph (Pvt)
Wells, Chester M. (Pvt) Messman.
Weschke, Leo (Pvt)
West, Chester T. (Pvt) KIA, 4 June 1918.
West, Harvey O. (Pvt)
Westcott, Percy D. (Pvt) KIA, 25 September 1918.
Westergren, Harry O. (Pvt) Orderly, 3rd Bn.
White, John A. (Sgt) Chiropodist.
Wiggins, Wayne (Pvt) Cook, 3rd Class.
Wilfert, Howard D. (Pvt)
Wilkerson, Sterling R. (Pvt) KIA, 15 September 1918.
Williams, Cranston, McC. (PFC)
Williams, Harry N. (Pvt) Regt'l Runner.
Williams, Perry F. (Pvt) Orderly, Regt'l Hq.
Williamson, Edward K. (Pvt) Cook, 2nd Class.

Wilson, Jinks C. (Cpl) National Naval Volunteer.
Wilson, William J. (Pvt) Messman.
Wimpner, Emmet (Pvt) KIA, 6 June 1918.
Wojozysnksi, A. (Sgt) KIA, 12 June 1918.
Wood, Dolph (Pvt) Regt'l Runner.
Wood, Moses (QmSgt)
Woodward, Lester C.T. (Pvt)
Wright, Charles C. (PFC) Band.
Young, Austin E. (Pvt)
Young, Vern W. (Cpl) Died of Wounds, 18 July 1918.
Zeitler, John A. (Pvt)
Zoerman, Henry C. (Cpl) Quartermaster Sgt.
Zooks, John H. (Pvt) KIA, 5 October 1918.

Supply Company

NAME (RANK) REMARKS

Puryear, Bennet, Jr. (Maj) Supply Co. Commanding Officer, Regt'l QM.
Dwight, Thomas (Cpt) Marine Corps Regular.
Holliday, Charles P. (Cpt) 3rd Bn QM, KIA, 5 August 1918.
McCaulley, Edwin P. (Cpt) Regt'l Transportation Officer, Co Gas Off.
Spencer, Ery M. (Cpt) 2nd Bn QM.
Grath, Patrick D. (2nd Lt) Reserve, Class 4.
Grealy, Patrick J. (2nd Lt) Reserve, Commissary.
Keenan, Joseph (2nd Lt) QM, 1st Bn, KIA, 9 November 1918.
McKittrick, Walter F. (2nd Lt) QM, 3rd Bn.
Scruggs, William (2nd Lt) QM Storeroom.

Enlisted

Hjortsberg, Alexander L. (1st Sgt)
Ady, Lewis J. (Cpl) Teamster.
Agostini, Camillo A. (Cpl) Teamster.
Agostini, Henry F. (Cpl) Teamster.
Alexander, Edward G. (Cpl) Teamster.
Anderson, August A. (Sgt)
Ashdown, Wallace K. (Pvt) Orderly.
Babcock, James G. (Pvt) Messman.
Baker, Robert O. (Cpl) Mechanic Blacksmith.
Baskins, Carl M. (Sgt) Asst to Vet.
Baucom, Wirt L. (Cpl) Teamster.
Bechtold, David M. (Cpl) Saddler.
Beck, George A. (Cpl) Teamster.
Bennett, Raymond F. (PFC) Commissary.
Berg, Edward (Pvt)
Best, James (Cpl) Teamster.
Binder, Julius C. (Cpl) Teamster.
Bowles, Charles L. (Cpl) Teamster.
Bowling, Joseph H. (Sgt) Mess Sgt.
Bradshaw, Clyde A. (Cpl) Teamster.
Calvert, Samuel S. (Pvt) Messman.
Campbell, Cranford (Pvt) Reserve, Commissary.
Campbell, Herbert L. (Cpl) Co Gas Officer.
Carlton, Henry W. (Cpl) Teamster.
Carnahan, Clarence D. (Cpl) Teamster.
Carroll, Jesse B. (Cpl) Teamster.

Clark, Warren (Cpl)
Coats, Edward N. (Pvt) QM.
Cohn, Myer (Sgt) Supply Sgt.
Cole, Milton L. (Cpl) Teamster.
Conrad, Herbert W. (Cpl) Teamster.
Conrad, John G. (Cpl) Teamster.
Cooper, William H. (Pvt)
Corey, Albert S. (Sgt)
Cox, Lewis O. (Cpl) Teamster.
Davis, Carl R. (Cpl) Teamster.
Davis, LeRoy F. (Cpl)
Dempsey, Earl L. (Cpl)
Dent, Thomas H. (Pvt) Teamster.
Despins, Louis J. (PFC) Orderly.
Dogan, Hubert H. (Pvt)
Douglass, Alfred C. (Cpl) Teamster.
Duke, William R. (Cpl) Cobbler.
Durbin, Edward (Pvt)
Engarde, Arthur B. (Cpl) Reserve, Class 2.
Fahey, James (Cpl) Teamster.
Fausz, Albert J. (Cpl) Teamster.
Fisher, Raymond K. (Cpl) Teamster.
Fluent, Lee R. (Cpl)
Fortner, Abner L. (Sgt)
Freudenberg, William H. (Cpl) Teamster.
Funnell, John L. (Cpl) Teamster.
Gabrielsen, Conrad B. (Cpl) Teamster.
Gane, Robert J. (Cpl) Marine Corps Reserve Class 2, Teamster.
Gates, Bruce H. (Cpl) Teamster.
Goodman, Edward (Pvt) Cook, 1st Cl.
Gray, John J. (Cpl) Teamster.
Green, Willard (Cpl) Teamster.
Greenlaw, Elmer E. (Sgt) QM Sgt 3rd Bn.
Grounds, Clarence A. (Cpl) Teamster.
Gwaltney, Thomas W. (PFC) QM.
Hall, John M. (Cpl) Teamster.
Harlan, Scott W. (Cpl) Teamster.
Harrison, Leo (PFC) Messman.
Hartman, John (Cpl)
Hawkins, Ray J. (PFC)
Heismann, Walter E.L. (Pvt) Company Barber.
Henderson, George (Pvt) Carpenter.
Hendricks, Charles B. (Cpl) Teamster.
Herbst, Herman A. (Cpl) Teamster.
Himelhan, Fred A. (PFC)
Hiner, Lewis E. (Pvt)
Hoffman, Albert F. (Cpl) Horseshoer.
Hogan, Freddrick L. (Pvt) QM Clerk.
Holland, Reginald R. (Cpl) Teamster.
Hollandsworth, Charles J. (Pvt)
Howard, Richard Z. (Cpl) Teamster.
Hudson, Howard (Cpl) Teamster.
Irons, Harold N. (Cpl) Teamster.
Jaroszewicz, Frank (Cpl) Teamster.
Jennings, Bert L., Jr. (Cpl) Teamster.
Johnson, Arthur T. (Cpl) Teamster.
Johnson, Edwin E. (Cpl) Teamster.
Johnson, LeVere H. (Cpl) Commissary.
Josey, Travis H. (Cpl) Mechanic.
Jung, Adrian A. (Cpl) Teamster.

Kauffman, Earl E. (Pvt)
Kearns, Andrew A. (Pvt)
Kendall, Elvin L. (Pvt)
Kindt, Harold D. (Sgt) QM Sgt, 3rd Bn.
Kinman, William T. (Cpl) Teamster.
LaHaye, Frank (Pvt)
Lahe, Philip H. (Sgt)Asst Wagonmaster, 2nd Bn.
Landowsky, George N. (Cpl)
LaQuay, Orville N. (Cpl) Teamster.
Larsen, Charles W. (Cpl) Teamster.
Laughlin, John M (Cpl) Teamster.
Lewicki, Stanley H. (Cpl) QM Stockroom.
Lewis, Charles B. (Cpl) Horseshoer.
Lillard, Richard (Cpl) Teamster.
Manning, James J., Jr. (Pvt)
Marold, Jack (Cpl) Teamster.
Martin, Charles R. (Pvt)
Martin, Sidney W. (Cpl) Teamster.
McCabe, James A., Jr. (Cpl) Teamster.
McCabe, William A. (Cpl) Teamster.
McCaffrey, Philip S. (Sgt)
McKittrick, Walter F. (Sgt)QM Sgt, 2nd Bn.
McLellan, John A. (Cpl)
Melcher, Raymond H. (Pvt) Teamster.
Midkiff, Ellis S. (Cpl) Teamster.
Milford, George (Sgt)
Miller, Claud D. (Cpl) Teamster.
Miller, Claude A. (Sgt) Stable Sgt.
Moran, Harley E. (Cpl) Teamster.
Moss, James (Cpl) Teamster.
Mote, Paul H. (Cpl) Teamster.
Moyer, Roy (Cpl) Teamster.
Musgrove, Robert (Cpl) Teamster.
Nelson, Joseph L. (Cpl)
Nelson, Otto C. (Pvt)
Nickle, Wilbur (Pvt) Messman.
O'Connor, Patrick J. (Cpl) Teamster.
O'Leary, Michael (Sgt)Wagonmaster.
Ogle, Hollie R. (Pvt) Teamster.
Olivier, Edward L. (Pvt) Commissary.
Pace, Thomas J.J. (Sgt) Asst Wagonmaster, 3rd Bn.
Patenaude, Joseph P. (Cpl) Teamster.
Pell, John T. (Cpl) Teamster.
Pixley, Russell (Pvt)
Poirier, Fielden L. (Cpl)
Potter, William B. (Cpl) Teamster.
Powers, Grant J. (Cpl) Marine Corps Reserve, Class 2.
Raulston, Samuel P. (Pvt) Teamster.
Reed, Russell M. (Cpl) Teamster.
Regan, Thomas (Cpl)
Reynolds, William W. (Cpl) Teamster.
Rhoades, Ralph O. (Cpl) Teamster.
Rhoads, Oby V. (Pvt) Teamster.
Richardson, Ralph D. (Cpl) Teamster.
Rinehart, Randolph R. (Cpl)
Robertson, Robert L., Jr. (Cpl)
Robertson, Robert (Pvt)
Rodefer, Bert A. (Cpl)
Rowan, James (Sgt) QM Sgt.
Rudderow, Howard C. (Pvt)
Sanderson, Floyd (Cpl) Teamster.

Savage, James A. (Cpl) Teamster.
Schmid, Lawrence J. (Pvt) QM.
Schneggenburger, Alfred (Cpl)
Schultz, Herman (Cpl) Teamster.
Shakespear, Donald D. (Cpl) Teamster.
Sheldon, George B., Jr. (Cpl) Teamster.
Skaggs, Roy W. (Cpl) Teamster.
Small, William (Cpl) Acting Police Sgt.
Smith, Odus H. (Cpl) Teamster.
Smithson, Ernest E. (Cpl) Teamster.
Stagge, Louis (Cpl) Teamster.
Stephens, James R. (Pvt) Teamster.
Stevens, Louis F. (Sgt) Asst Wagonmaster, 1st Bn.
Sturges, Thomas G. (Cpl) Teamster.
Sullivan, Frank J. (Pvt)
Sullivan, Thomas J. (Cpl) Commissary.
Sweeney, Edward F. (Pvt)
Taylor, Guss L. (HAp1) WIA, Belleau Wood.
Taylor, John C. (Cpl) Teamster.
Teems, William R. (Cpl) Teamster.
Thompson, Elmer D. (Pvt) Teamster.
Thompson, Milo W. (Cpl) Teamster.
Thompson, Robert (Pvt) Teamster.
Valleau, Harry O. (Cpl) Commissary.
VanBuskirk, George E. (Cpl) Teamster.
Vipham, John R. (Pvt) Cook, 2nd Cl.
Voitanis, Stanley F. (Pvt) Orderly.
Walters, Dewey C. (Cpl)
Wambach, Conrad, Jr. (Pvt) Messman.
Ward, William A. (Cpl) Teamster.
Ware, Harry F. (Cpl) Teamster.
Watson, Guy (Cpl) Teamster.
Weir, Frank B. (Cpl) Teamster.
Weiss, Oscar (Cpl)
Welch, William J. (Pvt)
Wills, William E. (Cpl) Asst Wagonmaster.
Wood, Griffith R. (Sgt)
Woods, Moses (Sgt)

8th Machine Gun Company

NAME (RANK) REMARKS

Fay, John H. (Cpl) Commanding Officer, 8th Co.
Nelms, James A. (Cpl) Commanding Officer, 8th Co,
   WIA at Belleau Wood.
Buchanan, Durant S. (1st Lt) WIA.
Garvey, James M. (1st Lt) WIA, 2 October 1918.
Nichols, John H. (Cpl) WIA at Belleau Wood.
Ashley, Thomas W. (2nd Lt) KIA, 6 June 1918.
Avery, Robert I. (2nd Lt) MC Reserve, Cl4.
Coverdell, Vern A. (2nd Lt) MC Reserve, Cl2, WIA.
O'Keefe, Raymond A.(2nd Lt) MC Reserve, Cl4, WIA.
Vasey, Bayard (2nd Lt) MC Reserve, Cl4.
Wilkinson, Alfred (2nd Lt) KIA, 5 October 1918.

Enlisted

Denney, John (1st Sgt)
Abercrombie, Lewis F. (Cpl)
Adamick, Albert (Pvt)

Addington, John L. (Pvt) WIA.
Adler, Maurice B. (PFC)
Alexander, Sterling (Pvt) KIA, 20 July 1918.
Allan, George D. (Sgt)
Altevogt, John W. (PFC)
Arnott, James B. (Pvt) KIA.
Atkins, Harold D. (Pvt) Marine Corps Reserve.
Austin, Edward (Sgt)
Avery, Robert I. (Sgt) Mess Sgt.
Bailey, Josiah F. (Pvt)
Banks, John F. (Sgt) MC Reserve, Cl 4, WIA.
Barnes, Charlie (Pvt)
Bartlett, Charles G. (GySgt)
Beekman, William V.D. (PFC)
Bennett, William H. (Cpl)
Bilas, Samuel (PFC) Cook, 2nd Cl.
Blair, Howard (Pvt) KIA, 12 June 1918.
Blood, Frank D. (Pvt)
Booth, Lawrence D. (Pvt) KIA, 4 October 1918.
Bounds, John D. (PFC) Reserve, Cl2, WIA.
Bowker, Walter J. (Pvt)
Boyd, Harold S. (Pvt) Marine Corps Reserve.
Bragg, Clem G. (PFC)
Breuer, William F. (Pvt)
Brown, Eugene M. (Pvt)
Brown, James S. (Pvt) Reserve, Cl2.
Brown, John (PFC)
Brown, Leonard L. (Pvt) MIA.
Brown, Norman B. (PFC) MC Reserve, Cl2.
Brown, Raymond T. (Pvt) Brunell, Arthur J. (Cpl)
Buchert, Luther R. (Cpl)
Burdick, Charles G. (Sgt)
Burns, Francis G. (Sgt)
Burns, Maurice N. (Pvt) Reserve, Cl2, WIA.
Byrne, George W. (Pvt) Marine Corps Reserve.
Canty, William M. (Pvt) WIA.
Carey, Miles H. (Pvt) Messman.
Carleton, William (Sgt) Co Stable Sgt.
Champerlain, Karl S. (Pvt) WIA.
Chappello, Joseph (Pvt)
Church, George, Jr. (PFC) MC Reserve, Cl2.
Churchill, Frank G. (Pvt)
Clarkston, Samuel (GySgt)
Cobeldick, John H. (Sgt) KIA, 19 July 1918.
Cochran, Joel L. (Cpl)
Cody, Emmett T. (Pvt) KIA, 20 July 1918.
Cole, Harry R. (PFC)
Collins, Dewitt (PFC)
Conolly, William J. (Pvt) Marine Corps Reserve.
Conway, James (PFC)
Cooley, Harold G. (Cpl) MC Reserve, Cl4, WIA.
Cornell, Ivan M. (Pvt) WIA.
Coverdell, Vern A. (Sgt)
Cowan, William R. (Pvt) Gassed.
Cox, George H. (Pvt)
Crum, Roy I. (Pvt)
Day, Stanley G. (Pvt)
Dennis, James B. (Sgt) MC Reserve, Cl4, WIA.
Dent, George H. (Pvt)
Depka, Charles W. (PFC) WIA.
Deschaseaux, John L. (Trumpeter)

Dobie, Henry G. (PFC)
Dorr, John A. (Sgt)
Downing, Abe L. (Pvt) MIA, rejoined.
Dunfee, William H. (Pvt)
Dunning, Thomas J. (Pvt)
Durant, Irving E. (Cpl) WIA.
Durden, Eddie (PFC)
Edelstein, Lester (Pvt) Marine Corps Reserve.
Edwards, Dewey J. (Pvt)
Eggert, Erwin H. (Pvt)
Eisele, Walter F. (Cpl)
Ellcott, Barton W. (Pvt)
Ellis, Ralph C. (Pvt)
Ely, Walter F. (Pvt)
Engle, Elwood F. (PFC) MC Reserve, Cl2.
Etzler, Henry C. (PFC) MC Reserve, Cl4.
Farley, Harley E. (Cpl)
Farley, Leonard G. (Pvt) KIA.
Ferdinandeen, John W. (Cpl) Company Saddler.
Ferris, Ira L. (Cpl)
Ferry, Ralph R. (Pvt)
Flader, John C. (Pvt) Flanagan, Charles M. (Pvt)
Fleisher, Abraham (PFC) MC Reserve, Cl2.
Flynt, Robert E. (Pvt) Ford, Daniel (Pvt) KIA, 4 October 1918.
Foulger, Arthur (Pvt) Reserve, Cl4, WIA.
Frampton, David W. (Pvt)
Francis, Loyd (Pvt)
Fullerton, George S. (Pvt)
Funk, Peter (PFC)
Gann, Ben O. (GySgt)
Gaume, Victor (Pvt)
Gehrke, Edward (Pvt) Messman.
Gisner, Oscar G. (Cpl)
Goff, Paul M. (Pvt) WIA.
Goodrich, George R. (Cpl)
Gordon, Vincent H. (Pvt)
Graff, Elmer R. (PFC)
Graham, David S. (Pvt) KIA, 6 June 1918.
Green, William C. (PFC)
Greenlee, Wendell W. (Pvt)
Grissom, Curtiss F. (Pvt) KIA, 4 October 1918.
Guider, Richard L. (Pvt)
Gunn, Raymond C. (Pvt) WIA.
Haggarty, Ira C. (Pvt)
Hall, Ralph M. (Cpl) KIA.
Hamm, Charles (Pvt) WIA.
Hamm, Walter L. (Cpl) Co Clerk.
Harrington, Richard C. (Pvt)
Harris, Ethan E. (Sgt)
Harris, Nay B. (Pvt)
Hatfield, Harry S. (Pvt) KIA, 2 November 1918.
Hawkins, Robert S. (Pvt) WIA.
Hayworth, Purl G. (PFC)
Hazelett, Hubert H. (PFC) WIA.
Healy, Ellis B. (Pvt) MIA, Joined Naval District.
Hedberg, Carl P. (Cpl)
Henderson, James S.H. (Cpl)
Henderson, Warren J. (Pvt) WIA.
Hendricks, Charles B. (Cpl) Teamster.
Hennessy, Henry M. (PFC) WIA.

Herby, John (Cpl) MC Reserve, Cl4, WIA.
Herrick, William L. (PFC)
Heryford, Guy F. (Cpl)
Hess, John L. (Pvt)
Hickey, Andrew (Pvt)
Hicks, Harry E. (Pvt)
Higgins, Joseph N. (Pvt)
Hill, Ralph S. (Cpl)
Hilton, Charles B. (Pvt)
Hobson, Vertis L. (Pvt)
Holland, James J. (PFC) WIA.
Homer, Joseph (Pvt)
Horton, Spencer R. (Pvt)
Horton, Willis B. (Pvt) Signalman, 1st Class.
Houston, Harry M. (Pvt) (KIA)
Howe, William R. (Sgt) MC Reserve, Cl4, WIA.
Humphrey, Ben (PFC)
Humphrey, Charles L. (Pvt)
Hutsell, Robert C. (Cpl)
Jackson, Joseph (Pvt) KIA, 4 October 1918.
Jackson, Marshall C. (Pvt)
Jacobs, Percy (Pvt) Messman.
Jacobs, Richard (Pvt) WIA.
Jacobs, Roy M. (Trumpeter) WIA.
James, Jack (Pvt) WIA.
Johnson, Carl H. (Pvt) WIA.
Johnson, Carl O. (Pvt) MC Reserve, Cl2.
Johnson, Clyde D. (Pvt) KIA.
Johnson, James E. (Pvt) KIA, 25 June 1918.
Johnson, Wymer E. (Pvt)
Jones, Allison L. (Pvt) WIA.
Jordan, Jack (Sgt)
Jordan, Thomas I. (Pvt) MIA.
Joyner, John R. (Pvt)
Kauf, William (Cpl)
Keate, Daniel L. (Pvt) MIA, KIA.
Keats, Julius R. (PFC) MC Reserve, Cl4.
Keller, Vernon E. (Pvt)
Kendel, Robert H. (Pvt) MC Reserve, Cl4.
Killin, Oscar J. (Pvt) KIA.
Knapper, Ernest C. (Pvt)
Knuck, Anthony P. (Pvt) KIA.
Korhumel, Frank P. (PFC)
Kreiner, Earle V. (Pvt)
Krogstad, Clarence M. (Pvt) WIA.
Kuebler, Henry R. (Pvt)
Kurant, Joseph (Pvt)
Kvernvik, Theodore (Pvt) WIA.
Lasker, Samuel (Pvt)
Lathrop, John E. (Pvt)
Lavelle, Joseph A. (Pvt) WIA.
Lee, Arthur W. (Pvt)
Leggett, Ben F. (Pvt)
Leonard, Joseph (Pvt)
LeQuatte, Lawrence L. (Pvt) WIA.
Lesh, George W. (PFC) MC Reserve, Cl4.
LeValley, Joseph O. (Pvt)
Lewter, Perley G. (Pvt) KIA.
Liesch, George A. (Pvt)
Little, Harvey B. (Pvt) WIA.
Logan, Clifford T. (PFC)

Lohr, Wilber M. (PFC) KIA.
Loomis, Myron A. (Pvt)
Louden, Bonn W. (Trumpeter)
Lozinak, Andrew (PFC)
Ludford, Harry C. (Pvt)
Luka, Peter (Sgt) MC Reserve, Cl4, WIA.
Lundquist, Enard T. (Pvt)
Lyon, Edwin A. (Pvt)
Madden, John A. (Pvt) MC Reserve, Cl4, MIA, WIA.
Malcom, Robert C. (Pvt)
Malloch, John A. (Cpl) MC Reserve, Cl4, WIA.
Maloney, George A. (Pvt) Reserve, Cl4.
Maltba, Harrison L. (Sgt)
Mangold, Norman (Sgt) MC Reserve, Cl4, WIA.
Mann, Freeman W. (Pvt)
Mannan, Dewey H. (Pvt) WIA.
Manwaring, Harold (Pvt) KIA.
Masters, Frederick M. (Pvt)
Matthews, Norbert T. (Cpl) KIA.
Mayer, Gordon C. (PFC) KIA, 3 October 1918.
McClelland, Edward B. (Pvt)
McClish, Milliard H. (Pvt) WIA.
McDonald Robert A. (Cpl) MC Reserve, Cl4, WIA.
McDonald, John R. (PFC)
McGee, Carl A. (Pvt)
McGinn, Frank (Pvt) Nat'l Naval Volunteer, Messman.
McGovern, Edgar B. (PFC)
McKague, Reynold (Pvt)
McKenney, Lloyd (Pvt) WIA.
McLaughlin, John (Pvt) WIA.
McLean, John (Pvt)
McNary, Glenn R. (Pvt)
McNelly, William J. (Pvt)
McPherson, John O. (Cpl)
McQueeney, Joseph J. (Pvt) Messman.
McReynolds, James A. (Cpl)
McTaggart, Lloyd G. (PFC)
Mellody, Joseph W. (Pvt)
Meyer, Lloyd H. (Pvt) WIA.
Mielka, Fred L. (Cpl) KIA, 4 October 1918.
Miller, Adam J. (Pvt) KIA, 18 July 1918.
Miller, Claud D. (Pvt)
Miller, John K., Jr. (Pvt)
Millsap, Mac C. (PFC)
Mitchell, Hugh B. (Pvt)
Mitchell, John H. (Pvt)
Moon, Harrison N. (Pvt)
Moser, Carl L. (Pvt)
Murphy, James E. (Pvt)
Myers, Theodore A. (Pvt)
Naugle, Harry G. (Pvt)
Neal, Raymond M. (PFC)
Neely, Ray M. (PFC)
Neilson, Olaf C. (Pvt)
Nichols, Ralph (Cpl)
North, Charles A. (Pvt) MC Reserve, Cl4.
O'Connors, Thomas (Pvt)
O'Donnell, Charles L. (Sgt)
Oaks, James A. (Cpl)
Odell, Robert E. (Cpl) Co Clerk.
Olson, John W. (Pvt) MIA, WIA.

Orem, Julian P. (Pvt)
Osbourn, Elver W. (Pvt)
Ostfeld, Irving (Pvt)
Overton, Thomas G. (Pvt)
Page, John D. (Pvt)
Palm, Louis H. (Pvt)
Palmer, William A. (Pvt)
Parkins, Edward W. (Pvt)
Parsons, Frank R. (Pvt)
Parsons, Idris T. (Pvt)
Payne, Major McK. (Pvt)
Perey, Francis L. (Pvt)
Perney, Sylvester (Cpl)
Perry, Willard H. (Pvt)
Peters, Anthony (PFC)
Peters, John W. (Pvt) WIA.
Pfrengle, Walter E. (Pvt) Signalman, 2nd Class, KIA,
    16 October 1918.
Phipps, Raymond L. (PFC)
Pichoff, Earl L. (Pvt)
Plumley, Ernest C. (Cpl) MC Reserve, Cl4.
Pojeske, John J. (PFC) WIA.
Pollock, Norman (Pvt) KIA, 1 November 1918.
Pope, James H. (Pvt) MIA, rejoined.
Pountney, Reuben I. (Pvt) WIA.
Prendergast, John J. (PFC) MC Reserve, Cl4.
Price, Charles W. (Drummer)
Pulfer, Cecil J. (PFC)
Pursley, Ernest R. (PFC)
Quirk, Alfred (Sgt) Mess Sgt.
Rae, John H. (Pvt)
Reardon, Michael (GySgt)
Reavis, Manly G. (Pvt)
Redmond, Claude E. (Pvt)
Richards, Lloyd T. (Pvt)
Roarabaugh, Harry R. (Cpl)
Roberts, Emmett T. (Pvt) MC Reserve, Cl2.
Roby, Robert R. (Pvt)
Roehrig, Ralph J. (Pvt) KIA, 16 June 1918.
Rogers, Malcolm G. (Pvt)
Rolph, William G. (Pvt)
Rosser, Bertram (Sgt) Co. Supply Sgt.
Rougier, William J. (Pvt)
Rourke, Arthur J. (Pvt) KIA, 2 November 1918.
Rutherford, Mack (PFC) WIA.
Ryan, Frank J. (Pvt) Cook, 2nd Class.
Salzer, John E. (Pvt)
Satterfield, Floyd (Pvt) KIA.
Sawyer, Arthur B. (Pvt)
Schaefer, Albert H. (Pvt)
Schmidt, Leo J. (Pvt)
Schulte, John H., Jr. (Pvt)
Schwab, Vincent M. (Sgt) KIA, 9 June 1918.
Scott, John W. (Cpl) MC Reserve, Cl4, WIA.
Scudder, Albert (Pvt)
Shelton, Grayson (Pvt) KIA, 6 October 1918.
Skaggs, Roy W. (Pvt)
Smith, Bert C. (Cpl)
Smith, Charles F. (Sgt) Supply Sgt.
Smith, Clarence E. (Pvt)
Smith, Frank (Pvt)

Smith, John F. (Pvt) Died of Wounds, 4 October 1918.
Smolenyak, John (PFC) WIA.
Smyth, Alvin E. (Pvt)
Snavely, Herbert L. (Pvt)
Steege, Otto H. (Pvt)
Stephens, Edward U. (Pvt)
Stevens, James C. (Pvt)
Stevens, Russell C. (Pvt)
Stough, Harold C. (Cpl) Company Horseshoer.
Strine, Otto H. (Pvt) WIA.
Tedesco, Lawrence (Cpl) MC Reserve, Cl4, WIA.
Thompson, George M. (Pvt)
Thompson, John E. (PFC) Co Corral.
Titus, Frank A. (Pvt)
Todd, Lee R. (Pvt)
Turley, Joseph O. (Pvt) MC Reserve, Cl4, WIA.
Ulrich, Frank S. (PFC)
Waidman, Albert M. (Cpl)
Walker, Leo F. (Pvt)
Walker, Orvel K. (Pvt) Messman.
Webster, Allen (PFC)
Wells, Harry R. (Pvt)
West, William E. (PFC) WIA.
Wicker, John C. (Pvt) WIA.
Wilcox, George W. (PFC)
Wilson, Ashley F. (Pvt) Messman.
Wilson, Sam J. (Pvt) WIA.
Womack, John H. (Pvt) WIA, 7 November 1918.
Woolley, John L. (Pvt)
Wulff, Irving (PFC) KIA.
Yancey, Cyrus (Pvt)
Yarema, Albert (GySgt)
York, Lex (Pvt) MIA, rejoined.

30th Replacement Company
(Disbanded, 15 October 1918)

NAME (RANK) REMARKS

LeBoeuf, Albert A. (Cpt) CO, 30th Co, 5th Regt'l.
Cochran, Harry K. (Cpt)
Wilson, Frank W. (Cpt)
Johnson, Earl F. (1st Lt)
Moore, Wyle J. (1st Lt)

Enlisted

Jessen, Emil (1st Sgt)
Adams, John (Pvt)
Albo, Dominic (Pvt)
Albus, Frank (Pvt)
Altman, John (Sgt)
Anselm, William B. (Pvt)
Armstrong, Percy N. (Cpl)
Arnett, Harry L. (PFC)
Atkinson, George A. (Pvt)
Bailey, Thomas R. (Pvt)
Baker, Eddie W. (Pvt)
Baker, Louis R. (Pvt)
Barner, Rae (Pvt)

Barron, Eugene E. (Pvt)
Bassett, Jay R. (Pvt)
Bates, Rolland B. (Cpl)
Bearden, John M. (Pvt)
Beck, Carl W. (Pvt)
Bell, Alonzo D. (Pvt)
Berve, Nelson E. (Pvt)
Birdsong, Lester D. (Pvt) Marine Corps Reserve.
Borden, Albert R. (Pvt)
Bosman, Frank (GySgt)
Bosse, Arthur (PFC)
Boyle, Frank R. (PFC)
Boyle, John J. (Pvt)
Brandies, Sidney (Cpl)
Briddon, Albert W. (Pvt) Marine Corps Reserve.
Bryant, Glenwin E. (Pvt)
Burfeind, Herbert (Cpl)
Burkhart, Charles F. (Pvt)
Burling, Alten (Pvt) Marine Corps Reserve.
Butler, Fred A. (Pvt)
Cady, Robert G. (PFC)
Cady, Theron G. (Pvt)
Cain, Robert J. (Pvt)
Califf, Harry W. (Pvt)
Cammell, Clarence T. (Pvt)
Card, Bertram (PFC)
Carne, James H. (PFC)
Carpenter, William M. (Cpl)
Casanova, Frank A. (Cpl)
Cashner, Roy (Pvt)
Centner, Earle W. (Pvt)
Chard, Elliott F. (Pvt) Marine Corps Reserve.
Cheney, Samuel A. (Pvt)
Chiantella, Michael (Pvt)
Church, Green M. (Pvt)
Clark, Paul D. (Pvt)
Clegg, Paul V. (Pvt)
Cobb, Fred (Cpl)
Coles, Harry A. (Pvt)
Counsil, Harry B. (Pvt)
Coverdale, Talmadge E. (Pvt)
Cromoga, John F. (Pvt)
Crosby, Wendell F. (Pvt)
Cunningham (Sgt)
Curtis, Fenley R. (Pvt) Marine Corps Reserve.
Danley, Harry H. (Pvt)
Davis, Harry E. (Pvt) Marine Corps Reserve.
Davis, James R. (PFC)
DeLaGrange, Geane (Pvt)
Dent, William D. (Pvt)
Deval, Glenn F. (Pvt)
Devoto, George L. (Pvt) Marine Corps Reserve.
Dick, Joseph E. (PFC)
Diehl, William (Pvt)
Dochter, Fred (Cpl)
Domm, Charles P. (Trumpeter)
Donohue, William A. (PFC)
Drumheiler, Samuel P. (Pvt) Marine Corps Reserve.
Dudley, Robert W. (Pvt)
Dysart, Samuel (Pvt)
Dziesko, Joseph P. (Pvt)

Ellis, Charles (Pvt)
Eplin, Frank L. (Pvt) KIA, 11 November 1918.
Etchegoen, Jean P. (PFC)
Ferm, Edmund H. (Pvt)
Fisher, Clyde B. (Cpl) Marine Corps Reserve.
Frederick, Louie E. (Cpl)
Fry, Ernest J. (Pvt)
Gaiowvnik, Michael W. (Pvt)
Garrett, Walter S. (Pvt)
Geltz, Frank J. (Pvt)
Gibbons, Edward M. (PFC)
Gill, Peter C. (Pvt)
Gillispie, William R. (Cpl)
Goeltz, George J. (Pvt)
Gooch, Eben W. (Pvt)
Gordon, John W. (Pvt)
Graham, Charlie F. (Pvt)
Graham, Manning L. (Pvt) Marine Guard Company.
Hardin, William A. (Sgt)
Harper, Fred J. (Pvt)
Harris, Roger A. (Trumpeter)
Harris, William O. (PFC)
Harshbarger, Wendell E. (Pvt)
Haynes, James A. (Pvt)
Hempstead, Joseph A. (PFC)
Heninger, Harold P. (Pvt)
Herron, William D. (Pvt)
Hively, Harley C. (Pvt)
Holcomb, Ira M. (Pvt)
Hoose, Eugene (Pvt)
Howes, Lewis L. (Sgt)
Hudkins, Lot (PFC)
Humphrey, Omer C. (PFC)
Hunt, Charles D. (Pvt)
Johnson, Homer (Cpl)
Johnson, Joe W. (Pvt) Marine Guard Company.
Johnson, John O. (Sgt)
Johnson, Oscar A. (Pvt)
Johnston, James J. (Sgt)
Jones, Arthur H. (Pvt)
Keefe, Martin J. (Pvt)
Keyes, Howard S. (Pvt)
Kilbourne, James G. (Pvt) Marine Guard Company.
Kilyshek, Bruno (PFC)
Kimball, Pardon C. (PFC)
King, Edward (Pvt)
Korb, Emil L. (Pvt)
Kosturos, George S. (Pvt)
Lacy, Perry A. (Pvt) Marine Guard Company.
Lady, Alfred J. (Pvt)
Landau, Joseph (Pvt)
LaRose, Donald A. (Cpl)
Larson, Arthur P. (Pvt)
Lawrence, Lewis C. (Cpl)
Lawrence, Thomas B. (Pvt)
Laws, Cecil R. (Cpl)
Leonard, Maynard (Pvt)
Lewis, James I. (Pvt) Marine Guard Company.
Lewis, Raymond D. (Pvt)
Lopez, Edmundo C. (Pvt)
Lowry, James M. (Cpl)

Lueben, Floyd J. (Sgt)
Lynch, Chadwick (Pvt)
Lynch, Joseph D. (Pvt)
Marriott, Chester N. (Pvt)
Marsh, Clinton (Pvt)
Marten, Fred H. (Pvt)
Marth, Frederick A. (Cpl)
Matson, Ben (Pvt)
Maxwell, Leonard M. (Pvt)
McArdle, Russell (Pvt)
McCague, John C. (Pvt) Marine Guard Company.
McCreary, Harry C. (Pvt) Marine Guard Company.
McCullah, Joseph O. (PFC)
McDonald, Harry (Pvt) Marine Guard Company.
McGrew, Edgar C. (Pvt) vt
McKitrick, Jessie H. (PFC)
McLaren, Myron (Pvt) Marine Guard Company.
McMurtrie, Alley L. (Pvt)
McSweeney, Gerard E. (Pvt)
McVeigh, William J. (Pvt)
Meschke, Carl (PFC)
Millard, Frank F. (Pvt)
Miller, Floyd D. (Sgt)
Miller, Frank J. (Pvt)
Mills, Stanley A. (Pvt) Marine Guard Company.
Montgomery, William G. (Pvt)
Moore, John C. (Pvt)
Moore, Williamson G., Jr. (Pvt)
Moran, Albert (Pvt)
Morris, John D. (Pvt)
Morse, Alvin B. (Pvt)
Mott, George C. (Cpl)
Musielski, John (Sgt)
Nelson, Louis (Pvt)
Nelson, Victor (Pvt)
Neville, Gilbert O. (Pvt) Marine Guard Company.
Niland, Thomas L. (Pvt)
Oldham, William (Pvt)
Olmstad, John (Pvt)
Olsen, Joseph C. (Pvt)
Olson, Oliver (Pvt)
Opial, Joseph (Pvt)
Osborn, Alfred (Pvt)
Osborn, John L. (Pvt)
O'Toole, Joseph P. (Pvt)
Owens, Daniel H. (Pvt)
Patten, Robert O. (Pvt)
Patterson, Isom L. (Pvt)
Paulson, Nils G. (Pvt)
Pearson, Albert S. (Cpl)
Perkins, Merlin (Pvt)
Perry, Frank D. (Pvt)
Pickle, Clarence H. (Pvt) Marine Guard Company.
Pike, Arthur (Pvt)
Pomeroy, Charles H., Jr. (Cpl)
Potter, Leon R. (Pvt) Marine Guard Company.
Powell, James B. (Cpl)
Prather, Eddy B. (Pvt)
Pruno, Elmer (Pvt)
Raymond, Drullard A. (Pvt)
Reed, Nathen L. (Pvt)

Reid, Hugh (Cpl)
Ricke, Henry A. (Pvt)
Roalson, Roy L. (Pvt)
Robbins, Duane H. (Cpl)
Rowley, Richard M. (Cpl)
Rudolph, Jacob B. (Pvt)
Rutledge, Lance (Pvt) Died of Wounds, 13 November 1918.
Scahill, William P. (Pvt)
Schave, Charles N. (PFC)
Schlupe, Carl C. (Pvt)
Schwartz, Bernard R. (Cpl)
Scott, James A. (Cpl)
Scott, Wallace J. (Cpl)
Sebastian, Ernest H. (Pvt)
Sellers, Don C. (Pvt)
Sheeley, Leslie T. (Pvt)
Shenk, Daniel J. (Pvt)
Sheridan, Albert E. (Pvt)
Shuster, Thomas C. (Pvt) Marine Guard Company.
Smith, Arnold C. (Pvt)
Smith, Daniel L. (Pvt)
Smith, Frank G. (Pvt)
Smith, Lon V. (Pvt)
Sowell, Vernon L. (Cpl) KIA, 1 November 1918.
Sparks, Clifford H. (Pvt)
Spence, Fred C. (Pvt)
Spence, Rosser (PFC)
Stafford, Raymond S. (Cpl)
Stahl, Chalmer A. (Trumpeter)
Stark, Raleigh D. (Pvt)
Stater, Roy (Pvt)
Stevens, Ralph F. (Pvt)
Stoneham, Robert M. (Pvt)
Story, Frank H. (Pvt)
Strickland, Benjamin H. (Cpl)
Stultz, Archie G. (Pvt) Marine Guard Company.
Tillotson, Budd (Pvt)
Toal, Frank (PFC)
Tobin, John P. (Pvt)
Tubbs, Alfred A. (Pvt)
Tucker, Leonidas L. (Pvt)
Tucker, Willie T. (Pvt)
Turner, Alfred T. (Pvt)
Van Dyke, Thomas J. (Pvt) Died of Wounds, 1 November 1918.
Van Sickle, Oliver T. (Pvt)
Vertrees, Richard L. (Pvt)
Vowels, Homer H. (Pvt) Marine Guard Company.
Waiss, Fred A. (Pvt)
Welch, Lyman G. (Pvt) Marine Guard Company.
West, Raymond T. (Pvt)
Wiedling, Theodore (Cpl)
Wilber, George H. (Pvt)
Williams, Arthur H. (Pvt)
Winfrey, Millard F. (Cpl)
Wissler, Jacob M. (Cpl)
Workman, Harold A. (Pvt)
Young, Henry (Pvt)

17th (A) Company, First Battalion

Name (Rank) Remarks

Denig, Robert L. (Maj)
Anthony, Robert C. (Cpt)
Hunt, LeRoy P. (Cpt) CO, "A" (17th) Co, 1st Bn.
Winans, Roswell (Cpt) Commanding Off, 17th Co.
Baston, Albert P. (1st Lt) WIA, 6 June 1918.
Blake, Robert (1st Lt)
Breckenridge, Leland D. (1st Lt)
Galliford, Walter T. (1st Lt)
Madison, Marshall P. (1st Lt)
Moore, Wyle J. (1st Lt)
Noblitt, Samuel M. (1st Lt)
Garvin, Earl W. (2nd Lt) Marine Corps Reserve.
Gassert, Howell A. (2nd Lt) Marine Corps Reserve.
Gissell, Bernhardt (2nd Lt) U.S. Army
Johnson, Gillis A. (2nd Lt) WIA.
Lienhard, Joseph (2nd Lt) Reserve, WIA.
Lindgren, Edward E. (2nd Lt) Reserve, WIA.
Norstrand, Carl J. (2nd Lt)
Paris, Augustus (2nd Lt)
Schwartzman, Edwin C. (2nd Lt) Reserve, WIA.
West, Eugene (2nd Lt) Reserve, Gas Officer.
Wilcox, Ralph McN. (2nd Lt)
Zinner, Fred J. (2nd Lt) Reserve, WIA.

Enlisted

Allen, Walter G. (1st Sgt)
Jessen, Emil (1st Sgt)
McDonald, George J. (1st Sgt)
Abelseth, John (Pvt)
Aldrich, Donald (Pvt)
Allen, Ernest L. (Sgt)WIA.
Ambler, Maxwell (Pvt)
Ames, Robert I. (Pvt)
Amick, Ira P. (Pvt)
Amsler, Maxwell (Pvt)
Anderson, Arvid P. (Pvt) MIA.
Andrews, James T. (Sgt)
Anthony, Charles (Sgt)
Applegate, Chauncey H. (Sgt)
Arnett, Harry L. (PFC)
Austin, Robert E. (Pvt)
Babb, Claud A. (Pvt) KIA, 15 June 1918.
Bailey, Paul (GySgt)
Balkenhol, Clarence F. (Sgt) WIA.
Bantz, Ernest M. (Sgt)
Bart, Edward A. (Sgt)
Bassett, Jay R. (Pvt)
Baume, John (CPhM)
Beam, Walter E. (Pvt)
Bearden, John M. (Pvt)
Beasler, Daniel (Pvt) WIA.
Beausoliel, Frederic (Pvt)
Becker, Floyd (Pvt)
Behr, William H. (Pvt)
Bell, Alfred A. (Pvt)

Beltz, Edwin H. (Pvt) WIA.
Berg, Louis A. (Pvt) Died of Wounds, buried in Somme, France.
Besherse, John W., Jr. (Pvt)
Bills, Dale A. (Pvt)
Birdsong, Lester D. (Pvt)
Bischof, Fred E. (Cpl)
Blackwood, Harold F. (Pvt) KIA, 8 June 1918.
Bohon, Ralph C. (Pvt)
Borah, Ernest (Pvt)
Boswell, Wilbur P. (Pvt)
Boyce, Archibald R. (Pvt)
Boyle, Frank R. (PFC)
Bozarth, Fremont (Pvt)
Brandt, Clayton D. (Pvt)
Breen, Kryn (Pvt) KIA, 4 October 1918, buried in the field.
Brennan, Clifford (Pvt)
Brewer, Nathan (PFC) KIA, 1 December 1918.
Briggs, Louis C. (Pvt)
Bring, Ivan W. (Pvt)
Brooks, Charles A. (Pvt)
Brooks, George C. (Pvt) Cook, 1st Class
Brown, Aden (Pvt) KIA, 9 June 1918.
Brown, Charles E. (Pvt)
Brown, Chester F. (Pvt) Nat'l Naval Volunteer.
Brown, Hogey (Pvt)
Brown, Leon (Pvt)
Buck, Charles W. (Pvt)
Buckman, Jewell (Pvt)
Budd, Stuart H (Pvt)
Budde, George W. (Pvt) KIA, 11 November 1918.
Burke, Clifford A. (Pvt) KIA, 9 June 1918.
Burling, Alten (PFC)
Burrows, Abner C. (Cpl)
Burrows, Charles A. (Cpl)
Bush, Marion L. (Pvt)
Butler, Fred A. (Pvt)
Cade, Paul T. (Pvt)
Campbell, Aldridge P. (Pvt) WIA.
Campbell, Cranford (Cpl) Reserve.
Campbell, Wade E. (Pvt)
Capwell, Samuel P. (Sgt)
Carson, Robert R. (Pvt)
Chase, Roscoe M. (Pvt)
Chason, Arthur A. (Pvt)
Cheatham, Clarence E. (Pvt)
Christensen, Peter, Jr. (Cpl)
Clark, Edwin B. (Pvt) WIA.
Clark, Edwin S. (Pvt)
Clark, James R. (Pvt)
Clift, James W. (Pvt)
Clore, Robert L. (Pvt)
Clowers, Raymond S. (Pvt)
Codes, Onnie J. (Pvt)
Colby, Martin (Pvt)
Collier, Lauren W. (Pvt)
Connolly, William E. (Pvt)
Cook, Marvill J., Jr. (Pvt) Died of Wounds.
Cooley, James E. (Sgt)
Coonan, John P. (Cpl)

Corbin, Francis B. (Cpl) KIA, 18 July 1918.
Corlett, Thomas J. (Pvt)
Corry, William B. (Trumpeter)
Couch, John V. (Pvt)
Cox, Richard W. (Pvt)
Cox, Roy E. (Cpl)
Cox, Smith (Pvt)
Cragg, Ralph A. (Pvt)
Craig, Clyde C. (Pvt)
Cremer, Leslie R. (Pvt)
Crippen, William H. (Pvt) KIA, buried in the field.
Cronk, Raymond E. (Pvt)
Crow, George B. (Pvt)
Cunningham, John (Sgt)
Curtis, Fenley R. (Pvt)
Custer, Earl E. (Pvt)
Damkjer, Walter (Sgt)
Davis, Roland O. (Pvt)
Debrott, William A. (Pvt)
DeGrange, Charles P. (Pvt)
Deiss, William J. (Cpl)
DeLaGrange, Geane (Pvt)
Demarest, Simon (Pvt)
Desmarais, Joseph L. (Pvt)
Dewitt, Raymond (PFC)
Dixon, Joseph (Pvt) Messman.
Doak, John W., Jr. (Pvt)
Dobrott, William A. (Pvt)
Donahie, William J. (Pvt)
Doughty, Shirley B. (Pvt)
Douglas, Ben W. (Pvt)
Downe, Parry L. (Pvt) WIA.
Drew, Charles E. (Pvt)
DroegKamp, Eugene A. (Cpl)
Drummond, Malcolm (Cpl)
Dubay, Louis H. (Pvt) Cook, 3rd Class.
Dumars, William W. (Pvt) KIA, 6 June 1918.
Duncan, Claud F. (Pvt)
Duncan, Frank (Cpl) KIA, buried in the field, 6 October 1918.
Dupree, Albert D. (Cpl)
Durr, Paul W. (Pvt) WIA.
Dysart, Samuel (Pvt)
Earnest, William V. (PFC)
Edwards, James W. (Cpl)
Elliott, Edward (Pvt)
Emig, Maurice D. (Pvt)
Enterline, Richard P. (Pvt)
Erbaugh, John W. (Pvt) Reserve.
Erwin, Joseph A. (Pvt) Died of Wounds in hospital, 4 October 1918.
Eschenbach, Henry A. (Pvt)
Fagan, Frank J. (Sgt)
Fahlow, Carl (Pvt) Gassed in line of duty.
Fairchild, Stanley S. (Pvt)
Fallow, Carl (Pvt)
Farmer, Houston B. (Cpl) KIA, buried in the field, 6 June 1918.
Farrar, Frank R. (Pvt)
Farrell, Frank A. (Cpl)
Ferguson, William J. (Cpl)

Fiala, Joseph T. (Pvt) WIA.
Figel, Paul P. (Cpl) WIA.
Finney, Benjamin F. (Pvt)
Finney, Benjamin F., Jr. (Pvt)
Fitch, Edward M. (Pvt) WIA.
Flemming, Walter E. (Pvt) WIA.
Fogell, Forest N. (GySgt) WIA.
Foran, Joseph F. (Pvt)
Ford, Thomas E. (Pvt)
Fowle, Royal E. (Cpl)
Fox, Claude A. (Pvt)
Fox, Daniel R. (Sgt) WIA.
Fox, Harris L. (Cpl)
French, Frank R. (PFC)
Frey, Abner B. (Pvt)
Frost, Henry S. (Pvt)
Gall, Paul W. (Pvt) Messman, KIA, 15 June 1918.
Gallogly, Floyd F. (Cpl)
Galvin, James J. (Cpl) Nat'l Naval Volunteer.
Ganslein, Augustine (Pvt)
Gardner, William H., Jr. (Pvt)
Garrison, Joseph D. (Pvt)
Garrison, Joseph N. (Pvt) WIA.
Gates, Ralph A. (Pvt)
Gebhardt, Herbert F. (Cpl)
Geraty, George C., Jr. (Pvt) WIA.
Giles, William N. (Pvt) KIA, buried in field, 5 October 1918.
Girard, John F., Jr. (Cpl)
Glenn, Clyde W. (Pvt) WIA.
Goodwin, Lewis J. (Pvt)
Grady, James W. (Pvt) Died of Wounds, 4 October 1918.
Graf, Robert E. (Pvt)
Graham, Lawrence A. (PFC)
Grange, Erwin M. (Pvt)
Greenberg, Samuel (Pvt) Shell shocked.
Greenleaf, Malcom F. (Sgt)
Greer, Hugh D., Jr. (Pvt)
Greer, Reed C. (Pvt) WIA.
Greer, William T.B. (Pvt)
Griffin, Jeremiah, J. (Pvt)
Grimes, Thomas W. (Pvt)
Grimm, Harry E. (Pvt)
Grimm, William A. (Cpl)
Gruner, Charles V. (Pvt) Reserve, WIA.
Gustafson, Lorne N. (Pvt)
Guth, Carl A. (Pvt)
Hagler, Harry H. (Pvt)
Hamlin, David W. (Pvt)
Hamman, Howard E. (Sgt)
Hammerton, Everett B. (Pvt)
Hannes, Harry J. (Pvt)
Hardin, William A. (Cpl)
Harper, Thomas B. (Pvt)
Harris, William B. (Pvt)
Hart, William J. (Trumpeter)
Hartman, John (Pvt)
Harvey, Dewey C. (Pvt)
Hathaway, Clarence D. (Pvt)
Hatton, Delbert J. (Pvt)
Haury, Edward F. (Pvt)

Haygeman, Ernest J. (Pvt) Cook.

Hays, Harry M. (Pvt) WIA.

Headings, Arthur S. (Pvt) WIA.

Hedian, Ralph V. (Pvt) WIA.

Heiss, George J. (Pvt) WIA.

Hempstead, Joseph A. (PFC)

Hendee, George M. (Pvt) WIA.

Hennen, Guy T. (Pvt) WIA.

Hess, Harry E. (Pvt) Died of wounds, 11 June 1918.

Hewitt, Eugene R. (Pvt)

Hicks, Donald E. (Pvt)

Hicks, John W. (Pvt)

Hildebrant, Joseph H. (Pvt)

Hill, Ralph R. (Pvt)

Hill, Thorn (Pvt)

Hilton, Peter V. (Pvt)

Hiner, Lewis E. (Pvt)

Hintzen, Bertram J. (Pvt)

Hitchcock, Andrew G. (Pvt)

Hockenberry, Cecil (Pvt) KIA, buried in the field, 4 October 1918.

Hoefle, August C. (Pvt)

Hoekstra, Theodore (Pvt)

Hoffman, Albert H. (Pvt) Gassed.

Hoffner, James B. (Pvt)

Hollander, Davis (PhM2)

Hollinshed, Percy L. (Pvt)

Holloway, Willie (Pvt)

Holmes, Frederick E. (Cpl)

Holsinger, Charles E. (Pvt)

Hoopes, Harlow R.F. (Pvt) Died of Wounds in hospital.

Horwitz, Herman H. (Pvt) MIA.

Hosack, Clarence F. (Pvt) Died of Wounds, 10 May 1919.

Howard, Jack (Pvt) Messman.

Howitz, Herman H. (Pvt)

Huddleston, William C. (Pvt)

Hudlow, Gilbert C. (Pvt)

Hudson, Edgar E. (Pvt)

Huey, Miles W. (Pvt)

Humiston, Clinton C. (Sgt)

Hunt, Charles D. (Pvt)

Imhoff, Laurence (Pvt)

Isherwood, Archibald M. (Pvt)

Jackson, Clifford N. (Pvt)

Jackson, Henry H. (Pvt)

Jacobson, Frank O. (Pvt) WIA.

James, Bushrod M. (Trumpeter) WIA.

James, William (Cpl)MIA.

Jameson, Alfred (Cpl)

Janca, Joseph J. (Pvt)

Jeffcoat, Horace G. (Pvt) Messman.

Jelinek, Emil B. (Pvt)

Johnson, Albert (Pvt) WIA.

Johnson, David A. (Cpl)Died of Wounds, 16 June 1918.

Johnson, Ned P. (Pvt)

Johnson, Neil P. (Pvt)

Johnson, Walter V. (Pvt)

Johnston, Ellis S., Jr. (Pvt)

Jones, Lee R. (Sgt)WIA.

Jones, Manly H. (Pvt)

Jones, Russel B. (Cpl)

Joyal, Joseph A. (Pvt) WIA.

Kaufmann, William J. (Cpl)

Keatley, William E. (Pvt) WIA.

Keefe, Martin J. (Pvt)

Keith, Frank G. (Pvt)

Keller, Alfred (Pvt)

Kelly, Paul J. (Pvt)

Kelly, William B. (Pvt)

Kelm, Edward J. (Pvt) Reserve, WIA.

Kennoy, Francis J. (Pvt)

Kernan, Charles E. (Pvt) WIA.

Kerr, Harold R. (Cpl)KIA, 15 June 1918.

Keyes, George I. (Pvt)Died of Wounds in hospital, Buried in Miomandre Military Cemetery, Marne.

Kiland, Edwin F. (Pvt)

Kilbourne, James G. (Pvt)

Killian, Edward A. (Pvt)

Kindig, Lester H. (Pvt)

King, John F. (Pvt)

Klawiter, Carl H. (Pvt)

Klinger, Ross L. (Pvt)

Klotz, Bert L. (Pvt)

Kness, Karl F. (Sgt)

Knott, George T. (Sgt) Company Supply Sgt, KIA, 18 July 1918.

Knutson, Omar J. (Pvt) WIA.

Korb, Emil L. (Pvt)

Kovar, John (Pvt) WIA.

Krakau, Earl E. (Pvt)

Labrie, Hector J. (Pvt)

Lake, Francis R. (Pvt)

Land, Reginald E. (Pvt)

Landau, Joseph (Pvt)

Langley, Charles E. (Pvt) KIA, 14 September 1918.

Lannigan, John L. (Pvt) WIA.

Larsen, Peter (Cpl)

Laughlin, Charles W. (Sgt)

Lawler, Loren L. (Pvt)

Lawrence, Anthony F. (Pvt)

Layman, Hollie J. (Pvt) Died of Wounds.

Layne, James H. (Pvt)

Layton, Joseph P. (Sgt) WIA.

Leaf, Helmer C. (Pvt)

Lee, Edgar E. (Pvt)

Lee, Robert G. (Pvt) WIA.

Leffler, John F. (Pvt) WIA.

Legnard, Frank J. (Sgt)

Legnard, John B. (Cpl) Died of Wounds, 6 October 1918.

Leonard, Fred D. (Pvt) WIA.

Leonard, Fred D., Jr. (Pvt) WIA.

Leonard, George L. (Pvt) WIA.

Leonard, Maynard (Pvt)

LePrell, Ambrose (Pvt) KIA, buried at St. Etienne.

Leyden, Leo T. (Pvt)

Lietka, George A. (Pvt)

Lindenmeier, Frank (Drummer)

Lipsky, Joseph (Pvt)

Livingston, Hautess K. (Sgt) WIA.

Loomis, Glenn S. (Pvt)
Lucas, James F. (Pvt)
Lybarger, Ernest R. (Cpl)
Lyle, Arch G. (Pvt)
Lytle, George E. (Pvt) WIA.
Macdonald, Cedrick A. (PFC)
Mackey, Harold F. (Pvt) Messman.
Madigan, Bernard A. (Pvt) Bn Runner.
Mady, Harold McL. (Cpl)
Mahar, Henry E. (Pvt)
Mansfield, Courtland S. (Pvt)
Marcus, Claus (Pvt)
Marks, Stanley H. (Pvt)
Marler, Elton (Cpl)
Marlow, David L. (Pvt)
Marshall, Albert R. (Pvt)
Matheny, Frank S. (Sgt)
Mathews, Frank M. (PFC)
Matthews, Roland J. (Cpl)
Maxwell, Norman T. (Pvt)
McCafferty, Ernest M. (Pvt)
McCarthy, Charles F. (GySgt) WIA.
McCarthy, John F. (Pvt)
McClain, Virgil E. (Pvt)
McClellan, William S. (Pvt) WIA.
McCormack, Clarence (Cpl)
McCune, Karl (Cpl)
McCurdy, Harold E. (Cpl)
McDonald, Walter G. (Pvt)
McGagus, John C. (Pvt)
McKendree, Dean G. (Pvt)
McKeone, James J. (Pvt)
McKinnon, Donald (Pvt)
McVeigh, William J., Jr. (Pvt)
Melody, George T. (PFC)
Melon, Eddie J. (Pvt) WIA.
Meric, Alcide L. (Cpl)
Meschke, Carl (PFC)
Meyer, August W. (Sgt)
Miller, Louis F. (Pvt) KIA, 18 July 1918.
Miller, Ralph (Pvt)
Mills, Stanley A. (Pvt)
Mobley, Troy B. (Pvt)
Moore, Edwin B. (Pvt)
Moore, Oscar J. (Cpl)
Morris, Fred H. (Pvt)
Mosall, John E. (Pvt) WIA.
Moser, John R., Jr. (Pvt)
Mottola, Thomas (Pvt)
Moutrey, Victor L. (Pvt)
Moxness, Arthur (Pvt)
Muller, Michael H. (Pvt)
Murphy, Clarence H. (Pvt)
Myer, August W. (Sgt) WIA.
Myers, Lewis F. (Pvt)
Naegle, Hans M. (Pvt)
Nagel, Edward B. (PFC)
Narusch, Anthony P. (Cpl)
Nash, Earl (Pvt)
Nason, Warren P. (Pvt)
Neal, Herbert (Pvt) WIA.

Nejedly, Boodie F. (Pvt)
Nelson, Louis (Pvt)
Newton, Byron E. (Pvt) WIA.
Niessen, Gerard J. (Pvt) WIA.
Oaks, Acie Therman (Pvt)
Obermiller, Arthur (Pvt)
O'Brien, Joseph J. (Pvt)
Ogle, Hollie R. (Pvt)
O'Hare, Peter C. (Pvt)
Oliver, John W. (Pvt) KIA, 19 July 1918.
O'Loughlin, John G. (Sgt)
Olsen, Joseph C. (Pvt)
Olson, Charles J.E. (Pvt) KIA, 15 September 1918.
O'Neal, Herbert (Pvt) MIA.
Orrill, William J. (Pvt) WIA.
Osborn, Alfred (Pvt)
Ouse, Carl C. (Pvt) Messman.
Oxford, George J. (PFC)
Palmer, Merlin E. (Pvt) KIA, 5 October 1918, Buried in
  the field.
Parker, Charles F. (Pvt)
Parks, Arthur W. (Pvt)
Parks, Harry M. (Pvt)
Patterson, James J. (Pvt)
Peake, Lester A. (Pvt)
Pedrick, Frank R. (Sgt) Company Clerk.
Pedro, Anthony (Pvt)
Peeples, Sam C. (Pvt) WIA.
Peggs, John C. (Sgt)
Peterson, Harold K. (Pvt)
Peterson, Harry W. (Pvt)
Phelps, William H. (Pvt) Messman.
Pickle, Clarence H. (Pvt)
Pierce, Merwin C. (Pvt)
Pine, Earl H. (Pvt)
Pitts, Granville E. (Pvt) WIA.
Pitts, Robert C. (Cpl)
Polhseno, Lewis (Pvt)
Poulson, John A. (Pvt)
Powers, Robert B. (Pvt)
Price, James W. (Pvt)
Pucciariello, Carmen (Pvt) WIA.
Pyle, Elmer R. (Pvt)
Pyle, Frank M. (Pvt) WIA.
Quinn, John J. (Pvt)
Rabe, Herbert G. (Pvt)
Ratchford, Arthur E. (Sgt)
Rawley, David A. (Pvt)
Reed, Eugene B. (PhM2)
Reid, Joseph J. (Cpl)
Reitz, Fred W. (GySgt) WIA.
Restle, August H. (Pvt) Messman.
Reynolds, John A. (Cpl)
Richardson, George K. (Cpl)
Riege, Paul E. (Pvt) WIA.
Riggs, John F. (Pvt)
Roberts, Sidney C. (Pvt) KIA, 15 June 1918.
Robertson, Howard G. (Pvt)
Robinett, Paul J. (Sgt)
Rohloff, John G. (Pvt) WIA.
Rose, Ernest W. (Cpl)

Rozean, Frank A. (Pvt)
Russell, Harry DeW. (Pvt)
Ryan, William J. (Pvt)
Sanders, Arthur J. (PFC)
Sanders, Noel, W. (Pvt)
Sandrok, Walter G. (Pvt) Messman.
Schaudt, Harry B. (Pvt)
Schomaker, John McQ (Pvt) WIA.
Scott, Milton R. (GySgt) WIA.
Seaman, John B. (Pvt)
Serres, Frank A. (Pvt)
Seymour, Alma E. (PFC)
Sherman, Arthur E. (Pvt)
Shiners, Clifford F. (PFC)
Sidwell, James D. (Cpl)
Sims, Amor L. (Sgt)
Skinner, Rufus H. (Pvt)
Slade, James R. (PFC)
Smith, Elmer D. (GySgt)
Smith, Ezra R. (GySgt)
Smith, George A. (Pvt)
Smith, George D. (Sgt) KIA, 3 October 1918. Buried in the field.
Smith, Howard (Pvt) Name change–Luke Henly.
Smith, Joseph L., Jr. (Pvt)
Smithers, James P. (Pvt)
Spangelo, Elmer (Pvt) WIA.
Spencer, George L. (Trumpeter) WIA.
Stach, William R. (Pvt) WIA.
Stasky, John F. (Pvt) WIA.
Steck, Joseph P. (Pvt) WIA.
Stine, Fay E. (Pvt)
Streck, Albert LeR. (Pvt)
Strehlow, Herbert A. (Pvt) KIA, 7 June 1918.
Stuart, Albert T. (Sgt)
Stuehr, Martin J. (Sgt)
Stunak, Arthur H. (Pvt)
Sulik, Anthony (Sgt) WIA.
Summerford, Robert D. (Pvt)
Suter, Jacob J. (Pvt)
Sutton, John (Pvt)
Swang, Harold A. (Pvt) WIA.
Sylvester, Albert (PFC)
Thomas, Parry A. (PFC) KIA, 15 November 1918.
Thomas, Theodore W. (Pvt) WIA.
Thompson, Paul K. (Cpl) MIA. Taken prisoner, but returned.
Tidwell, Phelon, Jr. (Sgt)
Tobin, Joseph J. (Pvt) WIA.
Tomaka, George (Pvt) KIA, 15 June 1918.
Tribolet, Herman G. (Pvt) Messman.
Trousdale, Emmette (Pvt)
Trusler, William (Pvt)
Turner, Alfred T. (Pvt)
Umstead, William C., Jr. (Pvt)
Uttley, Arthur (Pvt) WIA.
Valentine, Earl D. (Pvt)
Van Duesen, Robert R. (Sgt) Died of Wounds in hospital, 27 October 1918.
Van Natten, Milton E. (Pvt)
Varella, Victor (Pvt)

Venton, William R. (Pvt)
Wakefield, George H. (Pvt) WIA.
Wales, Thomas H. (Sgt)
Walker, Charley E. (Pvt)
Walleigh, Harry R. (Pvt) KIA, 18 July 1918.
Walls, Roy V. (Pvt)
Walsh, Edward P. (Pvt)
Walters, William E. (Pvt)
Ward, Calvin L. (Pvt) MIA.
Ward, William F. (Pvt) MIA.
Ward, William W. (PFC)
Warren, Clifford E. (Pvt)
Webb, Martin B. (Pvt)
Weichler, John (Pvt)
Weis, Edward J. (Pvt)
Weise, Walter D. (Pvt) WIA.
West, John P. (Cpl)
Whetstone, Sydney H. (Pvt)
White, Charles Jr. (Pvt) KIA, 2 November 1918.
White, Frank E. (Pvt) WIA.
White, Joseph T. (Cpl)
Whittemore, Starling (Pvt)
Wilcox, Raymond E. (Pvt)
Will, John D., Jr. (Pvt) Reserve.
Williams, George (Pvt) Died of Wounds, 3 November 1918.
Willis, George T. (Pvt) KIA, 6 June 1918.
Wissmann, George H. (Cpl) WIA.
Wolfe, William M. (Pvt)
Wolfers, John J. (Pvt)
Wood, Thomas B. (Pvt)
Wynne, Emmet H. (Pvt)
Yarella, Victor (Pvt) Died of Wounds in hospital. Buried in Miomandre Military Cemetery, Marne.
Young, Ralph A. (Pvt)
Zart, Harry S. (Pvt)
Ziegler, William G. (Pvt) MIA.

49th (B) Company, First Battalion

Name (Rank) Remarks

Hamilton, George W. (Cpt) Company CO, 49th Co.
Galliford, Walter T.H. (Cpt) Intelligence Off, 49th Co.
Gill, Charles C. (Cpt)
Kieren, Francis S. (Cpt) Commanding Off, 49th Co.
LeBeouf, Albert A. (Cpt)
Bogert, Edward O. (1st Lt)
Langford, Thomas A. (1st Lt) WIA.
Matthews, William R. (1st Lt) WIA.
Platt, Jonas H. (1st Lt) WIA, 6 June 1918.
Thomason, John W., Jr. (1st Lt)
Cannon, Adolphus (2nd Lt) Reserve.
Conner, Robert E. (2nd Lt) KIA, 3 October 1918.
Culnan, John H. (2nd Lt) Reserve.
Eastin, Fred C. (2nd Lt) WIA.
Frasier, Walter D. (2nd Lt) KIA.
Geer, Prentice S. (2nd Lt) Reserve.

Novak, Michael (2nd Lt) Reserve, WIA.
Peterson, William C. (2nd Lt) KIA, 6 June 1918.
Ross, Elbert W. (2nd Lt) Reserve.
Schneider, John G. (2nd Lt)
Somers, Vernon L. (2nd Lt) Marine Corps Reserve,
    KIA, 6 June 1918.
Talbot, Horace (2nd Lt) Marine Corps Reserve.

Enlisted

Anderson, Frank (1st Sgt)
Corbett, Murl (1st Sgt) WIA.
Tarker, Michael (1st Sgt)
Adams, James E. (Pvt) WIA.
Adams, Newton W. (Pvt)
Albright, Frederick J. (Pvt)
Allen, Lester W. (Pvt) KIA, 3 October 1918.
Allen, Lyle L. (Cpl)
Altman, John (Sgt)
Anderson, Victor M. (Cpl)
Atkinson, Abbie D. (Cpl)
Atkinson, George A. (Pvt)
Attaway, William J. (Pvt)
Augustine, Francis (Cpl)
Baines, Edwin A. (Pvt)
Barbee, Harry W. (Pvt) Evacuated to hospital.
Barger, George H. (Pvt) WIA.
Barnes, Rae (Pvt)
Barr, Ziba (Pvt)
Barrios, John E. (Pvt)
Barton, Howard H. (Pvt) MIA.
Bates, David (Sgt)
Beck, George H. (Trumpeter)
Beckett, William H. (Pvt)
Beevers, Frank A. (Pvt)
Benninger, Henry H. (Pvt)
Benson, Martin (Pvt)
Berenius, Anthony J. (Pvt)
Besterfeldt, Frank E. (Pvt)
Black, George O. (Pvt)
Blalock, John F. (Pvt) KIA, 6 June 1918.
Blood, Leo I. (Pvt)
Bloomer, Earnest (Pvt)
Boardman, Fred W. (Pvt) KIA, 4 November 1918,
    Reserve.
Bodwell, Frederick E. (Cpl) MIA.
Boehm, Christian (Pvt)
Bosic, Leo F. (Pvt)
Bosman, Frank (GySgt)
Bounds, Richard E. (Pvt)
Bovard, Sidney E. (Pvt)
Bowness, Harry (Sgt)
Boyd, William R. (Pvt)
Boyles, Charles P. (Pvt)
Bradish, Cyrus P. (Pvt) Reserve WIA.
Bradley, James J. (Pvt) WIA.
Bragg, Frank (Pvt)
Brandon, Eugene H. (Pvt)
Brandon, Ian (Pvt) KIA, 6 June 1918.
Breithaupt, Beryl (Pvt)
Brendle, William H. (Pvt)
Brewer, John H. (Pvt)

Brewer, Samuel O. (Pvt) WIA.
Briddon, Albert W. (PFC) Reserve.
Briggs, Willard (Pvt)
Brock, Robert S. (Cpl) Reserve.
Brooks, Harry V. (Pvt)
Brown, David E. (Pvt)
Brown, Edward L. (Pvt) Reserve, WIA.
Brown, Thomas (Pvt) KIA, 2 June 1918.
Broxup, John (Pvt) KIA, 5 November 1918, Reserve.
Brumbeloe, Algernon T. (PhM3) WIA.
Bruni, Emil (Pvt)
Brzozowski, William (Cpl) Signalman, 1st Class.
Buchanan, William E. (PFC)
Buck, Alonzo M. (Pvt)
Bullis, Everard J. (Pvt) WIA.
Burgert, John P. (Pvt) Reserve.
Burgh, Ernest A. (Pvt) Reserve.
Butcher, Christopher O. (Pvt)
Butler, Arthur R. (Pvt)
Cady, Robert G. (PFC)
Cain, Herman S. (Pvt)
Caldwell, James M. (Pvt)
Califf, Harry W. (Pvt)
Cameron, Roy E. (Pvt) Reserve.
Campbell, Dewey (Cpl) WIA.
Carlson, Harry V. (Pvt) Reserve, WIA.
Carter, Joe (Pvt) WIA.
Casey, John (Sgt) WIA.
Chard, Elliott F. (Pvt) Reserve.
Chiantella, Michael (Pvt)
Choinski, Leonard F. (Cpl)
Church, Glenn M. (Pvt)
Cleveland, Grover L. (Pvt)
Coate, John J. (Cpl)
Cobb, Fred W. (Cpl) KIA, 3 November 1918.
Cohen, David M. (Cpl)
Coldwell, Elijah H. (Cpl)
Colman, Carl W. (Pvt)
Colvin, Arthur G. (Pvt)
Comfort, Clifton C. (Pvt) Reserve.
Conge, Erving H. (Pvt)
Connolly, Walter T. (Pvt)
Conway, Peter (Sgt)
Cook, Herbert E. (Pvt)
Cook, Vivian (Pvt)
Coombs, Charles E. (Cpl)
Cooper, Aloysius P. (Pvt) Reserve, WIA.
Cornish, Paul W. (Pvt) Reserve, WIA.
Cotter, James T. (Pvt) KIA, 6 June 1918.
Coughlin, William H. (Pvt)
Counsil, Harry B. (Pvt)
Coverdale, Talmage E. (Pvt)
Crawford, Joseph A. (Pvt)
Cronin, Raymond P. (Sgt)
Cushman, Oliver W. (Pvt)
Cygan, William A. (Sgt)
Dacey, Joseph T. (Cpl)
Dale, Thomas DeW (Sgt)
Damico, Michael (Pvt)
Davidian, Dickran (Cpl) KIA, 2 November 1918.
Davis, Allen C. (Pvt)

Davis, Claude E. (Pvt)
Davis, Roger W. (Sgt)
Davis, Roy H. (Pvt) Reserve.
Dean, Ralph H. (Pvt)
Deans, James B. (Pvt) KIA, 4 October 1918.
Deere, Paul L. (Pvt)
Deluge, Henry (Pvt)
Denio, Ernest (Pvt) Reserve, WIA.
Dennin, William J. (Pvt)
Devoto, George L. (Pvt)
Dey, Claude M. (Cpl)
Dick, Joseph (PFC)
Diggins, Wilfred J. (Pvt)
Dillon, John R. (Pvt)
Domangue, Eanus J. (Pvt)
Donohue, James J. (Pvt)
Donohue, William A.(PFC)
Dowdle, Henry L. (Pvt)
Dudley, Robert W. (Pvt)
Dupes, Karl A. (Pvt)
Durrie, Howard S. (Pvt) WIA.
Dyer, James W. (Cpl) WIA.
Easter, James W. (Pvt) Died of Wounds, 15 July 1918.
Eckert, Albert L. (Pvt)
Edwards, Jessie T. (Pvt)
Edwards, William C. (Pvt)
Eiderson, William F. (Pvt)
Elsasser, John B. (GySgt) WIA
Ely, Robert L. (Pvt) KIA, 20 June 1918.
Estes, Jasper N. (Pvt) Died of Wounds, 1 November 1918.
Etchegoen, Jean P. (PFC)
Etheridge, Ottis R. (Pvt)
Evans, Arthur (Pvt) Reserve.
Evans, Ralph W. (Pvt) WIA.
Evans, Stanley F. (Pvt)
Exner, William P. (Pvt)
Faath, Lawrence J. (Cpl) MIA.
Fairclough, Frank D. (Pvt) KIA, 6 June 1918.
Farrell, James E. (Sgt) WIA.
Feinberg, Herman C. (Pvt)
Fennen, Timothy F. (Pvt)
Field, Harry, J.W. (Pvt)
Finn, Frank R. (Pvt)
Finnegan, Gerald R. (GySgt) KIA, 6 June 1918.
Fisher, Clyde B. (Cpl) Reserve.
Fisher, Raymond C. (Pvt)
Fistler, Arthur (Pvt)
Flaherty, Michael J. (Pvt) WIA.
Fleck, John W. (Pvt)
Fleenor, Nelson R. (Pvt)
Flynn, Edward J. (Cpl) MIA.
Foran, Claud J. (Pvt)
Forbes, John J. (Pvt)
Ford, Roy J. (Pvt) KIA, 6 June 1918.
Fort, William J. (Pvt)
Foster, Glen (Pvt)
France, Walter (Pvt)
Frederick, Eugene (Pvt)
Fremd, August W. (Pvt)
French, Louis N. (Pvt)

Fries, William B. (Pvt)
Gaddis, George D. (Pvt)
Gallagher, David E. (Pvt)
Gallup, Harley B. (Pvt) KIA, 4 October 1918.
Garrison, John N. (Pvt) KIA, 1 November 1918.
Garvey, Claude R. (Pvt) Died of wounds, 16 June 1918.
Garvin, Frank H. (Pvt)
Gavin, William A. (Sgt) Evacuated to hospital.
Geist, Abraham L. (Pvt) WIA.
Gentsch, Henry F. (Cpl) WIA.
Giles, Charlie W. (Pvt)
Gill, Edward (Cpl) WIA.
Gillingham, Henry (Pvt)
Gingrich, Charles (Cpl) WIA.
Glade, Edmund F. (Pvt)
Goff, Earl S. (Pvt)
Goldberg, Zell (Pvt)
Goldstein, Sam (Cpl)
Good, William J. (Pvt)
Gordon, John W. (Pvt)
Gorham, Samuel L.(Cpl) Reserve.
Gorsuch, Frank L. (Pvt) Reserve, WIA.
Goudy, George R. (Pvt)
Green, Harry (Pvt) Reserve.
Gregory, Harlan D. (Pvt) Evacuated to hospital.
Gridley, John S. (Cpl) MIA.
Griffin, Glen (Pvt)
Griffin, John (Pvt) Died of Wounds, 4 November 1918.
Groce, Arthur W. (Pvt)
Groce, David O. (Pvt)
Gruwell, Arthur B. (Cpl)
Hackman, Arlington F. (Pvt)
Hagen, Charles M. (Pvt) Reserve.
Hague, Edward A. (Pvt)
Hallum, George J. (Pvt) Cook 1st Class.
Halonen, Eino J. (Pvt)
Hamel, Edward G. (Pvt)
Hamilton, William W. (Sgt)
Hamlet, George O. (Pvt)
Hammerstrom, Knute W. (Pvt) WIA.
Hampton, William C. (Pvt)
Hand, John (Drummer) WIA.
Hanigan, Seth (Pvt)
Harding, Joel F. (Pvt) Reserve, WIA.
Harper, Victor E. (Trumpeter)
Harr, Clyde F. (Pvt)
Harrison, Thomas R. (Pvt)
Harshbarger, Wendell E. (Pvt)
Hart, Frank H. (Sgt)
Hartman, Raymond M. (Pvt)
Hawkins, Roy (Pvt)
Hay, Robert J. (Pvt) MIA.
Heald, William S. (Cpl) WIA.
Heaton, Herman M. (Pvt)
Henderson, Benjamin E. (Pvt) KIA, 6 June 1918.
Hennegan, Richard (Pvt)
Henry, James (Pvt) Reserve. In hospital.
Herbert, John F. (Pvt)
Herr, Russell G. (Pvt)
Herring, Claude R. (Pvt)
Higgins, James (Pvt) Reserve, WIA.

Hill, Earl T. (Pvt) MIA.
Hill, Herbert L. (Pvt) Died of Wounds, 7 June 1918.
Hill, Jewell T. (Pvt)
Hinchman, Clarence B. (Pvt)
Hockmuth, William J. (Pvt)
Hoeppner, Louis J. (Pvt)
Hoffer, Albert M. (Pvt)
Hoffman, Charles (GySgt)
Hogeboom, Kenneth D. (Pvt) WIA.
Holly, DeWitt H. (Pvt)
Holmes, Lewis A. (Pvt) Nat'l Naval Volunteer.
Hoose, Eugene (Pvt)
Horn, Milton E. (Pvt)
Houdak, Frank M. (Pvt) Reserve.
Hucobsky, John J. (Pvt)
Hughes, Ambrose (Cpl)
Humphery, Omar C. (PFC)
Hunter, Alexander M. (Pvt)
Hutchins, Walter (Pvt) KIA.
Hynett, Robert H. (Pvt)
Jacobs, George (Pvt)
Jacobson, Kenneth J. (Pvt)
Jenni, Clarence M. (Pvt)
Jodell, Clifford E. (Sgt) WIA.
Johnson, Frank G. (Pvt)
Johnson, George H. (Pvt)
Johnson, William M. (Pvt) KIA, 16 September 1918.
Johnston, Byron B. (Pvt) Reserve, WIA.
Jones, James W. (Pvt) WIA.
Jones, John F. (PFC) WIA.
Jones, Luther N. (Pvt)
Jones, Shattuc (Pvt)
Jordan, Laban M. (Pvt)
Kai, Frank F. (Pvt) Reserve.
Kaufman, Israel (Pvt) Nat'l Naval Volunteer.
Kayser, William F. (Pvt)
Keefe, Charles C. (Pvt)
Keller, John A., Jr. (Pvt)
Kellum, James B. (Pvt)
Kelly, Clarence H. (Pvt) Nat'l Naval Volunteer.
Keville, Timothy G. (Pvt) WIA.
Kew, Victor P. (Pvt)
Kidwell, Paul M. (Pvt) KIA, 6 June 1918.
Kilgore, James H. (Pvt) Evacuated to hospital.
Kilyshek, Bruno (PFC)
Kirschner, Conrad (Pvt)
Koch, Marion A. (Pvt) Reserve.
Kopka, Merland A. (Pvt) Reserve.
Kowalak, Anthony S. (Cpl)
Krapper, Viggo G. (Pvt)
Kukoski, John (Pvt) Cook, 2nd Class, WIA, 6 June 1918.
LaBonte, Edmond J. (Pvt)
Lamb, Hughey (Pvt)
LaPlante, Joseph (Cpl) WIA.
Latham, Livingstone (Pvt) WIA.
Lawrence, Thomas R. (Pvt)
Lawson, Everette R. (Pvt) Evacuated to hospital.
Leach, John W. (Pvt)
LeRoy, Jack C. (Pvt)
Levey, Benjamin (Cpl)

Lewis, Alban B. (Pvt)
Lewis, Graham M. (Pvt)
Lindgren, Edward E. (Cpl) Company Clerk.
Lomas, Norman S. (Pvt) Marine Corps Reserve.
Long, Albert W. (Pvt) WIA, Died of Wounds.
Louys, George C. (Cpl) MIA.
Lowe, Herman H. (Cpl) WIA.
Loy, Emmett (Pvt)
Luce, George W. (Pvt) Died of Wounds, 6 June 1918.
Luttrell, William E. (Pvt) Evacuated to hospital.
Lyng, Arthur E. (GySgt)
Lyon, Harry T. (Cpl) KIA, 6 June 1918.
MacMurray, John W. (Pvt)
Magill, Gerald P. (Cpl) KIA, 3 November 1918.
Martin, Charles R. (Pvt) WIA.
Martin, Clarence G. (Pvt)
Marx, Henry J. (Pvt)
Mason, Charles H. (Pvt)
Matson, Ben (Pvt)
Matt, James S. (Pvt) WIA.
Mattz, Herman (Pvt) KIA, 6 June 1918.
McAuliffe, Thomas C. (Cpl) WIA.
McBride, Arthur (Pvt)
McBroom, Walter H. (Pvt)
McClellan, Herbert C. (Pvt)
McClure, James E. (Pvt)
McCullah, Joseph C. (Pvt)
McDonald, Clyde A. (Pvt)
McDowell, Carl (Pvt)
McFarland, Charles E. (Sgt) WIA.
McGarry, John A. (Pvt)
McGraw, Charles J. (Pvt)
  WIA, Died of Wounds.
McGrew, Edgar C. (Pvt)
McGuckin, James A. (Pvt) KIA.
McManus, Thomas J. (Pvt)
McMillin, Janness C. (Pvt) WIA.
McMurtrie, Alley L. (Pvt)
McSweeney, Gerard F. (Pvt)
Meighen, Thomas V. (Pvt) Died from wounds, 19 October 1918.
Meinberg, Charles W. (Pvt)
Melburg, Elliott M. (Pvt)
Meyer, Clarence F. (Pvt)
Miles, Joseph M. (Pvt)
Miller, Floyd D. (Sgt)
Miller, Thomas A. (Pvt) Reserve, WIA, 4 October 1918.
Millsap, Mac C. (Pvt)
Miszkelis, Joseph (Pvt)
Mitchell, Earl (Pvt)
Mixon, Joseph W. (PFC)
Moffett, Robert G. (Pvt)
Morgan, Frank L. (Pvt)
Morgan, Robert D. (Cpl) KIA, 6 June 1918.
Morton, Clarence G. (Pvt) Reserve, WIA.
Mosby, Ira (Pvt)
Mrha, Rudolph A. (Pvt) Reserve.
Mullin, Samuel C. (Pvt)
Munney, Robert (Pvt) WIA.
Murphy, Arthur R. (Pvt)

Murphy, John F. (Pvt)
Myers, Fred (Cpl)
Myers, Robert H. (Pvt)
Naples, John S. (Cpl)
Neff, Eugene (Pvt)
Nelson, Allen R. (Cpl) MIA.
Nelson, Victor (Pvt)
Nice, William F. (Sgt)
Niersheimer, Walter E. (Pvt)
Norton, Wilbert H. (Pvt)
Nowak, Ignatius F. (Pvt) In hospital.
Nuttle, Harold D. (Pvt) In hospital.
O'Brien, William (Cpl)
O'Connor, Barney J. (Pvt)
O'Connor, Charles A. (Sgt) Property Sgt.
O'Neal, William C. (Pvt)
Oneal, William G. (Pvt) In hospital.
O'Neill, James E. (Pvt) Signalman, 2nd Class.
Osborn, John L. (Pvt)
Overstreet, Thomas P. (Pvt)
Paasch, Albert L. (Pvt)
Parker, John (Pvt)
Patnode, Nelson E. (Cpl)
Patterson, Everett P. (Pvt) Reserve.
Patterson, George (Pvt)
Pelham, James S. (Pvt)
Penney, Henry (Pvt)
Perkins, Earl F. (Pvt) WIA.
Perkins, James F. (Sgt) WIA.
Perkins, Marlin (Pvt)
Pitzer, Lee (Pvt)
Plummer, Lawrence M. (Pvt) WIA.
Pol, Cornelius (Pvt)
Posnak, William (Cpl)
Potter, Guy I. (Pvt)
Prawat, Bert E. (Pvt)
Price, Harrison E. (Pvt)
Proctor, David E. (Pvt) KIA, 6 June 1918.
Putnam, James B. (Pvt) Reserve, WIA.
Racey, Forrest N. (Pvt)
Rahm, Carl J. (Pvt) Reserve, WIA.
Ravenscroft, William J. (Pvt) Reserve, in hospital.
Reader, Arnold M. (Pvt) t
Reed, Clarence H. (Pvt)
Reid, Harold W. (Pvt) WIA.
Reilly, William L. (Cpl) Reserve.
Reister, Benjamin F. (Cpl) Died from wounds.
Renold, Carl E. (Pvt)
Rhodes, Armour A. (Pvt)
Ricks, Henry A. (Pvt)
Rieg, John (Pvt)
Riester, Benjamin F. (Pvt)
Rigsbee, Charles H. (Pvt)
Riley, Francis M. (Pvt)
Ritchey, Marshall (Pvt)
Ritter, John (Pvt)
Robbins, Duane H. (Cpl)
Rodgers, Ralph (Pvt)
Roff, Claude F. (Pvt)
Rogers, John A. (Pvt)
Roper, William A. (Pvt)

Ross, Stanley I. (Pvt)
Roth, John S. (Pvt)
Rourke, Thomas J. (Pvt) WIA.
Rowan, Harold W. (Pvt)
Rowland, Charles N. (Pvt) WIA.
Runyan, George H. (Pvt)
Runyard, Alonza R. (Pvt)
Russell, Arthur (Sgt)
St. Louis, Roland G. (Sgt) KIA, 19 July 1918.
Samaritan, Frank (Pvt)
Sanders, Dewey A. (Pvt)
Satterlee, L.V. (Pvt)
Satterlund, Sabin E. (Pvt)
Saul, Robert A. (Pvt) Reserve.
Schall, James S. (Pvt)
Schlumpberger, Alvin H. (Pvt) KIA, 20 June 1918.
Schmitz, John H. (Pvt) Reserve.
Schreiber, Walter T. (Pvt) Reserve.
Schroeder, Frank W. (Cpl) Reserve.
Schultz, Adolph C. (Pvt) WIA.
Schwald, Charles F. (PFC)
Schwarz, Bernard R. (Cpl)
Secoll, Myer (Pvt) Reserve.
Sedberry, John M. (Pvt)
Shaffery, William J. (Pvt)
Shanahan, James J. (Pvt) In hospital.
Sharpe, Maurice P. (Pvt) In hospital.
Sheeley, Leslie T. (Pvt)
Shepherd, Charles D. (Pvt) Nat'l Naval Volunteer.
Sheridan, Elbert E. (Pvt)
Sies, Harry J. (Pvt) In hospital.
Simpson, Thomas J. (Pvt) In hospital.
Sims, Sitman W. (Pvt)
Slife, Douglas M. (Pvt) In hospital.
Slover, Pleasant (Pvt)
Slover, Robert (Cpl)
Smith, Arthur B. (Pvt)
Smith, Clarence L. (Pvt)
Smith, Dewey F. (Pvt)
Smith, Earl C. (Pvt)
Smith, Earl O. (Pvt)
Smith, Frank G. (Pvt)
Smith, Harold B. (Pvt)
Smith, Walter H. (Pvt)
Snair, Bernard W. (Cpl) KIA, 18 July 1918.
Snair, Carl L. (Pvt)
Snyder, Emanuel F. (Pvt)
Snyder, Milo D. (Pvt)
Solarek, Frank J. (Pvt)
Southard, Samuel W. (Pvt) KIA.
Spence, Rossor E. (PFC)
Spencer, George L. (Trumpeter)
Sperry, Charles V. (Pvt)
Sprock, Howard M. (Pvt)
Stafford, Raymond S. (Cpl)
Stahl, Chalmer (Trumpeter)
Stahl, John J. (Sgt) Mess Sgt.
Stall, Richard J. (Pvt)
Stansberry, Luke (Pvt)
Steinkamp, Charles W. (Pvt) KIA, 20 June 1918.
Stephen, Robert A. (Cpl)

Stolipher, Emory R. (Pvt) Reserve.
Stubblefield, Earl V. (Pvt)
Swindler, Harold F. (GySgt)
Talbot, Shelby M. (Pvt) Reserve.
Tarlton, Raymond J. (Sgt) WIA.
Tartikoff, David (Pvt)
Taylor, Ernest J. (Pvt)
Taylor, Guss L. (Pvt)
Tenley, Eugene H. (HAp1) KIA, 4 October 1918.
Teuscher, William (Pvt) In hospital.
Tharalson, Benjamin W. (Pvt)
Thomas, David (Pvt) Reserve.
Thompson, George F. (Pvt) Reserve.
Thornsberry, Charles A. (Pvt)
Timmons, Chesley A. (Pvt)
Tollefson, Roy W. (Pvt) WIA.
Tompkins, Jessie G. (Pvt)
Tompkins, Wilbert N. (Pvt) Reserve, died, 4 October 1918.
Toulson, Joseph C. (Cpl) KIA, 6 June 1918.
Trankle, George (Pvt) WIA.
Tritt, Walter J. (Pvt) Died of Wounds, 18 July 1918.
Tucker, John W. (Cpl)
Tucker, Willie T. (Pvt)
Turnbow, Asmond (Pvt)
Turnor, Horace P. (Pvt)
Valentine, William C. (Pvt)
Vallon, Daniel (Pvt) Nat'l Naval Volunteer.
Van Galder, Edwin S. (Sgt)
Van Tassel, Fred (Pvt)
Van Train, William A. (Cpl)
Vedder, Rudolph A. (Pvt) Reserve.
Vertrees, Richard L. (Pvt)
Vest, Herbert McK. (Cpl)
Vestre, Willard E. (Pvt) KIA.
Vitale, Charles (Pvt) In hospital.
Vowels, Homer R. (Pvt) Reserve.
Wagner, William W. (Sgt)
Wainwright, William (Pvt)
Waiss, Fred A. (Pvt)
Waldraff, Howard D. (Pvt)
Walker, Uzell D. (Pvt)
Ware, Arthur F. (Sgt) KIA, 6 June 1918.
Wartham, Bryan M. (Pvt)
Watkins, Joe B. (Pvt)
Watson, James C. (Pvt) Reserve, WIA.
Watson, Marvin (Pvt) Cook, 3rd Class.
Wear, Eugene W. (Sgt) WIA, died of Wounds, 26 December 1918.
Webber, Michael P. (Pvt)
Webster, Fred W. (Pvt) WIA.
Weisbaker, Alfred E. (Pvt) KIA, 5 June 1918.
Wells, Charles E. (Pvt) WIA.
Wells, Harry E. (Cpl) MIA.
Weltz, Nathan (Pvt)
West, Alfred T. (Pvt) Reserve.
West, Raymond P. (Pvt)
Wetzell, George (Pvt)
White, Thomas J. (Pvt)
Wilkins, Walter D. (Pvt) WIA.
Williams, Francis E. (Cpl)

Williams, George E. (Pvt) KIA, 8 June 1918.
Williams, Perry A. (Pvt)
Wilson, Herman O. (GySgt) Died from wounds, 6 October 1918.
Wilson, Ray H. (Cpl)
Wilson, Raymond H. (Pvt) WIA.
Wilson, Robert L. (Cpl) MIA.
Winston, John W. (Pvt)
Wistrand, Ernest F. (Pvt) Reserve.
Witbeck, Alden M. (Pvt) KIA, 18 July 1918.
Wolf, Harry D. (Pvt)
Womack, Ernest F. (Pvt)
Wood, George H. (Pvt) Cook, 1st Class.
Wood, Jack J. (Trumpeter)
Woodle, Loren H. (Pvt)
Woodward, Henry T. (Cpl) WIA.
Workman, Harold A. (Pvt)
Wyss, Alfons J. (Pvt) Reserve.
Yager, Frank R. (Pvt)
Yensen, Christen B. (Pvt) Cook, 4th Class.
Zebre, Frank (Pvt)
Zeller, William G. (Pvt)

66th (C) Company, First Battalion

NAME (RANK) REMARKS

Blake, Robert (Cpt) CO, "C" Co.
Crabbe, William L. (Cpt) Company Commander.
Dirksen, Raymond R. (Cpt) WIA.
Gilfillan, Max D. (Cpt) WIA.
Thomason, John W., Jr. (Cpt)
Anthony, Robert C. (1st Lt)
Fleming, Hamilton, M.H. (1st Lt)
Godbey, Arnold D. (1st Lt) Battalion Intelligence Officer
Kelly, Francis J., Jr. (1st Lt)
Robinson, Ralph R. (1st Lt)
Sanderson, Richard O. (1st Lt)
Applegate, Chauncy H. (2nd Lt)
Bender, Daniel W. (2nd Lt) Gas Officer.
Corbett, Murl (2nd Lt) WIA.
Driscoll, Joseph F. (2nd Lt)
Giffels, Louis J. (2nd Lt)
Gilfilian, Max D. (2nd Lt)
Hulbert, Henry L. (2nd Lt) KIA, 4 October 1918.
McClain, Dave W. (2nd Lt) Reserve, Died of Wounds, 5 October 1918.
Moneypenny, Edward J. (2nd Lt)
Pitts, Robert C. (2nd Lt)
Rea, Leonard E. (2nd Lt) WIA.
Ross, Richard S. (2nd Lt) WIA.
Scott, Marvin (2nd Lt)
Thomas, Fred (2nd Lt)
Whitney, Harold W. (2nd Lt) Marine Corps Reserve.

Enlisted

Boone, William S. (SGM)
Carlson, John O. (1st Sgt)

McNulty, Thomas J. (1st Sgt) WIA.
Aarons, Morris A. (Pvt)
Airey, Ralph K. (Pvt) WIA.
Aldrich, George H. (Pvt)
Alexander, Orla C. (Pvt)
Allen, Joseph E. (Pvt) Reserve.
Anderson, Joseph L. (Pvt) KIA, 6 June 1818.
Anselm, William B. (PFC)
Anton, Cornelius (Cpl)
Armstrong, Eldon L. (Pvt) KIA, 4 October 1918.
Arnett, Thomas P. (Sgt) KIA, 6 June 1918.
Arnold, Sebren L. (Pvt)
Aschenbrenner, Joseph F. (Cpl)
Asprooth, Oscar M. (Pvt)
Atkins, Lonzele (Pvt)
Austin, Paul (Pvt) Messman.
Baccenelli, Ernest L. (Pvt) Nat'l Naval Volunteer.
Backer, Earl D. (Pvt)
Bailey, Edmond I. (Pvt)
Baker, Earl N. (Pvt)
Baker, Frank E. (Pvt) Reserve, WIA.
Baker, Harry I. (Sgt)
Baker, Roney S. (Pvt)
Ballou, Lawson (Pvt)
Banker, Marrion E. (Pvt)
Barnett, Stanley F. (Pvt) WIA.
Bartholomay, Henry (Pvt)
Baxley, Johnnie K. (Pvt)
Bayles, Raymond (Cpl) Shell shocked.
Bayman, Edward T. (GySgt)
Beach, Duncan J. (Pvt)
Beck, William R. (Pvt)
Beeman, Reitz F. (Pvt) WIA.
Bell, Jesse J. (GySgt) KIA, 5 November 1918.
Benson, Rodger W. (Pvt)
Bentzel, Paul M. (Pvt) Messman.
Bergerom, Calvin (Cpl) MIA, KIA, 4 October 1918.
Bevis, George W. (Pvt)
Bickley, John B. (Pvt)
Billman, George L. (Pvt)
Bishop, Otto R. (Pvt)
Blasco, Steven (Pvt)
Boaz, Fred O. (Pvt)
Bobovnyk, John A. (Cpl) WIA.
Boland, Leon J. (Pvt) MIA.
Bovee, Samuel A. (Pvt)
Bowers, Lawrence (Pvt)
Bradford, Algie D. (Cpl) MIA.
Bradshaw, Charles P. (Pvt)
Brennan, Eugene (Pvt) MIA.
Brennan, Michael G. (Pvt)
Brennan, William N. (Pvt)
Briesemeister, William (Pvt)
Brosseau, Paul A. (Pvt) KIA, 18 July 1918.
Brotherton, Walter (Pvt)
Brown, George W. (Pvt) WIA.
Brown, John E. (Pvt)
Buch, Harry (Sgt)
Buckley, Gerald T. (Pvt)
Burke, Herman L. (Pvt)
Burke, John C. (Pvt)

Burns, James J. (Pvt)
Burns, Oscar L. (Pvt)
Burns, Warren G. (Pvt)
Bynum, Joseph H. (Sgt)
Cadman, Seth C. (Pvt)
Callaway, Richard (Cpl)
Cameron, Clifford A. (Pvt)
Campbell, Charles R. (Pvt)
Campbell, Earl (Pvt) Sprained ankle.
Capps, James A. (Pvt)
Carpenter, Stanley D. (Pvt)
Carroll, Clarence E. (Pvt)
Carter, Jesse M. (Cpl)
Cartwright, George, Jr. (Cpl)
Caven, Robert M. (Pvt) WIA.
Caviness, William B. (Pvt)
Centner, Earle W. (Pvt)
Chandler, Allen (Pvt)
Chapman, George W. (Pvt) Mounted Orderly.
Chapman, Howard (Pvt)
Chartier, Louis E. (Pvt)
Chirdon, Clyde P. (Pvt)
Christie, Alexander (Pvt) Shell shocked.
Clark, Glen H. (Pvt)
Clarke, Bert (Cpl) Nat'l Naval Volunteer.
Clendenin, Kemp C. (Pvt) Wounded by accident.
Clingman, Harry L. (Pvt) Reserve, WIA.
Coats, Edward N. (Pvt)
Cochrane, Samuel R. (Pvt) Cook, 3rd Class.
Coffee, Joseph C. (PhM3)
Cole, Howard W. (Pvt)
Colehower, Horace T. (Pvt)
Coleman, William (Cpl)
Colliflower, Owen (Pvt)
Collins, Alfred B. (Sgt)
Colony, Alfred T. (Pvt)
Columbus, Ernest P. (Pvt)
Conaway, Hugh L. (Pvt)
Congdon, Sherry E. (PFC)
Connelly, Edward F. (Sgt) WIA.
Connolly, William E. (Sgt) Co Gas NCO.
Conrad, Grover C. (GySgt)
Cook, John A. (Pvt)
Cooper, Walter C. (Pvt)
Corrigan, John J. (Pvt) MIA.
Cowgill, Carl F. (Pvt)
Cowsert, Lewis T. (Pvt)
Cox, James McG. (Pvt) MIA.
Crane, Walter A. (Pvt) WIA.
Crawford, Lee H. (Pvt)
Crockett, Bert L. (Pvt) Reserve, WIA.
Crosta, James H. (Pvt)
Crowe, Morris E. (Cpl)
Crowe, Raymond J. (Pvt) MIA.
Cukela, Louis (Sgt)
Custock, Stephen A. (Pvt) Signalman, 1st Class.
Daniels, Silas A. (Cpl)
Davis, Cleo B. (Cpl)
Davis, Homer H. (Pvt) WIA.
Davis, Joseph H. (Pvt)
Davis, Lester L. (Cpl)

Decker, Roy W. (Sgt)
Degnan, John (Pvt)
Delaney, William H. (Pvt) Reserve, WIA.
DeMaio, John J. (Pvt)
Demarest, Walter E. (Cpl)
DeMott, Harry (Pvt) Messman.
Dick, George F. (Pvt)
Dodge, Chester E. (Pvt)
Donnell, William H. (Pvt)
Donnelly, Clarence W. (Pvt)
Donnerfeld, Samuel B. (Pvt) WIA.
Dotson, Elmer H. (Pvt) Gassed.
Dowling, Harold J. (Pvt)
Draughon, Robert W. (Pvt)
Drury, Albert B. (Pvt)
Dunipace, Harold M. (Cpl)
Dunn, Joshua D. (Cpl)
Eades, James E. (Pvt) Reserve, WIA.
Earley, August W. (Pvt)
Easley, Austin K. (Pvt) Reserve.
Edder, George W. (Pvt)
Edwards, Walter R. (Pvt)
Elliott, Paul C. (Pvt)
Ellis, Edward L. (Cpl)
Eskridge, John H. (Pvt) WIA.
Falkner, Murray G., Jr. (Pvt)
Fallon, Edward B. (Pvt)
Feigle, William M. (Pvt) Regt'l. Auto Driver.
Ferguson, Charles H. (Pvt)
Feriend, Lester L. (Pvt)
Ferrin, George C. (Pvt)
Fisher, Ernest A. (Pvt)
Fleeger, John W. (Pvt)
Flynn, James E. (Pvt) Messman.
Fontenot, Hampton (Pvt)
Ford, Myron F. (Pvt)
Forrester, Pairres J. (Pvt)
Forst, Solomon (Pvt)
Forsyth, Guy H. (Pvt) WIA.
Fort, Robert G. (Pvt) WIA.
Foster, Louis G. (Pvt) Reserve.
Foster, Paul E. (Pvt)
Francis, Max M. (Pvt) Reserve.
Francisco, Dwight W. (Cpl) Reserve.
Francisco, Harold (Pvt)
Frank, Jacob (GySgt) WIA.
Frantz, Lewis G. (Pvt)
Freeman, Lawson J. (Pvt)
Frost, David H. (Pvt)
Fuller, Irving W. (Sgt)
Fuqua, Claude (Pvt) Signalman, 2nd Class, KIA, 6
    June 1918.
Gallagher, Charles (Cpl) Company Clerk.
Gallagher, Herbert (Pvt) Messman.
Galvin, Owen P. (Pvt)
Gates, Bruce H. (Cpl)
Gaughran, George J.M. (Pvt)
Gaynor, William F. (Pvt)
George, Daniel W. (Pvt)
Gerage, Anthony (Pvt) MIA.
Gideon, William C. (Pvt)

Gillis, Francis J. (Pvt)
Gittings, Philip S. (Pvt)
Given, Raymond N. (Pvt) MIA, KIA.
Gladhill, Charles H. (Pvt) Gassed.
Golden, David (Sgt)
Goldworm, Jack (Pvt)
Goodwin, Warren (Cpl) WIA.
Gorin, Meyer E. (Pvt)
Gosney, Terrence I. (Pvt)
Gourley, Robert C. (Pvt) Died of Wounds, 8 June 1918.
Gowan, John H. (Pvt)
Grady, John D. (Pvt)
Graham, Manning L. (Pvt) Reserve.
Graves, Harvey C. (Pvt)
Grayson, Edley H. (Pvt) Gassed.
Green, Walter M. (Pvt) Gassed.
Greene, Enach F., Jr. (Cpl) WIA.
Gregory, Frank A. (Pvt)
Grisinger, Harrison M. (Pvt) WIA.
Gross, Bayard T. (Cpl)
Gruber, Augustas L. (Pvt) WIA.
Guidry, Walter J. (Pvt)
Gupton, Phillip L. (Pvt)
Guthrey, Casey G. (Cpl)
Haas, Louis C. (Pvt)
Haasis, Charles L. (Cpl) Nat'l Naval Volunteer.
Hachten, George C. (Pvt) WIA.
Hadley, Norman F. (Pvt) Marine Corps Reserve.
Haig, Russel J. (Pvt)
Hall, Leonard D. (Pvt)
Hall, Raymond S. (Pvt) Died of Wounds, 4 October
    1918.
Hall, William (Pvt)
Hammit, Mathew B. (Pvt)
Hampton, George E. (Sgt)
Hand, John (Drummer)
Handle, Clarence A. (Pvt)
Harding, Willard G. (Cpl)
Harper, Carey E. (Pvt)
Harrington, Steven J. (Pvt)
Harris, Leslie J. (Trumpeter)
Harris, Ralph C. (Pvt) Cook, 2nd Cook.
Harris, Wiley A. (Pvt) WIA.
Harsch, Joseph J. (Pvt) KIA, 5 October 1918.
Hartman, Clyde (Pvt)
Hawkins, Elmer J. (Pvt) Gassed.
Hawkins, William A. (Pvt)
Haynes, James A. (Pvt)
Healey, Edward F. (Pvt)
Heath, Donald L. (Pvt)
Heismann, Walter E.L. (Pvt)
Heller, Florian F. (Pvt)
Helwig, Charles H. (Sgt) Mess Sgt.
Henebury, Wilfred P. (Pvt)
Henkhaus, Henry E. (Pvt)
Henry, Curtis L. (Pvt) KIA, 18 July 1918.
Henshaw, Burton H. (Pvt) WIA.
Herzog, Albert E. (Cpl)
Hicks, John B. (Pvt)
Hilderbran, Hartwell F. (Pvt)
Hillebrandt, Clarence M. (Pvt)

Hirth, Alfred C. (Pvt)
Hobbs, Harry G. (Pvt) Messman.
Hockenberry, Ellis C. (Pvt)
Hoffman, Edward C. (Pvt)
Holiday, George G. (Pvt)
Holland, William L. (Pvt)
Hollaway, Ross (Pvt)
Holt, Fred (Pvt)
Holtz, John W. (Pvt) Reserve, KIA, 4 October 1918.
Hood, Charles B. (Pvt) Reserve, KIA.
Horgan, Roy L. (Pvt)
Hoy, Lawrence G. (Pvt)
Hudson, Howard (Cpl)
Hymel, Edgar J. (Pvt)
Jackson, William O. (Cpl)
Jacoby, Harry (Pvt)
Jamieson, Roland R. (PhM) KIA.
Joerger, Caspar J., Jr. (Pvt) Reserve.
Johnsen, Hans (Cpl) WIA.
Johnson, Elmer (Pvt) Reserve, WIA.
Johnson, Homer H. (PFC)
Johnson, Joe W. (Pvt) Reserve.
Jones, Daniel S. (Pvt)
Jones, Dewey J. (Pvt) WIA, Died of Wounds, 4 October 1918.
Jones, John T. (Pvt) WIA.
Jones, Ralph P. (Cpl)
Jones, Samuel S. (Pvt)
Joyner, Raymond S. (Pvt)
Kavanaugh, John W. (Pvt)
Keesee, Wallace B. (Cpl)
Kellum, Leon A. (Trumpeter)
Kelly, James P. (Sgt)
Kenuth, Charles E. (Pvt) Reserve, WIA.
Kerner, Eustis L. (Pvt)
Kerwin, Oliver M. (Pvt)
Kieffer, Arthur L., Jr. (Cpl)
Klamm, John L. (Pvt)
Klein, Joseph W. (Pvt)
Knight, Floyd C. (Sgt)
Knoblow, James L. (Sgt)
Kocak, Matej (Sgt) KIA, 4 October 1918.
Kopp, Louis G. (Cpl) WIA.
Kosturos, George S. (PFC)
Kron, Raymond F. (Pvt) Gassed.
Kunsemiller, Henry J. (Pvt) WIA.
Lancaster, Ralph L. (Pvt)
Law, Robert (Pvt)
LeBlanc, Frank (Pvt)
Lending, Theodore (Pvt)
Leontich, Antonio (Pvt) Nat'l Naval Volunteer.
Lewin, Eugene (HAp2)
Lewis, Bruce (Pvt)
Lind, Carl M. (Pvt)
Linder, Clarence H. (Pvt) Reserve.
Lloyd, Charles J. (Pvt)
Lowe, James M. (Pvt) Reserve, accident.
Lowry, Brents M. (Pvt)
Luttig, Fred (Pvt)
Lyttaker, Edward F. (Pvt) Reserve, WIA.
Mackinzie, John (Pvt)

Maden, Edward (Cpl)
Major, Edward J. (Pvt) Reserve.
Marriott, Chester M. (Pvt)
Marrone, Joseph (Pvt)
Marsh, Claire C. (Pvt)
Marsh, Clinton (Pvt)
Marth, Frederick A. (Cpl)
Mason, Wesley M. (Pvt)
Mathis, George J. (Pvt)
Maxwell, Leonard McK. (Pvt)
Mays, Alfred (Pvt) Messman.
Mays, Marion (Cpl)
McAllister, Deane J. (Pvt) Reserve.
McCabe, John C. (Sgt) MIA, KIA.
McCarthy, Herbert E. (Pvt)
McCarthy, Thomas A. (Pvt)
McCarty, Joseph E. (Pvt)
McClure, Jesse W. (Sgt)
McCracken, Arnold W. (Pvt)
McCreary, Harry C. (Pvt) Reserve.
McDowell, Irwin B. (Sgt) KIA, 6 November 1918.
McElroy, George C. (Pvt) KIA, 6 June 1918.
McIntyre, Clifton N. (Pvt) KIA.
McLaughlin, Joseph C. (Pvt)
McMichael, Stanley L. (Pvt) Reserve.
McNulty, James (Pvt) Messman.
Mercer, Ellsworth E. (Pvt) Reserve.
Meserole, Theodore C. (Pvt) Gassed.
Messanelle, Ray A. (PhM2)
Metzger, John A. (Pvt)
Michalski, John F. (Pvt) Reserve, in hospital.
Michalsky, Frank J. (Pvt) KIA, 4 October 1918.
Miller, John A. (Pvt) Reserve.
Millington, Fred M. (Pvt)
Milton, Henry R. (Pvt)
Moloski, Browny L. (Pvt)
Monagan, George C. (Pvt)
Mooney, Thomas (Pvt) Messman.
Moore, Williamson G., Jr. (Pvt)
Morgan, Arthur R. (Pvt) KIA, 10 November 1918.
Morgan, Francis J. (Pvt)
Mortensen, Ove E. (Pvt)
Mullinix, Layfatte (Pvt) Cook, 4th Class
Muns, Willie F. (Pvt) Messman.
Murphy, Arthur M. (Pvt)
Musolf, Edward J. (Pvt)
Nagle, Garry (Pvt)
Neail, Willis A. (Pvt)
Nicholson, Oscar E. (Pvt)
Nickel, Victor R. (Pvt)
Nigg, Casimir L. (Pvt)
Nolen, George W. (Sgt)
North, James F. (Sgt) WIA.
O'Bryan, Peter C. (Pvt)
Oelschlaeger, Edward E. (Cpl)
Oldroyd, Harold J. (Pvt)
O'Neill, John F. (Pvt)
Parker, Monroe S. (Cpl)
Parrett, Russell A. (Pvt)
Passmore, William F. (Pvt)
Patterson, Andrew A. (Pvt)

Patterson, Isom L. (Pvt)
Peco, Benjamin (Pvt)
Peeler, Benjamin A. (Pvt)
Pence, Thurston (Pvt) Reserve.
Perkins, William F. (Pvt)
Perry, Leon (Sgt) WIA.
Pike, Arthur (PFC)
Piskey, Anthony L. (Sgt)
Ponsar, Albert (Cpl) WIA.
Porter, Richard E. (Pvt)
Potter, Leon, R. (Pvt) Reserve.
Powell, Edward R. (Pvt)
Powis, Albert E. (Pvt) Cook, 4th Class.
Pruitt, Leonard P. (Pvt)
Pruno, Elmer (Pvt)
Pryde, John M. (Pvt)
Pyott, Russell P. (Pvt)
Rabet, George F. (Pvt)
Ranney, Glenn B. (Pvt)
Raphael, Orio V. (Pvt)
Raschke, Otto A. (Sgt) Mess Sgt.
Ratliff, George F. (Pvt) Cook. 1st Class.
Ream, Lynn (Pvt)
Reed, Elmer H. (Pvt)
Reed, Luther A. (Pvt)
Reever, Walter A. (Pvt)
Rhodes, Clarence B. (Cpl)
Richards, Paul (Pvt) Messman.
Richeson, Welby P. (Pvt)
Riker, Harry (Pvt) KIA, 18 July 1918.
Rindal, Arnold B. (Pvt)
Rivers, Norman R. (PFC)
Roark, Thurman B. (Pvt)
Roche, Edward C. (Pvt)
Rogoski, Charles (Pvt) Reserve, WIA.
Roop, Joseph W. (Pvt) WIA.
Rosenberg, Harvey G. (Pvt)
Rosenthal, Saul E. (Pvt) Died of Wounds.
Rowley, Richard M. (Cpl)
Rowold, Horace E. (Pvt)
Rudquist, Paul L. (Pvt) Cook, 3rd Class.
Sanders, Frank M. (Pvt)
Sanford, Jewell B. (Pvt)
Sawyer, John E. (Pvt) WIA.
Sayles, Claude E. (Pvt) KIA, 6 June 1918.
Schenk, Ray R. (Cpl) Wounded by gunshot.
Schilling, Edward C. (Pvt)
Schlum, Vincent A. (Pvt)
Schmitt, Cecil (Cpl) WIA.
Schneggenburger, John A. (Pvt)
Schorr, John A. (Pvt)
Schulze, George E. (Cpl)
Scott, John J. (Cpl)
Scott, William G. (Pvt)
Scroggs, James P. (Cpl)
Seselja, John (Cpl) Reserve, WIA.
Sheehan, Jeremiah J. (Pvt)
Shepherd, Wiley F. (Cpl)
Sheridan, Charles D. (Pvt) WIA.
Shield, Alexander R. (Sgt)
Shipley, Francis M. (Cpl)

Shirley, Charles L. (Cpl)
Shomer, Boris (Pvt)
Sickmier, Ernest A.J. (Pvt)
Simpson, Edward K. (Sgt)
Singleton, Roy E. (Pvt)
Slafter, Orren E. (Pvt) WIA.
Smead, Donald (Pvt)
Smith, Earl (GySgt)
Smith, Edward J.E. (Pvt) Messman, KIA, 10 November 1918.
Smith, Guy B. (Sgt) WIA.
Smith, Henry K. (Cpl)
Smith, Kenneth S. (Pvt)
Smith, Kirby R. (Pvt) KIA.
Sommers, Henry W. (Pvt)
Sommers, Marvin S. (Pvt)
Stearns, Martin L. (Pvt)
Stephens, Byron G. (Pvt)
Stephens, Roy W. (Pvt) WIA.
Stephens, Sam M. (Pvt)
Stone, Raymond O. (CPhM)
Strauss, Abe (Pvt)
Streeter, Ervin (Pvt)
Sussmilch, Don E. (Cpl) WIA.
Swartz, Edward B. (Pvt) WIA.
Taubert, Albert A. (Cpl)
Taylor, Albert L. (PFC) KIA, 10 November 1918.
Thieme, Robert L. (Cpl)
Thomas, William R. (Pvt) Gassed.
Thompson, Acors R. (Pvt)
Thompson, Fletcher W. (Pvt) Reserve.
Thompson, Howard J. (Pvt)
Thompson, William H. (Pvt)
Tinley, Bradford O. (Cpl)
Tintera, Louis (Pvt)
Tolle, Fred H. (Pvt)
Trigg, Raymond J. (Pvt)
Tronsar, Frank (Pvt)
Turbeville, Robert E. (Sgt)
Turner, John R. (Pvt)
Uhlitz, Harry P. (Pvt)
Updegraff, Charles J. (Cpl)
Van Dyke, Thomas J. (Pvt)
Van Vorhees, Alfred (Pvt)
Van Wicklin, Edward R. (Pvt)
Vercillo, Peter J. (Pvt)
Vernon, Jerome C. (Pvt) WIA.
Vogel, James J. (Cpl)
Von Lumm, William (GySgt) Died of Wounds.
Wade, John (Pvt)
Waliban, Roy E. (Pvt)
Ward, Fred (Pvt) WIA.
Warren, James P. (Pvt)
Webb, William (Pvt)
Weissinger, Rudolph (Pvt)
Weitzell, Joseph (GySgt)
Wells, Elbert (Sgt) Wounded by gunshot.
Welty, Frank G. (PhM2) KIA, 6 June 1918.
Welzel, Charles (Pvt)
Wiberg, Frederick H. (Pvt)
Williams, Owen McK (Pvt)

Williams, Russell L. (Pvt)
Willison, Everett E. (Pvt) Reserve.
Willson, James L. (Pvt)
Wilson, John E. (Pvt) WIA.
Wilson, Leonard J. (Pvt) Reserve.
Wing, Edwin S. (Pvt)
Witt, Frederick (Pvt)
Wood, Clarence L. (Pvt)
Wood, Emory S. (Pvt)
Woods, John G. (Pvt)
Woodward, George R. (Pvt)
Wright, Samuel O. (Pvt)
Wrigley, James F. (Pvt) Died of pneumonia.
Yeaton, Guy M. (Sgt) KIA.
Yoakam, Bernard (Pvt)
Young, Henry (Pvt)
Zeemin, John (Cpl)
Zimmerman, Virgil M. (Cpl) Company Clerk.

67th (D) Company, First Battalion

Name (Rank) Remarks

Cochran, Harry K. (Cpt) CO, "D" Company.
Dirkenson, Raymond F. (Cpt) Co Commander.
Keller, E. Rockey (Cpt) 1–31 May, Acting Adjt., 1st Bn.
Morse, Edmund H. (Cpt)
Whitehead, Frank (Cpt) Nat'l Naval Volunteer, WIA.
Beauchamp, Felix (1st Lt) Nat'l Naval Volunteer, WIA.
Crowther, Orlander C. (1st Lt.) Commanding Co., KIA, 6 June 1918.
Ferch, Aaron J. (1st Lt) KIA, 1 November 1918.
Johnson, Lester D. (1st Lt) WIA.
Ashley, Thomas W. (2nd Lt) KIA, 6 June 1918.
Bayman, Edward T. (2nd Lt)
Goodwin, Thomas A. (2nd Lt)
Gordon, Raymond (2nd Lt) Nat'l Naval Volunteer, WIA.
Kieren, Francis S. (2nd Lt)
Prather, Willis H. (2nd Lt) Nat'l Naval Volunteer.
Rinkevich, Anthony (2nd Lt)
Schubert, Richard H. (2nd Lt)
Thompson, Claude (2nd Lt) Nat'l Naval Volunteer, WIA.

Enlisted

Hunter, Daniel A. (1st Sgt) KIA, 6 June 1918.
Keag, Andrew (1st Sgt)
Abbott, Israel (Pvt) Nat'l Naval Volunteer, MIA.
Acuff, Robert E. (Cpl)
Agin, Lambert (Pvt)
Aitken, Malcolm D. (Pvt)
Akins, Patrick H. (Pvt) Marine Reserve.
Allen, Lon C. (Pvt)
Allen, Raphael C. (Pvt)
Altman, George W. (Pvt)
Ameling, William J. (Cpl)
Anderson, Arthur (Cpl)

Anderson, Fred W. (Pvt)
Anderson, Oliver O. (Pvt) Nat'l Naval Volunteer.
Anderson, Otmer O. (Cpl)
Anderson, William (Pvt)
Anthony, Harrison R. (Trumpeter)
Archer, Edgar F. (Cpl) Nat'l Naval Volunteer, WIA.
Argraves, Clyde I. (Pvt)
Armsey, Edgar S. (Pvt) Nat'l Naval Volunteer.
Atha, Thomas R. (Pvt)
Atkinson, Frank C. (Pvt)
Atkinson, William E. (Pvt)
Austin, Carl M. (PFC)
Bailey, Lazard (Cpl)
Baker, Joseph M. (Pvt)
Baker, Walter J. (Cpl) Nat'l Naval Volunteer, WIA.
Baldwin, Raymond H. (Pvt) Marine Reserve.
Balestriri, Peter (Pvt)
Barcus, Jesse (Cpl)
Barnes, John E. (Pvt)
Bazemore, Jackson F. (Pvt)
Beck, Robert (Pvt)
Becker, Bryan (Pvt) Nat'l Naval Volunteer, WIA.
Bell, Robert L. (Pvt)
Bellman, Ernest L. (Pvt) Cook, 3rd Class.
Bennett, Willis T. (Sgt)
Benson, Carl J. (Pvt)
Berg, Edward (Pvt) Nat'l Naval Volunteer.
Bernard, Rolland (Cpl) Marine Reserve, WIA.
Berry, Charles W. (Pvt)
Bessler, Paul J. (Pvt)
Birr, Alfred S. (Pvt)
Bishop, Robert H. (Pvt) Nat'l Naval Volunteer, WIA.
Blackwood, William D. (Pvt) Marine Reserve.
Blake, Hobart (Pvt) Marine Reserve.
Blake, John R. (PFC) KIA, 6 November 1918.
Blankenship, Richard L. (Cpl)
Bode, William O. (Pvt)
Bohanan, Harry R. (Pvt) KIA, 6 June 1918.
Bokosky, Frank J. (Pvt)
Bosse, Arthur (PFC)
Boterus, Anthony (Pvt)
Bowe, Melvin R. (Pvt) Marine Reserve.
Bowman, Alexander H. (Sgt) Quartermaster Sgt.
Bowman, Charles R. (Pvt) Nat'l Naval Volunteer, WIA.
Bowman, Ernest G. (Pvt) Nat'l Naval Volunteer, WIA.
Bramhall, Clyde H. (Cpl)
Brandau, Fred H. (Pvt) National Naval Volunteer.
Brannon, Rollo F. (Pvt)
Brantley, Beniette H. (Cpl) Nat'l Naval Volunteer, WIA.
Brennan, Francis J. (Pvt)
Brennen, Mortimer J. (Pvt)
Brichta, Edward (Pvt)
Britton, George (Pvt)
Brogdon, John E. (Cpl)
Brown, Edward L. (Cpl)
Brown, Lindsay (Pvt)
Brown, Willard L. (Pvt) Marine Reserve, KIA.
Brown, William C. (Pvt)
Browning, Clarence (Pvt) Nat'l Naval Volunteer.
Bryner, Charles (Cpl)
Buck, Kinsley C. (Pvt) KIA, 6 June 1918.

Burd, Vern V. (Pvt) Nat'l Naval Volunteer, Died of Wounds.
Burgess, John A. (PFC)
Burleigh, Bryan E. (Pvt) Marine Reserve.
Burris, Allen J. (Sgt) Supply Sgt.
Butler, Edward M. (Pvt)
Cain, Olna Y. (Cpl) KIA, 1 November 1918.
Caldwell, Joseph R. (Pvt) Marine Reserve, KIA.
Campbell, Samuel S. (Cpl)
Campbell, William H. (Pvt)
Capodice, Salvador A. (Pvt)
Cardiff, William J. (Pvt) Nat'l Naval Volunteer.
Carpenter, Oliver H. (Pvt) Marine Reserve, WIA.
Carpenter, Walter (Pvt) Nat'l Naval Volunteer, WIA.
Cary, Edwin K. (Pvt)
Case, Harold (Pvt) Nat'l Naval Volunteer, WIA.
Cathey, Daniel O. (Pvt)
Catlett, Harry E. (Pvt) Nat'l Naval Volunteer, WIA.
Challiss, Fred L. (Pvt)
Champion, Andrew (Pvt) Nat'l Naval Volunteer, WIA.
Charles, Ralph J. (Pvt)
Christ, James F. (Pvt)
Christian, Wesley J. (Pvt)
Christie, Harold J. (Pvt) KIA, 6 June 1918, Messman.
Christman, Joseph E. (Pvt) Marine Reserve, KIA.
Churchill, Edward H. (Cpl)
Cihak, Willis (Cpl)
Clark, Frank A. (Pvt)
Clayson, Frederick H. (Pvt)
Clevenger, Eugene (Pvt) Marine Reserve, WIA.
Close, Raymond E. (Cpl) Marine Reserve, WIA.
Cloud, John O. (PFC)
Cochran, Atlas C. (Sgt) Nat'l Naval Volunteer, WIA.
Combs, Charlie R. (Pvt)
Conerly, Thomas T. (Cpl)
Conrad, John G. (Pvt)
Conrad, Lynn H. (Pvt)
Cook, George F. (Pvt)
Cortright, Norman C. (Pvt)
Corwin, Albert F. (Pvt)
Costello, Frank M. (Pvt) Cook, 3rd Class.
Craver, John L. (Sgt)
Crout, Otis D. (Pvt) Marine Reserve, MIA.
Crowell, Truman M. (Pvt)
Cunningham, Bert (Pvt)
Cunningham, Smith (Pvt) Marine Reserve.
Curl, Roy E. (Pvt) Nat'l Naval Volunteer, WIA.
Curtice, Rex (Pvt)
Curtis, Harry (Pvt)
Dailey, Thomas W. (Cpl)
Daley, Lee J. (Pvt)
Daley, Raymond (Pvt)
Daniel, Leslie C. (Pvt)
Darby, Ira (Sgt)
Darmstadt, Edward H. (Cpl)
Davis, Cloyd K. (PFC) Nat'l Naval Volunteer, KIA.
Davis, Joseph M. (Pvt)
Davis, Roy R. (Pvt)
Dean, George P. (Pvt)
Dean, Howard R. (Pvt)
DeArmond, William O. (Pvt) Marine Reserve.

Dears, Frank J. (Pvt)
DeCou, Samuel S., Jr. (Pvt)
Delattre, Julien (Pvt)
Denman, Henry E. (Pvt)
Devaney, Jerome T. (Pvt)
Devlin, Bernard J. (Pvt) KIA, 4 November 1918.
Dibb, Harold J. (Pvt) Marine Reserve, WIA.
Diden, Jacob N. (PFC)
Dietrich, Neff T. (Pvt)
Donaghy, Harry J. (Pvt)
Donohue, James A. (Pvt)
Doriocourt, Charles (Pvt)
Dowdell, William H. (Pvt)
Drennan, Frank A. (Pvt)
Dressel, Edward A. (Pvt)
Drowty, Ray R. (Pvt)
Dudley, William P. (PFC)
Duffen, Harold R. (Pvt)
Duncan, Frank T. (Cpl)
Dutton, Peter W. (Cpl)
Duxbury, George H. (Pvt)
Dwire, William J. (Pvt)
Dyar, Thomas C. (Pvt)
Eagan, William F. (Pvt)
Eager, James H. (Pvt) Marine Reserve, WIA.
Easter, Rodney E. (Pvt) Pvt
Edge, Floyd (Pvt) KIA, 14 June 1918.
Edmunds, Robert A. (Cpl)
Edwards, Crawford W. (Cpl) Marine Reserve.
Egan, William F. (Pvt) Nat'l Naval Volunteer, WIA.
Eichler, Walter J. (Pvt)
Eilers, Henry H. (GySgt) Marine Reserve, KIA, 6 October 1918.
Eklund, Percival A. (Cpl)
Ellis, Harry H. (Cpl)
Epperly, Edgar M. (Pvt) Marine Reserve.
Ernst, Herman E. (Pvt)
Ernst, Lawrence F. (Pvt)
Evans, Austin H. (Pvt) Nat'l Naval Volunteer, WIA.
Evans, William H. (Pvt)
Faas, Laughlin J. (Pvt) Marine Reserve, WIA.
Fackey, John M. (Sgt)
Fanning, William (Pvt)
Farrell, Joseph (Pvt) KIA, 6 June 1918.
Feingold, Joseph (Pvt)
Ferris, James (Sgt) Marine Reserve, KIA, 1 November 1918.
Fesler, Charles E. (Pvt)
Ficklin, James G. (Pvt)
Ficklin, James T. (Pvt) Nat'l Naval Volunteer, WIA.
Fisher, Arthur J. (Pvt) Nat'l Naval Volunteer, WIA.
Fisher, James E. (Pvt) KIA, 6 June 1918.
Fitzgerald, John V. (Sgt)
Fitzsimmons, Joseph P. (Pvt)
Flader, Louis J. (Pvt)
Flaherty, William J. (Cpl)
Flynn, Harry (Pvt)
Foley, Joseph F. (Pvt) Cook, 2nd Class.
Forbeck, Richard P. (Pvt) Marine Reserve, KIA, 4 October 1918.
Ford, Fred (Pvt)

Foreman, James E. (Pvt) Nat'l Naval Volunteer, WIA.
Foster, Carl (Pvt)
Fox, Donald A. (Pvt)
Fox, Frederick H. (Cpl)
Fox, Marvin M. (Pvt) Marine Reserve.
Frantz, Glenn (Pvt)
Frantzen, Carl J. (Sgt) Mess Sergeant.
Fravell, Guy (Pvt)
Freudenthal, George W. (Cpl)
Fruin, Richard L. (Cpl)
Fullerton, John (Pvt)
Fulmer, Clifford J. (Pvt)
Galbraith, Russell (Cpl) Nat'l Naval Volunteer.
Gallagher, Osler D. (Cpl)
Gann, Bert D. (Cpl) KIA, 4 November 1918.
Garrett, Rudolf W. (Pvt)
Gates, Benjamin P. (Pvt)
Gates, Benjamin P., Jr. (Pvt)
Gebhard, Julius (PFC)
Geer, Prentice S. (Pvt)
Gidbey, Arnold E. (Cpl)
Giese, William H. (Pvt)
Giles, Samuel E. (Sgt)
Godbey, Arnold E. (Cpl)
Goddard, Adolphus L. (Pvt)
Goddu, Louis A. (Pvt) Nat'l Naval Volunteer.
Goldbeck, Eric A. (Pvt) Nat'l Naval Volunteer.
Goldsberry John V. (Pvt)
Gothard, Ira J. (Pvt) Nat'l Naval Volunteer.
Grabski, Leo (Pvt) Marine Reserve.
Grant, James H. (Pvt)
Graves, Harry H. (PFC)
Green, William (Cpl) Nat'l Naval Volunteer.
Greer, Frederick Z. (Pvt) Nat'l Naval Volunteer.
Grider, Douglas (Pvt)
Grimes, Lionel T. (Pvt)
Grosse, Otto H. (Pvt)
Groves, Philip A. (Pvt)
Grubman, Isidor (PFC)
Grucela, Mike T. (Trumpeter)
Grusich, Joseph (Pvt) Pvt
Guerrieri, Samuel (Cpl) Marine Reserve, WIA.
Gunther, Fred L. (Pvt) Nat'l Naval Volunteer, MIA.
Guthrie, Robert F. (Cpl) Nat'l Naval Volunteer, Gassed.
Gwin, Thurston D. (Pvt)
Haas, Eugene F. (Pvt) KIA, 6 June 1918.
Hackbarth, Gustav E. (Sgt)
Hackley, Sam J. (Pvt)
Haebe, George C. (Pvt)
Hagler, Walter H. (PFC)
Hale, Enoch R. (Pvt)
Hallberg, Roy (Pvt) Marine Reserve.
Haller, William (Pvt)
Haney, Charley L. (Pvt)
Hansen, Orville (Trumpeter)
Hapner, Kyle W. (Cpl) Nat'l Naval Volunteer.
Harbert, Roy C. (Pvt)
Harmon, Cecil (Pvt)
Harris, Harlan H. (Pvt) Marine Reserve.
Harris, Harvey M. (Pvt)
Harris, John (Pvt) WIA.

Harris, Levi M. (Pvt)
Harrison, Edward D. (Pvt) Nat'l Naval Volunteer.
Harville, Robert L. (Pvt)
Haupt, Clare B. (Pvt) Marine Reserve.
Hawkins, Charles G. (Sgt)
Haynes, Walter L. (Pvt)
Haywood, Walter M. (Pvt)
Hedden, Harvey P. (Pvt)
Henry, Walter (Pvt)
Hetrick, John F. (Pvt) Marine Reserve.
Hickey, Daniel E. (Pvt)
Higgins, Loren J.v (Pvt)
Hilsinger, Larry E. (Pvt) Nat'l Naval Volunteer.
Hinsdale, Russell L. (Pvt)
Hirsch, Charles F. (Sgt)
Hobson, Edwin L. (Pvt) Company Clerk.
Hoewner, Henry A. (Pvt)
Hoewner, Waldemar F. (Pvt)
Hohn, John (Pvt)
Hoover, Lyle I. (Cpl) Nat'l Naval Volunteer, WIA.
Hoover, Philip H. (Pvt)
Hopper, Arthur (Pvt) WIA, 6 June 1918.
Horner, George A. (Pvt) Cook, 4th Class.
Houston, James H. (Pvt)
Hubbard, Jesse G. (Pvt)
Hubbartt, Charles E. (Pvt)
Hundley, Carl S. (Cpl)
Huston, Harold G. (Pvt)
Hutchins, Russell McC (Pvt)
Hutton, George J. (Sgt)
Hutton, Harold J. (Pvt)
Hynes, Ralph E. (Pvt)
Ingham, Elmer E. (Pvt) Marine Reserve, WIA.
Isbell, Claude (Pvt)
Jacoby, Harry (Pvt) Nat'l Naval Volunteer, WIA.
Jewell, Charles L. Sgt
Jimerfield, Herbert W. (Pvt) KIA, 15 June 1918.
Johnson, Claude (PFC)
Johnson, Edgar L. (Pvt)
Johnson, George, Jr. (Pvt)
Johnston, Alexander J. (Pvt)
Johnston, John (GySgt)
Johnston, John (Sgt) Mess Sgt.
Jolly, Samuel J. (Pvt) Nat'l Naval Volunteer, WIA.
Jones, George A. (Pvt)
Jones, Herbert S. (Pvt)
Jones, Leslie F. (Pvt) Nat'l Naval Volunteer, KIA.
Jones, Merle L. (Pvt) Nat'l Naval Volunteer.
Jordy, Frederic (Pvt)
Judd, Philip A. (PFC)
Kahrimanis, William D. (Pvt)
Karhan, Frank (Sgt) Marine Reserve, WIA.
Kauffman, Earl E. (Pvt)
Keller, Arthur R. (Pvt)
Kelly, Thomas (Pvt)
Kenny, William A. (Pvt) Nat'l Naval Volunteer.
Kerns, Arthur R. (Pvt)
Kerrigan, Frank A. (Pvt)
Kessinger, Oscar M. (Pvt)
Kingcade, Charles E. (Pvt)
Kingsbury, Amos C. (Pvt) Marine Reserve.

Kirkwood, Ersel F. (Pvt)

Kitchens, Eric H. (Pvt) Nat'l Naval Volunteer.

Kitley, Charles R. (Pvt)

Knorr, George (Pvt) KIA, 6 June 1918.

Kraft, David F. (Pvt) WIA.

Krantz, Edward F. (Pvt)

Krohn, Edward M. (Pvt)

LaHaye, Frank (Pvt)

LaLone, Charles M. (Pvt)

Lamb, Leo D. (Pvt)

Landgon, William E. (Pvt)

Lane, Russell H. (Pvt)

Lang, Thomas A. (Pvt)

Lanning, Glencoe L. (Pvt)

Larison, Harrie H. (Pvt)

LaVelle, William H. (Pvt) Nat'l Naval Volunteer.

Lawrence, Eugene F. (Pvt)

Laxton, Oas (Cpl) Marine Reserve.

Leber, Paul R. (Pvt)

Lee, Ovelia, Jr. (Pvt)

LeGall, Louis (GySgt)

Lego, Amos E. (Pvt) Nat'l Naval Volunteer, WIA.

Lemon, Berrel A. (Pvt)

Lemons, Charles V. (Pvt)

Lewis, Charles A. (Pvt)

Ligon, Jowe W. (Pvt)

Limbert, Raymond W. (Pvt) KIA, 6 June 1918.

Linderborg, Karl (Pvt) WIA.

Lloyd, Harry E. (Pvt)

Loftus, Michael (Cpl)

Long, Ora (PFC)

Lowry, James M. (Cpl)

Lutz, Clarence F. (Pvt) Nat'l Naval Volunteer, WIA.

Lyman, Edwin L. (Pvt)

Lynn, Charles W. (Pvt)

Mackin, Elton E. (Pvt)

Mader, Robert (Pvt) Marine Reserve, KIA, 2 October 1918.

Mahoney, Frank J. (Pvt) Messman.

Malek, Frank (Pvt) Marine Reserve, WIA.

Marchand, Albert M. (Pvt) Messman.

Marold, Jack H. (Cpl)

Martin, William C. (Cpl)

Mason, William G. (Sgt)

Massey, Oth (Pvt)

Mather, Jacob A. (Pvt) Marine Reserve.

Mathis, Clarence E. (Cpl)

Mathuss, George M. (Drummer)

Maugans, Howard R. (Sgt)

Maxwell, Howard B. (Pvt)

Mayer, Charlie V. (Pvt)

Maynard, Marcus L. (Cpl)

McCandless, Earl S. (Pvt) Marine Reserve.

McCarrier, Joseph C. (Pvt) Nat'l Naval Volunteer.

McCarthy, Howard H. (Pvt) Nat'l Naval Volunteer, WIA.

McClurg, Reginald M. (Cpl)

McCoy, William D. (Pvt) Nat'l Naval Volunteer.

McDanel, Russell R. (Sgt) Bn Liaison.

McDill, Hardin B. (Pvt)

McDonald, John (Cpl) Nat'l Naval Volunteer, WIA.

McGaha, Robert C. (PFC)

McGarry, William R. (Pvt) Marine Reserve.

McGhee, William T. (Pvt) Marine Reserve.

McGuire, Brutus C. (Cpl)

McKuns, Herbert J. (Cpl) Marine Reserve, Died of Wounds.

McLean, Kenneth D. (Pvt) Nat'l Naval Volunteer, WIA.

McMenamy, Charles (Pvt) Messman.

McMichael, Linden (Pvt)

McMullen, Harry P. (Pvt) Nat'l Naval Volunteer, WIA.

McQuiddy, James E. (Pvt) Messman.

Meisner, James R., Jr. (Pvt)

Metcalf, Charles A. (PFC)

Metzger, Sidney (Pvt) Nat'l Naval Volunteer, WIA.

Michael, Lloyd E. (Pvt) Messman.

Middleton, Malcolm (Cpl)

Milewski, Joseph J. (Pvt) Marine Reserve, KIA.

Minton, Morton L. (Pvt)

Mitchell, Roy (Pvt) Nat'l Naval Volunteer, WIA.

Moles, Jacob H. (Pvt) Marine Reserve, Died of Wounds, 4 October 1918.

Montgomery, John T. (Pvt)

Moore, John T. (Pvt)

Moore, Otto (Pvt) Marine Reserve, KIA.

Moran, Lewis F. (Pvt)

Morash, George E. (Pvt)

Moscato, Pasco (Pvt)

Munns, Joe D. (Pvt) KIA, 6 June 1918.

Murphy, Charles M. (Cpl) Nat'l Naval Volunteer, WIA.

Murphy, Leo B. (Sgt) Nat'l Naval Volunteer, WIA.

Murray, Henry C. (Sgt)

Nelsen, Sophus F. (Pvt)

Nelson, Everett L. (Pvt)

Nelson, John D. (Pvt) Nat'l Naval Volunteer, WIA.

Newell, James E. (Pvt)

Nuttall, Henry R. (Pvt)

Obetz, Henry D. (Pvt) Bn Runner, Nat'l Naval Volunteer, WIA.

O'Brien, John F. (Pvt)

O'Brien, John J. (Pvt)

O'Donoghue, Michael T. (Pvt) Marine Reserve, KIA, 4 October 1918.

O'Gara, Edward H. (Cpl)

Olanie, Henry L. (Pvt) Nat'l Naval Volunteer, WIA.

O'Leary, John J. (Pvt)

Oliver, Joseph G. (Pvt)

Olstein, Abraham (Pvt)

Onecki, Stanley (Pvt)

Opial, Joseph (Pvt)

Ourant, Barry W. (Pvt)

Ourant, Harry W. (Pvt)

Ozier, John H. (Pvt)

Palmer, Carlisle R. (Pvt)

Park, James M. (Pvt) KIA, 6 June 1918.

Parker, James J. (Cpl)

Parker, Oliver (Sgt)

Parker, Pleas (Pvt) Nat'l Naval Volunteer, WIA.

Parran, William S. (Pvt)

Pavelka, Frank (Cpl)

Paxton, William D. (Pvt)

Peebles, Edmund E. (Pvt)

Peeler, Frank A. (Cpl)
Peterson, Elmer E. (Pvt) Nat'l Naval Volunteer, WIA.
Peterson, James A. (Pvt) Messman.
Peterson, Louis (Cpl)
Peterson, Nels J. (Pvt)
Petoskey, Howard (Pvt)
Phelps, Jay B. (Pvt) Nat'l Naval Volunteer.
Plageman, George (Pvt) Marine Reserve, WIA.
Pointer, Lewis S. (Pvt)
Pond, Philip M. (Cpl) Naval Volunteer, Died of
  Wounds, 16 October 1918.
Poole, Oscar B. (Pvt)
Porter, Charlie C. (Cpl)
Potter, Carl O. (Pvt) Marine Reserve, Died of Wounds.
Potter, Milo E. (Pvt) Marine Reserve, WIA.
Price, Russel (Pvt)
Pritchett, William F. (Pvt)
Privitt, Earl L. (Pvt)
Pugh, George A. (Cpl)Nat'l Naval Volunteer, WIA.
Pulkrabek, John (Pvt) Marine Reserve.
Quinlin, Louis T. (Pvt)
Radford, John (Pvt)
Ramey, Earl (Pvt)
Ramsey, Edward O. (Pvt)
Ray, Earl M. (Pvt) Marine Reserve.
Reeves, John W. (Pvt)
Reynolds, Walter H. (Pvt) Nat'l Naval Volunteer.
Rice, Harry (Cpl)
Rice, Omer A. (Pvt)
Richards, Clarence J. (Pvt) Nat'l Naval Volunteer.
Richards, Horace J. (Pvt)
Ritchie, Carl A. (Pvt)
Rives, Felix McW. (Pvt) Marine Reserve, WIA.
Roach, Pat (Pvt)
Roane, Lee R. (Pvt)
Robbs, James R. (Pvt)
Roberts, Victor (Pvt)
Rooker, James W. (Pvt) Nat'l Naval Volunteer.
Rose, Edwin F. (Cpl)
Rose, Jay F. (Pvt) Nat'l Naval Volunteer.
Rose, Richard W. (Pvt) KIA, 24 June 1918.
Rosenquist, George A. (Pvt) KIA.
Rothstein, Edgar (Pvt)
Rousseau, Eugene (Sgt) Police Sgt.
Roydon, Richard (Pvt)
Rozenski, Frank E. (Pvt) Marine Reserve, WIA.
Russell, John S. (Pvt) Nat'l Naval Volunteer, WIA.
St. Andre, Charles F. (Pvt)
Satterlund, Walter (Pvt)
Saunders, John D. (Cpl)
Schlatter, Edwin W. (Pvt)
Schmidt, Edward W. (Pvt)
Schmidt, Peter G. (PFC)
Schrook, Marcellus B. (Pvt)
Schuler, Charles A. (Pvt) KIA, 6 June 1918.
Scott, Wallace J. (Cpl)
Seitz, Frederick W. (Cpl) KIA, 2 November 1918.
Selinski, Frank (Cpl)
Semones, John F. (Pvt)
Senior, Russell E. (Pvt) Nat'l Naval Volunteer, WIA.
Sexton, Norman E. (Pvt) Nat'l Naval Volunteer, WIA.

Sheehan, Maurice C. (Pvt) WIA
Sheldon, William (Pvt) Nat'l Naval Volunteer, WIA.
Shelton, Nelson M. (Pvt)
Shepherd, Dewey E. (Pvt)
Shultz, Fred (Pvt)
Shultz, Herman L. (Pvt) Nat'l Naval Volunteer.
Simon, Pete E. (Pvt)
Simpson, Raymond F. (Pvt)
Sizemore, William McK (Pvt)
Smith, Boyce O. (Pvt) Nat'l Naval Volunteer.
Smith, Charles J. (GySgt)
Smith, Elmer R. (Pvt) Marine Reserve.
Smith, Peter S. (Pvt) Marine Reserve, Died of Wounds,
  5 October 1918.
Souder, William H. (Pvt)
Spicer, William E. (Pvt)
Steele, William (Pvt) Marine Reserve.
Stenmark, Nelson A. (Pvt) Marine Reserve, Died of
  Wounds, 5 October 1918.
Sterling, Calvin W. (Pvt)
Stern, Edgar (Pvt)
Sterner, Harry (Pvt)
Steuer, George E. (Cpl)
Stevens, Chester A. (PFC)
Stewart, Henry, Jr. (Cpl) Marine Reserve, WIA.
Stiles, George P. (Pvt)
Stouff, Octave P. (Pvt)
Stowers, John C. (Pvt) Nat'l Naval Volunteer, WIA.
Stroup, William L. (Pvt) Marine Reserve, KIA, 4 Octo-
  ber 1918.
Summers, Roy A. (Pvt)
Sweeney, Russell H. (Pvt) Nat'l Naval Volunteer, WIA.
Teague, Edward E. (Pvt)
Terry, William P. (Pvt)
Terry, William T. (Pvt)
Thomas, Harry (Pvt)
Thomas, William B. (Pvt)
Thompson, Joseph H. (Pvt) Nat'l Naval Volunteer, WIA.
Thompson, Tommy A. (Pvt) Marine Reserve, KIA, 4
  October 1918.
Tobbenboske, Frederick (Pvt) Nat'l Naval Volunteer,
  WIA.
Tonnies, Henry H. (Pvt) Nat'l Naval Volunteer, MIA.
Tousley, Reuben (Pvt) Nat'l Naval Volunteer.
Trauernicht, Walter (Pvt) Messman.
Troup, Judson R. (Pvt)
Turner, Benjamin R. (Pvt)
Ugland, Harold S. (Pvt) Nat'l Naval Volunteer, WIA.
Van Eman, Clare L. (Cpl) KIA, 6 June 1918.
Vernon, Emmett S. (Pvt)
Virgil, Joseph E. (Pvt) Nat'l Naval Volunteer.
Votey, Harold L. (Cpl) Marine Reserve, WIA.
Wagner, Howard A. (Pvt)
Wahl, Oscar E. (Pvt)
Wakefield, Russel J. (Pvt) KIA, 6 June 1918.
Wallis, George A. (Pvt) Nat'l Naval Volunteer.
Walters, Hugh A. (Pvt)
Warren, Elbert L. (Pvt)
Watts, William V. (Pvt)
Welch, John W. (Pvt)
West, Paul J. (Cpl)

White, Charles E. (Pvt)
Wilson, Arthur S. (Pvt)
Wilson, Earl P. (Sgt)
Winiecki, Edward L. (Pvt)
Winn, Carl F. (GySgt) KIA, 6 June 1918.
Wintering, Charles (Pvt) Marine Reserve.
Wiseman, Henry C. (Cpl)
Witherspoon, Charles W. (Pvt) Nat'l Naval Volunteer, WIA.
Wolter, Frank R. (Pvt) Messman.
Woodburg, Charles H. (Pvt)
Wright, Joseph E. (Pvt)
Yarbrough, James C. (Pvt)
York, Ralph L. (Pvt) Nat'l Naval Volunteer.
Young, Dewey O. (Pvt) KIA, 6 June 1918.

18th (E) Company, Second Battalion

NAME (RANK) REMARKS

Foster, John R. (Cpt) Commanding Off, Co. E.
Jackson, David T. (Cpt)
Wass, Lester S. (Cpt) Commanding Company, KIA 19 July 1918.
Godbey, Arnold D. (1st Lt)
Jackson, Gilbert D. (1st Lt)
Ashurst, William W. (2nd Lt)
Becker, Fred H. (2nd Lt) KIA, 18 July 1918.
Bradley, William A. (2nd Lt) Died of Wounds.
Collar, George C. (2nd Lt) WIA.
English, William (2nd Lt)
Fraser, Chester H. (2nd Lt)
Gassert, Howell A. (2nd Lt)
Hoskins, Harold B. (2nd Lt)
Hutchinson, William T. (2nd Lt) Marine Reserve, WIA.
Schaefer, Erwin F. (2nd Lt) Marine Corps Reserve.
Simmons, Marshall (2nd Lt)
Starkey, Joseph W. (2nd Lt) U S. Army.
Williams, Marshall B. (2nd Lt) Marine Reserve.
Zischke, Herman A. (2nd Lt)

Enlisted

Allen, Walter G. (1st Sgt)
Rhodes, Clarence D. (1st Sgt)
Adams, Raymond (Pvt)
Adams, Robert B. (Cpl)
Albert, Camille L. (Pvt)
Albert, Phillip L. (Pvt)
Aldrich, Fenton M. (Pvt)
Allen, Aubrey H. (Pvt)
Alscher, Abe (PFC)
Alterie, Louis J. (Pvt) Nat'l Naval Volunteer.
Altman, Guy (Pvt)
Ames, Robert I. (Pvt) Nat'l Naval Volunteer.
Amiotte, Albert (Pvt)
Amonette, William L., Jr. (Pvt)
Anderson, Charles E. (Pvt)
Anderson, Clarence G. (Pvt)

Anderson, Hewett B. (PFC)
Anderson, Oswald J. (Pvt)
Anderson, Richard W. (Pvt)
Anderson, Roy C. (Pvt)
Anderson, Walter S. (Pvt) WIA.
Anglin, Paul (Cpl)
Anson, Clarence B. (Pvt)
Antle, Russell J. (PFC)
Armour, Charles R. (Pvt) Marine Corps Reserve.
Arries, Major A. (PFC) MIA.
Ashlin, John R., Jr. (Pvt)
Atkinson, Frank W. (Cpl)
Auman, Wilson E. (Pvt)
Austin, Harry P. (Cpl)
Bacon, Harold D. (Sgt)
Bailey, Aurin H. (Pvt) Messman.
Bailey, Harry P. (Pvt)
Baker, Charles (Cpl)
Baker, Edward N. (Cpl)
Baker, Elmer C. (Pvt)
Ball, Joseph L. (Cpl)
Banister, Ira H. (Pvt)
Barber, Gordon C. (Pvt)
Barchus, Burras (Pvt)
Barnes, Charles N. (Pvt)
Barnes, Floyd T. (PFC) Marine Corps Reserve.
Barnum, Dean C. (Pvt)
Barry, Lewis W. (Pvt) KIA, 10 June 1918.
Bean, Charles S. (PFC)
Beavers, Albert A. (Pvt) KIA, 11 November 1918.
Becking, Alvin F. (Pvt) KIA, 12 June 1918.
Belk, Charles (Pvt) KIA, 10 June 1918.
Belles, Edwin C. (Pvt) Messman.
Berg, Leon W. (Pvt) Marine Corps Reserve.
Bergman, Lester (Pvt)
Bergstrom, Carl E. (Pvt) Marine Corps Reserve.
Best, Glen E. (Pvt)
Betz, Adolph L. (Cpl)
Bilski, Frank J. (Pvt)
Bishop, Anthony D. (Pvt)
Bishop, John S. (Pvt)
Bishop, Martin (Pvt) Messman.
Blackburn, William P. (Pvt) KIA, 12 June 1918.
Blackstock, Herbert F. (Pvt)
Blanchard, Bernard (Pvt)
Bleifus, Carl J. (Pvt)
Bolles, Steven (Cpl)
Bonner, Paul (PFC)
Bonnett, Stanley F. (Pvt)
Book, Emery C. (Pvt)
Borey, Frederick M. (Trumpeter)
Bornemann, Alfred H. (Pvt)
Borowiak, Paul L. (Cpl)
Bourn, George W., Jr. (Pvt)
Boyette, Amos M. (Pvt) Nat'l Naval Volunteer.
Braden, Fred M. (Pvt) WIA.
Bradley, Adelbert E. (Pvt)
Brennan, John (Pvt)
Brennen, Alphonsus C. (Pvt)
Breving, William (Cpl) WIA.
Brock, Joe M. (Pvt)

Brooks, Prosper R. (Pvt)

Brown, Arthur E. (Pvt)

Brown, Bergen T. (Pvt) MIA.

Brown, Charles A. (Pvt) Marine Corps Reserve.

Brown, James D. (Pvt)

Brown, Leonard E. (Pvt)

Brown, Paul W. (Cpl)

Brown, Robert A. (Cpl)

Brown, Royal (PFC) Marine Corps Reserve.

Bryan, Ralph E. (Cpl)

Bryce, Edward J. (Pvt)

Brylinski, Joseph F. (Pvt)

Bulman, William H. (Sgt) Died of wounds, 30 July 1918.

Burden, Murray (Pvt)

Burdick, Edward M. (Pvt) MIA, Died of Wounds, 12 October 1918.

Burns, Arthur F. (Pvt) Marine Corps Reserve.

Burwell, Stanley (Pvt) Bandsman.

Byce, Henry G. (Pvt)

Cain, Richard D. (Pvt)

Calhoun, George T. (Sgt) WIA.

Cameron, Robert C. (Pvt) KIA, 21 July 1918.

Campbell, William M. (Pvt)

Canady, Cecil L. (Pvt)

Cannon, Rollin M. (Pvt) KIA, 8 June 1918.

Cantrell, George M. (Pvt) WIA.

Carberry, Leo F. (Pvt)

Card, Arthur (Pvt)

Carey, James M. (Pvt)

Carl, Harry C. (Pvt)

Carr, Alva W. (Pvt)

Carr, Oliver B. (Sgt)

Carter, Daniel B. (Pvt)

Carter, Gilbert L. (Pvt) KIA, 21 July 1918.

Carter, Omer R. (Pvt) KIA, 6 October 1918.

Castle, Wayne H. (Cpl)

Cawthon, Charles L. (Pvt) Nat'l Naval Volunteer.

Chamberlain, Harry (Pvt)

Chipponeri, Joseph (Pvt)

Christie, William (Sgt)

Clark, William B. (Pvt)

Clarkson, Seth M. (Pvt)

Clemas, John (Pvt)

Cliver, Milton C. (Pvt)

Cole, Warren R. (Pvt) Marine Corps Reserve.

Collins, Wallace G. (Pvt)

Colon, George O. (Cpl) KIA, 21 July 1918.

Colvin, David P. (Pvt) KIA, 18 July 1918.

Conaway, Virgil J. (Cpl)

Conrad, Amos A. (Pvt)

Conroy, Martin J. (Cpl) Company Clerk.

Cook, Edward J. (Pvt)

Corbin, Bert R. (Pvt) Nat'l Naval Volunteer.

Cortright, Gerald R. (Pvt)

Courchane, Joseph J. (Pvt)

Couter, Howard E. (Pvt)

Cox, Thomas H. (Sgt)

Coyne, Paul P. (Cpl)

Crary, Harry D. (PFC)

Creager, Clyde (Pvt)

Crossen, Vernon J. (Sgt) KIA, 4 November 1918.

Crum, John R. (Pvt) Marine Corps Reserve, KIA.

Cullen, Thomas F. (Pvt)

Dahl, Albert R. (Pvt) WIA.

Daley, Joseph M. (Cpl) KIA, 10 June 1918.

Dawson, Wallace W. (Pvt)

Dean, William F. (Pvt) KIA, 4 October 1918.

Decatur, Alfred G. (Pvt) Marine Corps Reserve.

Degenhardt, John O. (Pvt)

DeGroff, Ephraim F. (Cpl)

DeVaney, Thomas F. (Pvt)

DeWitt, Fred J. (Pvt)

Dills, Robert J. (Pvt)

Dimmick, Howard O. (Pvt)

Dixon, Charles F. (Pvt)

Dobbins, George W. (Cpl) WIA.

Dodge, Miles H. (Sgt) Nat'l Naval Volunteer, KIA, 1 June 1918.

Donaldson, William H. (Pvt)

Donohoe, Charles E. (Sgt) Died of Wounds.

Dooley, George W. (Cpl)

Downhour, Harry E. (Pvt) MIA.

Ducey, James A. (Sgt)

Dudley, George M. (Cpl) Marine Corps Reserve.

Dunn, Gordon R. (PFC) Marine Corps Reserve.

Dwyer, Joseph A. (Pvt)

Easton, Ora James (Cpl) MIA.

Edlin, Alvin P. (Pvt)

Edwards, Dewey C. (Pvt)

Eggert, Elmer J. (PFC) MIA.

Elbe, Rudolph (Pvt)

Elkin, Cecil F. (Pvt) Gassed.

Elliott, Herman J. (PFC) WIA.

Ellis, Alton B. (Pvt)

Enochson, Arthur L. (Pvt)

Entgelmeier, Arthur (Pvt)

Eulert, Karl (Pvt) Gassed.

Evans, Alva L. (Pvt)

Evans, John T. (Pvt)

Fehrs, Lester I. (Pvt)

Feinberg, Wolfe W. (PFC)

Fellenbaum, Edward C. (Pvt)

Field, Harry B. (Cpl) KIA, 6 June 1918.

Finnell, Albert M. (Pvt) WIA.

Finney, Emmet O. (Pvt)

Fischer, William A. (Pvt)

Fowler, Victor O. (Pvt) Nat'l Naval Volunteer.

Fox, Daniel R. (Cpl) Company Clerk.

Fraser, Gilbert D. (Pvt) KIA, 12 June 1918.

Fritts, Jacob B. (PFC) Marine Corps Reserve.

Frost, George (Pvt)

Fuller, Albert L. (Cpl) Marine Corps Reserve.

Gabriel, Joseph A. (Pvt)

Gadreau, Joseph (Sgt)

Gilman, Frank H. (Pvt) Nat'l Naval Volunteer.

Gilman, John C. (Pvt)

Glenn, Eugene I. (HAp2)

Goode, Harry (Pvt) Messman.

Gorney, Frank (Pvt)

Gorsuch, Ralph K. (Pvt)

Grebbien, Henry W. (Pvt) Messman.

Grimes, Lawrence (PFC) MIA.
Gross, Lee L. (Sgt) WIA.
Gruver, Fred B. (Pvt) KIA, 21 July 1918.
Gruver, Harry W. (Pvt) Nat'l Naval Volunteer.
Hall, Burton (Pvt)
Hammerling, Loren E. (Pvt)
Hansen, Melvin K. (Pvt)
Hardiman, Michael J. (Cpl)
Harris, Clifford J. (Pvt)
Harris, Edwin V. (Pvt)
Harris, Orville (Pvt)
Harris, Robert L. (Pvt)
Hartley, Edwin C. (Pvt) Marine Corps Reserve.
Hartman, David R. (PFC) Marine Corps Reserve.
Hawkins, James A. (Pvt) Cook, 3rd Class.
Hazzard, Bert F. (Cpl)
Heller, Pearl E. (PFC)
Hemmerling, Loren A. (Pvt) KIA, 4 November 1918.
Hendricks, John (Cpl) KIA.
Heninger, Henry A. (Pvt)
Henry, Noah (Pvt)
Herrick, Donald A. (Cpl)
Herron, Sterling J. (Cpl)
Hettel, Henry A. (Pvt) MIA.
Hibbard, Frederick J. (Pvt)
Hill, Louis (Pvt) Died of wounds, 15 September 1918.
Hill, Robert (Pvt)
Hillman, Walter (GySgt)
Hitter, Leonard A. (Cpl) MIA, Died of Wounds.
Hoffmeier, Harry B. (Pvt)
Hoffschmidt, Joseph J. (Pvt)
Hoke, Graydon A. (Pvt) MIA.
Holmes, Alfred P. (Pvt)
Holmes, Noah H. (Cpl)
Horne, Leon W. (Trumpeter)
Horne, Robert S. (Pvt)
Howard, William M. (Sgt) WIA.
Hunter, Charles J. (Pvt)
Husk, Brenton L. (Pvt)
Hydrick, James T. (Pvt)
Illien, Elbert W. (Pvt)
Irwin, Cecil A. (PFC)
Isaly, Earl W. (Pvt) KIA, 7 October 1918.
Jack, Warren D. (Pvt) Messman.
Jacobs, Harry V. (Cpl)
James, Henry G. (Sgt)
Jeppson, Doras S. (Pvt)
Johnson, Arthur C. (Cpl)Marine Corps Reserve.
Johnson, Paul T. (Pvt) KIA, 4 October 1918.
Johnson, Russell T. (PFC)
Jones, Alton C. (Pvt)
Jones, Anselm P. (PFC) MIA, Died of Wounds.
Jones, John W. (Pvt) Marine Corps Reserve.
Jones, William H. (Cpl)
Joubert, Gaudias J. (Pvt) Messman.
Kaplan, Michael (PFC) Marine Corps Reserve.
Kaub, Arthur L. (Cpl)
Keene, Roy S. (Drummer)
Keller, Joseph R. (Cpl) Marine Corps Reserve.
Kelley, Bernard J. (PFC) Marine Corps Reserve.
Kelly, Earl A. (Cpl)

Kennedy, Lawrence W. (Cpl)
Kennedy, William A. (GySgt)
Kinney, Cecil H. (Pvt) Nat'l Naval Volunteer.
Klien, Joseph (Pvt)
Knebel, Andrew (PFC) MIA.
Knowlton, Frederick T. (Pvt) Nat'l Naval Volunteer.
   Messman.
Kolson, Francis E. (Pvt) KIA, 8 June 1918.
Koressel, Herman J. (Pvt)
LaBelle, Joseph T. (Pvt) MIA.
LaCoste, Warren J. (Sgt) Gassed.
Langlan, Joseph G. (Pvt)
Lanterman, Gilbert (Pvt)
Lasher, Roy C. (Pvt) WIA.
Lasure, Harry A. (Cpl)
Lawson, Valentine (Pvt) Messman, KIA, 11 June 1918.
Leary, George T. (Pvt) Gassed.
Lenhart, James E. (Pvt)
Lidstad, Guy N. (Cpl)
Lind, Charles (Pvt)
Lockwood, Ralph P. (PFC) Marine Corps Reserve.
Lodal, Alf H. (Pvt)
Lubers, Harry L., Jr. (Pvt) Died of Wounds.
Luck, Harry J. (Pvt)
Lull, John S. (Pvt)
Lyman, Guy E. (Pvt) Marine Corps Reserve.
Lyons, Glen C. (Pvt)
MacHatton, Joseph P. (Pvt) Died of Wounds.
MacSparran, William T. (GySgt) KIA, 31 October 1918.
Mann, Arthur (PFC) MIA.
Marine, George A. (Pvt)
Marovitz, Maurice (Cpl)
Mayes, John J. (Pvt)
McAllister, Joseph F. (Pvt) Nat'l Naval Volunteer.
McArdle, Leo B. (Cpl)
McArthur, Charles V. (Pvt)
McBride, Kenneth E. (PFC)
McCasland, Arthur L. (Cpl) MIA.
McCauley, John L. (Cpl) KIA.
McConagha, William A. (Pvt)
McCormick, Patrick (Pvt)
McDonald, Evans, Jr. (Pvt)
McDonald, Frederick J. (Pvt)
McIlhenny, John E. (Pvt)
McKay, Leslie B. (Cpl) KIA, 10 June 1918.
McKenna, Walter J. (Pvt)
McNally, Harry (Pvt)
Meister, George E. (Pvt)
Melville, Wilbur J. (Pvt)
Mesisca, Anthony (Pvt)
Messinger, Edgar L. (Pvt)
Metzger, Charles S. (Pvt)
Miller, Earl D. (Pvt)
Minch, Rudolph (Sgt) MIA.
Mitchell, Kent A. (Pvt)
Mitchke, Irvin E. (Pvt)
Monkevicz, Alex P. (Sgt)
Moody, Lewis H. (Cpl)
Moore, Tell (Pvt)
Morgan, Chester D. (Pvt)
Morgan, Felix T. (Pvt) MIA.

Morris, Anthony A. (Pvt) WIA.

Morris, Joseph L. (Pvt)

Mullarkey, John J. (Pvt)

Murphy, Joseph C. (Pvt)

Murray, James C. (Pvt)

Nash, Mickie F. (Pvt)

Neely, Oliver L.M. (Sgt) Gassed, died in hospital, 16 October 1918.

Nellis, George (Pvt)

Nelson, Otto C. (Pvt)

Nelson, Peter A. (Pvt)

Newell, Charles G. (Pvt)

Newman, Fred (Pvt)

Newton, Bertie B. (Pvt)

Newton, Ralph E. (Pvt)

Nickerson, Leslie D. (Pvt)

Nilsen, George (Pvt)

Nolan, Vincent A. (PhM3)

Norman, Wesley O. (Pvt) WIA.

North, Roy O. (Pvt)

Norwood, Henry H. (Pvt) Gassed.

Novick, Edward F. (Sgt) MIA.

Novick, Frank P. (Sgt) WIA.

Ohrt, Ralph J. (Pvt)

Olds, Arthur (Sgt)

Olin, Charlie M. (Pvt)

Olsen, Carl A. (Pvt)

Opheim, Irving M. (Pvt) Marine Corps Reserve.

Osborne, Vivian N. (Pvt)

Ostreim, Rudolph M. (Pvt)

Oyler, Arthur A. (Pvt)

Painter, Charles C. (Pvt)

Palusis, John C. (Cpl)

Panko, Andrew (Sgt)

Parlette, Vincent P. (Pvt)

Parmley, William B. (Sgt) KIA, 6 June 1918.

Patton, James B. (Sgt)

Peck, Frederic W. (Pvt) WIA.

Pegues, Josiah E., Jr. (Pvt)

Peltoniemi, Walter (Pvt) vt

Perrault, John A. (Cpl)

Perrin, Lester M. (Pvt)

Perrot, Linwood H. (Pvt) MIA.

Perry, Lester V. (Pvt)

Perussina, Michael B. (Pvt)

Peterson, Frank E. (Pvt)

Petoskey, Edward (Cpl) Marine Corps Reserve.

Pettegrew, Arlando R. (Pvt)

Peyton, Leland K. (Cpl)

Phelps, Jay B. (Pvt)

Phillips, Harvey C. (Pvt) KIA, 18 June 1918.

Pickering, Harry L. (Pvt) Marine Corps Reserve.

Pidcoe, Clifford W. (Pvt)

Pixley, Clifford W. (Pvt)

Porter, Baker T. (Pvt)

Postelwaite, Clarence L. (Pvt)

Prescott, Harold B. (Pvt)

Prunty, Hugh J. (Sgt)

Pryke, Donald W. (Pvt) Marine Corps Reserve.

Pugh, Eugene (PFC) Marine Corps Reserve.

Rachlin, David (PFC) MIA.

Randall, Alfred H. (Pvt)

Reading, Elwood J. (Pvt)

Ream, Lynn (Pvt)

Reddington, Richard J. (Pvt)

Reed, Edward W. (Pvt)

Reed, Frank A. (Pvt)

Reed, Wheeler K. (Pvt)

Reid, John La (Pvt)

Reimann, August (Pvt)

Renshaw, Alger L. (Pvt)

Rhode, Leon C. (Pvt) Cook, 1st Class.

Rice, Omer A. (Pvt)

Richardson, Darrington (Pvt)

Richardson, George C. (Pvt) Nat'l Naval Volunteer.

Richardson, Lowell (Pvt) KIA, 13 June 1918.

Richardson, Turner (Pvt) Messman.

Rickettes, Langdon L. (Cpl) KIA, 4 October 1918.

Riddle, Guy E. (Pvt) WIA.

Rigg, Harve (Pvt) Marine Corps Reserve.

Rink, Walter S. (Pvt)

Roach, Eugene F., Jr. (Pvt)

Robarge, Albert A. (PhM1)

Robb, William J., Jr. (Pvt)

Robertson, George P. (GySgt)

Robertson, John (Pvt)

Robinson, Cecil B. (Pvt)

Rock, Phillip (Pvt) Messman.

Rodenburg, John H. (Pvt)

Rogers, Thomas E. (Pvt)

Rosenblum, Isadore (Pvt)

Roth, William L. (Pvt) Messman.

Roush, Lyman P. (Cpl)

Row, Pinkney S. (Pvt)

Ruf, James C. (Pvt)

Rumpa, Anthony P. (Sgt)

Salmon, Marcues B. (Pvt) Messman.

Sanderson, Alton (Pvt)

Sandmeyer, Edward F. (Pvt) WIA.

Sands, Kenneth C. (Pvt) Nat'l Naval Volunteer.

Sarle, Joseph M. (Pvt)

Scalf, Chester C. (Pvt)

Schaber, Allyn B. (Cpl) KIA.

Schiani, Alfred (Pvt) WIA, 13 June 1918.

Schlenk, Robert J. (Pvt)

Schlereth, Walter W. (Pvt) Marine Corps Reserve.

Schmidt, Arthur F. (Sgt)

Schneider, William J. (Cpl) KIA.

Schooley, James A. (Pvt) Marine Corps Reserve.

Schultz, Rudolph M. (Pvt) Messman.

Schwartzman, Edwin G. (Sgt)

Scott, Marvin (GySgt)

Scroggs, James P. (Pvt) Nat'l Naval Volunteer.

Seale, Clyde W. (Cpl) WIA, Died of Wounds, 4 October 1918.

Secrist, John W. (Pvt)

Seewerker, Joseph F. (Sgt) WIA.

Seibert, George (Pvt)

Seiffert, John (GySgt)

Sennish, John W. (Pvt)

Sharkey, Robert B. (PFC)

Shedd, Owen D. (Cpl)

Sheinker, Abraham (Pvt)
Sherman, Whitney D. (Cpl)
Shine, George W. (PFC)
Shiverdecker, James M. (Pvt)
Shover, Oscar E. (Pvt) KIA, 10 June 1918.
Shubert, John J. (Pvt) MIA.
Sincock, Harold R. (Pvt)
Singer, Charles M. (Cpl) Marine Corps Reserve.
Skinner, Perry E. (PFC) Marine Corps Reserve.
Sklar, Reuben (Cpl)
Smith, Edward S. (Pvt)
Smith, George J. (Sgt)
Smith, Robert A. (PFC)
Spell, Edward R. (Cpl)
Stahlbrodt, Paul T. (Cpl) Marine Corps Reserve.
Staight, Milton E. (Sgt)
Stanfill, Joseph D. (Pvt) Nat'l Naval Volunteer.
Steiner, Winfred (Pvt)
Stensson, Carl H. (Pvt) KIA, 3 October 1918.
Stewart, Merwin C. (Pvt)
Stickney, Guy C. (Sgt)
Stiles, Guy C. (Pvt)
Stiles, William A. (Pvt) Messman.
Stover, Isaac A. (Cpl)
Streety, Sidney B. (Pvt)
Stricker, Clarence E. (Pvt) WIA.
Strong, Curtis W. (Pvt)
Struthers, Charles B., Jr. (Pvt) KIA, 4 November 1918.
Sturm, Thomas O. (Pvt) WIA.
Sullivan, Michael G. (Pvt)
Sweet, Glen A. (Sgt)
Sweitzer, Leon I. (Pvt) Marine Corps Reserve.
Swensen, Sidney S. (Pvt) Marine Corps Reserve.
Swinney, Oram J. (Pvt) MIA.
Taylor, Benjamin F. (Pvt)
Taylor, George M. (PFC)
Taylor, Stephen B. (Trumpeter)
Tennant, Charles W. (Pvt)
Tharp, James P. (Pvt)
Thomas, Joe A. (PFC)
Thomas, Thomas V. (Pvt) KIA, 13 June 1918.
Thornburg, Ollie B. (Pvt) Cook, 4th Class.
Thornlow, Percy R. (Pvt)
Tipps, George T. (Pvt)
Tischer, William F. (Pvt)
Trapp, Donald L. (Pvt) KIA, 12 June 1918.
Tucker, James R. (Pvt) MIA.
Uszko, Joseph P. (Sgt) Cook, 1st Class.
Utz, Lee N. (Pvt)
Van Sickle, Raymond B. (Pvt)
Vance, Jerry M. (Pvt)
Vanderhoof, William H. (Pvt)
Villars, Roy L. (Pvt) MIA.
Villegas, Ernest D. (Pvt)
Wade, Mason D. (Cpl)
Wallace, John (Pvt) Cook, 2nd Class.
Walsh, John R. (Sgt) WIA.
Walter, Joseph (GySgt)
Walters, Charles C. (Pvt) Cook.
Warsocki, Paul J. (Pvt)
Watkins, Ray L. (Pvt)

Watson, Francis W. (Trumpeter)
Watts, John F. (Cpl) Company Mechanic.
Webb, Posey L. (Pvt)
Wegenast, Fred A. (Pvt) Died of Wounds, 9 June 1918.
Wegenast, Herbert R. (Cpl)
Weigle, Door H. (Pvt)
Weiner, Karl S. (Sgt)
Weisshaar, Carl A. (Pvt)
Wells, Allen J. (Cpl) Marine Corps Reserve.
Wempner, Emment (Pvt)
Wennisch, William J. (Pvt)
White, Wesley G. (Pvt)
Whited, James L. (Pvt)
Wilds, Joseph Jr. (Pvt) MIA.
Willett, Richard P. (Pvt) WIA, 7 June 1918.
Williams, Chester E. (Pvt)
Williams, Lewis R. (Pvt)
Wilmot, Harry (Pvt)
Wilson, George D. (Pvt)
Winchenbaugh, Wolcott (GySgt)
Woerter, Raymond (Pvt)
Wojczynski, Anthony (Sgt)
Wojtkowiak, Steve J. (Pvt) Nat'l Naval Volunteer.
Wolfmuller, Harry (PFC) MIA.
Wood, Edward M. (Pvt)
Workman, Ellsworth (Cpl)
Worth, Henry J. (Cpl)
Yates, George E. (PFC)
Yezek, Joseph (PFC)
Young, George H. (PFC) MIA.
Zein, Frank H. (Pvt) KIA, 4 October 1918.
Ziegler, Hobart W. (Pvt) Gassed.
Zitko, Nicholas (Sgt)

43rd (F) Company, Second Battalion

NAME (RANK) REMARKS

Dunbeck, Charley (Cpt) WIA, F Co
Massie, Nathaniel H. (Cpt)
Murray, Joseph D. (Cpt)
Milner, Drinkard B. (1st Lt)
Stockton, James R. (1st Lt) WIA.
Thayer, Sydney, Jr. (1st Lt) WIA, 11 November 1918.
True, Norman E. (1st Lt)
Cannon, Adolphus (2nd Lt) Marine Reserve.
Glendinning, Henry P. (2nd Lt) Served as Battalion
    intelligence officer.
Legendre, James H. (2nd Lt)
Ross, Elbert W. (2nd Lt) Marine Reserve.
Stockes, George F. (2nd Lt) Marine Corps Reserve.
Williams, Robert O. (2nd Lt) Marine Corps Reserve.

Enlisted

Harding, Kenneth W. (SGM)
Burns, Harold F. (1st Sgt)
Lyons, Walter S. (1st Sgt)
Abbott, Claude T. (Pvt) KIA, 11 June 1918.

Abrams, Edward B. (Cpl) KIA, 11 June 1918.
Andrews, John (Pvt) Signalman, 3rd Class.
Arensen, Joseph E. (Pvt)
Ashcraft, Roscoe S. (Pvt)
Aston, Thomas J. (Pvt) Marine Corps Reserve.
Ault, Harris A. (Pvt)
Aument, Stephen J. (Pvt)
Ayers, Nathaniel W. (Pvt) Signalman, 2nd Class.
Azarovitz, Joseph (Pvt)
Balcom, Fred L. (Pvt)
Baldwin, Howard W. (PFC)
Bankston, Charles M. (PFC)
Bard, John E. (Pvt)
Barrett, Floyd E. (PFC) KIA.
Barry, John P. (Sgt)
Bartik, Anton A. (Pvt)
Batema, Orlo H. (Pvt)
Baur, William C. (Pvt)
Beach, Frederick D. (PFC)
Bell, Thomas H. (Pvt) KIA, 14 June 1918.
Belzarini, Louis (Pvt)
Bennett, Frederick S. (Cpl)
Bennett, William E. (Pvt) MIA, 13 June 1918.
Bergholtz, Henry K. (Cpl)
Bernstein, David (Cpl)
Betts, Harry R. (Cpl)
Birmingham, Francis W. (PFC) Messman.
Bishop, Otis R. (Pvt) Marine Corps Reserve.
Blick, Henry F. (Pvt) Officer's Orderly.
Bluhm, Herbert C. (GySgt)
Boecking, Guido C. (Pvt)
Boehmer, John A. (Cpl)
Bondurant, Lloyd H. (Pvt) Marine Corps Reserve.
Boots, Wade A. (Pvt) Marine Corps Reserve. Battalion
    Runner.
Bosckis, Peter (Pvt)
Boudeau, Louis J. (Pvt) Marine Corps Reserve.
Bowyer, Robert C. (Cpl)
Boyd, William B. (Pvt)
Bracken, Harry (Pvt)
Bramblette, Roy E. (PFC) Marine Corps Reserve.
    Cook 4th Class.
Brougher, Theophilus C. (Pvt)
Brown, Constant (Pvt) Marine Corps Reserve.
Bruhn, Erik E. (Pvt) Messman.
Brunelle, Wilfred (Pvt)
Buck, Joseph H. (Pvt)
Buck, Walter B. (Pvt)
Budlong, William T.R. (Pvt)
Bunnell, Benjamin O. (Pvt) Marine Corps Reserve.
Burch, Roy (Pvt) Marine Corps Reserve, WIA.
Burlison, Franklin C. (Cpl)
Burton, Emory S. (Pvt) WIA.
Bush, Francis H. (Pvt) Died of Wounds.
Butler, Eustice E. (Pvt)
Bywaters, Edward F. (Pvt)
Campbell, William E. (Sgt) WIA.
Canfield, John R. (Pvt)
Canfield, Roger I. (Sgt)
Carey, John J. (Pvt)
Cartwright, Richard J. (Pvt)

Casey, John (Pvt)
Cassidy, John H. (PFC)
Castaing, Henry J. (Pvt)
Champion, John G. (Pvt)
Chandler, Charlie M. (Sgt)
Chandler, George I. (Pvt) KIA, 11 June 1918.
Chapman, George C. (Pvt)
Chapman, Ramsey B. (Pvt) Signalman, 1st Class.
Christensen, LeRoy C. (PFC)
Churchill, Chester A. (Cpl)
Clark, Guy H. (Cpl)
Clark, Hugh S. (Pvt) Cook, 4th Class.
Clawson, Harry A. (Pvt) Marine Corps Reserve.
Clifford, James H. (PFC) Reserve, KIA.
Collette, Clyde H. (Pvt) Marine Corps Reserve, WIA.
Colville, Franklin A., Jr. (Pvt)
Connelly, Peter A. (Cpl)
Connelly, Samuel F. (Pvt)
Conover, Kenneth S. (Pvt)
Conway, William T. (Pvt) Marine Corps Reserve.
Cook, Paul N.P. (Pvt) Officer's Orderly.
Cook, Samuel O. (Pvt)
Cook, Walter (GySgt)
Coombs, Arthur J. (Cpl)
Coombs, Leroy (PFC) Battalion Intelligence Detail,
    WIA.
Cornelius, Lee E. (Pvt)
Correia, Charles L. (PFC)
Cossman, Otto J. (Pvt)
Courtney, James (Sgt)
Cowley, Richard (Cpl)
Coy, Gordon L. (Cpl)
Crabtree, Hugh O. (Cpl)
Crale, Joseph (Pvt)
Crampton, William J. (Cpl)
Crommett, Arthur L. (Cpl)
Cunningham, Edward J. (Cpl)
Curry, Charles F. (Pvt)
Curtis, Robert L. (Pvt) Marine Corps Reserve. Battal-
    ion Intelligence Detail.
Cushing, William I. (PFC) Marine Corps Reserve.
Dahme, Gilbert C. (Pvt)
Daniele, Leo H. (Pvt)
Darst, Rollie P. (Pvt) Marine Corps Reserve, WIA.
Daum, Edward R. (Pvt)
Davis, Fred M. (PFC)
Davis, George H. (Sgt)
Davis, Thomas R. (Pvt) Marine Corps Reserve.
Davis, Ward C. (PFC) Marine Corps Reserve. Battal-
    ion Intelligence Detail.
Dawes, Lyell C. (Pvt)
Decker, Emil F. (Pvt) Reserve, MIA, died.
DeHart, Louis A. (Pvt) Officer's Orderly.
DeLima, Clarence A. (Cpl) WIA.
Dellatore, Herman (Pvt)
Dellinger, William H. (Pvt)
Demmler, Harry O. (Sgt)
Dentel, Martin A. (Pvt)
DesForges, Major G. (Pvt)
Devlin, Bert W. (PFC)
Dienstel, Edward A. (Pvt)

Doble, Percy R. (Pvt)
Dockstader, Gordon L. (Sgt)
Donnelly, James H. (Pvt)
Doss, Henry G. (Pvt)
Douglas, Erastus (Pvt)
Downard, Louis J. (Pvt)
Driscoll, Joseph F. (Cpl)
Duffield, Harry C. (Pvt)
Dunphy, William N. (Pvt) Marine Corps Reserve, WIA.
Durocher, Eugene J. (Pvt)
Dutcher, Allen V.R. (Pvt) Marine Reserve, Died of Wounds, 18 November 1918.
Dygert, Raymond W. (Pvt)
Edmonds, John L. (Cpl)
Ellsworth, Buster A. (Pvt)
Erlando, George N. (Pvt)
Essex, Robert M. (Pvt)
Evans, John F. (Cpl)
Ezell, Herbert A. (Pvt)
Fagan, Frank F. (Cpl)
Farrow, Rogers G. (Pvt)
Fasano, Joseph (Pvt) KIA, 11 June 1918.
Faust, Herbert J. (Pvt)
Fisher, William H. (Pvt) Marine Corps Reserve, WIA.
Flanigan, Joseph B. (Cpl) Marine Corps Reserve.
Flemming, Arthur W. (Pvt)
Fletcher, Walter L. (Pvt)
Flowers, John (Pvt)
Flynn, James J. (Pvt)
Foreman, Louis A. (PFC)
Foster, David B. (Cpl)
Foster, Patrick (Cpl)
Fowler, Frank J. (Pvt)
Franczek, Frank W. (Cpl)
Frank, Fred, Jr. (Pvt) Marine Corps Reserve, WIA.
Fresh, Frank D. (Pvt)
Fritz, Charles L. (Cpl) KIA, 5 November 1918.
Frock, Maurice E. (Pvt) Died of Wounds, 12 June 1918.
Gallivan, James (MarGun)
Gardner, George W. (Sgt) Marine Corps Reserve.
Geard, Albert (Pvt)
Geiger, John C. (Cpl)
Genader, Edward (Pvt) Battalion Medical Officer's Orderly.
Gest, Sydney G. (Cpl) Marine Corps Reserve.
Gidley, Irving Y. (Sgt)
Gillies, William J. (Cpl)
Glaser, Jacob (Pvt)
Glen, Fred B. (Pvt)
Glover, George W. (Cpl)
Gogue, Paul R. (Pvt) Battalion Intelligence Detail.
Goldmeier, Herbert M. (Pvt)
Goodrich, Louis H. (Cpl)
Goodwyn, Nathaniel B. (GySgt)
Gorman, Henry (PFC) Battalion Runner, WIA.
Gravenhorst, Clement B. (Pvt)
Gray, Frank H. (Sgt) KIA, 12 June 1918.
Gray, Kenneth E. (Pvt)
Green, Morton (Pvt)
Greening, William J., Jr. (Cpl)
Griffin, Ray B. (Pvt) Marine Corps Reserve.

Grimm, Howard L. (PFC)
Gross, George G., Jr. (Pvt) Marine Corps Reserve, gassed.
Groves, Ermy W. (Pvt)
Gulbrandsen, Erling E. (Pvt) KIA, 13 June 1918.
Gunter, Abslom P. (Pvt) Battalion Runner.
Hacker, William C. (Pvt) Marine Corps Reserve, WIA.
Hagaman, Will J. (Pvt)
Hagle, William C. (Pvt)
Hall, Earl J. (Pvt) Marine Corps Reserve, gassed.
Hall, Roy H. (Pvt)
Halstead, Roy G. (Pvt)
Hamilton, Donald (Sgt)
Hamilton, Richard J. (Pvt) KIA.
Hanes, Francis R. (Pvt)
Hansen, Max J. (Pvt)
Harper, William B. (Pvt)
Harrington, William M. (Pvt) Marine Reserve.
Hart, Pearl O. (PFC) Marine Corps Reserve, WIA.
Hays, George W. (Cpl) Marine Corps Reserve, WIA.
Healy, James J. (Pvt)
Heeran, John (Pvt) Marine Corps Reserve, WIA.
Heller, Arthur C. (Pvt)
Henderson, John S. (PFC) Cook, 2nd Class.
Henderson, Walter M. (Pvt) Officer's Orderly.
Hennen, Leo H. (GySgt)
Henry, Joseph (Cpl)
Herrick, Otto M. (Pvt)
Hight, Thomas A. (Pvt)
Hill, Samuel E. (Pvt) Cook, 2nd Class.
Hillery, David J. (Pvt)
Hodges, James S. (Pvt) KIA, 3 June 1918.
Hoffman, William (Sgt)
Holt, Dean G. (Pvt) Reserve, MIA.
Holtmeyer, George F. (Pvt)
Howell, James J. (PFC) Marine Corps Reserve.
Huff, Warren C. (Pvt)
Huntzinger, Joseph W. (Pvt)
Hurst, Azzie H. (Pvt) Marine Corps Reserve, WIA.
Hurst, Harvey (Pvt) Marine Corps Reserve, WIA.
Hustch, John W. (Pvt)
Iago, John J. (PFC) Marine Corps Reserve, WIA.
Ince, Robert H. (Cpl)
Inman, Lawrence C. (Pvt)
Inman, Leon W. (Sgt) Marine Corps Reserve, WIA.
Jackson, Thomas J. (Sgt) Marine Corps Reserve, WIA.
Jameson, William (Pvt)
Jarrell, John W. (Pvt)
Jarzemsky, Paul J. (Pvt)
Jennings, Blandford (PFC)
Jennings, Edward (Pvt)
Jennings, Virgil (PFC)
Jesperson, Elmer V. (Pvt)
Johnson, Arthur H. (Pvt) Marine Corps Reserve, WIA.
Johnson, Carl A. (Sgt)
Johnson, Charles B. (Cpl)
Johnson, Harry M. (Pvt) Marine Corps Reserve.
Johnston, Lemuel L., Jr. (Pvt)
Johnston, Venerable E. (HAp2)
Joinville, Victor E. (Pvt) KIA, 9 June 1918.
Jones, Elmer E. (PFC) Messman.

Jones, Robert L. (Cpl)
Jones, Warren C. (Pvt)
Jones, William R. (Pvt)
Kaboska, Joseph B. (Pvt)
Kahn, Albert H. (Pvt) Messman.
Kamp, Charles P., Jr. (Pvt)
Keefover, Walter L. (Pvt)
Keeney, Charles H. (Pvt) KIA, 14 June 1918.
Kendrick, John R. (Pvt)
Kerndl, Charles A. (Pvt)
Kerr, George J. (Pvt)
Kershner, Ira D. (Pvt)
Keyes, Edward J. (Pvt) Marine Corps Reserve, WIA.
Kirkendall, Harley S. (Pvt)
Kish, Steve F. (PFC) Marine Corps Reserve, WIA.
Klay, Carl (Pvt)
Knecht, Albert J. (Pvt)
Koch, Harry E. (Pvt)
Koehl, Walter S. (Pvt)
Kohlmorgen, Harry F. (Cpl) Marine Corps Reserve, WIA.
Kowker, Anthony J. (Cpl)
Krohn, Elmer (Pvt) Reserve, MIA.
Kwiakouski, Ray J. (Pvt)
Lacey, Charles G. (Sgt)
Lang, Fred A. (Pvt)
Lange, Walter E. (PFC)
Langkabel, Frank (PFC)
LaPine, Jesse R. (Cpl) Marine Corps Reserve, WIA.
LaPoint, John F. (Cpl)
Latzsch, Kenneth M. (Pvt)
Lavenau, Paul A. (Pvt) WIA.
Lee, Leonard T. (Pvt)
Lee, Will H. (Cpl)
Lee, William B. (PFC) Officer's Orderly.
Leepa, Andrew (Sgt) Mess Sgt.
Leithauser, Carl F. (Cpl)
Lindley, Ralph (Pvt) Marine Corps Reserve, WIA.
Linroth, Frank R. (Pvt) Marine Corps Reserve.
Lisko, Stephen, Jr. (Pvt)
Little, Roy W. (Pvt)
Lockhart, George W. (Pvt) Died of Wounds, 11 June 1918.
Lockridge, Conard (Pvt)
Lorentz, John (Pvt)
Love, Arthur F. (Pvt)
Lucey, John H. (PFC)
Luloff, Zalme (PFC)
Lundquist, Carl E. (Pvt)
Luther, Sam C. (Pvt) Marine Corps Reserve.
Lyman, John R. (Pvt)
MacDonald, Percy (Sgt)
Mackintosh, Samuel E. (Pvt)
Magin, Henry (Pvt)
Maher, Joseph F. (Sgt) KIA, 4 October 1918.
Mahler, Anthony E. (Pvt)
Maresca, Joseph (PFC)
Marion, Alton J. (Pvt)
Martin, Joseph A., Jr. (Pvt)
Martin, William C. (Pvt) Marine Corps Reserve.
Mason, Lester F. (Pvt)

Mathewson, Milledge R. (Pvt) Marine Corps Reserve, WIA.
Mathias, Jean (Pvt)
Mattson, Manny (Pvt)
McCarty, Richard W. (GySgt)
McClane, Arthur (Pvt)
McClure, Jesse W. (Sgt)
McCormick, Harry S. (Pvt)
McCormick, James A. (Pvt) KIA, 14 June 1918.
McDonald, Edward J. (Pvt) Marine Corps Reserve, WIA.
McDonald, Frank (Pvt)
McDow, Milton R. (Pvt)
McFarland, Andrew G. (Pvt)
McJunken, Howard B. (Pvt)
McKeon, Richard A. (Cpl)
McLure, Timothy B. (Cpl)
McNamara, John F. (Pvt)
Meadors, Johnny A. (Pvt) Marine Corps Reserve.
Meagher, Frank T. (Pvt)
Merkel, Edmo E. (PhM2) WIA, 4 October 1918.
Mertens, Frank J. (Pvt)
Meyer, Julius H. (Pvt)
Meyers, Kallman (Pvt)
Michel, Harold H. (PFC)
Miller, Earl S. (Pvt)
Miller, Frank L. (Pvt)
Milner, Malin D. (Pvt)
Minor, Dewey (Pvt)
Mitchell, Graham (Pvt)
Mitchell, William E. (Pvt)
Moizo, Phillip A. (Pvt)
Moore, Albert S. (Sgt) Marine Corps Reserve.
Moore, George (Pvt)
Moreinis, William (Pvt)
Morgan, Arthur W. (Cpl) Marine Corps Reserve, WIA.
Morse, Raymond E. (Pvt)
Morton, Elliott R. (Pvt)
Moseley, Benjamin F. (Pvt) KIA, 12 June 1918.
Motchman, Robert B. (Pvt)
Mudek, Joseph S. (Pvt)
Muscatell, Frank L. (Pvt)
Muschamp, William (Pvt)
Myers, Ernest R. (Cpl) Marine Corps Reserve.
Nash, James (Sgt)
Neffe, Victor E. (Pvt)
Neider, Frank (Pvt)
Nelson, Alvin R. (Cpl)
Nessly, Earl E. (PFC) Marine Corps Reserve, WIA.
Newman, Kenneth I. (Pvt)
Newman, Marion W. (Pvt)
Nickin, Howard D. (Cpl) Marine Corps Reserve, WIA.
Norris, Donald C. (Pvt)
Novak, Michael (Sgt)
O'Hara, Carl W. (Pvt)
Oldeen, Norman L. (Cpl) Marine Corps Reserve.
Olsen, August (Pvt)
O'Malley, Louis W. (Pvt) Marine Corps Reserve.
Oswald, Charles R. (Pvt) Marine Corps Reserve.
Overholser, Othov (PFC)
Paulson, Harry W. (Pvt) Marine Corps Reserve, WIA.
Peterson, Lind J. (Pvt)

Peterson, Walter C. (Pvt)

Petrie, Gerald R. (Cpl)

Phillips, Donald F. (Pvt)

Phillips, William B. (Pvt) Died, pneumonia, 19 September 1918.

Pickens, Clifford J. (Pvt) Officer's Orderly.

Pickett, Julius U. (Pvt) Battalion Runner.

Plumley, John S. (Pvt)

Pohl, Ernest G. (Pvt) Marine Corps Reserve.

Poland, Chandler U. (Cpl) Marine Corps Reserve.

Powers, Anselm L. (Cpl)

Prange, Ernst M. (Pvt)

Prickett, Frank (Pvt)

Priest, George S. (Pvt) Marine Corps Reserve, WIA.

Purvis, Charles G. (Pvt)

Quinn, Joseph F. (Pvt) Battalion Runner. Marine Corps Reserve, WIA, Died.

Rademacher, Richard L. (Pvt)

Rankin, Charlie H. (Cpl)

Raub, Russell M. (Cpl)

Rawlings, Rexall J. (Pvt)

Reath, Thomas R. (Sgt) Marine Corps Reserve, KIA, 12 June 1918.

Reed, Harry J. (Pvt)

Reed, Milton (Pvt)

Reed, Ronald A. (Pvt) Marine Corps Reserve, WIA.

Rice, Guy W. (Pvt) Marine Corps Reserve.

Richards, Osgood S. (Cpl)

Richmond, Clarence L. (Pvt) Marine Corps Reserve.

Riffert, Edward H. (Trumpeter)

Ringer, Stanley A. (Sgt)

Roach, George E. (Cpl) Marine Reserve, WIA.

Roberts, George E. (Pvt)

Roberts, Joseph K. (PFC) Marine Corps Reserve, WIA.

Roberts, William S. (Pvt)

Robertson, George M. (Cpl) Marine Corps Reserve.

Robinson, George Mc. (Pvt)

Rochford, John D. (Pvt)

Rodgers, John W. (Sgt) KIA, 6 June 1918.

Rogers, James L. (Pvt)

Rogers, Wolbert A. (Pvt) Marine Corps Reserve.

Roggelien, Herman O. (Pvt) Marine Corps Reserve, WIA.

Root, Harold E. (Pvt)

Root, Lemuel T. (Sgt)

Rothstein, Edgar (Pvt)

Rubin, Carleton J. (Pvt)

Rudge, Charles H. (Sgt) Marine Corps Reserve.

Rudge, Richard C. (GySgt)

Runevitch, Stanley B. (Pvt)

Russ, Frank L. (Pvt) Marine Corps Reserve. Regimental Runner.

Russell, John M. (Pvt)

Russell, Thomas N. (PhM3) WIA, 4 October 1918.

Ryan, John T. (Pvt)

Sager, Henry S. (Pvt)

Salisbury, Fred M. (Pvt) Marine Corps Reserve. Battalion Intelligence Detail.

Sapp, George A. (GySgt)

Saunders, Ernest G. (Trumpeter)

Schaich, John W. (Sgt)

Schaub, Herman L. (Pvt)

Schaufele, Raymond F. (Pvt)

Schierenbeck, Herbert K. (Pvt) Marine Corps Reserve, WIA.

Schmanke, William T. (Pvt)

Schofield, Jack M. (Pvt)

Scholey, Edward C. (Cpl)

Schonteich, Harry (Pvt)

Schrader, Henry (Pvt) Messman.

Schulmeister, Leonard A. (Pvt)

Seay, Joseph J. (PFC) Messman.

Seitz, Lester E (Pvt) Marine Corps Reserve, WIA.

Sewell, John H. (Cpl)

Shontz, Charles M. (Pvt) Battalion Runner.

Shriver, Harry L. (Pvt)

Sieg, Robert E. (Pvt) Marine Corps Reserve.

Simpson, Edward K. (Pvt)

Sims, Thomas B. (Pvt)

Singer, Maurice P. (Cpl)

Smith, Frank R. (Pvt)

Smith, Lincoln T. (PFC) Marine Corps Reserve.

Smith, Ralph M. (Sgt)

Snow, Edward C. (Pvt) Marine Corps Reserve.

Snyder, Clarence E. (Pvt)

Sokira, Birt (PFC)

Somers, James A., Jr. (Pvt)

Sparks, John C. (Pvt) Marine Corps Reserve, WIA.

Sprinkles, Walter L. (Pvt)

Stapleton, John (Cpl) Trumpeter.

Starns, Murrell W. (Pvt)

Still, Ralph D. (Pvt)

Stilley, James H. (PFC)

Stott, John G. (Cpl)

Stoughton, Ralph H. (Pvt)

Strickler, Jacob H. (Pvt)

Strike, Frederick W. (PFC)

Strong, Wayland M. (Pvt) Marine Corps Reserve.

Summers, Henry W. (Pvt)

Summers, Russell A. (Pvt) Marine Corps Reserve.

Swartz, James M. (Pvt)

Tate, James C. (Pvt) KIA, 11 June 1918.

Taylor, John W. (Pvt)

Teander, Roy (Cpl)

Tegeler, Vernon W. (Pvt) Marine Corps Reserve.

Thomas, Frank E. (Trumpeter)

Thompson, Daniel O. (Pvt)

Tiernan, Andrew L. (Pvt)

Tomlin, George D. (Pvt) Marine Corps Reserve, WIA.

Toms, David E. (PFC)

Torgerson, James A. (Pvt) Died of Wounds, 12 June 1918.

Tormey, William F. (Pvt) Company Commander's Orderly.

Towns, Jesse (Cpl)

Trimble, Harry A. (Pvt)

Trimble, Matt (Pvt)

Trusler, William (Pvt)

Turosky, John (Pvt)

Vaughn, Roy C. (Pvt)

Veith, Harry O. (Sgt)

Vernon, Samuel H. (Pvt)

Vogala, Fred (Pvt)

Wagner, Francis A. (Pvt)
Walczak, William (Pvt)
Wallis, George A. (Pvt)
Wallis, Otis L. (Pvt)
Walter, Frank H. (Sgt)
Watson, Roderick D. (Cpl) Marine Corps Reserve.
Weatherby, Alexander (Pvt)
Webber, Floyd H. (Cpl)
Weddell, George J. (PFC)
Wells, Roy W. (Pvt)
Werner, Bernard (Pvt) KIA, 6 June 1918.
Westlake, Charles S. (Sgt)
Wheeler, Marshall E. (Pvt) Marine Corps Reserve.
Whiteman, George H. (Pvt) Marine Corps Reserve, WIA.
Whitman, Louis C. (Cpl)
Wiese, Otto A. (Pvt)
Wilken, Berthold H. (Sgt)
Willhoit, Louis J. (Pvt) Marine Corps Reserve.
Williams, Harry W. (Cpl)
Wilson, Grant O. (Pvt)
Wilson, Joseph E. (Pvt)
Winter, Alvin R. (Pvt)
Wodarezyk, Mike (GySgt)
Wolford, Jerry (Cpl) Marine Corps Reserve.
Woodfield, Virgil H. (Pvt)
Wunder, William C. (Pvt)
Wyman, Elmer C. (Pvt)
Young, William M. (Pvt)
Zemaitis, Mindow L. (Pvt) KIA, 13 June 1918.
Zima, John (Pvt) Marine Corps Reserve, WIA.
Zoller, Charles (Pvt)

51st (G) Company, Second Battalion

NAME (RANK) REMARKS

Corbin, Willie O. (Cpt) Commanding Company, Member, Special Court.
Cumming, Samuel C. (Cpt) Commanding, G Co.
Williams, Lloyd W. (Cpt) Commanding Company, Died of Wounds, 11 June 1918.
Hagan, Joseph A. (1st Lt)
Massie, Nathaniel H. (1st Lt)
Montague, Robert L. (1st Lt)
Wagoner, Tolbert (1st Lt) WIA, 11 June 1918.
Brewer, James C. (2nd Lt) KIA, 11 June 1918.
Johnson, Gillis A. (2nd Lt)
Loughborough, R.H. (2nd Lt)
Keiter, William A. (2nd Lt) Marine Reserve.
Ross, Elbert W. (2nd Lt) Marine Reserve.
Wood, Egbert J. (2nd Lt) Marine Reserve.

Enlisted

Ballentine, Joseph C. (SGM)
Burton, Taressa C. (1st Sgt)
Kieren, Francis S. (1st Sgt)
Stockes, George F. (1st Sgt)

Abbott, Roy S. (Pvt)
Abrams, Curtis B. (PFC)
Airhart, Ralph J. (Pvt)
Alifeld, Arthur (Pvt)
Althoff, Paul J. (Sgt)
Angelo, Charles P. (Pvt)
Applebee, Edward G. (Pvt)
Applebee, William J. (Pvt)
Applegate, Julian E. (Pvt)
Ashe, Arthur J. (Pvt) KIA 11 June 1918.
Atkinson, William (Pvt) Messman.
Ault, Arthur E. (Pvt)
Austin, George P. (Pvt)
Auwerter, Andrew L. (Pvt)
Babbitt, Lawson M. (Pvt) KIA, 11 June 1918.
Bamforth, Jack (Pvt)
Bancroft, Sheridan (Pvt)
Bangs, Theodore E. (Pvt) KIA, 11 June 1918.
Banning, Henry A. (Cpl)
Barthlow, Harry E. (Pvt)
Bassett, John R. (Pvt)
Beaty, Alvin G. (Cpl)
Beck, Edward J. (Pvt)
Becker, Eugene B. (PFC)
Bell, Carl R. (Pvt) KIA, 2 July 1918.
Benson, Raymond R. (Pvt)
Benton, William A. (Pvt) Messman.
Berg, Johnnie N. (Pvt)
Berry, Glenn A. (Pvt)
Beyer, John W. (Pvt)
Biggerstaff, John W. (Pvt)
Blais, Emile (Pvt)
Blanke, Frederick A. (Pvt) Messman.
Bluhm, Carl (Pvt)
Bock, Fred E. (Pvt) KIA, 11 June 1918.
Bodine, George (Pvt) Marine Reserve.
Bonzales, Daniel (Cpl)
Boone, Isaac N. (Pvt) Messman.
Borck, John (Pvt)
Bradley, Hallie M. (Cpl) Marine Reserve.
Brandenburg, Arthur H. (Cpl)
Bray, William K. (Pvt) KIA, 11 June 1918.
Bridgford, John V. (Pvt) Orderly.
Briggs, Howard R. (Pvt) Marine Reserve.
Brouillette, Herby (Pvt)
Brown, Perry J. (Pvt)
Bruce, Herman (Pvt) Cook, 1st Class.
Buchardi, Adolph C. (Pvt)
Burns, Robert S. (Pvt) KIA, 10 June 1918.
Byrd, Wallace (PFC)
Callender, James C. (Pvt)
Carlisle, George E. (Pvt)
Carlisle, George K. (Pvt)
Carr, Joseph F. (Pvt)
Carter, Sidney T. (Pvt)
Caudle, James W. (Pvt)
Clark, Ernest C. (PFC) KIA, 10 November 1918.
Clark, Myron A. (PFC) Marine Reserve.
Clauson, Nicholas E. (GySgt)
Clave, Louis E. (Pvt)
Clayton, James A. (Pvt)

Cleveland, Jesse C. (Pvt) Marine Reserve.

Cleveland, William R. (Sgt) Died of wounds, 11 June 1918.

Coe, Philip H. (PFC) Regimental Chaplain's Orderly.

Colby, Elwood L. (Cpl)

Collins, Timothy F. (Pvt)

Commons, Harry E. (Pvt)

Connelly, Raymond F. (Cpl)

Conner, Robert N. (Pvt) Cook, 3rd Class.

Cook, Harry J. (Cpl)

Cook, Judson M. (Pvt) Marine Reserve.

Cook, Langdon A. (Sgt)

Cooper, Charles H. (Pvt)

Cooper, Samuel L. (Pvt)

Corrington, John W. (Pvt)

Craft, Boykin W. (Pvt) Cook, 2nd Class.

Craig, Horace J. (Pvt)

Craig, Raymond H. (Pvt)

Crim, Charles B. (Pvt)

Crossman, John L. (Pvt)

Crumb, Chester L. (PFC)

Cundy, Miles S. (Cpl)

Curley, Thomas J. (Sgt) Mess Sgt.

Davis, Carl W. (Pvt)

Davis, Homer H. (Pvt)

Davis, Patrick H. (Pvt)

Delaney, Edward (Pvt)

Deshazer, Charles H. (Pvt)

Dibbert, Robert R. (Pvt)

Diket, Joseph H. (Pvt)

DiNoto, Salvatore (Drummer)

Dixon, Arthur G. (Cpl)

Dodd, James I. (Pvt) KIA, 6 June 1918.

Donahue, William A. (Pvt) KIA, 1 November 1918.

Dorris, John L. (Pvt)

Downey, John L. (Pvt)

Dreher, Carl L. (Pvt)

Dumm, Walter C. (Pvt)

Duncan, John F. (Pvt)

Dunlap, Glenn H. (Pvt)

Eaton, Robert H. (Pvt)

Edenton, Charlie V. (Pvt)

Edge, Edward T. (Pvt) KIA, 11 June 1918.

Elchinger, George H. (Pvt)

Ellison, Sherman A. (Pvt)

Enix, James A. (GySgt)

Erickson, Earl E. (Cpl)

Erwin, Walter C. (Pvt) Messman.

Etoch, Will A. (Pvt)

Falslev, Marinus J. (Pvt) Messman.

Faries, Roswell R. (Pvt)

Farrar, William M., Jr. (Pvt)

Faulkner, George D. (Sgt) WIA.

Ferranti, Ernest J. (Pvt) KIA, 11 June 1918.

Ferson, Paul D. (PFC)

Finley, Vernon T. (Pvt)

Fisher, Roland (Cpl) Died of disease, 23 February 1919.

Fitzgerald, Maurice J. (Pvt)

Flaherty, Louis (Pvt)

Fletcher, Fred (Pvt)

Ford, Wilford R. (PFC)

Forner, Peter C. (Pvt)

Foster, Ferris U. (Cpl)

Fowler, Mark P. (Pvt)

Francis, Lester L. (Pvt)

Freer, Roy (GySgt)

French, George C. (Pvt)

Gallagher, Thomas J. (PFC)

Ganzel, Charles C. (Pvt)

Gates, Ralph M. (Pvt)

Gee, David C. (Drummer)

Ginsberg, Charles (Pvt)

Gladstone, Leo (Pvt) WIA.

Glenn, Rollie D. (Pvt)

Gonzales, Daniel (Pvt)

Gordon, Raymond H. (Pvt) Pay & Muster Roll Clerk.

Gothard, Ira J. (Cpl) Wounded, 11 June 1918.

Graham, Loyal Y., 3rd (Pvt)

Grannan, Thomas F. (Pvt)

Grant, Albert M (Cpl)

Gray, Frank (Sgt)

Green, William (Pvt)

Greider, Earl C. (Pvt)

Guillod, Frank L. (Sgt)

Guterl, William P. (Pvt)

Haller, George W. (Cpl)

Hanna, Raymond P. (Pvt)

Hansen, George E. (Pvt)

Harbright, Walter (Cpl)

Harden, William (Pvt)

Harmon, Michael V. (Cpl)

Harney, Arthur P. (Pvt)

Harper, Roy A. (Pvt)

Harrington, Henry A. (Pvt) Messman.

Harrison, Edward D. (Cpl)

Hart, Edward J. (Pvt)

Haselbeck, Matthew F. (Pvt)

Hayden, William T. (Pvt)

Heck, Thomas E. (Pvt)

Hensiek, Alonzo C. (Cpl)

Hewes, Cyrus A. (Pvt) Messman.

Hiers, William J. (Pvt)

Hill, Daniel H. (Pvt)

Hill, Everett L. (Pvt)

Hillabush, George F. (Sgt)

Himmelberger, Fred (Cpl)

Hinckley, Joel C. (Pvt)

Hobright, Walter H. (Sgt)

Hogdon, Lester W. (Sgt)

Hogan, Thomas (GySgt) WIA.

Holder, Arthur (Cpl)

Holt, Jeston E. (Pvt)

Holton, Andrew H. (Pvt)

Hopkins, Lum O. (Pvt) Marine Reserve.

Howe, Cecil L. (Pvt)

Hughes, Richard J. (Pvt) Marine Reserve.

Hutcheson, Stuart (Pvt)

Jackson, Stephen D. (Cpl)

Jacobs, Derwin H. (Pvt)

Jacobs, Walter O. (Pvt) Messman.

Jennings, Raymond G. (Sgt)

Jernigan, Gus M. (Pvt) Cook, 1st Class.

Jocobensky, Stephen (Pvt)
Jolly, Willis L. (Pvt)
Josephson, Charles A. (Pvt)
Jump, Elmer L. (Sgt)
Kapoostanski, Owse (Cpl) WIA.
Kennedy, Joseph A. (Pvt)
Kennedy, William H. (Pvt) KIA, 10 November 1918.
Kezar, Glenn A. (Pvt)
Kinnear, Lyle D. (Pvt)
Kirsch, Joseph M. (Pvt) Messman.
Klebe, William E. (Pvt)
Klingenberg, Arthur (Pvt)
Koeneman, Arthur (Pvt)
Koeppe, Paul D. (Pvt)
Konkel, Charles (Pvt)
Kovalchek, Jacob S. (Pvt)
Krasowski, Simon (Pvt)
Kretzer, Leo W. (Pvt)
Kuechenmeister, Henry A. Pvt
Kurzawski, John (Pvt) KIA, 21 July 1918.
Lalor, Lawrence (PFC)
Lambeth, George D. (Sgt)
Largen, Otis (Pvt)
Lavelle, William H. (Cpl)
Lawhon, Claude (Pvt)
Lawrence, John R. (Pvt) KIA, 11 June 1918.
Lazzara, Antonio (Cpl)
Lee, William E. (Pvt)
Legg, John W. (Pvt)
Lemon, Gilbert W. (Cpl) KIA, 11 June 1918.
Lochbehler, George (Pvt)
Locke, Karl W. (Cpl) KIA, 3 June 1918.
Logan, Harold S. (Pvt) Messman.
Lowell, Louis A. (Pvt)
Lundachen, Harvey C. (Pvt)
Lusader, Maurice S. (Pvt) KIA, 10 November 1918.
Lyman, John R. (Pvt)
Lyon, Russell G. (PFC) KIA, 11 November 1918.
Lyon, Stephen R. (Pvt)
MacBean, Hector W. (Cpl)
Manning, Edward E. (Pvt) Messman.
Markling, Frank J. (Pvt)
Marshall, Hugh E. (Pvt)
Marshall, James L. (PFC)
Marshall, Walter S. (PFC)
Marter, Timothy E. (Pvt)
Martin, Edward (Pvt)
Martin, George M. (Pvt)
Mason, Harry B. (Pvt)
Mathews, Bernard R. (Pvt)
Mayer, Frederick J. (Pvt) Messman.
McCarrel, Vern M. (Pvt)
McColm, William J. (Sgt) KIA, 6 June 1918.
McCorkle, Louis G. (Cpl)
McCormack, John J. (Pvt)
McCullough, William R. (Pvt)
McCurry, Lewis M. (Pvt) KIA, 25 June 1918.
McGartland, Clarence F. (Pvt)
McGee, Joe (Pvt)
McGovern, Philip M. (Pvt)
McKee, Harry C. (Pvt)

McKenna, Daniel T. (Cpl)
McKenna, James J. (Pvt) KIA, 7 June 1918.
McLean, Amos A. (Pvt)
McLeod, Murdock E. (Cpl)
McMasters, Ezra (Pvt)
McMillen, Ewell E. (Pvt)
McNearny, Joseph R. (Pvt)
McReynolds, William F. (Pvt)
Meinsohn, George D. (Pvt)
Mejia, Raymond (Pvt)
Miley, John B. (Pvt)
Miller, Archibald (Sgt)
Miller, Dewey (PFC) WIA, 4 October 1918.
Mills, Verne E. (Pvt)
Mitchell, William O. (Pvt)
Monroe, Ezra C. (Pvt)
Moore, Alva E. (Pvt)
Moore, Orval C. (Cpl)
Moore, William B. (Pvt)
Moorefield, Harold E. (PFC)
Morgan, James D. (Pvt) KIA, 12 July 1918.
Morris, Ernest R. (Cpl)
Morrison, Frank (Pvt)
Moss, William M. (Pvt) KIA, 11 June 1918.
Mulligan, Edward H. (Cpl)
Murphy, David J. (Cpl)
Naegelen, Charles A. (Pvt) KIA, 11 June 1918.
Naud, Earl E. (Sgt)
Nelson, Charles E. (Pvt)
Nelson, John (Sgt) Police Sgt. Supply Sergeant.
Nelson, Solon A. (Pvt)
Newitt, George R. (Pvt)
Noblett, Elmer A. (Pvt)
Nolan, William T., Jr. (Pvt) KIA, 11 June 1918.
Noles, Richard L. (Pvt)
Norton, Walter V. (Pvt) KIA, 11 June 1918.
Novess, Robert L. (Pvt)
Nowak, Peter (Cpl)
Ogden, Stanley D., Jr. (Pvt)
O'Hara, Frank D. (Pvt)
O'Hern, John E. (Pvt)
Olesinski, Steve (Pvt)
Olson, Alex W. (Pvt)
Ommundsen, Abraham L. (Pvt)
O'Sullivan, Thomas M. (Pvt)
Otten, Paul A. (Pvt)
Ouzts, Joseph P. (Pvt) KIA, 11 June 1918.
Owens, William J. (Pvt) Marine Reserve.
Owings, Joseph O. (Pvt)
Owings, Sam W. (Pvt) Marine Reserve.
Palmer, Harold T. (Cpl)
Palwick, Joseph (Sgt) Muster Roll Clerk.
Paradis, Emile P. (Pvt)
Parish, Herbert I. (Pvt)
Parry, William (Pvt) Barber.
Parsons, James H. (Sgt)
Patten, James R. (Pvt)
Patterson, John A. (Pvt)
Paxson, Darrel (Pvt)
Paxton, William F. (Pvt) Marine Reserve.
Pearoe, Robert R. (Pvt)

Peffly, Calvin (Cpl)
Perash, Andrew M. (Sgt) WIA.
Perry, William F. (Pvt)
Petro, Frank H. (Pvt)
Philhower, Louis S. (Trumpeter)
Phillips, Eldridge D. (Pvt)
Phillips, Henry K. (Pvt) Marine Reserve.
Phillips, Owen R. (Pvt)
Pickering, James H. (Pvt)
Pillsworth, Thomas S. (Pvt)
Plunkett, Edward J. (Pvt)
Pomeroy, Robert O. (Cpl)
Pople, Charles S. (Pvt)
Powers, James G. (Pvt)
Pownall, John W. (Cpl) SD Mechanic
Pratt, Jesse L. (Pvt) KIA, 2 November 1918.
Price, Ivan L. (Pvt) KIA, 3 November 1918.
Pritchett, John A. (Pvt)
Pross, Gustav A. (Pvt) Marine Reserve.
Puffer, Richard W. (Cpl)
Pugh, Herschel D. (Pvt)
Quam, Carl E. (Pvt)
Racinowski, Stanley (Pvt)
Reardon, Richard J. (Pvt)
Reichard, Carl (Pvt)
Remonda, Elias E. (Pvt) Cook, 3rd Class.
Reynolds, Edwin F. (Pvt)
Reynolds, Walter H. (Pvt)
Rhodes, Merrill R. (Pvt)
Richards, James A. (Pvt)
Richardson, Clarence E. (Pvt)
Richardson, Oard (Pvt)
Roach, Charles L., Jr. (Pvt)
Roberts, Benjamin F. (Pvt)
Roberts, James H. (PFC) KIA, 10 November 1918.
Rogers, Raymond P. (Pvt) Gassed, WIA.
Rohrbaugh, Richard M. (Pvt)
Rolfe, Ward A. (Pvt)
Romick, Charles (Pvt)
Rosen, Edward W. (Pvt)
Ross, Richard S. (GySgt) WIA, Shell Shock.
Rothauser, John (Pvt)
Ruark, Edward D. (Cpl) Marine Reserve.
Runa, John F. (PFC)
Russell, John F., Jr. (Cpl)
St. Clair, Charles H. (Pvt)
Sandberg, Max (Pvt)
Savercool, David (Cpl) KIA, 12 June 1918.
Sayre, Harvey N. (Pvt)
Schifferer, George (Sgt)
Schild, Harry W. (Pvt)
Scholz, Edward T. (Pvt)
Schrader, Carl F. (Trumpeter)
Schramm, Frederick (Cpl) KIA, 6 June 1918.
Schreiber, Carl S. (Pvt)
Schreiber, Karl C. (Pvt)
Schulz, William L., Jr. (PFC)
Schulze, Claude H. (Pvt) Marine Reserve.
Schutt, Vern W. (Pvt) Messman.
Schwabe, Calvin W. (Pvt)
Seger, Herbert D. (Pvt)

Selbach, Frank B. (Pvt)
Sever, John J. (Pvt)
Shanafelt, Saylor D. (Pvt)
Shawe, Merwyn C. (Pvt)
Sheehan, Daniel H. (Pvt)
Sheehan, John H. (Pvt)
Shepard, Percy L. (Cpl)
Sherman, John J. (PFC) Marine Reserve.
Shimandle, Fred E. (Pvt)
Shipe, Orme S. (Pvt)
Siefert, Frederick A. (Cpl)
Silvers, Samuel E. (Pvt)
Simkins, Norman A. (Pvt)
Simms, Arthur W. (Pvt)
Skala, Leon F. (Pvt)
Skinner, Charles L. (Pvt)
Slaughter, Lester (Pvt)
Slivey, Matthew C. (Pvt)
Smith, Alfred J. (Pvt)
Smith, LeClair (Sgt)
Smith, Ralph D. (Pvt)
Smith, Stacy K. (Pvt)
Smith, William C. (Pvt)
Snavely, Glenn A. (Pvt) WIA.
Snodgrass, Howard (Pvt)
Soddy, William C. (Pvt)
Spear, Walter C. (Pvt)
Spears, Rex W. (PFC)
Spencer, Warren G. (Pvt)
Spinley, Joseph (Pvt)
Stamps, Ira H. (Pvt)
Stanton, Claude A. (Pvt)
Steck, Frederick F. (Pvt)
Steen, William H. (Pvt) Marine Reserve.
Stewart, Albert D. (Pvt) KIA, 11 June 1918.
Stockman, John (Pvt) Marine Reserve Cl2.
Stoffel, James E. (Pvt)
Strasser, Walter F. (Pvt)
Streator, Paul M. (Sgt)
Strob, Galusha A. (Pvt)
Stultz, Garr W. (PFC) Marine Reserve.
Sullivan, Andrew J. (Pvt)
Sullivan, George W. (Pvt)
Sutherland, Earl L. (Cpl)
Sutherland, Jim W. (Sgt)
Swank, Harry L. (Sgt)
Swanson, Harry A. (Pvt)
Swesey, Lawrence E. (GySgt) WIA, Belleau Wood.
Swope, Walter B. (Pvt)
Taunt, Clarence (Cpl) Marine Reserve Cl2.
Taylor, Willie C. (Pvt)
Thacher, Howard L. (Pvt)
Thigpen, Luscious H. (Pvt)
Thoburn, Archie C. (Pvt)
Thomas, Hal B. (Pvt)
Thompson, David A.R. (Sgt)
Thorn, Raymond S. (Pvt) KIA, 11 June 1918.
Tipton, George V. (Sgt)
Tisdale, Arlo W. (Pvt)
Tobin, Ralph A. (Pvt) Marine C. Reserve Cl2.
Tooze, Roff (Cpl)

Tracy, Joseph E. (Pvt)
Tucker, Russell E. (Pvt)
Turner, Charles R. (Cpl)
Turner, James C. (Pvt) Marine Reserve.
Upson, James D. (Pvt)
Valerio, Raphael (Pvt)
Vinyard, Howard (Cpl) KIA, 11 June 1918.
Voorhees, Perry (Pvt)
Wagoner, Tolbert W. (Cpl)
Watts, William R. (Pvt)
Weeks, Dewey E. (Pvt)
Weeks, William E. (Pvt) KIA, 15 June 1918.
Wells, Harvey L. (Pvt)
Whelan, Ray A. (Pvt)
Whittington, Odell (Pvt)
Wilkison, Guy F. (Pvt)
Williams, Cecil A. (GySgt) WIA at Belleau Wood.
Williams, Forest (Pvt)
Williams, Harold (Sgt)
Williams, Lewis L. (Pvt)
Williams, Roy (Pvt)
Williams, Thomas D. (PFC)
Willums, Milford W. (Pvt)
Wilson, Henry E. (Pvt)
Winn, Joseph L. (Pvt) Cook, 2nd Class.
Wise, James H. (Pvt)
Withers, Charles E. (Sgt) Police Sergeant.
Witte, John K. (Pvt)
Wnuk, Joseph F. (Cpl) WIA at Belleau Wood.
Wojoiak, Ignatius (Pvt)
Wolfe, Russell B. (Pvt)
Wood, John D. (Pvt)
Woodruff, Wilbert A. (Pvt)
Woodward, Clarence (Pvt)
Wortley, George E. (Pvt) Messman.
Yates, Belton C. (Cpl)
York, Earl J.B. (Pvt)
Zinner, Fred J. (Sgt)

55th (H) Company, Second Battalion

Name (Rank) Remarks

Butler, Henry M. (Maj)
Blanchfield, John (Cpt) Commanding, 55th Co. Died of wounds, 8 June 1918.
Cornell, Percy D. (Cpt) Commanding, 55th Co.
Peck, Dewitt (Cpt)
Baylis, Charles D. (1st Lt)
Cooke, Elliott D. (1st Lt) WIA.
Mathews, William R. (1st Lt) Battalion Intelligence Officer.
Shepherd, Lemuel C. (1st Lt) WIA.
Wilson, Frank W. (1st Lt)
Brady, Vincent A. (2nd Lt) Marine Reserve. Died of wounds, 14 November 1918.
Cannon, Adolphus (2nd Lt) Marine Corps Reserve.
Carhart, Joseph (2nd Lt) WIA.

Corriveau, Paul E. (2nd Lt) KIA, 6 October 1918.
Gassert, Howell A. (2nd Lt)
Johnson, Clell G. (2nd Lt) Marine Corps Reserve.
Lane, Harry G. (2nd Lt)
Lyle, Lucius Q.C.L. (2nd Lt)
Maher, Joseph F. (2nd Lt) Reserve, KIA.
Palmer, Harold T. (2nd Lt) KIA, 3 October 1918.
Vose, Howard L. (2nd Lt) WIA, Died of Wounds, 8 October 1918.
Waterhouse, William F. (2nd Lt) KIA, 13 June 1918.
Williams, Marshall B. (2nd Lt) Marine Corps Reserve.

Enlisted

Brown, Stephen (1st Sgt)
Burnett, John T. (1st Sgt) KIA, 13 June 1918.
Aasland, John E. (Cpl)
Abrisch, Hall N. (Pvt)
Adams, William F. (Pvt)
Albert, Sarvaul H. (Pvt) Marine Reserve, WIA.
Alexander, Richard B. (Pvt)
Allan, John W. (Pvt)
Alspach, Luther J. (Pvt) Marine Reserve.
Anderson, Claude S. (PhM1)
Anderson, Howard E. (Pvt)
Angell, Ralph M. (Pvt) Marine Reserve, WIA.
Applebee, William J. (Pvt) Marine Reserve.
Arabie, Fernand (Pvt)
Armstrong, Percy D. (Pvt)
Arnold, William H. (GySgt) WIA.
Ashdown, Wallace K. (Pvt)
Assland, John E. (Cpl)
Atkinson, Oscar I. (PFC)
Auerback, Frederick P., Jr. (Pvt)
Augusta, Roe O. (PFC)
Auten, Lawrence L. (Pvt) KIA, 4 October 1918.
Bailey, William O. (PFC)
Baker, Russell W. (Pvt)
Baldwin, Ralph W. (Cpl)
Ball, Earle M. (Pvt) Messman.
Bankard, Charles W. (Pvt)
Barczykowski, Frank J. (Pvt) WIA.
Barnett, Bryan J. (Pvt)
Barrows, Albert E. (Cpl)
Barry, James F. (PFC) Messman.
Barth, Herbert J. (Pvt) MIA.
Basso, Michael T. (Pvt)
Baubie, Edward F. (Pvt)
Bauchmann, Otto C. (Pvt)
Baughman, Victor K. (Pvt) Died of Wounds.
Baylis, Joseph B. (GySgt) MIA.
Bean, John W.L. (Pvt) MIA.
Beddow, Paul M. (PFC)
Behr, Frederick G. (Pvt) KIA, 8 June 1918.
Belcher, Stanley K. (Pvt) Marine Reserve, WIA.
Bell, Ernest E. (Cpl) Clerk, Regimental Headquarters.
Benoit, Albert (Pvt)
Benson, Albert E. (Pvt)
Benton, Arthur C. (Sgt)
Benz, George E. (Pvt) KIA.
Bergdahl, Carl F. (Cpl) KIA, 4 October 1918.
Bergey, John St. C. (Pvt)

Bergstrom, Walter R. (Sgt) WIA.

Bielecki, William E. (Pvt)

Biglow, Leslie (Pvt) KIA, 10 June 1918.

Birkes, William H. (Cpl)

Bloomquist, John W. (Cpl) KIA, 8 June 1918

Bluhm, Fred H. (Pvt) Marine Reserve, WIA.

Bobby, Andy (Cpl)

Boeckel, Thomas F. (Sgt) Battalion Intelligence Section.

Bolton, Walter E. (Pvt) MIA.

Bonitz, Raymond W. (Pvt)

Bonner, Paul (Pvt)

Bonney, Homer W. (Cpl)

Boston, Edgar D. (PFC)

Boyd, Donovan E. (Pvt)

Bradbury, Eoen, Jr. (Pvt)

Bradford, Robert E.L. (Cpl)

Brant, Orville J. (Cpl) KIA.

Britton, Paul W. (Sgt) KIA, 6 October 1918.

Brown, Dilmus (Pvt) KIA, 12 June 1918.

Brown, George F. (Pvt)

Brown, Perry J. (Pvt) Marine Reserve, WIA.

Bryan, Bates (Pvt)

Buchanan, Orville C. (Pvt)

Buchlein, Edward R. (Pvt)

Buford, David L. (GySgt) KIA, 13 June 1918.

Burgesser, George W. (Pvt) Battalion Orderly.

Burke, Philip J. (Pvt) Died, pneumonia.

Burns, Paul P. (Pvt) Marine Reserve, WIA.

Burnside, Harry M. (Pvt) Messman.

Cabell, Edward E. (Cpl)

Cady, Ray L. (Pvt)

Cairns, David D. (Pvt)

Callahan, John J. (Pvt)

Callahan, Thomas C. (Pvt)

Campbell, Albert D. (Pvt)

Campbell, Daniel M. (Pvt) Sig., 3rd Class. Battalion Runner.

Campbell, James E. (Cpl) MIA.

Canfield, Hector J. (Pvt)

Cannon, Leonard I. (Pvt) Marine Corps Reserve, WIA.

Cardarella, Marco (Pvt)

Carew, Gerald A. (Pvt) Battalion Runner.

Carter, George A. (Pvt)

Cartwright, Dewey S. (Pvt) Marine Corps Reserve.

Caston, Carey T. (PFC) Marine Reserve, WIA.

Chamberlain, Earle H. (Pvt) Wounded, Died of Wounds.

Chandler, George R. (Pvt) Marine Corps Reserve.

Chandler, John H. (Pvt) Marine Corps Reserve, WIA.

Charland, Harry N. (Pvt)

Chefetz, Harry (Cpl) KIA, 18 July 1918.

Childs, William W. (Pvt) Marine Corps Reserve, WIA.

Clark, Thayer H. (PhM1)

Cody, Alfonso L. (Pvt)

Colberg, Edward (Pvt) Cook, 4th Class.

Colliflower, Owen (Pvt)

Colterjohn, Gilbert D. (Cpl)

Conger, Charles A. (PFC) WIA.

Conlon, Irving J. (Pvt)

Connolly, Thomas M. (Pvt) WIA.

Conroe, George E. (Pvt) Marine Corps Reserve. Messman.

Cooper, Charles H. (PFC) Marine Reserve, KIA.

Coppenger, George W. (PFC)

Cornprobst, Charles C. (Sgt)

Corson, Almer R. (Pvt)

Corson, Horace V. (Pvt)

Costage, Alexander E. (Cpl)

Coulter, Frank L. (Pvt) Marine Corps Reserve.

Courtney, Robey K. (Pvt) Marine Reserve, WIA.

Coyle, Joseph C. (Pvt)

Crepeau, Louis J. (Pvt) C.C. Orderly. Battalion Interpreter.

Crichton, John C. (Pvt) Batt. orderly.

Critchfield, Roland A. (Pvt) Marine Corps Reserve.

Crose, James E. (PFC)

Crossett, Hobart B. (Pvt)

Crump, George W. (Pvt)

Cunningham, Charles F. (Pvt) KIA, 21 July 1918.

Cunningham, Virgil (Pvt)

Curtis, William W. (Pvt)

Dadini, Grutly S. (Pvt) Marine Corps Reserve.

Daley, Arthur J. (Cpl) Died of disease.

Dargitz, Carl E. (Pvt) Marine Reserve, WIA.

Davis, James E. (Pvt)

Davis, Jerry M. (Pvt)

Davison, Harold E. (PFC) Marine Corps Reserve.

Dean, William McK. (PFC)

DeChant, Henry J. (Pvt)

DeGabain, Edward D. (Pvt) Marine Corps Reserve.

Degnan, James F. (Cpl) Marine Reserve, KIA, 10 November 1918.

DeLuca, James (Pvt)

DeMaio, John J. (Pvt)

Demaree, Ralph G. (Pvt)

Denn, Alexander (Pvt) KIA, 12 June 1918.

Dixon, Harry S. (PFC)

Dobovitz, Abe (Pvt)

Dockx, Francis J. (Cpl) KIA, 5 June 1918.

Dodd, Earl P. (Pvt)

Donaldson, Thomas H. (Sgt) WIA.

Donnell, William H. (Pvt)

Donovan, William E. (Pvt) Battalion Intelligence Section.

Doody, John (Cpl)

Dorsey, Edward (Pvt) KIA, 5 October 1918.

Dorsey, Howard S. (Cpl) KIA, 5 October 1918.

Douthit, Leland E. (Cpl)

Dowd, John J. (Pvt)

Doyle, Edward T. (Cpl) Marine Reserve, KIA.

Drake, Frank E. (Pvt)

Dudley, Earl S. (Pvt)

Dunfee, Alton L. (Pvt) Battalion Orderly.

Durant, Charles E. (Pvt)

Duzienski, William (Pvt)

Dwyer, George P. (Sgt)

Dyrhaug, Melvin (Pvt) Marine Reserve.

Eagan, Alonzo (Pvt)

Edwards, Fred M. (Pvt)

Ellett, George A. (PFC)

Ellis, Earl T. (Pvt) Marine Reserve, WIA.

Elmore, Theodore (Drummer)
Emmerson, Emil (Pvt) Marine Corps Reserve.
Engel, William F. (Sgt)
Evans, Walter O. (Cpl)
Evans, William (PFC)
Everett, Harold E. (Cpl)
Fallon, James (Sgt) Mess Sgt.
Farley, John J. (Pvt) Messman.
Faulkner, Charles B. (Pvt)
Fauver, William C. (Pvt) Messman.
Felker, Charles L. (Pvt)
Field, Harold (Pvt) MIA.
Fisher, Harry C. (PFC) Marine Reserve, WIA.
Flagler, Clifton (Pvt)
Floyd, James R. (Cpl)
Ford, William L. (PFC)
Foster, Durward G. (Pvt)
Foulkes, William J. (PFC)
Fountain, James H. (Pvt) Died of Wounds, date not known.
Foy, Joseph J. (Pvt)
Frank, Guy W. (Cpl)
Franz, John H. (Pvt)
Frazee, Walter E. (Pvt) Messman.
Fredericks, Neil W. (Pvt)
Fuller, Edward A. (Pvt)
Gallagher, Frank P. (Pvt)
Gallagher, Osler D. (Cpl)
Galvin, Owen A. (Pvt)
Garrett, Charles G. (Pvt) Battalion Orderly.
Garrett, John M. (Sgt) Battalion Orderly.
Gascovitch, Isaac (Pvt)
Geiger, Ray F. (PFC) WIA.
Geores, Carl H. (PFC)
Gerrik, Lewis W. (Pvt) Marine Corps Reserve, WIA.
Gilbert, Leslie T. (Pvt) WIA, 4 October 1918.
Ginsberg, Charles (Pvt) Marine Reserve.
Gleason, Vincent J. (Sgt) Mess Sergeant.
Glover, Harry L. (Pvt)
Glover, William L. (Pvt)
Godfrey, Albert P. (Pvt)
Godshaw, Samuel G. (Pvt)
Goerke, George A. (PFC) WIA.
Goldeen, Samuel S. (PFC) MIA.
Golden, Leo P. (Pvt)
Goodwin, Harry (Pvt)
Gorby, Marion (Pvt)
Gorman, Edwin M. (Pvt) KIA, 18 July 1918.
Gorshel, David H. (Pvt)
Gosman, Kenneth W. (Pvt)
Gould, Leon W. (Pvt) MIA.
Gowen, Eddie S. (Pvt)
Graham, Edwin L. (Pvt)
Grannan, Thomas F. (Pvt) MIA.
Grau, Henry G. (Pvt) Marine Corps Reserve.
Gravener, John N. (Pvt) KIA, 12 June 1918.
Green, Charles N. (Pvt) KIA, 12 June 1918.
Greenberg, Abe (Pvt)
Greene, Benjamin S. (PFC)
Greene, Frank A. (Pvt)
Gregg, Thomas J. (Pvt) Died of Wounds, 19 July 1918.

Grife, Bernard L. (Pvt)
Griffith, Chester D. (Pvt)
Gross, Alton (Pvt) Marine Corps Reserve
Gumbert, Charles M. (Pvt)
Haines, Lyle M. (Pvt)
Hale, Jerry F. (Pvt)
Hale, John J. (Pvt)
Haley, John D. (PFC)
Hamann, Fred (Pvt)
Hamilton, George W. (Pvt) Marine Reserve, WIA.
Hamilton, Irving G. (GySgt)
Haney, John S. (Pvt) Marine Corps Reserve
Hannah, Stanford (Pvt) MIA.
Harden, William (Pvt) Marine Reserve, WIA.
Harper, Glenn E. (Pvt) WIA.
Harralson, Aymard C. (Pvt) KIA.
Harrington, Daniel R. (Pvt)
Hart, Murray E. (Trumpeter)
Hartzog, Hal L. (Cpl) Battalion Intelligence Section.
Harvey, John J. (Pvt) MIA.
Harwell, Malcolm L. (Pvt)
Hasely, Charles F. (Trumpeter) Marine Reserve, WIA.
Hatfield, Monroe S. (PFC)
Hathaway, Ben H. (Cpl)
Hawk, John F. (Pvt)
Haybeck, Charles Jr. (Cpl) KIA, 12 June 1918.
Hayden, William T. (Cpl) Marine Reserve, KIA.
Heath, Hobart (Pvt)
Heavrin, Irwin B. (Pvt) WIA.
Heffley, Jake L. (Pvt)
Henderson, Edgar A. (Pvt)
Hendron, Harold H. (Pvt) Marine Corps Reserve.
Henning, Herbert W. (Pvt) MIA.
Heyer, Delbert D. (Pvt) Marine Reserve, WIA.
Hickok, James A. (Pvt) WIA.
Higbee, Chester A. (Pvt)
Hiller, Walter S. (PFC)
Hirst, Samuel C. (Pvt) WIA.
Hodgdon, Lester W. (Sgt) WIA.
Hodgen, Grover C. (PFC) Marine Reserve.
Hoffman, Ralph E. (Pvt)
Hoffman, Valentine P. (Pvt) WIA.
Hoffman, William C. (Pvt) Marine Reserve, WIA.
Holder, Arthur (Sgt) WIA, Died of Wounds.
Holland, Thomas J. (Pvt)
Hopkins, Elmer E. (Pvt)
Hopkins, Farrell E. (Pvt)
Hopta, Joseph L. (Sgt) KIA, 4 November 1918.
Hornor, Kenneth (Pvt) Marine Corps Reserve, WIA.
Horstmann, Paul F. (Cpl) KIA, 21 July 1918.
House, Calvin (Cpl) Battalion Intelligence Section.
Howard, Arthur S. (Pvt)
Howd, George C. (Pvt)
Hruby, Joseph (Pvt) Marine Reserve, WIA.
Hunnewell, Ralph E. (Sgt) Battalion Intelligence Section.
Hunt, Raymond F. (Pvt)
Hunter, Ernest B. (Pvt) WIA.
Hurley, Paul T. (Cpl)
Hurley, William (Pvt)
Hutchison, Paris (Cpl)

Hutt, Henry W. (Cpl)
Hynek, Charles M. (Pvt) MIA.
Imes, Isaac E. (PFC) Marine Corps Reserve.
Ireland, Albert C. (Cpl) WIA.
Irwin, Samuel D. (Sgt)
Ishee, George F. (Pvt) Marine Corps Reserve. Messman.
Ishee, Howard L. (Pvt)
Jackson, Leonard J. (Pvt)
Jacobensky, Stephen (Pvt) KIA.
Jacobs, Derwin H. (PFC) MIA.
Jamison, Russell (Pvt)
Janson, Howard L. (Pvt)
Jarosik, Jacob F. (Pvt) KIA, 12 June 1918.
Jeter, Joseph W. (PFC) Cook, 1st Class.
Johnson, Arthur T. (PFC)
Johnson, Earl L. (Pvt)
Johnson, Edwin J. (Pvt) Messman.
Johnson, Ralph W. (Pvt) KIA, 11 November 1918.
Johnson, William (Pvt)
Johnston, Frederick G. (Pvt) MIA.
Jolliff, Karl L. (Pvt) Marine Corps Reserve, WIA.
Jones, Clarence A. (Sgt)
Jones, George (GySgt) Marine Reserve.
Jones, Paul H. (Pvt)
Josephs, Howard W. (Pvt)
Joy, John J. (Pvt) Marine Reserve. Died of Wounds, 4 October 1918.
Justesen, William A. (Pvt) Marine Corps Reserve.
Kammeraad, Leonard (Pvt)
Kane, Tony W. (Sgt)
Katzenberg, George W. (Cpl)
Kaulsky, Frank (Pvt) WIA.
Kavesky, Joseph (Pvt)
Kee, Glen S. (Cpl) WIA.
Kelly, Leo B. (Pvt) Messman.
Kelly, Leo S. (Pvt) Cook, 3rd Class.
Kennedy, John J. (Pvt) Company Clerk.
Kesl, Leon P. (Pvt) Marine Corps Reserve.
Kienholz, Alfred W. (PFC)Marine Corps Reserve.
King, Owen L. (Pvt) WIA. Battalion Runner.
King, William O. (Pvt)
Kizer, William (Pvt) Marine Corps Reserve.
Klingenberg, Arthur H. (Pvt) Marine Reserve.
Kmiec, Stanislaus (Sgt) Died of Wounds.
Kneil, Lawrence H. (Cpl)
Knell, Lawrence B. (Cpl)
Knepp, Clarence C. (Sgt)
Knight, Asa F. (Pvt)
Koehler, George W. (Pvt) KIA.
Kowalski, Frank J. (Pvt) Marine Reserve.
Kownacki, Charles G. (Pvt) Marine Reserve.
Kriger, Walter F. (Cpl) WIA.
Kurtz, Raymond J. (Pvt)
Lambeth, George D. (Sgt) WIA, Died of Wounds.
Lasell, Richard B. (Pvt) WIA.
Latsko, Martin J. (PFC) Marine Reserve, KIA, 4 October 1918.
Laudenberger, Frank A. (Pvt)
Lawlor, Valentine A. (Pvt) Marine Reserve.
Layton, Harold M. (Pvt) Marine Reserve.
Lazzara, Antonio (Sgt) Marine Reserve.

Leader, Albert K. (Pvt)
Leary, John D. (Sgt)
Lee, Cyrus B. (Pvt)
Lewis, Albert M. (Pvt) KIA, 4 October 1918.
Lewis, Amos W. (Cpl) Marine Corps Reserve.
Lewis, Clayton B. (Pvt)
Lewis, Wheatley D. (Pvt)
Liller, Marion G. (Pvt)
Linderborg, Karl (Pvt)
Lindsey, Raymond E. (Sgt) WIA.
Linton, Willie (PFC) KIA, 4 October 1918.
Little, Jake (Pvt)
Little, William J. (Pvt)
Livingston, Leo (Pvt)
Lockhart, Dan A. (Pvt) KIA, 3 June 1918.
Lodowski, Joseph (Pvt)
Loitved, Lester L. (Pvt)
Love, Ernest R. (Sgt)
Ludgate, Robert D. (Pvt)
Lustgraaf, Ferdinand P. (Pvt)
MacDonald, Dalvin F. (Pvt) Marine Reserve, WIA.
Madden, Ira W. (Pvt)
Madison, William (Cpl)
Maginness, Charles E. (Pvt)
Marco, James J. (Sgt) Died of Wounds, 6 October 1918.
Markusic, Fred (Pvt) Battalion Communications Cook.
Markuske, Walter W. (Pvt)
Martin, Arsene J. (Pvt)
Martin, Augburn D. (Pvt)
Martin, Charles F. (Pvt) Marine Reserve.
Martin, Oscar E. (Pvt) Battalion Intelligence Section. WIA, Belleau Wood.
Martin, Robert E. (PFC) Marine Reserve, WIA.
Marx, John H. (Pvt)
Massey, Jesse J. (Pvt)
Mathis, Arthur M. (Pvt)
Mattix, Elbert C. (PFC)
May, Dorsey D. (Pvt)
Mayer, Adrian H. (Pvt) Marine Reserve, WIA.
McCane, Karl (Cpl)
McCarthy, James (Pvt) KIA.
McCleary, James E. (Pvt) Sig., 2nd Class.
McCooey, John H. (Pvt) Messman.
McCook, Martin J. (Pvt) KIA, 12 June 1918.
McCormick, Francis H. (PFC)
McCoy, Frank A., Jr. (Cpl)
McCoy, Martin E. (Cpl)
McCune, Karl (Cpl)
McDermott, George (GySgt)
McDermott, Joseph J. (Pvt) Reserve, KIA.
McDole, Riley J. (Pvt) Messman.
McFadden, Willis B. (PFC)
McFarland, Oland M. (Pvt)
McGinnis, Charles R. (Sgt) KIA, 13 June 1918.
McGrath, Joseph J. (Pvt) KIA, 12 June 1918.
McGrew, George B. (Pvt) MIA.
McIlhiney, Allan F. (Pvt)
McIntyre, William (Pvt)
McKean, James P. (PFC)
McLaughlin, Theodore H. Pvt
McMurray, Hugh J. (Pvt)

McNiff, James C. (Pvt)
Meador, Garland P. (Pvt)
Meador, Luther M. (Pvt)
Medine, Clifford G. (Pvt)
Meikle, William T. (Pvt)
Meinhardt, Walter J. (Pvt) Marine Reserve.
Melchior, Charles (Pvt)
Meredith, Harry C. (Pvt) Battalion Orderly.
Merritt, George F. (Pvt) Marine Reserve, WIA.
Merryman, George S. (Sgt) Marine Reserve.
Messinger, Elias J. (Pvt) Marine Corps Reserve.
Michalek, Walter F. (Pvt)
Mignacco, Attilio J. (Pvt) Died of Wounds, 8 June 1918.
Miller, Minor D. (PFC) Marine Reserve, KIA.
Miller, Robert H. (Pvt) KIA, 7 October 1918.
Miller, Walter B. (Cpl)
Mincey, George A. (Cpl)
Miner, Paul E. (Pvt) MIA.
Moeller, Ernest L. (Pvt)
Montag, Bernard W. (Cpl)
Monteith, Ray (Pvt)
Mooney, Charles J. (Cpl)
Morgan, Edris (Pvt) Cook, 1st Class.
Morgan, Julian G. (Pvt)
Morrill, Frank E. (Pvt)
Morrison, Frankv (Pvt) MIA.
Morrow, Hugh (Pvt) Marine Reserve, WIA.
Morrow, Ronald G. (Pvt) Cook, 3rd Class.
Mueller, Eldor G. (Pvt)
Mullen, Russell W. (Pvt) KIA, 11 June 1918.
Mullenix, Jessie B. (Pvt)
Murlin, Joseph R. (Pvt)
Murphy, Felix P. (Pvt) MIA.
Murr, Albert C. (Pvt)
Myers, William E. (Pvt)
Narvane, Arnold E. (Cpl)
Nash, Harry C. (Sgt) WIA.
Nation, Harry L. (Pvt) WIA.
Negri, John P. (Pvt)
Nelson, Austin A. (PFC)
Nelson, Harvey D. (Pvt) Marine Corps Reserve. Battalion Intelligence Section.
Nelson, Oscar V. (Cpl) Marine Reserve.
Netke, Joseph A. (Sgt) Marine Reserve, WIA.
Newell, Edward G. (Cpl)
Newnham, Chester J. (Pvt)
Nickerson, Howard L. (Pvt)
Nobles, Virgil W. (Pvt) Clerk at Regimental Headquarters.
Noblett, Elmer A. (Pvt) Marine Reserve, KIA.
Noblitt, Massey G. (Pvt)
Norton, Harold C. (Pvt)
Nyen, Oscar A. (Pvt) MIA.
Oakes, Bernard F. (Sgt) WIA.
O'Bannon, Ernest H. (Pvt)
O'Berske, William R. (Pvt)
O'Connell, Richard C. (Pvt) WIA, Died of Wounds, 11 October 1918.
O'Hare, William J., Jr. (Pvt) WIA.
O'Hern, John E. (Pvt) Marine Reserve.
O'Lear, Walter (Pvt)

O'Leary, Eugene D. (Pvt)
O'Leary, John D. (Sgt)
O'Neal, Henry (Pvt)
O'Neill, Arthur C. (Pvt) KIA.
O'Rourke, John J. (Pvt)
Ostby, William O. (Pvt) MIA.
Osterhout, Harold P. (PFC)
Packard, Samuel F. (PFC) Marine Corps Reserve .
Page, John A. (Sgt)
Palmer, Philip P. (Pvt)
Pangburn, William B. (Pvt) KIA.
Parker, Clayton A . (Pvt) Marine Corps Reserve .
Parker, John H. (GySgt)
Parsons, Erwin E. (Cpl)
Parsons, James H. (Sgt) Marine Reserve, WIA.
Passen, John J. (Pvt)
Patient, James R. (Pvt) KIA, 3 June 1918.
Patrick, Lloyd (PFC)
Patterson, Frank D. (Pvt)
Pearce, Alvin (Pvt)
Peck, Harold E. (Pvt)
Peden, Guy H. (PFC) Marine Reserve, KIA.
Pelletier, Willis H. (Pvt)
Perash, Andrew M. (Sgt) Marine Reserve, WIA.
Perrotti, Patsy (Pvt)
Perry, Aubrey H. (Pvt) KIA, 12 June 1918.
Peterson, Emil (Pvt)
Pew, Arthur, Jr. (Pvt)
Phelps, Cecil C. (PFC)
Philips, John M. (GySgt) Died 13 May 1919 while on Rhine River Patrol.
Phillips, Harvey I. (Pvt)
Phlegar, John N.H. (Pvt)
Piland, Finnes E. (Pvt) Reserve.
Pillsworth, Thomas S. (PFC) Marine Reserve, KIA.
Poirier, Paul E. (Sgt)
Poole, William L. (Pvt)
Portner, Ferris D. (Sgt)
Powers, John J. (Pvt) Marine Reserve, WIA.
Powers, Richard A. (Pvt)
Powers, Richard A., Jr. (Pvt) Messman.
Pownall, John W. (Cpl) Marine Reserve, KIA.
Price, Ernest C. (Pvt) KIA, 4 October 1918.
Priddy, Forrest C. (Pvt) WIA.
Pruitt, Ballard L.E. (Pvt)
Puceta, Andrew (PFC) Marine Reserve, WIA.
Quinn, Jerome P. (Cpl) Marine Corps Reserve.
Rager, George C. (Pvt)
Ramey, Fred W. (Pvt) Marine Corps Reserve.
Randall, Clyde C. (Pvt)
Rankin, William C. (PFC) Marine Reserve, KIA.
Ray, Robert H. (Pvt) Marine Corps Reserve.
Reichle, Edward J. (Pvt)
Rennekamp, Henry A. (Pvt)
Reynolds, Carson G. (Cpl)
Richards, John (Pvt)
Richards, John H. (Pvt) Marine Reserve.
Richardson, Littleton E. (Pvt) Marine Corps Reserve. Battalion Intelligence Section.
Richardson, Mayrant D. (Trumpeter)
Richmond, Charles H. (Cpl)

Rieke, Ray E. (Pvt)
Riggs, Russell (Pvt) KIA.
Rinker, Charles F. (Pvt)
Rippy, Henry S. (Pvt)
Roberson, James N. (Pvt)
Robinson, Samuel G. (Pvt) Marine Reserve, WIA.
Roe, Walter E. (Pvt) Marine Reserve, WIA.
Rogstad, Joseph (Pvt)
Rolfe, Ward A. (PFC) Marine Reserve.
Romine, Samuel S. (PFC)
Rosecrans, Harold E. (Cpl)
Rosier, Hoy B. (Pvt) Died of Wounds.
Roska, Victor J. (Pvt)
Ross, John W. (Pvt)
Russell, Lloyd R. (Pvt) Marine Reserve.
Rutty, Philip H. (Pvt)
Ryan, James S. (Pvt)
St. Clair, Charles H. (Pvt) MIA.
St. Clair, Kenneth L. (Sgt)
Samples, Jesse A. (Pvt) Marine Reserve, WIA.
Samples, Leslie H. (Pvt) WIA.
Samuels, Sidney (Pvt) Marine Corps Reserve.
Saunders, Franklin A. (Pvt)
Saylor, Marshall B. (Pvt) Marine Reserve, WIA.
Schanda, Edward (Pvt) MIA.
Schaub, William J. (Pvt)
Schlieman, Frank F. (Pvt)
Schmelzer, Edwin E. (Pvt)
Schmidt, John A. (Cpl) Marine Reserve, KIA, 4 October 1918.
Scholler, Harold (Pvt) KIA, 4 October 1918.
Scholz, Edward T. (PFC) Marine Reserve, WIA.
Schreiter, Walter E. (PFC) Battalion Intelligence Section.
Schriber, William G. (Pvt)
Schroeder, Ralph W. (Pvt)
Schuppel, Arthur (Pvt)
Schwartz, William J. (Pvt) WIA.
Scott, Benjamin H. (Pvt) WIA.
Sempf, William R. (Cpl)
Sharp, Horace H. (Pvt)
Shively, Lee M. (Pvt) Messman.
Shorten, Steve N. (Pvt) Marine Corps Reserve.
Shue, James H. (Pvt)
Simerson, Ervin (Pvt) WIA.
Simms, Arthur W. (PFC) Marine Reserve, WIA.
Simon, Michael P. (Pvt)
Simons, Leo J. (Pvt)
Sinclair, Wilbert W. (PFC)
Singleton, Eugene R. (Pvt) Marine Reserve, WIA.
Sinramm, Otto S. (Pvt) Reserve, MIA.
Slawson, Lloyd J. (Pvt) Marine Reserve, WIA.
Smith, Boyce O. (Pvt)
Smith, Clifford F. (Pvt) Marine Corps Reserve.
Smith, Herman F. (Pvt)
Smith, Marvin (Pvt)
Smith, William B. (GySgt)
Smith, William C. (Pvt) Marine Reserve, WIA.
Snead, William H. (Pvt)
Sniadecki, John (Pvt)
Snow, Palmer P. (Cpl) Company Clerk.
Snyder, Francis S. (Pvt) Marine Reserve, WIA.

Snyder, James H. (Pvt) Messman.
Spaulding, Gillman (Pvt)
Spinley, Joseph (Cpl) Marine Reserve, KIA.
Spohn, Russell J. (Pvt) Marine Corps Reserve. Messman.
Stahl, Harold (Sgt)
Stanley, Judson L. (Pvt) Marine Reserve, WIA.
Stealey, Arthur L. (Cpl) MIA.
Steinemann, Bert (Pvt) Marine Reserve.
Steinmiller, William F. (Sgt)
Stevens, Felix J. (PFC) Marine Reserve, WIA.
Stien, Henry F. (Sgt)
Still, Arthur C. (Pvt) Messman, KIA, 5 June 1918.
Strait, William M. (Cpl)
Strait, William M., Jr. (Pvt) Batt. Orderly.
Strange, James C. (Pvt)
Stratton, George U. (Pvt)
Strayer, Dwight L. (Pvt) Marine Reserve, WIA, died.
Strickland, Charles E. (Pvt)
Strong, Frank J. (Pvt) KIA, 4 October 1918.
Stuewe, Frank A. (Pvt) Marine Corps Reserve.
Stumm, Robert S. (Pvt)
Summers, Arthur (Pvt)
Sussenguth, Harold F. (Pvt)
Sutman, Joseph L. (GySgt)
Suynnott, Joseph A. (GySgt)
Swallow, George E. (Pvt) Marine Corps Reserve.
Sweetman, Joseph A. (Pvt)
Sweeney, Edward L. (PFC) Marine Reserve, WIA.
Sylvester, Lewis H. (Pvt)
Tausch, Steven (Pvt) Marine Reserve, WIA.
Taylor, Lewis W. (Pvt)
Taylor, Richard O. (Pvt)
Terry, Ellis G. (Sgt) WIA.
Terwilliger, Percy D. (Pvt) Battalion Intelligence Section.
Tharau, Herman (GySgt) KIA, 8 August 1918.
Thayer, William F. (Pvt) WIA.
Theis, John H. (Pvt) Reserve, MIA.
Thomas, Bennie O. (Pvt) KIA, date not known.
Thomas, Eugene R. (Cpl) Marine Corps Reserve.
Thomas, Frank E. (Trumpeter)
Thomas, George E. (Pvt)
Thomas, George W. (Pvt)
Thompson, David A. (Sgt) Marine Reserve, WIA.
Thompson, John W. (Pvt)
Thompson, Rexford L. (PFC) Marine Reserve, WIA.
Thompson, Walter N. (Cpl) Marine Reserve, KIA.
Tilton, Charles A. (Pvt) MIA.
Tipp, William H. (Pvt) Marine Reserve, WIA.
Toothaker, Leroy G. (Pvt)
Trachsel, Walter (Pvt) Marine Corps Reserve.
Trainer, Leo G. (Sgt)
Trivette, Harter H. (PFC) MIA.
Tronsor, Frank (Pvt) MIA.
Turner, Allan G. (Pvt)
Valerio, Raphael (Pvt) Marine Reserve, WIA.
Van Dame, Felix (Pvt) Marine Corps Reserve.
Van Gorder, Grant E. (Cpl)
Vierbuchen, William J. (GySgt)
Walden, William C. (Pvt)
Walker, Earl B. (Pvt)
Wallraff, Louis E. (Pvt) Marine Reserve.

Walter, Stephen M. (Pvt)

Warnecke, Francis (Pvt) Cook, 1st Class.

Washburn, Horace D. (Cpl)

Watermolen, Alphonse (Cpl) MIA.

Weaver, Walter S. (Pvt)

Webb, Walter W. (Pvt)

Weber, William C. (Cpl)

Weis, Richard A. (Pvt) Marine Corps Reserve.

Weitzel, Charles S. (Pvt) Marine Corps Reserve.

Welk, George T. (Pvt) Reserve, MIA.

Wells, Harvey L. (Pvt) Marine Reserve, WIA.

Welty, Clayton E. (Pvt)

Weschke, Leo (Pvt) Died, pneumonia.

Westfall, Wilbur O. (Pvt)

Weston, Floyd L. (Pvt)

Wetzel, Earl J. (Pvt) Marine Reserve.

Wilbur, Eugene E. (Pvt)

Wilcox, William (Pvt)

Wilkins, William (PFC)

Williams, Charlie P. (Pvt) Reserve, MIA.

Williams, James H. (Pvt)

Willson, James L. (Pvt) Reserve.

Wishart, Theophilus D. (Pvt) Marine Reserve. Died of Wounds, 14 December 1918.

Wistrand, Harry E. (Pvt) MIA.

Woerter, Raymond F. (Pvt)

Wood, Clayton (Pvt)

Wood, Dolph (Pvt) WIA.

Wooll, Ernest A. (Trumpeter)

Wooten, Jerome A. (Pvt) KIA, 4 October 1918.

Wright, Gilbert (Cpl)

Wyatt, Albert E., Jr. (Pvt)

Wyatt, Delbert (Pvt) MIA.

York, Asa C. (Pvt) Marine Reserve. Died of Wounds.

Young, Frank W. (Pvt)

Young, Howard H. (Sgt)

Young, Robert (Sgt) WIA.

Zalmanowski, Stanley A. (Pvt)

Ziegler, William G. (Pvt)

16th (I) Company, Third Battalion

NAME (RANK) REMARKS

Yowell, Robert (Cpt) Commanding 16th Co.

Rorke, James F. (Cpt) Regular. Additional Duty: Summary Court Officer.

Yarborough, George H., Jr. (Cpt) Died of wounds, 26 June 1918.

Duckham, William A. (1st Lt)

Hash, Kyle C. (1st Lt) Marine Reserve. Died of Wounds, 19 October 1918.

Bernier, Oliver D. (2nd Lt) Marine Reserve.

Foster, James E. (2nd Lt) Marine Corps Reserve, WIA.

Foster, John T. (2nd Lt)

Parsons, Miller V. (2nd Lt) Marine Reserve.

Pinkham, Harold N. (2nd Lt) WIA, 23 June 1918.

Sweet, Walter (2nd Lt) Marine Reserve.

Thomas, Fred (2nd Lt) Marine Corps Reserve, WIA.

Toekelson, Timon J. (2nd Lt)

Enlisted

Davis, Harry (1st Sgt)

McClintock, Henry (1st Sgt) Company 1st Sgt.

Abrams, Harold C. (Pvt)

Adams, Arthur V. (Pvt) Marine Corps Regular. WIA.

Addante, Frank W. (Pvt) KIA, 7 June 1918.

Ahrens, Nickolas J. (Pvt) MC Reserve, Class 4.

Aitchison, Walter E. (PFC) Marine Corps Regular. WIA.

Alberth, Louis (Pvt)

Albertson, Carl E. (Pvt)

Alcorn, Robert M. (Pvt)

Amerson, Benjamin P. (Pvt)

Anderson, Emil W. (Pvt)

Armagost, George B. (Pvt)

Bagby, Orville E. (Cpl)

Baker, Henry W. (PFC) Marine Corps Regular.

Ball, Henry S. (Sgt)

Ball, Walter J. (Pvt) Marine Reserve.

Bankston, George M. (Pvt)

Barnaby, Floyd (Cpl)

Barron, Edward H. (Pvt)

Barron, Eugene E. (Pvt)

Barron, William L. (Pvt) Died of disease, 29 August 1918.

Barth, Jacob P. (Pvt)

Barton, Charley A. (Pvt)

Batt, C.A. (Pvt) KIA, 25 June 1918.

Beach, Dewey H. (Pvt)

Beasley, Erna R. (HAp1)

Beaupre, George E. (Pvt)

Beck, Elmer T. (Pvt)

Bell, Joe (Sgt)

Bemberg, Henry (Pvt) KIA, 23 June 1918.

Biederstadt, Cordt F. (Cpl)

Birttnen, Gust A. (Pvt)

Bliven, Raymond E. (Cpl) KIA, 23 June 1918, Nat'l Naval Volunteers.

Bobal, George J. (Pvt)

Bobick, Michael (Pvt) KIA, 23 June 1918.

Boissiy, Eddie A. (Cpl) Nat'l Naval Volunteers.

Bolender, Hugh E. (Cpl) KIA, 23 June 1918.

Boline, Johann A. (GySgt)

Bookout, Charlie H. (Pvt)

Bowers, John F. (Cpl)

Brady, Frank (PFC) Naval Volunteer, WIA.

Brittnen, Gust A. (Pvt)

Brooke, Lester J. (PFC)

Brown, Clell G. (Pvt)

Brown, Ivan A. (Pvt)

Bruce, Willie H. (Pvt)

Brugger, Johnny H. (PFC) Marine Corps Regular.

Buchheister, Ernest L. (Pvt) KIA, 23 June 1918.

Burns, Harry T. (Sgt) WIA.

Cady, Theron G. (Pvt)

Campbell, Elvis (Pvt)

Campbell, Richard M. (GySgt) Marine Corps regular. WIA.

Cannon, Roger W. (Pvt)

Cappuccio, Salve (Pvt)

Capwell, Chester K. (Pvt)

Carlson, Ralph C. (Sgt) Naval Volunteer, WIA.

Carr, John F. (Sgt) In charge of Arms and Accoutrements.

Carrington, Fred (Sgt) Marine Corps regular. WIA.

Carroza, Harry P. (Pvt)

Carson, Charles O. (Sgt)

Chmielewski, Felix J. (Pvt)

Christ, Charles W. (Sgt)

Christner, Edward (Cpl)

Christophersen Elmer B. (Pvt)

Clancy, Thomas D. (GySgt)

Cleveland, George E. (Pvt) KIA, 23 June 1918.

Cluney, James L. (Pvt)

Cockreham, Ralph (Sgt) In charge of Arms and Accoutrements.

Collins, James B. (Pvt) Marine Corps Regular, MIA.

Colvin, Harry W. (Pvt)

Constantinides, George D. (Cpl)

Cook, John M. (Pvt)

Cooke, Ralph (Pvt) KIA, 12 June 1918.

Cottrell, Oscar (Pvt)

Coulter, Claude R. (PFC) Marine Corps Regular. WIA.

Coulter, Edwin C. (Cpl) Marine Corps Regular, KIA, 4 October 1918.

Courtney, Edward J. (Sgt) Marine Corps Regular. WIA.

Coyle, Harry F. (Cpl)

Cromoga, John F. (Pvt)

Crotinger, Melvin G. (Pvt)

Crum, Louis C. (GySgt)

Cuffel, Floyd A. (Pvt)

Culbertson, William E. (Pvt) Marine Corps Regular. WIA.

Culver, Cleo R. (Pvt)

Cunningham, John B. (Pvt) Marine Corps Regular.

Currie, Edmund (PFC) Marine Reserve. Messman.

Cutchinson, W.E. (Pvt)

Daymude, Thomas B. (Cpl)

Decker, Claud A. (Pvt)

Degnan, William J. (Pvt)

DeHaven, John F. (Pvt) KIA, 23 June 1918.

Dell'Ermo, James (PFC)

Demarest, Samuel E. (Pvt)

Denson, Henry O. (Pvt)

Devney, Bernard H. (Pvt)

DeWitt, Douglas (Pvt) Marine Corps Regular, MIA.

Deyon, Joseph R. (Pvt) Marine Corps Reserve, Class 4, KIA, 15 June 1918.

DiBucci, Antonio (PFC) Messman.

Dixon, Roy M. (Pvt)

Doherty, George F. (Pvt)

Domado, Fritz (Cpl)

Donlin, James (Pvt)

Dorman, George J. (Pvt) WIA.

Dougherty, James D., Jr. (Pvt) KIA, 25 June 1918.

Douglas, Ralph S. (Pvt)

Douglass, Mertie L. (Pvt)

Dow, David M. (Cpl)

Drain, Joseph F., Jr. (Pvt)

Drewes, William P. (Pvt) KIA, 25 June 1918.

Driscoll, Edward P. (PFC)

Duffy, James A. (PFC) Marine Corps Regular, WIA.

Dunbar, Lewis E. (Pvt) Marine Corps Regular, KIA, 4 October 1918.

Dunlap, James J. (Pvt)

Durbin, Walter H. (Cpl)

Dwyer, Frank M. (Pvt)

Dwyer, Martin J. (Pvt)

Dyer, Thomas (Cpl)

Earl, Clifford E. (Pvt) Marine Corps Regular. WIA.

Earle, Herbert A. (Pvt) Marine Corps Regular. WIA.

Easton, Carl K. (Pvt)

Eberle, Edward C. (Pvt)

Eddy, Noel H. (Pvt) Marine Corps Regular.

Edgar, Ernest P. (Pvt) Marine Corps Regular. WIA.

Edgar, William R. (Pvt)

Eichenfeldt, Daniel C. (Cpl) Naval Volunteer, WIA.

Elberson, John D. (Pvt) Marine Reserve.

Elftmann, Frederick W. (PFC) Marine Corps Regular. WIA.

Ellis, George S. (Pvt)

Elstad, Clarence W. (Pvt) KIA, 6 June 1918.

Evans, Frederick T. (Pvt)

Evans, Robert A. (Pvt)

Fackrell, Hugh (Pvt) KIA, 23 June 1918.

Faino, Victor (Pvt)

Farnham, Waldo H. (PFC) Marine Corps Regular, KIA, date not known.

Fee, John H. (Pvt)

Ferg, Francis X., Jr. (Trumpeter)

Finley, Roy (Pvt)

Fishbaugh, Maurice V. (PFC) Marine Reserve.

Flanigan, John P. (Pvt)

Florentine, Anthony (Cpl) Naval Volunteer, WIA.

Flori, August M. (Cpl)

Fox, John B. (Cpl) Marine Corps Regular. WIA.

Fox, Wade H. (Pvt)

Frankey, Clarence J. (Pvt) Messman.

Fridenmaker, Arthur B. (Pvt)

Gallagher, John (Cpl)

Gallagher, Martin L. (Pvt)

Gamber, Charles L. (Cpl)

Gately, John E., Jr. (Pvt)

Gaviglia, Joseph (PFC) Marine Corps Regular. WIA.

Gehringer, Albert N. (Pvt) Marine Corps Reserve, MIA.

Gerard, Harold F. (Pvt)

Geselle, Albert J. (Pvt)

Gift, Charles A. (Pvt)

Gillen, Arthur A. (Pvt)

Gillespie, Thomas M. (Cpl)

Goetz, Frederick J. (Pvt)

Goodman, Howard (Pvt)

Gospodarski, Alexander (Pvt) Marine Corps Regular.

Gould, Joel (Pvt)

Grade, Martin (Sgt)

Grainge, Howard E. (Sgt) Marine Reserve.

Graves, Walter P. (Pvt)

Gray, Thomas A. (Pvt)

Greenberg, Isidore (Pvt) Gassed.

Greenberg, Israel M. (Sgt)

Greenman, Earl F. (PFC) Naval Volunteer, WIA.
Grollman, Herman (Cpl) KIA, 23 June 1918.
Gunderson, Edwin C. (PFC) Marine Reserve.
Gustafson, John A. (Sgt)
Hall, Olin (Pvt)
Hall, Robert E. (Pvt) Marine Corps Regular. WIA.
Hamilton, Terrence G. (Cpl) Company Clerk.
Haney, David A. (Pvt)
Hanrahan, Edward A. (Pvt) Marine Corps Regular. WIA.
Hansen, Albert W. (Pvt) Marine Corps Regular. WIA.
Hansucker, Carroll J. (Sgt)
Harlow, Albert L. (Pvt) vMarine Reserve.
Harris, Charlie L. (PFC) Cook, 2nd Class.
Harris, William B. (Cpl)
Hastings, George F. (Cpl)
Hausen, George O. (Pvt)
Healy, Augustine (Pvt)
Heisel, James E. (Pvt) Messman, KIA, 23 June 1918.
Henderson, Ernest L. (PhM) U.S. Navy, WIA.
Herbitz, Harry (Pvt)
Hernan, Patrick (PFC) Messman.
Herrick, Benjamin E. (Pvt)
Herwick, William L. (Pvt)
Hewes, Charles S. (Cpl)
Higgins, Andrew J. (Pvt) KIA, 3 June 1918.
Higgins, James A. (Cpl)
Higgins, Thomas F. (Pvt) Marine Reserve.
Hildebrand, Carl E. (PFC)
Hilliard, Howard G. (Cpl) KIA, 9 November 1918.
Hillix, Harry (Cpl) KIA, 23 June 1918.
Hinton, Irving E. (Pvt)
Hirn, William (GySgt) Marine Corps Regular. WIA.
Hochreiter, William (Pvt)
Hoggatt, Ralph M. (PhM3) USN.
Holland, Delbert D. (Pvt) Marine Corps Regular.
Holmquist, Harry C. (Pvt)
Hoover, Henry J. (Pvt)
Horak, Edward G. (Pvt)
Horbitz, Harry (Pvt)
Horton, William D. (Pvt) Marine Reserve.
Houghton, John J. (Pvt)
Houser, Joe F. (Pvt)
Houston, Harry M. (Pvt)
Howett, Drexel (PFC)
Hubley, Charles E. (Pvt)
Hudson, Alfred E. (Pvt) Marine Corps Regular. WIA.
Hughes, Clyde E. (Pvt)
Hults, Frederick (Cpl) Nat'l Naval Volunteers.
Hurt, John W. (Pvt)
Hutchinson, Maurice L. (Pvt)
Imeson, Thomas H. (Cpl) Nat'l Naval Volunteer.
Indergard, Carl (PFC)
Irminger, James P. (Pvt) KIA, 25 June 1918.
Irminger, Victor E. (Pvt)
Jacobs, Darnell M. (Pvt)
Jacobs, Orville E. (Pvt)
Jacobson, George W. (Pvt)
Jamick, Edward (PFC) Messman.
Jenney, Charles W. (Pvt)
Jewell, Paul W. (Sgt) Nat'l Naval Volunteers, KIA, 6 June 1918.

Johns, Edward (Cpl)
Johns, Odis (Pvt) Marine Corps Reserve.
Johnson, Carl E. (Pvt)
Johnson, Carl P. (Pvt)
Johnson, Frank W. (Pvt) KIA, 25 June 1918.
Johnson, Frederick W. (Pvt)
Johnson, Harry H. (Pvt)
Johnson, Karl F. (Pvt)
Johnston, Roy R. (Cpl)
Jones, Clarence W. (Pvt)
Jones, Hubert R. (Cpl) Nat'l Naval Volunteers, WIA.
Jones, Leon B. (Pvt)
Jones, Richard E. (Pvt)
Jones, Roy L. (PFC)
Jones, William C. (Pvt)
Josberger, Philip A. (PFC)
Karsten, Ernest E. (Pvt)
Kaylor, Julius F. (Pvt)
Kearney, Bernard J. (Pvt)
Keener, Clark W. (Sgt)
Keirn, Otha S. (Pvt) KIA, 6 June 1918.
Kellerman, Herman (Pvt) Messman.
Kelley, George W. (PFC)
Kelley, Jeremiah M. (Pvt) Marine Corps Regular.
Kelly, John W. (Pvt)
Kennedy, Charles A., Jr. (Pvt) Marine Corps Regular, gassed.
Khun, John L. (Cpl)
Kiestler, Realis C. (Pvt)
Kimball, Pardon C. (PFC)
Kimball, Richard (Pvt) KIA, 25 June 1918.
Kinnick, Joseph, Jr. (Pvt) Marine Corps Regular. WIA.
Kinzel, Charles D. (Pvt)
Kirchman, Leonard W. (Pvt) Marine Corps Regular. WIA.
Kirnard, Charles H., Jr. (Pvt)
Kishler, Edwin P. (Pvt) KIA, 25 June 1918.
Klamm, Walter (Cpl)
Koblentz, Vern F. (Pvt)
Korman, Frank A. (Pvt)
Korskey, Joseph W. (Cpl) KIA, 23 June 1918.
Kowalak, Albert (Pvt)
Kraus, Earl A. (Pvt)
Kuhr, Harvey A. (Pvt)
Kyser, Dewey W. (Pvt)
LaBudde, Raymond E. (Pvt)
Landon, Joseph (Pvt) Marine Corps Regular.
Lang, George F. (Pvt) Marine Corps Regular. WIA.
Larson, Arthur P. (PFC)
Larson, Fred (PFC) Cook, 1st Class.
Lawrence, William H. (Pvt)
Laws, Cecil R. (Cpl)
Le Roy, Alfred E. (Pvt)
Leavens, Carl F. (PFC)
Lenert, Henry P. (Pvt)
Lenihan, Emmet R. (Pvt)
Lester, Eugene R. (Pvt)
Lewis, William F. (Pvt)
Lindsay, Parley L. (Pvt) Marine Reserve.
Little, Victor J. (Pvt)
Lloyd, Hugh (PFC) Marine Reserve.

Lonergan, Harry O. (Pvt)
Long, Riley M. (GySgt)
Long, Will S. (Pvt)
Louden, Bonn W. (Trumpeter) Marine Corps Regular.
Lover, James H. (Sgt) Marine Reserve.
Lubawski, Paul (Pvt) Marine Corps Regular. WIA.
Lynch, Chadwick N. (Pvt)
Lynch, Ralph F. (Cpl) Marine Corps Regular. WIA.
Macofsky, Raymond (Pvt) Messman.
Malick, George E. (Pvt) Marine Corps Regular. WIA.
Mann, Harry J. (Pvt)
Manning, Joseph M. (Cpl) Marine Reserve. Company
    Clerk.
Manning, William H. (Pvt) Marine Corps Regular. WIA.
Marquering, William C. (PFC) Naval Volunteer, gassed.
Marten, Fred H. (Pvt)
Martin, John W. (Pvt)
Mason, James E. (Pvt) Marine Corps Regular. WIA.
Mathias, John F. (PFC)
Matthews, Leo F. (Pvt)
Matthews, Roy E. (Pvt)
McCarthy, Joseph E. (Pvt)
McCastline, Metler A. (Pvt)
McCoy, Andrew J., Jr. (Pvt)
McCurdy, James E. (Pvt)
McDaniel, Dee H. (Pvt)
McDermott, Philip A. (Pvt)
McGlumphy, Hallis G. (Pvt)
McLaren, Myron (Pvt) Marine Reserve.
McMonagle, John J. (Pvt)
McQuain, Adam (Pvt) Marine Corps Regular. WIA.
McSpadden, Calvin R. (Pvt)
Memey, Lester J. (Pvt)
Memmer, Isador W. (Pvt)
Mercer, Frank E. (Pvt)
Mercurio, Charles P. (Pvt)
Merritt, Harold B. (Pvt)
Metcalfe, Robert L. (Cpl)
Meyers, Wilber J. (Pvt)
Millard, Frank F. (Pvt)
Miller, Ferrin C. (Pvt) Marine Corps Regular, MIA.
Miller, John C. (Sgt)
Miller, Leonard (Pvt)
Milligan, David K. (Pvt)
Milsted, Henry (Pvt)
Minerd, George E. (Pvt)
Montgomery, Claude H. (Pvt) Marine Corps Regular,
    KIA.
Montgomery, Herbert S. (Pvt)
Moody, Norman B. (Pvt)
Moore, Frank R. (Pvt)
Moore, James A. (Cpl)
Moore, Robert T. (Pvt) WIA, 22 June 1918.
Moran, Joseph M. (Pvt)
Morehead, Nelson L. (Pvt) Marine Corps Regular. WIA.
Morgan, Frank (Cpl)
Morgensteen, Max (Pvt)
Morre, Robert T. (PFC)
Morrison, William J. (Pvt)
Mullally, Clinton C. (Pvt)
Mullery, James J. (Pvt)

Mulvihill, John F. (Sgt)
Murphy, Arthur A. (Cpl)
Murphy, Eugene F. (GySgt) Marine Corps Regular.
    KIA, 4 October 1918.
Nehring, Walter A. (Pvt)
Nelson, Harry A. (Pvt)
Newhouse, Peter W. (Cpl)
Newton, Harold G. (Pvt)
Nicastro, Peter (Pvt)
Nice, William E. (Pvt)
Nicholson, Fred E. (Pvt)
Nickerson, Elwood (Pvt)
Noell, James A. (Pvt)
Nye, Frank W. (Sgt) Marine Reserve.
O'Donnell, James T. (Pvt)
Olmstad, John (Pvt)
O'Malley, Lawrence A. (Pvt)
Orr, Harley D. (Pvt)
Orum, Louis C. (GySgt)
Paine, Edward G. (Pvt) Marine Corps Regular, Died of
    Wounds.
Palagrove, Howard P. (Pvt)
Pallatroni, Louis J. (Pvt) Nat'l Naval Volunteer.
Palsgrove, Howard P. (Pvt) Marine Corps Regular, MIA.
Parker, Eugene J. (PFC) Naval Volunteer, WIA.
Parker, Lawrence F. (Pvt) Marine Corps Regular.
Partington, George C. (PFC)
Patterson, James A. (Sgt) KIA, 6 June 1918.
Patton, Emmett L. (Pvt)
Pearson, Albert S. (Cpl)
Perry, Cecil W. (Pvt)
Peters, Ray (Pvt)
Pfannerstill, George J. (Sgt)
Phelan Francis (HAp1)
Phipps, Paul D. (Pvt)
Pierce, Jack (Pvt)
Pifer, Amon W. (PFC)
Pivoda, Fayette W. (Cpl) Marine Corps Regular. WIA.
Plantz, Clarence L. (Pvt) Marine Reserve.
Pleisch, Cecil W. (Pvt) KIA, 25 June 1918.
Pointer, John H. (Pvt)
Pomeroy, Charles H., Jr. (Cpl)
Porter, Wilbur H. (PFC)
Powell, James B. (Cpl)
Puleo, Thomas (Sgt)
Quinn, Eric D. (Pvt) KIA, 23 June 1918.
Rader, Guy (Cpl)
Raymond, Drullard A. (Pvt)
Readhead, Nicholas D. (Pvt)
Regan, Gerald V. (Cpl) Marine Corps Regular, KIA, 4
    October 1918.
Reihl, Philip J. (Pvt) KIA, 6 June 1918.
Reiley, John D. (Pvt)
Rhine, Drumond (Pvt)
Rhoades, Burton (Cpl) Marine Corps Regular. WIA.
Rice, Robert T. (Sgt)
Rich, Peter P. (Cpl)
Richards, Clyde N. (Pvt) Marine Corps Regular, MIA.
Riddle, Lin P. (Pvt)
Rider, Walter K. (Pvt)
Riehl, Philip J. (Pvt)

Rigler, Anthony W. (Cpl)

Riley, Mark F. (Cpl) KIA, 25 June 1918.

Rippey, Delmer (Cpl) Marine Reserve.

Rishel, Joseph L. (Pvt) KIA, 25 June 1918.

Robb, Thompson E. (Pvt) Marine Corps Regular. WIA.

Robbins, Lloyd A. (Pvt)

Robertson, Lowell R. (Pvt)

Robertson, Robert L. (Pvt)

Robison, Cleatus W. (Pvt) Marine Corps Regular.

Robison, Elon C. (Pvt)

Ross, Emmett C. (Pvt)

Row, Ralph McC. (Pvt) Marine Reserve.

Ruff, David (Drummer)

Ruff, Sterling L. (Sgt)

Rulong, Maurice E. (Pvt)

Rumpke, Henry W. (Sgt)

Russell, Herbert C. (Pvt)

Ryan, John E. (Cpl) Marine Corps Regular. WIA.

Ryerson, Harry D. (Sgt) Marine Corps Regular. WIA.

Sadowski, Walter (Pvt)

St. George, Herbert (Cpl) KIA, 6 June 1918.

Salmon, Dana C. (Cpl)

Saunders, John A. (Pvt)

Sawedzki, Anton G. (Pvt)

Scahill, William P. (Pvt)

Schellenberg, Albert (Pvt) Marine Corps Regular. WIA.

Schierholz, Herman H. (Pvt)

Schnicke, Herbert C.F. (Pvt)

Schueman, Martin C. (Pvt)

Schwartz, William E. (Pvt)

Searcy, Charley A. (Pvt)

Sebastian, Ernest H. (Pvt)

Seidler, Arthur A. (Pvt)

Seifert, Frank H. (Pvt)

Seney, Raymond A. (PFC) Messman.

Seurig, Walter A. (Pvt)

Sexton, Clark McL. (Pvt)

Shafer, Fred L. (Pvt)

Sharpe, William B. (Cpl) Marine Corps Regular. WIA.

Shauberger, Gale B. (Pvt)

Sheehan, Grant B. (PFC)

Sherman, William H. (Pvt)

Sherry, James W. (Pvt)

Shields, Roy D. (Pvt)

Shillingburg, Condon G. (Cpl) Marine Corps Regular. WIA.

Sims, Ralph P. (Pvt)

Sister, Frank McK. (Pvt)

Skeen, Earl F. (Cpl)

Skeen, Ralph (PFC)

Skidmore, Robert J. (Pvt) Marine Reserve.

Sleight, Morris G. (Cpl)

Sloan, Charles E. (Cpl) Marine Corps Regular.

Smith, Albert E. (Pvt) MC Reserve, Class 2.

Smith, Charles R. (Pvt)

Smith, Clarence T. (Pvt)

Smith, Daniel L. (Pvt)

Smith, Floyd L. (Pvt)

Smith, George T. (Pvt)

Smith, Guy W. (Pvt) Marine Corps Regular.

Smrekar, Mathias (Pvt) Marine Corps Regular. WIA.

Snider, Henry C. (Pvt) KIA, 23 June 1918.

Snider, Sidney R. (Cpl) Marine Corps Regular, WIA, Belleau Wood.

Snyder, George R. (Pvt) MC Reserve, Class 2.

Sojourner, Martin (Cpl)

Sondstrom, Warner W. (Pvt)

Spaulding, Gilman (Pvt) Marine Corps Regular.

Stamer, Ernest (PFC) Marine Reserve, Died of Wounds, 23 October 1918.

Stanton, Joseph J. (Pvt) Marine Reserve.

Stanton, Willard E. (Cpl)

Stegena, Andrew (PFC)

Stevens, Clare C. (PFC)

Stewart, William K. (Pvt)

Stone, John F. (Sgt) KIA, 4 November 1918.

Stoneham, John (Cpl)

Stoneham, Robert M. (PFC)

Stoughton, Charles E. (Pvt)

Strain, John H. (Pvt) Died of Wounds, 23 June 1918.

Strickland, Benjamin H. (Cpl)

Stroka, Alexander (Sgt)

Stroman, George L. (Pvt)

Stuteman, Warren K. (Pvt) Marine Corps Regular. WIA.

Stuth, Wilfred H. (Cpl)

Sullivan, William (Pvt)

Sullivan, William G., Jr. (Pvt)

Swain, Grover C. (Pvt) KIA, 23 June 1918.

Swanson, Thorval (Pvt)

Sweeney, Harvey O. (Pvt)

Sypniewski, Bernard (PFC)

Szczepanski, Peter (Pvt)

Tax, M.H. (Pvt)

Telford, Estil R. (Pvt)

Thomas, Guy (Pvt)

Thompson, Ira C. (PhM) U.S. Navy.

Thompson, Preston E. (Pvt)

Thompson, William C. (Pvt)

Toner, James L. (Trumpeter) Marine Corps Regular.

Trainor, Emmett F. (Pvt)

Trinkner, Clarence A. (Pvt) Marine Corps Regular.

Trusler, Henry E. (Pvt)

Tubbs, Albert A. (PFC)

Tucker, Thomas B. (Cpl) Marine Corps Regular.

Turner, Arthur L. (Pvt)

Turner, Benjamin F. (Cpl) KIA, 23 June 1918.

Ulrich, John F. (Pvt)

Van Gemert, Henry (Pvt)

Van Schoor, Harold (Pvt) Marine Corps Regular. WIA.

Vaughan, James A. (Pvt) WIA.

Vencil, Carl W. (Sgt)

Vogt, John O. (Pvt) Died of Wounds, 25 June 1918.

Voliva, John L. (Pvt) Reserve, Died of Wounds.

Walker, Francis L. (Pvt) Marine Corps Regular. WIA.

Walker, James M. (Sgt)

Walker, Merrill E. (Pvt) Marine Corps Regular, gassed.

Walsh, Joseph (Pvt)

Walters, Charles T. (Pvt)

Walton, George H. (Pvt)

Wardrope, Ralph (Cpl)

Waters, Thomas J. (Pvt)

Watkins, Dewey T. (Pvt)

Watson, Clarence J. (Cpl) Fleet Reserve.
Weaver, Chauncey O., Jr. (Pvt)
Weaver, Courtney M. (Pvt) Marine Corps Regular.
Weed, Sam L. (Pvt)
Weller, Sidney (Pvt) KIA, 25 June 1918.
West, John B. (Pvt)
Wettre, Erling C. (Pvt)
Wheatley, Charles E. (Pvt)
White, Melville C. (Pvt)
White, Raymond C. (Pvt)
Wilkins, Ralph E. (Sgt)
Wilson, Floyd W. (Pvt)
Winter, Clarence (Pvt)
Wolf, Ralph (PFC) Marine Corps Regular, MIA.
Wood, Howard B. (Cpl) KIA, 23 June 1918.
Young, Gilbert W. (Pvt) KIA, 6 June 1918.
Zimmer, Edmond J. (Pvt)
Zwinge, Albert B. (PFC) Marine Reserve.

20th (K) Company, Third Battalion

NAME (RANK) REMARKS

Collier, Eugene F.C. (Cpt)
Fisk, Francis (Cpt) CO, K Company.
Jackson, Gilder D. (Cpt) Marine Corps Regular, WIA.
Platt, Richard N. (Cpt) Commanding Officer, 20th Co.
DeVries, Thurston J. (1st Lt)
Elmore, Arthur T. (1st Lt) KIA, 13 July 1918.
Babcock, Robert C. (2nd Lt) KIA, 1 November 1918.
Batten, George B. (2nd Lt) Marine Corps Reserve.
Burris, Allen H. (2nd Lt) Marine Corps Reserve.
Coppinger, Harry M. (2nd Lt) U.S. Army, KIA, 25 June 1918.
Lowe, William O. (2nd Lt)
Lubers, Bruce G. (2nd Lt)
Martineau, Earl T. (2nd Lt)
Potter, Hal N. (2nd Lt)
Silverthorn, Merwin H. (2nd Lt) Marine Corps Regular, WIA.
Toomey, Ernest (2nd Lt) U.S. Army. Wounded at Belleau Wood.
Wilson, Percival L. (2nd Lt) Wounded at Belleau Wood.
Wirthington, James S. (2nd Lt) Marine Corps Reserve.

Enlisted

Dittmore, Charlie W. (1st Sgt)
Grant, John (1st Sgt)
Higgins, James A. (1st Sgt)
Aanes, Hans G. (Cpl)
Acaley, Samuel, Jr. (Pvt) Marine Corps Regular.
Adams, Eli (PFC)
Adams, Herbert C. (Pvt)
Adams, John (Pvt)
Adams, Louis C. (Cpl)
Adie, James L. (Pvt)
Albrecht, Harry (Pvt) Marine Corps Regular, WIA.
Alguire, Hiram J. (PFC) Marine Corps Regular, WIA.

Allbritton, Roy (Pvt)
Allcorn, Don (Pvt)
Allen, Robert L. (Pvt)
Allen, Bernard D. (Pvt)
Allen, Charles L. (Pvt)
Allen, James N. (Pvt) KIA, 6 June 1918.
Allen, Sammie E. (Pvt)
Allen, Walter (HAp) U.S. Navy.
Allen, Willard J. (Pvt)
Allspaugh, Bert W. (Pvt)
Altman, Theodore W. (Sgt) Died, pneumonia.
Andersen, Harvey F. (Pvt)
Anderson, Archie (Pvt) Marine Corps Regular, WIA.
Anderson, Burt M. (PFC)
Anderson, George L. (PFC)
Anderson, John W. (Pvt)
Anderson, William (Pvt)
Andrews, Roy V. (Pvt)
Arbogast, Ray C. (Pvt)
Archbold, Chester M. (Pvt) Marine Corps Regular, WIA.
Arnold, Emery E. (Pvt)
Arthur, Edward J. (Pvt)
Aschmann, Charles O. (Pvt)
Ashbaugh, William L. (Pvt)
Atkinson, Marion L., Jr. (Pvt) Marine Corps Regular, WIA.
Auer, Charles (Cpl) KIA, 6 June 1918.
Auer, Ora H. (Pvt)
Ault, Elias V. (Pvt)
Baber, William G., Jr. (Pvt) Battalion Commander Clerk Office.
Bacon, Lonnie J. (Pvt)
Bailey, Claud W. (Pvt)
Baldwin, Robert R. (Cpl)
Banks, John (Pvt)
Bannkratz, Ellis H. (Sgt)
Barkhausen, Harry (Pvt)
Barnes, Robert D. (Pvt) Marine Corps Regular, KIA.
Barry, Clarence F. (Pvt)
Barry, Martin L. (Pvt) Marine Corps Regular, WIA.
Bartlett, Emery A. (Pvt) KIA, 12 June 1918.
Barwick, Thomas C. (Pvt)
Baur, Walter C. (Pvt)
Baxter, James B. (Pvt)
Becker, John H. (Pvt)
Beebe, John (Pvt) Marine Corps Regular, KIA.
Begert, Rudolph W. (Pvt)
Begg, William (Pvt) MIA.
Belcher, Fred (Cpl)
Belcour, Charles J. (Pvt) Marine Corps Regular, WIA.
Bell, Justus S. (Cpl)
Bellona, Levi L. (Pvt)
Belz, Joseph W. (Pvt) Marine Corps Regular, WIA.
Bennett, Christopher F. (Pvt)
Bennett, John J. (PFC)
Bennett, Walter L. (Pvt)
Bennett, Winfield A. (Pvt) Marine Corps Regular, WIA.
Bigley, Walter S. (Pvt) KIA, 8 June 1918.
Bisonette, George O. (Cpl) WIA.
Blackden, Earl B. (Cpl) KIA, 7 June 1918.
Blalack, Cleo (Pvt)

Blomberg, Edward F. (Pvt) Marine Corps Regular.
Boeke, Carleton F. (Cpl)
Bond, Sterling P. (Pvt)
Borg, Benjamin W. (Pvt)
Borror, Charles D. (Pvt) Marine Corps Regular, WIA.
Boyce, Irving L. (Pvt)
Boyd, Leland E. (Pvt)
Bradgate, Raymond E. (Pvt)
Bradley, Joseph H. (Pvt)
Bradshaw, Thomas J. (Trumpeter)
Brandies, Sidney (Cpl)
Brandt, Joseph (Pvt) Marine Corps Regular.
Brash, Cedric (Trumpeter)
Braswell, Louis B., Jr. (Pvt) KIA, 6 November 1918.
Bredesen, Osuld (Cpl)
Brennan, James (Pvt)
Brennan, James G. (Cpl)
Brewer, Leo D. (Cpl)
Bridge, Joseph (Pvt)
Brines, John R. (Pvt) Marine Corps Regular, WIA.
Britton, Curtis (PFC) Marine Corps Regular, WIA.
Brock, Charles W. (Pvt) Marine Corps Regular, WIA.
Brockhoff, Edward J. (Pvt)
Brody, John J. (Cpl) Marine Corps Regular.
Brophy, Aloysius L. (Pvt)
Brower, Verne J. (Pvt)
Brown, Edward D. (Pvt)
Brown, Frank (Pvt)
Brown, Thomas W. (Cpl)
Brown, Wilburt S. (Pvt) Marine Corps Regular, WIA.
Brunbaugh, William (Pvt)
Brunner, Walter D. (Pvt)
Bucker, Elliotte E. (PFC)
Bucklew, William S. (Pvt)
Buli, Albert N. (Pvt)
Burnside, George H. (Pvt) Marine Corps Regular, WIA.
Butler, Thane O. (Pvt)
Byron, Harold G. (Pvt)
Cahn, Louis K. (Pvt)
Calhoun, Charles J. (Pvt)
Cameron, Duncan J. (Pvt)
Campbell, Roe E. (Pvt)
Candito, Vincent J. (Pvt)
Cantlon, Sherman W. (Pvt)
Carlson, Clarence O. (Pvt)
Carlton, Richard B. (Pvt)
Carpenter, James C. (Cpl)
Carper, Dwight (Pvt)
Carroll, Thomas G. (Pvt)
Carter, William L. (Pvt)
Case, William G. (Sgt)
Cathers, Joseph (Sgt)
Cervinski, Roman (Pvt)
Cesmat, Albert A. (Pvt)
Chadwick, James R. (Pvt) KIA, 7 June 1918.
Chapin, Raphel T. (Pvt)
Chapman, Fred L. (Cpl)
Chapman, Wilbur D. (Pvt)
Chase, Bruce G. (Pvt) KIA, 6 June 1918.
Christopher, John D. (Cpl)
Christopher, John K. (Pvt)

Clark, Garrie (Pvt) Messman.
Cleary, Joseph A. (Pvt)
Cluff, Denton F. (PFC)
Cohen, Sidney (Pvt)
Cole, Charles B. (PFC)
Collins, Jesse L. (Pvt)
Collins, Neal J. (Pvt)
Cooper, Auburn F. (Pvt)
Cooper, Oscar M. (PFC)
Cooper, Truman (Pvt)
Copman, W.E. (Pvt)
Counts, Ole E. (Pvt)
Cox, Wayne (PFC)
Crangle, James C. (Pvt)
Crimmins, Edward J. (PFC)
Crist, George R. (Pvt)
Cromer, Wilfred S. (Pvt)
Crossley, Clarence S. (Pvt)
Crosswy, Walter D. (Pvt)
Curtis, Chester L. (Pvt)
Curvan, James J. (Pvt)
Damond, Francis D., Jr. (Pvt)
Davey, Roland W. (Pvt)
Davis, Albert L. (Sgt)
Davis, Ernest W. (Pvt) KIA, 4 October 1918.
Davis, Henry L. (Pvt) Marine Corps Reserve.
Davis, Murry H. (Cpl)
Dees, Arthur A. (Pvt)
DeVoe, Charles E. (Pvt)
Digby, Russell B. (Pvt) Died of Wounds, 15 July 1918.
Dingle, Richard W. (Pvt) KIA, 6 June 1918.
Distel, Harold (Pvt) Marine Corps Regular, WIA.
Distel, Roy C. (Cpl)
Dobbertin, John J. (MarGun) Marine Corps Regular.
Dobbins, Worthy E. (PFC)
Dochter, Fred (Cpl)
Dogan, Hubert H. (Pvt)
Douglass, Ora J. (Pvt)
Dressler, Milo (PFC) Marine Corps Regular, WIA.
Duda, Walter F. (Sgt) KIA, 22 June 1918.
Dunphy, James P. (Pvt) Marine Corps Regular, KIA.
East, Walter A. (PFC)
Eckler, Elmer (Pvt)
Edwards, Henry C. (PFC) WIA, gassed.
Edwards, Stephen L. (Pvt)
Empey, Hollis E. (Cpl) KIA, 10 November 1918.
Engler, George (Sgt)
Erickson, Donald E. (Pvt) Died of Wounds, 13 June
   1918.
Ermer, Leo A. (Pvt)
Erwin, Richard F. (Pvt)
Evans, Guy G. (Pvt)
Fagan, Harvey (Pvt)
Faught, Roy K. (Pvt)
Fehr, John D. (Pvt) Died of Wounds, 26 June 1918.
Ferguson, Hugh Mc. (Pvt) MIA.
Ferguson, John R. (Pvt)
Ferguson, Thomas A. (Pvt)
Field, Danforth W. (Cpl) Marine Corps Regular, WIA.
Fischer, Robert M. (Cpl) KIA, 6 June 1918.
Fisher, Earl H. (Pvt)

Fisk, Leon W. (GySgt)
Fitzwater, James O. (Cpl)
Flynn, Francis J. (GySgt) KIA, 6 June 1918.
Forbes, Edward P. (Pvt)
Foren, Irving W. (Pvt) Died of Wounds, 6 June 1918.
Foster, Lewis E. (Pvt)
Francis, William A. (PFC) Marine Corps Reserve.
Fraser, Alexander R. (Pvt)
Fry, Lee L. (Pvt)
Fulmer, Clinton W. (Pvt)
Fultz, George C. (GySgt)
Funderburk, Clyde W. (Cpl)
Gahring, Roland A. (Cpl)
Gay, Harry (GySgt) Marine Corps Regular, WIA.
Gibson, John W. (Pvt)
Gilbraith, Lester J. (Pvt)
Gilhisen, Morris E. (Pvt)
Glasco, Robert L. (Pvt)
Goen, Ralph E. (Pvt)
Gomez, Charles F. (Pvt)
Grau, Wayne W. (PFC) Marine Corps Reserve.
Green, Francis E. (Cpl)
Green, Parnell (PFC) Marine Corps Regular, WIA.
Greer, William J. (PFC)
Grenier, Joseph A. (Pvt)
Grinen, Steven (Pvt)
Gross, Arthur (Trumpeter) Marine Corps Regular, WIA.
Growe, Harold (Pvt) Messman, KIA, 6 June 1918.
Grue, Louis A. (Pvt) Marine Corps Regular, WIA.
Guenther, Clayton A. (Pvt)
Gustafson, Arthur S. (PFC)
Gwaltney, Thomas W. (Pvt)
Haggarty, Ira C. (Pvt)
Hall, Orvil (Pvt)
Hall, Russell W. (PhM) U.S. Navy.
Hamilton, Grover C. (PFC) Marine Corps Regular, WIA.
Hamilton, William A. (Pvt)
Hansen, William (Pvt) KIA, 6 June 1918.
Hardwick, Hendon H. (Pvt)
Hardy, Edward V. (PFC)
Hasty, John A. (Pvt) Marine Corps Reserve.
Hebert, Clarence H. (Pvt)
Heggen, Reuben (Pvt)
Hendershot, Charles R. (Cpl)
Hendershot, George (Pvt)
Henderson, James W. (PFC)
Henderson, William D. (Cpl)
Herring, Val (PFC)
Hess, Robert B. (Cpl)
Hewitt, Harold H. (Pvt)
Heymann, Henry P. (Sgt) KIA, 23 June 1918.
Hill, Frederick B. (Pvt) Messman.
Himelhan, Fred A. (Pvt)
Hixon, John (PFC)
Hobbs, Robert H.J. (Pvt)
Hodapp, Philip H. (Pvt) Marine Corps Reserve.
Hoffman, Edwin W. (Pvt) Marine Corps Regular, WIA.
Hollingshead, Charles (Cpl) WIA, 24 June 1918.
Horton, Donald C. (Pvt)
Hovis, Watson E. (Pvt)
Hughes, George D. (Cpl)

Hull, Edwin D. (Cpl) Clerk, Batt Comdr Office.
Hyke, Frank H. (Cpl)
Iah, Rex W. (Sgt)
Ingebritson, Reuben (Pvt)
Ives, John H. (PFC) Messman.
Jacobson, Howard C. (Cpl)
Jahnke, Irving F. (Pvt)
James, Joseph H. (PhM) U.S. Navy.
John, Thomas (Cpl)
Johns, Jerome W. (Cpl) Company Clerk.
Johnson, Herbert A. (Cpl)
Johnson, Joseph D. (Pvt) Marine Corps Regular, WIA.
Johnson, Raymond C. (PFC) Marine Corps Regular, WIA.
Johnson, Victor E. (Cpl)
Jones, Eddie E. (Cpl)
Kanouse, Simon W. (Pvt) KIA, 6 June 1918.
Kaskey, Henry Y. (Sgt)
Kelley, Fred A. (Pvt)
Kelley, Leo (Pvt)
Kellum, Charles (Pvt) Cook, 1st Class.
Kennedy, Earl V. (Sgt)
Kiemme, Carl J. (PFC) Marine Corps Regular, MIA.
Kinkel, Edwin P. (PhM3)
Kippley, William L. (PFC)
Kitzmann, Francis R. (Pvt)
Klapp, Joseph G.W. (Cpl)
Kleinman, Moroni (Pvt) KIA, 25 June 1918.
Klemme, Carl J. (Pvt)
Klohe, John M. (Pvt)
Knapp, George L. (PFC)
Knaub, Chester E. (PFC)
Koch, Edwin H. (Pvt)
Kounovsky, Albert J. (Pvt)
Krasch, Roy R. (Pvt) Marine Corps Regular.
Kriege, Andrew A. (Pvt)
Kubilus, Raymond (Pvt)
Kyle, Charley, Jr. (Pvt)
Lamb, Walter S. (PFC)
Langway, Henry W. (Pvt)
Lantz, Charles I. (Pvt)
LaTour, Douglas T. (Pvt) Marine Corps Reserve. Messman.
Laundrie, Edward (Pvt)
LaValley, Marcellis (Pvt)
Lawson, Henry F. (Pvt)
Lawton, William R. (PFC)
Layton, Rush (Pvt)
Leavitt, George E. (Pvt)
Ledoux, Joseph (Pvt)
Lee, Harry D. (Cpl)
Lee, Louis E. (Pvt)
Leger, Ranold E. (Pvt) Marine Corps Regular, WIA.
Lehman, Charles H. (Pvt)
Leissure, George W. (HAp1)
Lendy, Richard L. (Pvt)
Lenz, William H. (Pvt)
Leonhard, Walter E. (Pvt) Marine Corps Regular, WIA.
Lewis, Joyce S. (Pvt)
Lewis, William T. (Pvt)
Lighthart, Norman F. (Pvt)

Lindsay, Thomas W. (Cpl)
Lindsy, Donald B. (Pvt)
Linnert, Robert H. (Pvt) Marine Corps Regular, WIA.
Little, George L. (Pvt)
Lloyd, Robert E. (Sgt)
Lockwood, Harry M. (Pvt) KIA, 23 June 1918.
Logghe, Julius L. (Pvt)
Lopez, Edmundo C. (Pvt)
Loubiere, Anthony (Pvt)
Lovejoy, Robert E. (Pvt)
Lowe, George M. (Pvt) Cook, 4th Class.
Ludy, Jack (Pvt)
Lueban, Floyd J. (Sgt)
Lukins, Fred T. (Sgt) KIA, 6 June 1918.
Lynch, Joseph D. (Pvt)
Lyon, Cedric E. (Pvt)
Mack William H. (GySgt) KIA, 19 July 1918.
Madden, James D. (PFC) Marine Corps Regular, WIA.
Magnus, Paul N. (Pvt)
Maloy, Glen E. (Pvt)
Mangin, Howard (Pvt)
Manning, Joseph E. (GySgt)
Martin, Paul N. (PFC)
Martin, Ralph E. (Pvt)
Martindale, Charles P. (Pvt)
Mathes, James C. (Pvt)
Mattingly, Randel A. (Pvt) KIA, 6 June 1918.
Mayfield, Ollie A. (Pvt) Marine Corps Regular, WIA.
McCarron, Edward F. (Pvt)
McColly, Charley D. (Pvt)
McConnell, Charles F. (Cpl)
McCulloch, George (Pvt)
McGinn, James E. (Pvt) Messman.
McGraw, Thomas P. (Pvt)
McKenzie, James H. (Pvt)
McMurtrie, Claude (Pvt)
McPherson, John A. (Pvt)
McWhirter, William L. (Pvt) KIA, 12 June 1918.
Melby, Almer J. (Cpl)
Mercer, Howard B. (Pvt) Marine Corps Regular.
Miller, Frank D. (Pvt)
Miller, Frank L. (Pvt)
Miller, Menthley R. (Pvt)
Miller, Neilson R. (PFC)
Mills, Carl B. (Pvt)
Milne, Marion R. (Cpl)
Mitchell, William (Pvt)
Mock, Jack O. (Pvt)
Mock, Rex C. (Pvt)
Moore, Earl W. (Pvt)
Moore, Ernest E. (Pvt)
Moore, John P. (Pvt)
Morton, Earl W. (Pvt) Marine Corps Reserve.
Mott, George S. (Cpl)
Muhlstein, Louis I. (Pvt)
Mullin, William L. (Pvt)
Munger, Chester L. (Pvt)
Munroe, Theodore R. (Pvt)
Murphy, Robert N. (Pvt)
Myer, George E., Jr. (Sgt)
Nadeau, William J. (Pvt) Marine Corps Regular, WIA.

Nathans, Francis J. (Pvt)
Neeser, Harry F. (Pvt)
Neil, Allan W. (Pvt)
Nelsan, Orville A. (Pvt)
Ness, Gunval (Pvt)
Nichol, Andrew A. (Pvt)
Ningard, Joseph L. (Pvt) Marine Corps Regular.
Nolte, William V. (PhM1)
Nordaan, Andrew (Pvt)
Oaks, Grover C. (Sgt)
O'Donnell, Patrick A. (Pvt)
Orfanpos, Kunstantinos (Pvt)
Oster, Henry A. (Cpl) Marine Corps Regular, WIA.
Ott, John H. (Cpl) Marine Corps Reserve.
Owen, Ward E.G. (Pvt)
Patterson, Eugene (Pvt)
Patyk, Jacob F. (Pvt)
Payne, Boyd J. (PhM3)
Peck, John (Sgt)
Pell, Howard M. (Pvt) Messman.
Perkins, Leonard (Pvt)
Perrine, Henry C. (Sgt)
Phillips, Charles M., Jr. (Pvt) Marine Cps Res, Class 2
Pilcher, Luther W. (Sgt) KIA, 6 June 1918.
Pitts, James T. (PFC) Marine Corps Regular, WIA.
Plumlee, Hugh C. (Pvt) Cook, 1st Class.
Polane, Chester H. (Sgt
Pope, James H. (Pvt)
Porter, Francis R. (Pvt)
Potts, David Jr. (Pvt) KIA, 2 November 1918.
Powell, Walter E. (Pvt) KIA, 1 November 1918.
Powers, Etheridge (Pvt)
Prather, Eddy B. (Pvt)
Pressley, Henry (Pvt)
Price, Roy V. (Pvt)
Prince, Edward B. (PFC) Marine Corps Regular, WIA.
Quinn, Roland W. (Pvt) Marine Corps Regular, WIA.
Radcliffe, John (Pvt)
Radloff, Charles J. (Sgt) Marine Corps Regular, WIA.
Ramsey, LaVerne G. (Pvt) Marine Corps Regular.
Reck, John (Cpl)
Redmond, Paul C. (Pvt)
Rednick, Cecil F. (Pvt)
Reed, Harry E. (Pvt)
Reed, Russell M. (Pvt)
Reeves, Tom P. (Pvt) Cook, 3rd Class.
Reid, Hugh (Cpl)
Renaldi, James (Pvt) Cook, 2nd Class.
Rhea, Charles J. (Pvt)
Richardson, Bert A. (Cpl)
Roberts, Harry C. (Pvt) KIA, 2 November 1918.
Robinson, Dayton H. (Pvt)
Rodefer, Bert A. (Cpl)
Rodgers, George H. (Pvt) Marine Corps Regular, WIA.
Rogers, John G. (Pvt)
Ronsky, Otto J. (Pvt)
Rowley, Thomas (Cpl) Marine Corps Regular, WIA.
Rummell, Willie W. (Pvt) Marine Corps Regular.
Rusconi, Ferdinand (Pvt)
St. Leon, Roy E. (Cpl)
St. Louis, Harry H. (Pvt)

Schlagster, Merle D. (Pvt)
Schleppegrell, Thorald W. PFC
Schmidt, Joseph W. (Pvt)
Schorner, Joseph F. (PFC)
Schroeder, Benjamin B. (Pvt) Marine Corps Reserve.
Scott, Claude E. (Cpl)
Segalini, Paul S. (Pvt) Marine Corps Regular, MIA.
Seifert, Paul (Pvt) Marine Corps Regular, WIA.
Sellars, George B. (Pvt)
Severns, Sidney (Pvt) KIA, 6 June 1918.
Shannon, Patrick A. (Pvt)
Sherman, Stephen G. (Sgt) KIA, 6 June 1918.
Sherritt, Aaron R. (Cpl) WIA, Belleau Wood.
Shotwell, Robert L. (Pvt)
Sicora, Michael R. (Cpl)
Sidders, Frank (Pvt)
Silverston, Albert (Pvt)
Simms, William E. (Pvt)
Simpson, Everett P. (PFC)
Simpson, John A. (Pvt)
Smith, Fred A. (Pvt)
Smith, Guy L. (Cpl)
Smith, Jay D. (Pvt)
Smith, John J. (PhM) U.S. Navy.
Smith, Leslie H. (Pvt)
Smith, Lester D. (PFC)
Smith, Raymond W. (Pvt)
Smithmeyer, Rudolph R. (Pvt)
Snyder, Joseph (PFC)
Solins, Emanuel (Pvt)
Sothern, Cedric D. (Pvt) Marine Corps Regular.
Souza, Julius (Pvt)
Spitzbardt, Gustave (Pvt) Marine Corps Regular, KIA, 5 October 1918.
Stark, Raleigh D. (Pvt)
Stearns, Stanley (Cpl)
Stegin, Frank E. (Pvt) Marine Corps Regular, WIA.
Stephens, Samuel D. (Pvt)
Stevens, Ralph F. (Pvt)
Stoley, Frank (Pvt)
Strain, Sherman A. (Pvt)
Strange, Clarence O. (Pvt)
Sutherland, Robert P. (Pvt)
Swanland, Oscar F.W. (Pvt)
Swanson, Clarence V. (Pvt)
Swenson, Sigurd M. (Pvt)
Talaska, John (Pvt)
Taylor, Ross A. (PFC)
Terwilliger, Floyd E. (Pvt)
Thieme, Frank R. (PFC)
Thomas, Clarence G. (Pvt)
Thomas, Maxwell S. (Pvt)
Thomson, Clarence G. (PFC)
Thomson, Lawrence W. (Pvt)
Thorne, Joseph W. (Pvt)
Thornquist, August M. (Pvt)
Thorpe, Byron McK. (Cpl)
Tidwell, Jessie N. (Pvt)
Tierney, Edward O. (Pvt)
Tigner, Elmer E. (Pvt)
Trewartha, Oliver T. (PFC)

Trinka, Frank (Pvt) Died of illness, 25 November 1918.
Troutman, Paul W. (Pvt) Marine Corps Reserve.
Tryon, Stewart E. (Cpl)
Tupa, Frank J. (Cpl)
Twiggs, Cecil D. (Pvt)
Tyer, Elmer L. (Pvt)
Updike, Hubert (Sgt)
Utter, Emerson (Pvt)
Vehe, Reuben F. (Pvt) Marine Corps Regular, MIA.
Venable, Garrett (Pvt)
Vogel, Louis (Pvt)
Vorschimer, Robert (Pvt) Marine Corps Regular.
Wagner, William A. (Pvt)
Waldman, Theodore J. (Trumpeter)
Waldrop, Victor H. (Pvt)
Walker, James A. (Pvt) Marine Corps Regular.
Wallace, John (Pvt)
Warnecke, Francis (Sgt)
Warren, Robert H. (Pvt) Marine Corps Regular.
Weaver, Benjamin W. (PhM) Marine Corps Regular.
Webb, Vernon L. (Pvt)
Webster, Horace P. (Cpl)
Wells, Rowland B. (Pvt)
White, Harry G. (Sgt) Marine Corps Reserve.
Whitney, Charles H. (Pvt)
Williams, Harry N. (Pvt) Marine Corps Regular.
Williams, Marshall B. (Cpl)
Williams, Oliver (Pvt)
Williams, Ray B. (Pvt)
Williams, Rush (PFC)
Wilson, Everett V. (Pvt) Marine Corps Reserve.
Wilson, Robert D.A. (Pvt) Died of Wounds, 23 June 1918.
Winfrey, Millard F. (Cpl)
Wolfhegel, Charles (GySgt) Marine Regular, Died of Wounds, 14 November 1918.
Woods, Emmett N. (Pvt)
Worstall, Thurman E. (Pvt)
Wryess, Henry J. (Pvt)
Young, Ralph E. (Pvt) Marine Corps Reserve.
Zimermann, Henry W. (Sgt)

45th (L) Company, Third Battalion

Name (Rank) Remarks

Conachy, Peter (Cpt) Commanding Off., 45th Co.
Hope, Edward B. (Cpt) WIA, 6 June 1918.
Quigley, Thomas (Cpt) WIA.
Rorke, James F. (Cpt) CO, L Company.
Wilson, Frank W. (Cpt)
Bennett, Floyd W. (1st Lt) Commanding 1st Platoon.
Blanton, John F. (1st Lt)
Davies, Thurston J. (1st Lt)
Johnson, Earl F. (1st Lt)
Readey, Daniel J. (1st Lt)
Butler, Edward M. (2nd Lt) WIA.
Conroy, Edward E. (2nd Lt)

Gustafson, John A. (2nd Lt) Commanding 2nd Platoon.
Holljes, Herman R. (2nd Lt)
Kesel, Jacob J. (2nd Lt) WIA.
Miles. Thomas H., Jr. (2nd Lt) KIA, 6 June 1918.
Parker, John H. (2nd Lt) Gassed.
Shepherd, Wiley F. (2nd Lt) WIA.
Wilson, Claggett (2nd Lt)

Enlisted

Boden, Austin W. (1st Sgt)
Higgerson, William P. (1st Sgt) KIA, 6 June 1918.
Myers, Charles A. (1st Sgt) Marine Corps Reserve.
Abell, William F., Jr. (Pvt)
Abercrombie, Albert R. (Pvt) WIA.
Abrams, Albert E. (Pvt) Gassed.
Acker, Francis F. (Pvt) KIA, 4 October 1918.
Adams, Edward R. (Pvt)
Adkins, Harvey G. (Pvt)
Adkins, Richard M. (Pvt)
Agostini, Camillo A. (Cpl) Wagoner.
Albus, Frank (Pvt)
Alexander, James N. (Pvt)
Allen, Andrew B. (Pvt)
Althouse, Ira C. (Pvt)
Alton, Charles T. (Pvt)
Andis, Jesse J. (PFC)
Anthony, George A. (Pvt) Cook, 1st Class.
Atkinson, Louis D. (Pvt)
Austin, Wayne G. (Pvt)
Ayers, Burl C. (Pvt)
Bailey, Caskie L. (Cpl)
Bailey, Thomas R. (Pvt)
Baines, Roscoe K. (Sgt) WIA.
Baird, Joseph W. (Pvt)
Baker, Wilbur L. (Pvt)
Baldwin, James L. (Pvt)
Baldwin, Otha L. (PFC)
Ballinger, William E. (Pvt)
Balogh, John (Drummer)
Barbour, Thomas A. (Sgt) WIA.
Barden, Thomas M. (Pvt)
Barlow, Joel C. (Pvt) KIA, 9 November 1918.
Barnes, George I. (Pvt)
Barr, Charles C. (GySgt)
Barrington, Warren M. (PhM)
Batcher, Harry W. (Sgt)
Bates, Rolland B. (Cpl)
Baucom, John C. (Pvt)
Beach, Joseph M. (Pvt) KIA, 9 July 1918.
Beasley, Lancelot R. (PhM3) U.S. Navy.
Beck, Carl W. (Pvt)
Bennett, Mont (Pvt)
Berline, Ross W. (Cpl)
Berry, George F. (Pvt) WIA.
Beuhler, Edward (PFC) WIA.
Beyer, Alfred G. (Pvt)
Biedenbender, Richard (Pvt) WIA.
Bill, Edward C. (Pvt) Messman.
Bishop, Franklin O. (Pvt) WIA.
Black, Glen W. (Cpl) WIA.
Boazman, Joe J. (Pvt)

Boland, Andrew J. (Pvt)
Bonday, Robert (Pvt) Battalion Runner.
Boner, John H.H. (PFC)
Bonfils, Sylvester F. (Pvt)
Bonifacino, Charles (Cpl)
Bowers, Grover C. (Pvt) Messman.
Bowman, Raymond W. (Pvt)
Boyle, John J. (Pvt)
Brasfield, Gale R. (Pvt)
Braudwell, Leslie J. (Pvt) Gassed.
Braun, Albert R. (Pvt)
Brautigam, George F. (Cpl) WIA.
Brendel, August A. (Cpl)
Brice, Francis W. (Pvt)
Brink, Melvin P. (Pvt)
Briscoe, Harry O. (PFC) Reserve, MIA.
Brown, Elmer (Pvt)
Brown, Francis W. (Pvt)
Brown, James J. (Cpl)
Brown, Robert D. (Pvt) WIA.
Bruce, Thomas G. (GySgt)
Brush, Izaak W. (Pvt) Died of Wounds, 4 October 1918.
Bryar, Morrison A. (Pvt)
Buck, Francis H. (Pvt) Gassed.
Burnett, George W. (Pvt) WIA.
Burns, James H. (Pvt)
Burns, Leo W. (Pvt)
Burns, Thomas F. (Pvt)
Byrley, Howard E. (Sgt)
Byron, Thomas A. (Pvt)
Callibrece, Carl (Pvt)
Cameron, Henry H. (Pvt)
Campbell, Lowell D. (Pvt) WIA.
Carpenter, William M. (Cpl)
Carson, Nathan B., Jr. (Pvt)
Carson, Willard J. (Cpl)
Carter, Omar R. (Pvt) KIA, 6 October 1918.
Casanova, Frank A. (Cpl)
Case, Joseph R. (Pvt)
Casey, Walter (Sgt) Supply Sergeant.
Cashner, Roy (Pvt)
Center, Harland B. (Pvt)
Centrell, Charles (Pvt)
Chavido, Carlos (Pvt) WIA.
Christenson, Christian O. (PFC) Marine Corps Reserve.
Christofferson, Axel P. (Sgt)
Clark, Dean C. (Cpl) KIA.
Clark, Paul D. (Pvt))
Claxon, Ora S. (PFC
Close, Frederick L. (Pvt) Reserve, WIA.
Cofield, Walter C. (Pvt)
Colby, Rolland (Pvt)
Coleman, John F., Jr. (PFC)
Confer, Harry E. (Pvt)
Connoly, George W. (Pvt)
Corcoran, Timothy J. (Pvt) WIA.
Cordes, Edrick J. (Pvt) WIA.
Craig, Robert H. (Pvt)
Crandall, Harry (PFC)
Croft, Clarence (PFC)
Crotty, John F. (Pvt)

Crow, Paul M. (PFC)
Crow, Paul N. (Pvt)
Crowder, Eulie B. (PFC) Gassed.
Crowder, William A. (Pvt)
Cryderman, James A. (Pvt)
Cummings, Frank A. (Pvt)
Cumming, Kenneth L. (Pvt) Gassed.
Curnan, Michael (Sgt)
Cushing, Leo H. (PFC)
Cushman, Clifford S. (Cpl) KIA, 6 June 1918.
Dahl, Albert R. (Pvt) WIA.
Dahlquist, Ernest L. (Pvt)
Dance, Powhatan R. (Pvt)
Danley, Harry H. (Pvt)
Darwin, Thomas M. (Pvt) WIA.
Davis, Henry H. (Pvt) Messman.
Davis, James T. (Pvt) Marine Corps Reserve.
Davis, Ralph A. (PFC)
Day, Hobson E. (Pvt)
Day, Thompson E. (Pvt)
Dean, Chester A. (PFC)
DeKay, Robert H. (Pvt)
Denny, Francis, Jr. (Sgt)
Deschaseaux, John L. (Trumpeter)
Deveney, John F. (Pvt)
DeVeney, John S. (Pvt)
Dickerson, Howard H. (Pvt)
Dollens, Leon (Cpl)
Donohue, James J. (Pvt)
Donovan, John L. (Cpl)
Doran, John P. (Pvt)
Dorsey, William O. (Pvt)
Dost, Franklin L. (Sgt)
Douglas, Abbey H. (Pvt)
Duckworth, Carl (Pvt)
Duffy, Robert J. (Pvt)
Dunham, Herbert L. (Pvt)
Dyer, William J. (PFC)
Early, George T. (Sgt)
Eaton, William V. (PFC)
Eckel, Melton B. (Pvt)
Elder, Lewis C. (Pvt)
Elliott, Thomas D. (Pvt)
Ellis, Charles (Pvt)
Ennis, Allen M. (Pvt)
Ensign, Wilbur P. (PFC)
Evans, Alva (Pvt) MIA.
Evans, Richard H. (Pvt)
Evers, Wallace J. (Sgt)
Fagan, Joseph F. (Pvt) KIA, 13 June 1918.
Farrar, Glen B. (Cpl) WIA.
Ferguson, Orville C. (Pvt)
Ferriso. John D. (Pvt)
Fhy, Joseph E. (Pvt)
Fincher, Julian H. (Pvt)
Fink, Harry W. (Cpl)
Fisher, David M. (Pvt)
Fitch, Prosper E. (Pvt)
Flaum, George (Pvt)
Fletcher, James F. (Pvt) MIA.
Florian, Frederick W., Jr. (Pvt) KIA, 6 June 1918.

Foote, Robert D., Jr. (Sgt)
Forton, Edward F. (Pvt)
Fowler, Robert C. (Pvt)
Fox, James J. (Pvt) Messman.
Frandsen, Arthur C. (Pvt)
Franko, John A. (Pvt) Died of Wounds.
Frehse, Charles J. (Pvt) KIA, 6 June 1918.
Fritsch, Harry C. (Pvt) WIA.
Gabriel, Reginal L. (Pvt)
Gallagher, Peter B. (Pvt)
Gates, Francis E. (Pvt)
Gaynor, Charles F. (Pvt)
Geary, Benjamin B. (Sgt)
Gehler, Edward C. (Pvt)
George, Alexander W. (Pvt) WIA.
George, Malcolm H. (Pvt) Reserve, Class 2.
Gess, Frank E. (Pvt)
Gibbons, James J. (Sgt) KIA at Belleau Wood.
Gibbs, Lacey (Pvt)
Gibson, Lyle A. (Cpl)
Gilder, Wade H. (PFC)
Gill, Homer E. (Pvt)
Gillette, Gerald M. (Pvt) Battalion Intelligence.
Gleason, Edward F. (Pvt)
Goelz, George J. (Pvt)
Goldsmith, Joseph R. (Pvt)
Goodman, Julius (Pvt)
Gordon, Charles R. (Cpl) Died of Wounds, 4 October
   1918.
Gordon, Fred (GySgt)
Gorsky, Frank E. (PFC)
Gosney, Charles W. (Pvt)
Gower, Frank N. (Pvt)
Grant, Oscar P. (Cpl)
Gray, Grover C. (Pvt)
Gregg, Hobart (Pvt)
Griffen, William L. (Cpl)
Gross, Charles (Pvt) Gassed.
Grounds, Clarence A. (Cpl) Wagoner.
Gunderson, Andrew E. (Pvt)
Gustafson, Herbert C. (PFC)
Haeft, Albert E., Jr. (Pvt)
Hagedorn, Henry C. (PFC) Marine Corps Reserve.
Hanson, Albert I. (Cpl) WIA.
Hanson, Carl F. (Pvt)
Hardcastle, William (Cpl)
Harding, Otto L. (Pvt)
Harned, LeRoy (Pvt)
Hartley, Paul F. (Pvt) Reserve, Class 2.
Haury, Edward F. (Pvt) WIA.
Hausler, Walter A. (Cpl) Reserve, Co Clerk.
Haverson, Gutman W. (Pvt)
Heglin, Harry M. (Pvt) WIA.
Heninger, Harold P. (Pvt)
Henry, George E. (Pvt)
Hensley, Emmett T. (Pvt) WIA.
Herman, Charles A. (Pvt)
Hess, Raymond J. (Pvt)
Hess, Rollin (Pvt) WIA.
Hewett, Charles W., Jr. (Cpl) Reserve, Co Clerk. KIA,
   6 June 1918.

Hewson, Franklin N. (Pvt) Reserve, Class 2.
Higgs, Elmer E. (Pvt)
Higley, Robert F. (Pvt)
Hill, Andrew J. (Pvt)
Hilliar, Leon H. (Pvt)
Hinton, John (Pvt)
Hoagland, Elmond (Pvt)
Hoch, Adam, Jr. (Pvt)
Hoffman, Errol H. (Pvt)
Holman, Howard B. (Pvt)
Hoppe, William G. (Pvt)
Horan, William A. (Pvt)
Hoskins, Percy H. (Pvt) Reserve, Class 2.
Hotchkiss, Russell (Pvt)
House, Robert C. (PFC)
Houston, Herbert M. (Pvt)
Hoyt, Timothy (Cpl)
Hudson, Otis L. (Pvt) Died of flu, 25 Feb 1919.
Huling, Warren R. (Pvt)
Hull, Roy E. (HAp1) U.S. Navy.
Hulton, Thomas (Pvt)
Humphrey, William W. (Pvt)
Hutnik, John (PFC)
Hyde, George F. (Pvt)
Inden, Clarence E. (Pvt) KIA, 6 June 1918.
Isaac, John A. (Pvt)
Jackson, Honel A. (Cpl)
Jackson, Howard A. (Pvt)
Jackson, John W. (Pvt)
Jacquess, John R. (Pvt) KIA.
Jagosz, Stanley (Pvt)
Jarvis, James L. (Pvt) Reserve, WIA.
Jenkins, Homer (Sgt) KIA, 6 October 1918.
Jett, Harry C. (Pvt)
Johnson, Albert F. (PFC)
Johnson, Albert S. (Cpl)
Johnson, Edgar E. (PFC) KIA.
Johnson, Gustavis E. (Pvt) Reserve, WIA.
Johnson, James E. (PFC) WIA.
Johnson, John N. (Pvt)
Johnson, Richard E. (Pvt)
Johnston, Arthur H. (GySgt) KIA, 15 August 1918.
Jones, Felix W. (Sgt) Died of Wounds, 5 October 1918.
Jordan, George J. (Pvt) WIA.
Julian, Timothy J. (Pvt)
Kaesler, Gerd A. (Pvt)
Kearns, Frederick F. (Pvt)
Keenan, Willie A. (Pvt) WIA.
Keeton, Ewing D. (Pvt)
Kelleher, James P. (GySgt)
Keller, George H. (Pvt)
Kelly, Paul (Pvt)
Kemp, Amma D. (PFC)
Kerley, Parks (Pvt) WIA.
King, Benjamin H. (Sgt)
Kingston, Frederick J. (Pvt) Messman.
Kirscht, Adam B. (Pvt)
Klay, Albert R. (PFC) Gassed.
Kleins, Robert J. (Pvt)
Knight, Lester C. (Pvt) Died of Wounds.
Knopp, Fred J. (Pvt)

Kraps, Harry C. (Pvt)
Kruger, Henry (Pvt) Marine Corps Reserve.
Kups, William (Pvt) WIA.
Kus, Martin J. (Cpl)
Lane, Walter A. (Pvt)
LaRose, Donald A. (Cpl)
Larson, Oscar N. (Sgt) Mess Sergeant.
Lasecki, Walter C. (Pvt)
Laughlin, James L. (PFC)
Lawing, Holland H. (Pvt) WIA.
Lawrence, Harry F. (PFC)
Lawrence, Lewis C. (Cpl)
Laws, Harley (Pvt)
Lazar, Frank (Cpl)
Lee, Harry L. (Pvt)
Lemieux, Samuel J. (Pvt)
Leonard, Oliver R. (Pvt)
Leveridge, Walter E. (Pvt)
Linendoll, Ray L. (Pvt)
List, Fred A. (Pvt) WIA.
Little, George W. (Trumpeter) WIA.
Lloyd, Allen T. (Pvt)
Lobb, Lorin C. (Cpl)
Locke, Frederick G. (Pvt)
Louis, Thomas (Sgt)
Lumaree, LeRoy W. (Pvt) KIA, 26 June 1918.
Luzack, Thomas G. (Sgt)
MacGillivray, Daniel J. (Cpl) WIA.
Maddox, Rexford L. (Pvt)
Malbin, David L. (Pvt)
Maloney, Joseph C. (Pvt) KIA.
Manchester, William (Pvt)
Manning, Stephen A. (Pvt) Reserve. Died of Wounds,
    date not known.
Marble, Ralph S. (Pvt) Reserve, Gassed.
Marcum, Henley P. (Cpl) Reserve, WIA.
Marlow, Thomas F. (Pvt)
McCarthy, Frank (Pvt)
McCreary, Carl T. (Pvt) Marine Corps Reserve.
McDaniel, Robert E. (Pvt)
McDermott, Peter J. (Pvt) WIA.
McDonald, Harry (Pvt) Marine Corps Reserve.
McGhee, Robert H. (GySgt)
McGinnis, Christian I. (Pvt) WIA.
McGoveran, Thomas H. (Cpl)
McHenry, Michael K. (Cpl)
McMahon, John C. (PFC) WIA.
McMillan, John S. (Pvt)
McNerney, William R. (Pvt) WIA.
McVeany, Arthur P. (PFC)
Meek, Harry (Sgt)
Mellon, John E. (PFC)
Merrill, George W. (Pvt) KIA, 6 October 1918.
Milburn, Charles W. (Pvt)
Millage, Frank (Pvt)
Miller, Frank J. (Pvt)
Miller, Paul S. (Pvt)
Millin, Richard B. (Pvt)
Montgomery, Ollie P. (Pvt)
Moody, Francis B. (Pvt)
Moore, Robert T., Jr. (Pvt)

Moreland, Harry C. (Cpl) WIA.

Morris, James B. (Pvt)

Muhlean, Walter J. (Pvt)

Mutch, Harvey A. (PFC)

Myers, Everett J. (Pvt)

Myles, Edward F. (Pvt)

Nash, Guy N. (Pvt)

Natue, Fred J. (PFC)

Nau, Henry (Pvt)

Neal, Robert U. (Cpl)

Neary, Leo E. (Pvt)

Nelson, John (Pvt) Gassed.

Neuneker, William (Pvt) Died of Wounds, 4 October 1918.

Nevling, Ruben M. (Sgt)

Newell, Loren E. (Pvt) KIA, 13 June 1918.

Noblit, Clifford H. (Cpl)

Noel, James F. (Pvt)

Norton, Omer H. (Pvt) WIA.

Nussbaum, Leon E. (Pvt)

O'Connel, Daniel J. (Pvt)

O'Connel, Hugh (Pvt)

Offen, Albert I. (Pvt) MIA.

Oliver, Harold S. (Pvt)

O'Neil, Henry (Pvt)

Ontko, Andrew (Cpl) WIA.

Ormsby, Emmett T. (Pvt)

Orr, Joseph L. (Pvt)

Orr, Norval W. (Pvt)

O'Toole, Joseph P. (Pvt)

Ott, Barton H. (Pvt)

Otto, William H. (Cpl) KIA, 6 June 1918.

Page, Joe J. (PFC)

Paget, Willis T. (Pvt)

Paine, Harry M. (Pvt)

Palmer, Frank F. (Pvt)

Parshall, Wilbur (Pvt) WIA.

Paulsen, John C. (Pvt)

Pearce, John J. (Pvt)

Pecsenye, Edward J. (Pvt)

Pence, Fred L. (Pvt)

Peterson, John O. (Cpl) WIA.

Phillips, Gail O. (Pvt) Orderly, KIA, 18 June 1918.

Pierce, Harold D. (Pvt)

Pierce, Walter W. (Pvt)

Piper, Ralph E. (Pvt) WIA.

Pitcher, Morgan I. (Pvt)

Placek, Joseph T. (Pvt) KIA, 24 June 1918.

Platt, Chester E. (Cpl)

Ploger, Claude (Pvt) Gassed.

Poirier, Daniel (Pvt)

Pospisil, George R. (Pvt)

Poston, Rollin H. (Pvt)

Powell, Silas, Jr. (Pvt)

Prescott, Walter P. (PFC)

Presley, Dread D. (PFC)

Prevost, Stevens (Sgt) Reserve, Gassed.

Pry, Robert E. (Pvt)

Pyle, Guy L. (Sgt)

Ralston, Frank S. (Pvt) Cook, 3rd Class.

Ramold, John (Pvt)

Randall, Henry N. (Pvt) WIA.

Randolph, John (Pvt) Company Runner.

Ratinski, Walter W. (Pvt)

Rausch, John E. (Pvt)

Rea, Frank A. (Pvt) KIA, 7 June 1918.

Reavy, George H. (Pvt)

Reis, Gabriel O. (Pvt)

Renn, Leo (Pvt)

Reuter, Edward H. (Cpl)

Reynolds, Richard S., Jr. (Pvt) KIA, 13 June 1918.

Rhodes, Robert J. (Pvt) KIA, 6 June 1918.

Rhodes, Willard B. (Pvt)

Rice, Frederick L. (PFC)

Richards, George B. (PFC)

Richardson, Joe (Pvt)

Rigger, Louis (Pvt)

Riton, Oscar (Pvt)

Rives, Glen M. (Pvt)

Robbins, Ernest C. (PFC)

Robbins, Wayne (Pvt) Messman.

Robinson, William L. (Pvt)

Robison, William L. (Pvt)

Rogers, Carl W. (Cpl) Marine Corps Reserve.

Rollar, Glen M. (Pvt)

Roller, William G. (Pvt)

Rominger, Oscar J. (Pvt)

Rosecrans, Lyle D. (Pvt)

Rosenberg, Harry (Cpl)

Rosenstein, Myron (Pvt) Marine Corps Reserve.

Ross, Erving (Pvt)

Rottmeyer, Herman (Pvt)

Rousay, Richard R. (Pvt) Reserve, Gassed.

Rouse, Reginald R. (Pvt)

Rowles, Charles G. (Pvt)

Roycroft, Loyd C. (Cpl)

Ruleford, William A. (Sgt)

Rupert, George W. (Pvt)

Russell, John B. (Pvt) Company Runner.

Rutherford, Percy J. (Pvt)

Ryan, John J. (Pvt) Company Runner.

Ryan, Neil (Pvt)

Ryhn, Victor (PhM3) U.S. Navy.

Ryrie, James W. (Pvt)

Sadler, George H. (Pvt)

Sahm, John M. (Pvt)

Salisbury, George E. (PFC)

Sanders, Harley (Pvt)

Sangren, Ray H. (Pvt)

Sarret, Eugene J. (Pvt)

Schaefer, Clarence (Pvt)

Schaefer, Erwin F. (Pvt) Cook, 1st Class.

Schaffer, Clarence (Pvt)

Scheyanski, Francis T. (Pvt)

Schmidt, Edward A. (PFC)

Schrader, Howard S. (PFC)

Scoresone, Michael (Pvt)

Seasongrod, John C. (Pvt)

Seward, Wallace A. (Pvt)

Shaull, Reed F. (Cpl)

Sheets, Edgar (Pvt) Died of Wounds.

Sheldon, Arthur L. (PFC) KIA.

Sheline, Andrew L. (Pvt) WIA.
Shelton, Raymond C. (Cpl)
Shepard, Paul E. (Sgt) Gassed.
Shotwell, Howard (Pvt)
Simmons, Joseph S. (Cpl)
Simmons, Wenfred S. (Pvt)
Slater, George L. (Cpl)
Slusser, Glen D. (Sgt)
Slussher, William N. (Pvt)
Smeal, Roy S. (Pvt)
Smith, Charles A.H. (Pvt)
Smith, Charles W., Jr. (Cpl)
Smith, Lon V. (Pvt)
Smith, Robert T. (Pvt)
Smith, Russell A. (Cpl)
Smith, Stuart J. (Pvt)
Smithana, Theodore R. (Cpl)
Smoot, Herman C. (Pvt)
Sollock, Chas. T. (Cpl)
Spaeth, Vernie B. (Pvt) Marine Corps Reserve.
Spall, Adam J. (Pvt) WIA.
Sparks, Walter T. (Pvt) Marine Corps Reserve.
Spencer, Frank P. (Pvt) Reserve.
Sponsel, William F. (Pvt)
Spotswood, Joseph (Cpl) KIA.
Spring, Ira L. (Cpl) KIA, 14 June 1918.
Stagner, Dale Don C. (Pvt) WIA.
Stanley, Gervase V. (Pvt)
Starlin, Jasper H. (Cpl)
Steinker, Fred G. (Pvt)
Stent, William A. (Pvt)
Stephens, Anthony C. (Pvt)
Steves, John B. (Pvt)
Stickney, Iven C. (Pvt)
Stielke, Carl (Pvt) KIA, 2 July 1918.
Storer, Prentice E. (Pvt)
Story, Frank H. (Pvt)
Strain, Benjamin T. (Pvt) KIA, 6 June 1918.
Stricker, Timothy F. (Sgt)
Struble, Stanley E. (Cpl) Reserve, MIA.
Stuart, Kenneth (Pvt)
Stuart, Martin (Cpl)
Stultz, Archie G. (Pvt) Marine Corps Reserve.
Sullivan, Edward P. (Pvt)
Sutherland, Jim W. (GySgt) WIA.
Swanson, David C. (PFC)
Sweeney, Edward J. (Pvt)
Taarland, Peter (Pvt)
Tarves, Eben C. (Pvt) Gassed.
Teat, Lee R. (Pvt)
Templeton, John A. (Cpl) Fleet Marines, Gassed.
Terry, Leon F. (PFC)
Thayer, Samuel H. (Pvt)
Their, Luke, Jr. (Pvt)
Thomas, David R. (Pvt) WIA.
Thompson, Donald (Pvt) Messman.
Thompson, Edward C. (Pvt)
Thornton, Fred A. (Pvt)
Throdahl, Edgar M. (Pvt)
Tigner, Richard E. (Pvt)
Tilson, Luther O. (Pvt)

Tobin, John P. (Pvt)
Todd, Harold (GySgt) KIA, 6 June 1918.
Tosh, Charles A. (Pvt)
Townsend, Herbert H. (Pvt)
Trammell, James M. (Pvt) Marine Corps Reserve.
Turner, Ross J. (Pvt) WIA.
Turnure, Harold R. (Pvt)
Underwood, Thomas M. (Pvt)
Upole, Lawrence H. (Pvt) MIA.
Upton, William H. (Pvt)
Usray, Joe F. (Pvt)
Vail, Edwin F. (Pvt)
VanDerhoff, Wm. W. (PFC)
Vanderhoven, Frank J. (Pvt)
Vanek, Adolph T., Jr. (Pvt)
Varnell, Fred E. (Pvt)
Vergalletto, Frank P. (Pvt) WIA.
Vierling, Edward, Jr. (Pvt)
Voorhees, Bernard T. (Sgt)
Wade, Irvin (Pvt) KIA, 13 June 1918.
Wagner, Joseph W. (GySgt)
Waldrop, Frank H. (Pvt)
Walker, Elbert O. (Pvt) WIA.
Walters, Dewey C. (Pvt)
Wanberg, Wilford R. (Pvt) KIA, 2 November 1918.
Webber, Claude E. (Pvt)
Webber, Henry A. (Pvt)
Wedding, Jerome W. (Cpl)
Welch, William F. (Pvt) Messman.
Wells, William A. (Pvt) KIA, 6 June 1918.
Wentz, Robert W. (Pvt) WIA.
Westerman, Theodore C. (PFC)
Whitcomb, Jack (Trumpeter)
White, Frank J. (Cpl)
Wickwire, Henry J. (Pvt) KIA.
Wilfong, Charles E. (Pvt)
Williams, Charlie O. (Cpl)
Williams, Lionel E. (Pvt) WIA.
Williams, Robert O. (Cpl)
Wood, George E. (Pvt) Marine Corps Reserve.
Young, Lafe S. (PFC)

47th (M) Company, Third Battalion

Name (Rank) Remarks

Case, Philip T. (Cpt) Commanding, 47th Co.
Ball, Clarence (Cpt) CO, M Company.
Barker, Frederick A. (Cpt)
Moseley, Gaines (Cpt) Commanding Company,
    Marine Reserve, WIA.
Duckham, William A. (1st Lt)
Hoffman, Stanford W. (1st Lt)
Knapp, Raymond E. (1st Lt)
Carbary, James (2nd Lt) Marine Corps Reserve.
Clauson, Nicholas E. (2nd Lt) Marine Corps Reserve.
Cukela, Louis (2nd Lt) Marine Corps Reserve.
Fuller, Melvin E. (2nd Lt) Marine Corps Reserve.

Heckman, Jacob H. (2nd Lt) Marine Cps Reserve, Cl4.
Hurtt, Reuben, Jr. (2nd Lt) WIA.
LeGette, Curtis W. (2nd Lt) Marine Corps Reserve, WIA.
Murray, Henry C. (2nd Lt) Marine Corps Reserve.
Schmidt, William H., Jr. (2nd Lt) Marine Reserve, KIA, 4 October 1918.
Stallings, Laurence T. (2nd Lt) WIA, 6 June 1918.
Synnott, Joseph A. (2nd Lt) Marine Cps Reserve, Cl4. KIA, 7 June 1918.

Enlisted

Gilpatrick, Bernie (1st Sgt)
Madsen, Edmund T. (1st Sgt) KIA, 6 June 1918.
Markley, George (1st Sgt) Marine Reserve, KIA, 4 October 1918.
Paget, Charles (1st Sgt) Marine Corps Reserve.
Adam, Joseph E. (PFC) Marine Corps Reserve, Gassed.
Albo, Dominic (Pvt)
Allen, Fred G. (Pvt)
Ames, Bert E. (Cpl) Died of Wounds, 25 June 1918.
Anderson, Harry C. (Pvt) Marine Cps Reserve, Cl 4.
Anhalt, William H. (Pvt)
Argust, Thomas B. (Pvt) Marine Corps Reserve.
Ashmore, James E. (Pvt)
Atkinson, Joseph M. (Cpl)
Austin, Edward S. (Pvt)
Bache, Mike L. (Pvt)
Bagley, Kilmer S. (PFC)
Baier, Arthur R. (Pvt) Marine Corps Reserve.
Baker, Elmer F. (Pvt)
Baker, Omer W. (Pvt) Fleet Marine Corps Reserve.
Bannan, Francis H. (Pvt)
Barnes, Guy E. (Pvt)
Barrell, Arthur W. (Pvt)
Bass, Kenneth A. (Pvt)
Bayly, George F. (Pvt)
Beard, Dwight M. (Pvt)
Beasley, Joseph D. (Pvt)
Beaughan, Ernest A. (Pvt) Marine Corps Reserve, WIA.
Bell, Alonzo D. (Pvt)
Benson, Raymond (Pvt) Marine Corps Reserve.
Bernier, Oliver D. (Sgt)
Berve, Nelson E. (PFC)
Bigham, Jesse S. (Pvt)
Bishop, George T. (Cpl)
Black, Preston (Pvt) Marine Corps Reserve.
Blankenship, Wayne (Cpl)
Bleasdale, Harry C. (Pvt)
Bloche, Arthur E. (Pvt)
Bolstrum, Peter E. (Pvt)
Bonnell, Roy I. (PFC)
Borrelli, Tony (Pvt)
Boston, Thomas C. (Pvt)
Bostwick, P.I. (HAp1)
Bowman, Harry (Pvt) Marine Corps Reserve.
Boyce, Earl B. (Pvt) Marine Corps Reserve.
Brewer, Edmund (Pvt)
Brewington, Clarence W. (Cpl)
Britteau, Alfred S. (Sgt)
Brodkin, Gilbert (Pvt)

Brooks, John W. (Pvt)
Brose, Robert J. (Pvt)
Brown, Charles V. (PFC) Marine Reserve. Died of Wounds, 24 October 1918.
Brown, Gordon R. (GySgt) Marine Corps Reserve, WIA.
Brown, Joseph D. (Pvt)
Brown, Raimer (Pvt)
Bruno, Arthur H. (Pvt) Marine Corps Reserve.
Bryant, Glenwin E. (Pvt)
Burfeind, Herbert (Cpl)
Burgess, Roland W. (PFC)
Burgett, Albert A. (PFC) Marine Corps Reserve.
Burgett, James B. (Pvt) Marine Corps Reserve.
Burhans, Robert A. (Cpl) KIA, 23 June 1918.
Burns, Charles R. (Pvt) KIA, Belleau Wood.
Busch, Roy H. (Cpl) KIA, 16 August 1918.
Bush, John J. (Pvt) Marine Reserve, KIA.
Butler, Daniel J. (Pvt)
Cain, Robert J. (Pvt)
Cammell, Clarence T. (Pvt)
Campbell, Robert L. (Pvt)
Carbary, James (GySgt)
Card, Bertram (PFC)
Carne, James H. (PFC)
Carr, Henry J. (Pvt)
Carraway, Thomas J. (Cpl) WIA.
Carter, Herbert (Pvt)
Carter, William E. (Pvt)
Cary, Clarence W. (Pvt)
Case, Forrest L. (Pvt)
Case, George B. (Cpl) Marine Corps Reserve, WIA.
Caylor, Joseph B. (Pvt)
Cernik, Godfrey (Pvt)
Chance, Henry B. (Pvt)
Chaney, Samuel A. (PFC)
Choinski, Leonard F. (Cpl)
Christiansen, William E. (PFC) WIA.
Clarity, R.M. (HAp1)
Clark, Gerald B. (Pvt)
Clark, James L. (Pvt) WIA, 6 June 1918.
Clausen, Fred J. (Pvt) Marine Corps Reserve.
Claypool, Dennis P. (GySgt)
Clegg, Paul V. (Pvt)
Clem, Ross A. (Pvt) Marine Corps Reserve.
Cobbett, Philip W. (Pvt)
Coffey, Clarence D. (Pvt)
Colberg, John R.L. (Pvt) Marine Corps Reserve, WIA.
Coleman, Cecil (Pvt)
Collins, Merritt S. (Pvt)
Collopy, Christie (Sgt)
Comer, William P. (Pvt) Marine Reserve, MIA, gassed.
Cook, Archie N. (Pvt) Marine Corps Reserve, WIA.
Cooke, Lester B. (Pvt) Marine Corps Reserve, WIA.
Cookson, Paul D. (Pvt) Marine Corps Reserve, WIA.
Cooper, Harley R. (Pvt) Marine Corps Reserve.
Corcoran, Vincent P. (Pvt)
Corey, Walter C. (Cpl)
Cox, Ben O. (PFC)
Coy, Walter M. (Pvt)
Crawford, Ernest R. (Sgt)

Crosby, Wendell F. (Pvt)
Crosley, Louis (Cpl)
Cross, Jay W. (Pvt)
Cunningham, Earnest L. (Pvt)
Daley, Harold F. (Pvt) Marine Cps Reserve, Cl4.
Dana, Gerard S. (Pvt) Marine Corps Reserve.
Danford, Erwin (Sgt) Died of Wounds, 23 July 1918, Gas NCO.
Davies, Robert C. (Pvt)
Davis, Alden I. (Pvt)
Davis, Harry E. (Pvt) Marine Corps Reserve.
Davis, James R. (PFC)
Day, Joseph (Pvt)
DeHaan, Gerrit (Sgt)
Delayo, Joe (Pvt)
Diehl, William (Pvt)
Dittmar, John S. (Cpl)
Diveley, George W. (PFC) Marine Corps Reserve, WIA.
Dobbertin, John J. (MarGun)
Dobbins, Clarence R. (Pvt)
Dodds, John W. (Pvt) Marine Corps Reserve, WIA.
Doize, Sidney P. (Pvt)
Donley, Grover C.J. (Pvt)
Dorando, Frank S. (Pvt)
Douglas, Earl B. (Pvt) Signalman, 1st Cl.
Dowling, Joseph E. (Pvt)
Dragoo, Elza M. (Pvt)
Duncan, Thomas (Sgt) WIA.
Dunn, Michael T. (Pvt) Marine Corps Reserve, WIA.
Dunphey, Frank W. (Sgt) Marine Corps Reserve, WIA.
Durr, Stephen (PFC) Marine Corps Reserve, Gassed.
Dyer, Edward T. (PFC)
Ecay, Clarence (Cpl)
Egan, John S. (Pvt)
Epperson, Vergil T. (Pvt)
Erbaugh, Cecil H. (Pvt)
Evans, Lynn (Pvt)
Fabinski, Joseph C. (Cpl)
Fagan, Clarence (Pvt)
Fahey, Martin P. (PFC) Marine Corps Reserve. Died of Wounds.
Fairweather, James M. (Pvt)
Feckar, Joseph (PFC) Marine Reserve, MIA, gassed.
Fellenbaum, Edward C. (PFC)
Ferm, Edmund H. (Pvt)
Ferson, Joseph R. (Sgt) Marine Corps Reserve, WIA.
Fien, Tigbert A. (Pvt)
Fitzgerald, Thomas J. (Cpl) KIA, 1 November 1918.
Flinn, John E. (Sgt) Marine Reserve, KIA.
Fluent, Leeroy (Pvt)
Fogle, William E. (Pvt) Marine Corps Reserve, WIA.
Fore, Wiley D. (Pvt) Cook, 3rd Class, KIA, 6 June 1918.
Forton, Robert J. (Pvt) Marine Corps Reserve, WIA.
Foster, William E. (PFC)
Frankforther, Glenn A. (Pvt) Messman.
Frederick, Louis E. (Cpl)
Gahr, Albert L. (Pvt)
Gaines, Charlie W.M. (PFC)
Galvert, Samuel E. (Pvt) Marine Corps Reserve.
Gardner, Verne W. (Pvt) KIA, 6 June 1918.

Garrett, Walter S. (Pvt)
Geiger, Harold C. (Pvt)
Gerhard, William G. (PhM)
Gibbons, Edward M. (PFC)
Gibbs, James S. (Pvt)
Gill, Peter C. (Pvt)
Goetze, Hugo C.W. (Cpl)
Gooch, Eben W. (Pvt)
Graham, Charlie F. (Pvt)
Graham, Clarence N. (Pvt)
Granning, Edward R. (Pvt) Cook, 1st Class.
Gray, Franklin H. (Cpl)
Griffin, Benjamin E. (Pvt)
Griffin, Matt (Sgt) Marine Corps Reserve, Gassed.
Griffin, Roger M. (Pvt)
Grimes, Roy (Pvt) Messman.
Grimsey, Roy P. (Pvt) Pvt
Griswald, Henry J. (Pvt)
Gullickson, Otto (Pvt)
Gunderson, Ole (Pvt)
Guyton, Joseph A., Jr. (Pvt)
Gygax, Louis (Pvt)
Hafner, Charles G. (Pvt) Messman.
Hall, Jesse (Pvt)
Hall, John M. (Cpl)
Hampton, Harold (PFC) Marine Corps Reserve, WIA.
Harper, Fred J. (Pvt)
Harring, L.H. (HAp1)
Harris, William O. (PFC)
Harrold, Owen M. (Pvt)
Hartwell, Leo E. (Pvt) Marine Corps Reserve, WIA.
Hatch, Robert A. (Pvt) Marine Corps Reserve. Died of Wounds.
Hathaway, Harry F. (Pvt) KIA, 26 June 1918.
Hayes, Daniel W. (Pvt) Marine Corps Reserve, WIA.
Hefner, Fred (Pvt) Marine Reserve.
Heiserman, Leon L. (PFC) Marine Corps Reserve, WIA.
Herman, Erven C. (Pvt)
Hickey, John J. (Cpl)
Higgins, Henry E. (Pvt) KIA, 25 June 1918.
Hill, Arsey W. (Pvt)
Hill, Carroll F. (Pvt) Marine Reserve, WIA.
Hill, Ralph O. (Pvt) Marine Cps Reserve, Cl 4.
Hively, Harley C. (Pvt)
Hoff, Milford J. (Pvt)
Hoffman, Hugh E. (Pvt)
Holcomb, Ira M. (Pvt)
Holland, Archie T. (Pvt)
Holland, Cecil C. (Pvt) Marine Reserve, MIA, gassed.
Holman, Charlie J. (Pvt) Marine Reserve, KIA.
Hoppstein, Theodore J. (Pvt) Cook, 1st Class.
House, John O. (Pvt) Marine Reserve, KIA, 4 October 1918.
House, Lisle S. (Pvt) Marine Reserve, Died of Wounds, 16 October 1918.
Howell, Thomas (Pvt) Marine Reserve, WIA.
Howes, Lewis L. (Sgt)
Hubbard, Dick H. (Pvt)
Hubert, Victor J. (Pvt)
Hudkins, Lot (PFC)
Hunt, Grant J. (PFC) Marine Corps Reserve, Gassed.

Hutchinson, Raymond K. (Pvt) Marine Corps Reserve, Shell Shocked.

Hyde, Irving F. (PFC) Marine Corps Reserve, WIA.

Ichniowski, Vincent J. (Pvt)

Isselbacher, Irving (Pvt) Marine Corps Reserve, Concussion.

Jackson, Kenneth L. (Pvt)

Jackson, Lyle (Pvt) Marine Corps Reserve, WIA.

Jacobi, Alfred J. (Pvt)

Jacobs, Frank M. (Pvt)

Jacoby, William A., Jr. (Pvt)

James, Charles H. (Cpl) Marine Cps Reserve, Cl4, WIA, 25 June 1918.

Janke, Robert R. (PFC) Marine Corps Reserve, WIA.

Javins, R.M. (PhM3)

Jefferies, George E. (Pvt)

Jeffers, Clarence J. (Pvt) Marine Corps Reserve.

Jeffress, Willie R. (Sgt) Marine Corps Reserve, KIA, 6 June 1918.

Johnson, Clarence F. (Pvt) Marine Corps Reserve.

Johnson, Harold G. (Pvt)

Johnson, Harry (Pvt)

Johnson, John (Pvt)

Johnson, Oliver (Pvt)

Johnson, Reuben J. (Pvt)

Johnson, William A. (PFC)

Johnston, Oral D. (PFC) Marine Corps Reserve.

Jones, Albert E. (Pvt) Marine Corps Reserve, Cl 4, KIA.

Jones, Ralph D. (Pvt)

Jones, Victor (Pvt)

Jonte, Herbert H. (Pvt)

Jordan, Delbert R. (Pvt) KIA, 2 November 1918.

Jordan, Philip M. (Pvt)

Jorden, Oscar E. (GySgt)

Joyce, Thomas H. (Pvt) KIA, 24 June 1918.

Kadel, Alfred G. (Pvt)

Kass, George G. (Pvt) Marine Corps Reserve, WIA.

Katz, Max (PFC) Marine Corps Reserve, WIA.

Kearins, Edward F. (Pvt)

Kehoe, William J. (Pvt) KIA.

Kellar, John E.T. (Cpl)

Keller, Theodore (Sgt)

Kellner, Jacob J. (Pvt) Marine Reserve, KIA, 4 October 1918.

Kelly, Clarence W. (Sgt)

Kemble, Frank W. (Pvt) KIA, 26 June 1918.

Kemp, Claud (Cpl) Marine Reserve, KIA, 4 October 1918.

Kemp, John L. (Pvt)

Kendall, Elvin L. (Pvt)

Kenny, John F. (Pvt) Marine Corps Reserve, WIA.

Kerr, Ira E. (PFC) Marine Reserve, MIA, gassed.

Kerr, Ira R. (Pvt)

Keyes, Howard S. (Pvt)

Keyser, James M. (Cpl) Marine Reserve, MIA.

Kilgellon, John E. (Sgt) KIA, 25 June 1918.

Kime, Curtis M. (Pvt) Marine Corps Reserve, WIA.

King, Edward (Pvt)

Kite, Joseph B. (Pvt) Marine Reserve.

Klima, Otto (Pvt) Messman.

Knox, Charley M. (Pvt)

Knutson, Arnold S. (Pvt) Marine Corps Reserve, WIA.

Kraul, Edwin K. (Cpl)

Kretschmar, Charles H. (Pvt) Marine Corps Reserve.

Krigbaum, Harry J. (Pvt) Marine Corps Reserve.

Kuster, Charlie S. (Pvt) Marine Corps Reserve.

Kuster, Frederick E., Jr. (Pvt) Cook 3rd Class.

Kutz, Harry (Pvt)

LaBoissiere, Arthur J. (Pvt) Marine Corps Reserve, WIA.

Lacy, Perry A. (Pvt) Marine Corps Reserve.

Lacy, Thomas W. (Pvt) Marine Corps Reserve, WIA.

Laidlaw, Harold A. (PFC) Marine Corps Reserve, WIA.

Lampley, Ollie E. (Pvt)

Landreth, Victor M. (Sgt)

Lange, Roy B. (Pvt) Marine Corps Reserve, Died flu.

Larch, John F. (Pvt) Marine Corps Reserve, Died flu.

Laul, Jacob S. (Sgt) Marine Corps Reserve, WIA.

LeGrange, Clifford J. (Pvt)

Lerch, John F. (Pvt)

Lewis, Charles H. (Drummer) Marine Corps Reserve, WIA.

Linck, Fred L. (Sgt) Marine Corps Reserve, WIA.

Lincoln, Francis L. (Pvt)

Litherland, James E. (Pvt)

Littley, Daniel J. (Cpl) Marine Corps Reserve.

Livingston, Jay (Pvt)

Lochbihler, George (Pvt) Marine Reserve.

Loesch, Martin P. (Pvt)

Longenecker, Walter D. (Cpl)

Lord, John J. (Pvt)

Lorentz, Leroy R. (PFC)

Loveland, Roelif A. (PFC) Marine Corps Reserve, Shell Shocked.

Luce, Floyd E. (Pvt)

Lynch, Frank J. (Pvt) KIA, 6 June 1918.

MacGregor, Lewis A. (Pvt) Died of Wounds, 27 June 1918.

Madison, George F. (Cpl)

Magda, Andrew S. (Pvt)

Manning, James E. (HAp1)

Mallion, John A. (Pvt)

Manton, Robert W. (PFC)

Maphis, Andrew F.W. (Pvt) Marine Reserve.

Markwell, Charles (Pvt)

Marsh, Norman W. (Sgt) Marine Corps Reserve.

Marshall, George T. (Cpl)

Martin, Benton M. (PFC)

Martin, John (Pvt)

May, Edwin (Pvt)

May, Russell B. (Pvt)

McCann, Joseph E. (Pvt)

McCoy, Guy E. (Sgt) Marine Corps Reserve, Gassed.

McCullough, John A. (Pvt) Teamster.

McCullough, William J. (Pvt)

McEntee, Bernard C. (Sgt)

McFarland, Charles P. (Sgt)

McKee, John E. (Pvt) Marine Corps Reserve, WIA.

McKitrick, Jessie H. (PFC)

McMenamin, Daniel L. (Pvt) Marine Reserve.

McNeil, Donald J. (Cpl)

McPherson, Lewis R. (Pvt)

Mearaviller, Arthur (Pvt)

Melcher, Edward J. (Cpl) WIA, 25 June 1918.

Mercer, Harry R. (Pvt) Marine Corps Reserve.

Metzinger, Lester S. (Pvt) Marine Corps Reserve, Died of flu.

Meyer, Alfred F. (Pvt)

Michael, George E. (Pvt) Marine Corps Reserve, Died of flu, 27 June 1918.

Michels, Adrian J. (Pvt) Died of Wounds, 6 June 1918.

Miller, Charles A. (Sgt)

Miller, Earl F. (Cpl)

Milton, William E. (Pvt) Marine Corps Reserve.

Minikowski, Jerome J. (Pvt)

Mitchell, Leslie B. (Pvt) Marine Corps Reserve, WIA.

Moe, John R. (Sgt) Marine Corps Reserve, WIA.

Monahan, William H. (Pvt) Marine Cps Reserve, Cl 4.

Montgomery, William G. (Pvt)

Moore, John C. (Pvt)

Moore, William F. (Pvt)

Moran, Albert (Pvt)

Moran, Harry N. (Pvt) Marine Corps Reserve, WIA.

Morgan, Ralph E. (PFC)

Moriarty, John S. (Sgt)

Morris, John D. (Pvt)

Morris, Walter (Pvt) Marine Reserve, WIA, Belleau Wood.

Morrison, John L. (Pvt) Messman.

Morse, Alvin B. (Pvt)

Muncey, Alton E. (Pvt)

Murphree, George M. (Sgt)

Murphy, Harry (PFC) Marine Corps Reserve, WIA.

Murphy, John W. (Pvt) Marine Reserve, MIA, gassed.

Mursch, Emil C. (Pvt) Messman.

Myers, Harry T. (Pvt) Marine Corps Reserve.

Mynatt, Burlie G. (Pvt)

Nalley, Roscoe J. (Pvt)

Nelson, Charles A., Jr. (Pvt) Battalion Storeroom Keeper.

Newberry, Paul R. (PFC)

Nicholson, Jackson P. (Cpl)

Nielson, Claude M. (Sgt) WIA.

Nold, Everett G. (PFC) Marine Corps Reserve.

Oberle, John E. (Pvt) Messman.

O'Brien, Alfe T. (Sgt) Supply Sgt.

O'Brien, Henry M. (Pvt)

O'Donnell, Gordon S. (Pvt)

O'Donnell, Harold J. (Pvt) Marine Reserve, MIA, gassed.

Ogle, Houston E. (Pvt)

O'Leary, Neal (Pvt)

Oliver, William R. (Sgt) Marine Corps Reserve, WIA.

Olson, Oliver (Pvt)

Orchard, Thomas M. (Pvt)

Orlofski, Frank W. (Cpl)

Osterhage, Bernard H. (Pvt)

Overly, Raymond D. (Cpl) Marine Corps Reserve.

Page, Allison M. (Cpl) KIA, 25 June 1918.

Park, William M. (Pvt)

Parker, Clifford E. (Pvt)

Parker, Wheeler H. (Cpl) Marine Reserve.

Parmerton, Foster (Pvt) Marine Reserve, KIA.

Parson, Martin L. (Pvt)

Parsons, Clyde E. (Pvt) Marine Reserve, KIA, 4 October 1918.

Parsons, Isaac W.W. (Cpl) Marine Cps Reserve, Cl 2.

Patten, Robert O. (PFC)

Patterson, I.W. (PhM3)

Paulson, Nels G. (Pvt)

Perkins, Parley (Pvt)

Perry, Irvin (Pvt)

Perry, Keith E. (Pvt) Marine Corps Reserve.

Peterson, George I. (PhM3)

Pfanner, Robert (Pvt)

Piere, Alfred J. (Pvt)

Pollock, John H. (Pvt)

Popka, David A. (Pvt)

Porter, James W. (Pvt)

Prast, Harry W. (Pvt)

Quaidy, Chester L. (Pvt) Marine Corps Reserve, WIA.

Quinlan, James F. (Pvt)

Ratte, John T. (GySgt)

Rebscher, William E. (Pvt)

Reckitt, Harry G. (Pvt) Marine Reserve.

Redffern, David (Pvt)

Reed, Nathen L. (Pvt)

Reed, Rexton K. (Pvt)

Reese, John (Pvt)

Resendes, William J. (Pvt) KIA, 25 June 1918.

Rhodes, James E. (Pvt)

Rindeau, Arthur J. (GySgt) KIA, 6 June 1918.

Roalsen, Roy L. (Pvt)

Roan, George B. (Sgt)

Robinson, Andrew F. (Pvt) Marine Reserve.

Robinson, William S. (Pvt)

Rodgers, Martin S. (GySgt) Marine Corps Reserve, WIA.

Romans, Ernest (Cpl) WIA, Belleau Wood.

Rose, John A. (Sgt) Marine Corps Reserve, Gassed.

Rosmarck, George (Sgt) Marine Corps Reserve, WIA.

Ross, Charles W. (Pvt)

Ross, Warren L. (PFC) Marine Reserve, Gassed.

Roth, Lewis J. (Pvt) In Charge of Corral.

Rowland, Chester L. (Pvt)

Ruck, Charles E. (Pvt)

Ruckert, William (Pvt)

Rudderow, Howard C. (Pvt) Marine Reserve.

Rudolph, Frank P. (PFC)

Rudolph, Jacob B. (Pvt)

Rupp, John N. (Pvt) Cook 2nd Class.

Ryan, Daniel C. (Pvt)

Rylander, Thor A. (Pvt)

St. Claire, William A. (Pvt) Marine Corps Reserve, WIA.

Sacks, Howard (PFC) Marine Reserve, Died of Wounds, 4 October 1918.

Sanderson, Joseph (Pvt) Marine Reserve.

Scales, Yewell D. (Cpl)

Schenck, Hugh V. (Pvt)

Schenk, Ferdinand C. (Pvt)

Schmelzer, Walter H. (PFC)

Schmidt, Edward C. (Pvt)

Schmidt, William H., Jr. (GySgt)

Schuler, Louis B. (HAp1) KIA, 26 June 1918.

Schultz, Theodore A. (Pvt) Shell Shock.

Schuster, Edward (Pvt) Marine Reserve, MIA, WIA.

Schwend, John E. (Pvt) Marine Corps Reserve, WIA.

Seyd, August F. (Pvt) Marine Corps Reserve, WIA.

Shaw, Gerhardt W. (Pvt)

Shaw, Guy W. (Pvt) Motorcycle Driver.

Shaw, Hugh B. (Pvt) WIA, Belleau Wood.

Shepherd, Walter F. (Pvt) Marine Corps Reserve, WIA.

Shoemaker, Gregg L. (Cpl)

Short, Alexander, Jr. (Pvt) Marine Corps Reserve, Cl4.

Showers, William L. (Pvt)

Shuman, Joseph H., Jr. (Sgt) Marine Corps Reserve, WIA.

Shuster, Thomas C. (Pvt)

Silvers, Elbert (Sgt) Marine Corps Reserve, Gassed.

Simpson, Roy H. (Pvt) Marine Reserve, KIA, 12 June 1918.

Sincavitz, Joseph (Cpl)

Skidmore, Van Rensselear (Pvt) Marine Corps Reserve, Cl4, KIA, 24 June 1918.

Slumba, Mike J. (Pvt)

Smith, Ambrose E.C. (Pvt)

Smith, Arnold C. (Pvt)

Smith, Benjamin F. (Pvt) Marine Corps Reserve, WIA.

Snyder, William R. (Pvt) Marine Corps Reserve.

Sockel, Frank (Cpl) KIA, 19 July 1918.

Sone, James R. (Pvt) Marine Reserve, KIA.

Sorg, Walter W. (Pvt)

Sorrels, Henry A. (Pvt)

Souder, Herbert H. (Pvt) Marine Reserve, KIA, 17 June 1918.

Spang, Benjamin J. (Pvt)

Speedy, Wilbur C. (Pvt)

Spence, Fred C. (PFC)

Spencer, Guy H. (PFC) Marine Corps Reserve, Died of Wounds.

Staake, William F. (Pvt) Marine Reserve.

Stanton, E.C. (HAp1)

Stark, Cecil (Pvt) Marine Reserve, MIA.

Steger, Athol B. (Pvt) Marine Corps Reserve.

Steven, John J. (Cpl) KIA, 15 September 1918.

Stevens, Charles L. (Pvt) KIA, 6 June 1918.

Stevens, William E. (Pvt)

Stevenson, Charles R. (Pvt)

Stranahan, J. Willard (Pvt)

Stuart, Fred (Sgt)

Stutzman, George F. (Pvt) Marine Corps Reserve, Gassed.

Sullivan, Maurice W. (Pvt) Marine Corps Reserve.

Swanson, John E.G. (Trumpeter)

Sweeney, Edward F. (Pvt) Marine Reserve, MIA.

Taylor, Bert G. (Pvt) Died of Wounds, 7 June 1918.

Taylor, Edward L. (Sgt) Marine Corps Reserve, Shell shocked.

Terwillegar, Earl E. (Pvt) Marine Corps Reserve.

Thompson, James W. (Pvt)

Tillotson, Budd (Pvt)

Toal, Frank (PFC)

Todd, Glenn E. (PFC) Marine Corps Reserve, WIA.

Tomlinson, John R. (Pvt)

Towson, Charles A. (Pvt)

Tranor, Frank E. (Pvt)

Tross, Eugene J. (Pvt)

Tucker, Leonidas L. (Pvt)

Underwood, Shirley S. (PFC)

Vansickle, Oliver T. (Pvt)

Vaughn, Grover C. (PFC)

Wagner, Willard J. (Pvt) Marine Reserve, KIA, 4 October 1918.

Walker, Ishmeal P. (Pvt) Marine Reserve, WIA.

Walker, Ivan C. (Pvt) KIA, 28 July 1918.

Walker, James T. (PFC)

Walker, William J. (Pvt) KIA, 6 June 1918.

Walser, Reed D. (Pvt)

Walton, James P. (Pvt)

Ware, Grover C. (Pvt)

Warner, Melvin (Pvt)

Waters, Robert A. (Cpl) Marine Corps Reserve, Died of Wounds.

Watson, Ernest J. (PFC) Marine Corps Reserve.

Watts, Heilliard B. (Pvt)

Waugaman, Lewis (Cpl)

Webb, Wilbur A. (Pvt)

Weidner, Harry L. (Sgt) Marine Corps Reserve.

Weingart, George W. (Pvt)

Weiss, Clarence E. (Pvt)

Weisz, Ivan S. (Pvt)

Wekwert, Louis (Pvt) Marine Reserve, KIA.

Welch, Lyman G. (Pvt) Marine Corps Reserve.

Welsh, Emil E. (Pvt) Marine Reserve.

West, Aaron W. (Pvt)

West, Henry (Cpl)

Westlund, Conrad J. (Pvt) Marine Corps Reserve.

Wheeler, Neil E. (Pvt) KIA, 17 June 1918.

White, William C. (Pvt)

Whitman, Ralph F. (Pvt)

Wiedling, Theodore (Cpl)

Wightman, Walter H. (Pvt)

Wilbanks, William D. (Pvt)

Wilber, George H. (Pvt)

Wilcox, Charley A. (Pvt)

Wildeboer, William H. (Pvt)

Wilkie, Philip B. (Trumpeter) WIA at Belleau Wood.

Willey, Stanley (Pvt)

Williams, Arthur H. (Pvt)

Williams, Clarence (Pvt)

Williams, Edgar T. (Pvt)

Williams, Jack G. (Pvt)

Williams, James L. (Pvt)

Willmot, William H. (GySgt) Marine Corps Reserve.

Wilson, Claud W. (Sgt)

Wilson, Roy (Cpl)

Winn, Harlan H. (Pvt)

Wissler, Jacob M. (Cpl)

Woelfer, Rudolph C. (Pvt) Marine Corps Reserve, WIA.

Wolbrecht, Henry A. (Pvt) Marine Corps Reserve.

Wood, Jeremiah R. (Pvt) KIA, 6 June 1918.

Woodward, Carl (Pvt)

Wright, John C. (Sgt) Marine Corps Reserve.

Wright, John L. (Pvt)

Wright, John S. (Pvt)

Wright, Marvin H. (Pvt)

Wright, Roy (Pvt)

Wrote, Joseph N. (Pvt)
Wurm, Richard A. (Pvt)
Yates, William (Pvt) Marine Corps Reserve, WIA.
Young, Frank (Pvt)
Young, Fred C. (Pvt)
Young, Louis J. (Pvt)

Youngs, Howard J. (Pvt) Marine Reserve, KIA, 4 October 1918.
Ziehm, William V. (Pvt)
Zilier, Frederick C. (Pvt)
Zimmerman, Harvey W. (Pvt)
Zimmerman, Lysle J. (Pvt)

Chapter Notes

Preface

1. It was also called the Paris Gun, but Big Bertha and the Paris Gun were actually two different weapons. The Germans were in the process of dismantling and shipping the weapon back to Germany in August 1918.

2. Richard Cleveland to Helen Ericson, 12 August 1918.

3. The French boxcars could hold forty men or eight horses, which led to the title forty by eights. They had no springs and were very uncomfortable. Everyone wanted to get close to the door to see the scenery and get fresh air. See Dick Camp's book *The Devil Dogs at Belleau Wood: U.S. Marines in World War I* (Minneapolis: Zenith Press, 2008), page 32.

Introduction

1. George B. Clark, *The American Expeditionary Force in World War I: A Statistical History, 1917–1919* (Jefferson, NC: McFarland, 2013), 55.

2. Edwin N. McClellan, *The United States Marine Corps in the World War* (Washington, DC: Headquarters, USMC, 1920), 9. McClellan lists 70 officers and 2,689 Marines as the totals in the 5th Marine Regiment that sailed for France in June 1917, but to these are added to the regiment replacements and others during its stay in France and Germany.

3. The monthly rosters were compiled and typed in 1931. They were later converted to microfilm that can be viewed today at the USMC Historical Division, Quantico, Virginia. I have omitted the remarks about minor offenses in the Appendix D listing to save space in an already lengthy appendix.

Chapter 1

1. George B. Clark, *The American Expeditionary Force in World War I: A Statistical History, 1917–1919* (Jefferson, NC: McFarland, 2013), 5.

2. U.S. Government, "Documents," http://www.our documents.gov/doc_large_image.php?flash=true&doc= 15 (accessed 18 March 2015).

Chapter 2

1. Some estimates indicate six thousand Belgians were killed plus twenty-five thousand homes and other buildings in 837 communities destroyed.

2. Virginia Schomp, *Letters from the Battlefield, World War I* (New York: Benchmark Books, 2004), 11–12.

3. U.S. Archives, "Education/Lessons," http://www.archives.gov/education/lessons/zimmermann (accessed 18 March 2015).

4. This author went through the same effort to enlist nearly forty years later. My two brothers were serving in the Korean war and I wanted to enlist to fight. I was underage and had terribly bad eyesight. I was nearly six feet tall and weighed less than 120 pounds. The army did not care about my weight but had problems with my bad eyesight and the fact that I was underage. I went to the Minnesota National Guard and was accepted. The National Guard did not have a problem with my bad eyesight. Later, when I applied to West Point and failed the eye exam, a kindly army doctor signed off on the paperwork saying that I must have strained my eyes studying for my final exams in high school. Of course I said, "Yes, sir." In fact, I don't think I ever studied a day in my life in high school.

5. Raymond P. Rogers, *Memoirs as Told to His Daughters,* 1.

6. Peter F. Owen, *To the Limit of Endurance: A Battalion of Marines in the Great War* (College Station: Texas A&M University Press, 2007), 3.

7. Charles Terry, *Wilson's War: America in the First World War* (Lexington, 2011), 60.

8. Paris Island was later renamed Parris Island.

9. Owen, *To the Limit of Endurance,* 3.

10. Ibid.

11. Ibid.

12. Louis C. Linn, *At Belleau Wood with Rifle and Sketchpad* (Jefferson, NC: McFarland, 2012), 4.

13. Barbara W. Tuchman, *The Guns of August* (New York: Ballantine Books, 1962), 197.

14. Owen, *To the Limit of Endurance,* 4.

15. Terry, *Wilson's War,* 52.

16. J.E. Rendinell and George Pattullo, *One Man's War: The Diary of a Leatherneck* (New York: J.H. Sears, 1928), 1–7.

17. James R. Scarbrough, *They Called Us Devil Dogs* (Scarbrough: 2005), 2.

18. Frederick Wise and Meigs O. Frost, *A Marine Tells It to You* (New York: J.H. Sears, 1929), 156.

19. During World War II, men of ages eighteen through sixty-five were required to register and eighteen through forty-five were subject to military service. Over 10 million were inducted between 1940 and 1947. It was a wider war.

20. Terry, *Wilson's War*, 57.

21. Robert B. Asprey, *At Belleau Wood* (Denton: University of North Texas Press, 1996), 11.

22. Ibid., 23.

23. Scarbrough, *They Called Us Devil Dogs*, 135–136.

24. The Maxim machine gun (called the Maschinengewehr) was the primary German defensive small-arms weapon, but it was patented in the United States between 1883 and 1885 by Hiram S. Maxim before he moved his experiments to the United Kingdom. The Maxim was adopted by the Germans and other belligerents, but not the United States.

25. Mark Mortensen, *George W. Hamilton, USMC: America's Greatest World War I Hero* (Jefferson, NC: McFarland, 2011), 48–50.

26. Asprey, *At Belleau Wood*, 8.

27. Edwin N. McClellan, *The United States Marine Corps in the World War* (Washington, DC: Headquarters, USMC, 1920), 13.

28. Ibid., 15.

29. Owen, *To the Limit of Endurance*, 2.

30. Some such as Smedley Butler and Daniel Daly had two Medal of Honor awards before serving in France. Pershing denied a third Medal of Honor award for Daly because he thought that no one deserved a third Medal of Honor.

31. McClellan, *The United States Marine Corps in the World War*, 9.

Chapter 3

1. *American Experience: Influenza 1918*, PBS, 1998.

2. John M. Barry, *The Great Influenza: The Story of the Deadliest Pandemic in History* (New York: Penguin Books, 2004), 4.

3. *American Experience: Influenza 1918*, PBS, 1998.

4. Susan Kingsley Kent, *The Influenza Pandemic of 1918–1919: A Brief History of Documents* (Boulder: University of Colorado, 2013), 3.

5. Alfred W. Crosby, *America's Forgotten Pandemic: The Influenza of 1918* (New York: Cambridge University Press, 2003), 113.

6. Virginia Schomp, *Letters from the Battlefield, World War I* (New York: Benchmark Books, 2004), 61.

7. Carol F. Byerly, *Fever of War: The Influenza Epidemic in the U.S. Army During World War I* (New York: New York University Press, 2005), 73.

8. Ibid., 74.

9. Ibid., 75.

10. Ibid.

11. Camp Oglethorpe was closed after World War II.

12. U.S. Army Medical Department, "Office of Medical History," http://history.amedd.army.mil/books docs/WW I/VolVII/ch02part1.html (accessed 9 November 2014).

13. Verner S. Gaggin to Mrs. Verner S. Gaggin, 19 October 1918.

14. Verner S. Gaggin to Mrs. Verner S. Gaggin, 24 October 1918.

15. Kent, *The Influenza Pandemic*, 7–8.

16. *American Experience: Influenza 1918*, PBS, 1998.

17. Ibid.

18. Crosby, *America's Forgotten Pandemic*, 25.

19. Byerly, *Fever of War*, 72.

20. Raymond P. Rogers, *Memoirs as Told to His Daughters*, 1.

21. Crosby, *America's Forgotten Pandemic*, 27.

22. John Keegan, *The First World War* (New York: Vintage Books, 2000), 408.

23. Byerly, *Fever of War*, 73.

24. Crosby, *America's Forgotten Pandemic*, 158.

25. Byerly, *Fever of War*, 11.

26. Ibid., 10.

27. *American Experience: Influenza 1918*, PBS, 1998.

28. Ibid.

29. Barry, *The Great Influenza*, 247.

30. Kent, *The Influenza Pandemic*, 11.

31. Byerly, *Fever of War*, 181.

Chapter 4

1. Mark Mortensen, *George W. Hamilton, USMC: America's Greatest World War I Hero* (Jefferson, NC: McFarland, 2011), 54.

2. Ibid., 47.

3. Ronald J. Brown, *A Few Good Men: A History of the Fighting Fifth Marines* (Novato, CA: Presidio Press, 2001), 16.

4. Brig. Gen. Edwin Howard Simmons, USMC (Ret), and Col. Joseph H. Alexander, USMC (Ret), *Through the Wheat: The U.S. Marines in World War I* (Annapolis: Naval Institute Press, 2008), 53.

5. Brown, *A Few Good Men*, 22.

6. Simmons and Alexander, *Through the Wheat*, 53.

7. Louis C. Linn, *At Belleau Wood with Rifle and Sketchpad* (Jefferson, NC: McFarland, 2012), 45–46.

8. Raymond P. Rogers, *Memoirs as Told to His Daughters*, 1.

9. James R. Scarbrough, *They Called Us Devil Dogs* (Scarbrough, 2005), 45–46.

10. Robert B. Asprey, *At Belleau Wood* (Denton: University of North Texas Press, 1996), 26.

11. Scarbrough, *They Called Us Devil Dogs*, 52.

12. In Vietnam half a century later, the story was the same. At night on our defensive perimeter if you stepped on a rat it would squeal like a pig. The rats would hang around us. All they wanted was a snack (a piece of your leg). You couldn't shoot them because they would give away your position, so we spent the night kicking at them and they just waited for a chance to have a snack.

13. Asprey, *At Belleau Wood*, 27.

14. Ibid.

15. Linn, *At Belleau Wood with Rifle and Sketchpad*, 59.

16. Gilbert Hart, *Citizen Soldier I: World War I Recollections of Private James E. Hatcher, USMC*, 19–20.

17. Ibid., 19–20. Fifty years later this author had an opportunity to experience a slight bit of Markham's experience. In Vietnam I was running as fast as I could when a shell impacted right next to me. It was big, a 122mm rocket. I should have been riddled, but there was not a scratch on me. Instead I was lifted yards into the air and landed on my head. Shells do squirrelly things. A guy yards farther away was badly wounded.

18. Scarbrough, *They Called Us Devil Dogs,* 49–50.

19. Douglas V. Johnson II and Rolfe L. Hillman, Jr., *Soissons 1918* (College Station: Texas A&M University Press, 1999), 7.

20. Virginia Schomp, *Letters from the Battlefield, World War I* (New York: Benchmark Books, 2004), 63.

21. Johnson and Hillman, *Soissons 1918,* 7.

22. Asprey, *At Belleau Wood,* 32.

23. Ibid., 35.

24. Ibid., 50.

25. David Bonk, *Château Thierry & Belleau Wood 1918: America's Baptism of Fire on the Marne* (New York: Osprey, 2007), 40.

26. Simmons and Alexander, *Through the Wheat,* 82–84.

27. Asprey, *At Belleau Wood,* 43.

28. Bonk, *Château Thierry & Belleau Wood 1918,* 40.

29. Ibid., 14.

30. Ibid., 41

31. Ibid., 40–42.

32. Albertus W. Catlin, *"With the Help of God and a Few Marines": The Battles of Chateau Thierry and Belleau Wood* (Yardley: Westholme, 2013), 74–75.

33. John W. Thomason, Jr., *The United States Army Second Division Northwest of Chateau Thierry in World War I,* ed. G.B. Clark (Jefferson, NC: McFarland, 2006), 42.

Chapter 5

1. Elton E. Mackin, *Suddenly We Didn't Want to Die,* ed. G.B. Clark (Novato, CA, CA: Presidio Press, 1993), 25. The cry came from the wounded being evacuated as they watched the Marines moving forward to the front.

2. John J. Pershing, *My Experiences in the World War,* vol. 2 (New York: Harper and Row, 1931), 89–90.

3. James R. Scarbrough, *They Called Us Devil Dogs* (Scarbrough, 2005), 94.

4. Mark Mortensen, *George W. Hamilton, USMC: America's Greatest World War I Hero* (Jefferson, NC: McFarland, 2011), 75.

5. John W, Thomason, Jr., *The United States Army Second Division Northwest of Château Thierry in World War I,* ed. G.B. Clark (Jefferson, NC: McFarland, 2006), 47.

6. Mortensen, *George W. Hamilton,* 75.

7. Thomason, *The United States Army Second Division,* 38.

8. George B. Clark, *The Second Infantry Division in World War I: A History of the American Expeditionary Force Regulars, 1917–1919* (Jefferson, NC: McFarland, 2007), 45.

9. George B. Clark, *Devil Dogs Chronicle: Voices of the 4th Marine Brigade in World War I* (Lawrence: University Press of Kansas, 2013), 136–137.

10. Peter F. Owen, *To the Limit of Endurance: A Battalion of Marines in the Great War* (College Station: Texas A&M University Press, 2007), 39.

11. Clark, *The Second Infantry Division in World War I,* 46.

12. Ibid.

13. Thomason, *The United States Army Second Division,* 67.

14. Ibid., 69.

15. Brig. Gen. Edwin Howard Simmons, USMC (Ret), and Col. Joseph H. Alexander, USMC (Ret), *Through the Wheat: The U.S. Marines in World War I* (Annapolis: Naval Institute Press, 2008), xxiii; Ronald J. Brown, *A Few Good Me: A History of the Fighting Fifth Marines* (Novato, CA: Presidio Press, 2001), 28.

16. George B. Clark, *Devil Dogs, Fighting Marines of World War I* (Novato, CA: Presidio Press, 1999), 92.

17. Henry Berry, *Make the Kaiser Dance: Living Memoirs of the Doughboy* (New York: Arbor House, 1978), 79–80.

18. George B. Clark, *Decorated Marines of the Fourth Brigade in World War I* (Jefferson, NC: McFarland., 2007), 95.

19. Robert B. Asprey, *At Belleau Wood* (Denton: University of North Texas Press, 1996), 123.

20. Ibid., 122.

21. Frederick Wise and Meigs O. Frost, *A Marine Tells It to You* (New York: J.H. Sears, 1929), 206.

22. Ibid., 133.

23. Brown, *A Few Good Men,* 26.

24. Ibid., 27.

25. One account attributes the saying to L. Cpl. Brian A. Tanner while another says it was Colonel Neville and the 2nd Battalion Commander, Wise, claims that he said it. Williams was not alive to refute their claims.

26. Mackin, *Suddenly We Didn't Want to Die,* 6.

27. Thomason, *The United States Army Second Division,* 70.

28. Clark, *The Second Infantry Division in World War I,* 51.

29. Thomason, *The United States Army Second Division,* 71.

30. Alan Axelrod, *Miracle at Belleau Wood: The Birth of the Modern U.S. Marine Corps* (Guilford: Lyons Press, 2007), 112.

31. Clark, *Devil Dogs,* 98.

32. Harbord was right. The value of hachures was virtually nil. All they indicated was that something was there (see maps included in this history). The French maps were also old, made in 1832 and updated in 1912. They were 1:500000 scale, which was of little military value. Other military maps are better, showing elevation using contour lines, but the French maps were deceptive.

33. Asprey, *At Belleau Wood,* 140.

34. Clark, *The Second Infantry Division in World War I,* 52.

35. Clark, *Decorated Marines,* 111.

36. Albertus W. Catlin, *"With the Help of God and a Few Marines": The Battles of Chateau Thierry and Belleau Wood* (Yardley: Westholme, 2013), 105.

37. Axelrod, *Miracle at Belleau Wood,* 113.

38. Clark, *Devil Dogs,* 111.

39. Mortensen, *George W. Hamilton,* 78–79.

40. U.S. Navy, "History, Medal of Honor Recipients," http://www.history.navy.mil/search.html?q=medal+of+honor (accessed 18 March 2015).

41. Hamilton to Commandant Barnett, 19 November 1919, National Archives.

42. Mackin, *Suddenly We Didn't Want to Die*, 17–18.

43. Ibid., 44.

44. Axelrod, *Miracle at Belleau Wood*, 115–116.

45. Clark, *Decorated Marines*, 49.

46. Asprey, *At Belleau Wood*, 159.

47. Ibid., 152–153.

48. Ibid., 205.

49. Ibid.

50. Clark, *Decorated Marines*, 19.

51. Mortensen, *George W. Hamilton*, 76.

52. Thomason, *The United States Army Second Division*, 85.

53. Ibid., 93.

54. Simmons and Alexander, *Through the Wheat*, 103.

55. Brown, *A Few Good Men*, 36.

56. Asprey, *At Belleau Wood*, 162.

57. Brown, *A Few Good Men*, 36.

58. Years later and several wars after Belleau Wood when I took command of my battalion, the brigade commander cautioned me that if I wanted to be informed of what was going on don't rely on reports, get with the troops. I did.

59. Simmons and Alexander, *Through the Wheat*, 104.

60. The helmets provided protection and weighed two pounds. Years later I claimed that my similar helmet gave me a short neck and wore out the hair on my head.

61. Charles Anthony Wood, *Clifton Bledsoe Cates 1893–1970: Register of His Personal Papers* (Washington, DC: Headquarters, U.S. Marine Corps, 1985), 4.

62. Dick Camp, *The Devil Dogs at Belleau Wood: U.S. Marines in World War I* (Minneapolis: Zenith Press, 2008), 93.

63. Clark, *Decorated Marines*, 133.

64. Asprey, *At Belleau Wood*, 180.

65. Ibid., 197.

66. Ibid.

67. Ibid., 182.

68. Clark, *Devil Dogs*, 128.

69. Clark, *Decorated Marines*, 133.

70. Asprey, *At Belleau Wood*, 185.

71. Gilbert Hart, *Citizen Soldier I: World War I Recollections of Private James E. Hatcher, USMC*, 39.

72. J. Robert. Moskin, *The Story of the U.S. Marine Corps* (New York: Paddington Press, 1979), 113.

73. Clark, *The Second Infantry Division in World War I*, 54.

74. U.S. Navy, "History/Photos," http://www.history.navy.mil/photos/pers-us/uspers-o/w-osborn.htm (accessed 18 March 2015).

75. Clark, *Devil Dogs*, 89.

76. Asprey, *At Belleau Wood*, 204.

77. Clark, *The Second Infantry Division in World War I*, 64.

78. Clark, *Devil Dogs*, 145.

79. Don V. Paradis and Peter F. Owen, *The World War I Memoirs of Don V. Paradis, Gunnery Sergeant, USMC* (2010), 50–51.

80. Asprey, *At Belleau Wood*, 261.

81. Clark, *Decorated Marines*, 110.

82. Asprey, *At Belleau Wood*, 265.

83. Clark, *Decorated Marines*, 35.

84. Ibid., 198.

85. Wise and Frost, *A Marine Tells It to You*, 240–241.

86. Asprey, *At Belleau Wood*, 316.

87. Mackin, *Suddenly We Didn't Want to Die*, 50.

88. Scarbrough, *They Called Us Devil Dogs*, 101.

89. Brown, *A Few Good Men*, 49.

90. Camp, *The Devil Dogs at Belleau Wood*, 124.

91. Eric Ludendorff, *Ludendorff's Own Story, August 1914–November 1918*, vol. 2 (New York: Harper & Brothers, 1919), 269.

92. Pershing, *My Experiences in the World War*, 89–90.

93. Asprey, *At Belleau Wood*, 234–235.

94. George B. Clark, *The American Expeditionary Force in World War I: A Statistical History, 1917–1919* (Jefferson, NC: McFarland, 2013), 23.

95. Raymond P. Rogers, *Memoirs as Told to His Daughters*, 1.

96. Brown, *A Few Good Men*, 51.

97. The rumor was that selection was based upon uniform appearance, but a few members of the 5th went for other reasons. Henry Lenert of the 3rd Battalion went to be decorated for single-handedly capturing a German machine-gun company. He preferred to see the ladies in Paris instead and so he took French leave (went AWOL).

Chapter 6

1. Douglas V. Johnson II and Rolfe L. Hillman, Jr., *Soissons 1918* (College Station: Texas A&M University Press, 1999), A 6–7.

2. The French equivalent of the U.S. Independence Day.

3. Johnson and Hillman, *Soissons 1918*, 14–15.

4. Ronald J. Brown, *A Few Good Men: A History of the Fighting Fifth Marines* (Novato, CA: Presidio Press, 2001), 52.

5. Johnson and Hillman, *Soissons 1918*, 40.

6. Camions had small wheels and no springs and were usually driven by French colonial troops who seemed to enjoy the pain that they inflicted when hitting every pothole. Nevertheless, camions were better than a long foot march.

7. Johnson and Hillman, *Soissons 1918*, 62.

8. Mark Mortensen, *George W. Hamilton, USMC: America's Greatest World War I Hero* (Jefferson, NC: McFarland, 2011), 99.

9. Louis C. Linn, *At Belleau Wood with Rifle and Sketchpad* (Jefferson, NC: McFarland, 2012), 99.

10. Brown, *A Few Good Men*, 53.

11. U.S. Navy, "History, Medal of Honor Recipients," http://www.history.navy.mil/search.html?q=medal+of+honor (accessed 18 March 2015).

12. U.S. Navy, "History, Medal of Honor Recipients," http://www.history.navy.mil/search.html?q=medal+of+honor (accessed 18 March 2015).

13. George B. Clark, *Decorated Marines of the Fourth Brigade in World War I* (Jefferson, NC: McFarland, 2007), 104.

14. Brown, *A Few Good Men,* 57.

15. Linn, *At Belleau Wood with Rifle and Sketchpad,* 110–111.

16. Brown, *A Few Good Men,* 58.

17. Ibid.

18. Raymond P. Rogers, *Memoirs as Told to His Daughters,* 2.

Chapter 7

1. Elton E. Mackin, *Suddenly We Didn't Want to Die,* ed. G.B. Clark (Novato, CA: Presidio Press, 1993), 139–140.

2. Ronald J. Brown, *A Few Good Men: A History of the Fighting Fifth Marines* (Novato, CA: Presidio Press, 2001), 58–61.

3. American Battle Monuments Commission, *American Armies and Battlefields in Europe: A History, Guide and Reference Book* (Washington, DC: Government Printing Office, 1938), 105–107.

4. Louis C. Linn, *At Belleau Wood with Rifle and Sketchpad* (Jefferson, NC: McFarland, 2012), 141.

5. Mark Mortensen, *George W. Hamilton, USMC: America's Greatest World War I Hero* (Jefferson, NC: McFarland, 2011), 108.

6. George B. Clark, *The Second Infantry Division in World War I: A History of the American Expeditionary Force Regulars, 1917–1919* (Jefferson, NC: McFarland, 2007), 122.

7. Linn, *At Belleau Wood with Rifle and Sketchpad,* 144–145.

8. George B. Clark, *Devil Dogs, Fighting Marines of World War I* (Novato, CA: Presidio Press, 1999), 276.

9. Ibid., 280.

10. U.S. Navy, "History, Medal of Honor Recipients," http://www.history.navy.mil/search.html?q=medal+of+honor (accessed 18 March 2015).

11. Clark, *The Second Infantry Division in World War I,* 131.

12. Clark, *Devil Dogs,* 283.

13. Brown, *A Few Good Men,* 62–63; Clark, *Devil Dogs,* 285.

14. Paul Gardner to Mr. and Mrs. Chas Gardener, 16 September 1918. Paul Gardner was a dispatch rider and proud of his Indian motorcycle.

Chapter 8

1. George B. Clark, *Decorated Marines of the Fourth Brigade in World War I* (Jefferson, NC: McFarland, 2007), 6.

2. George B. Clark, *The Second Infantry Division in World War I: A History of the American Expeditionary Force Regulars, 1917–1919* (Jefferson, NC: McFarland, 2007), 139–143.

3. American Battle Monuments Commission, *American Armies and Battlefields in Europe: A History, Guide and Reference Book* (Washington, DC: Government Printing Office, 1938), 352.

4. Clark, *The Second Infantry Division in World War I,* 144.

5. Peter F. Owen, *To the Limit of Endurance: A Bat-*

talion of Marines in the Great War (College Station: Texas A&M University Press, 2007), 108.

6. U.S. Navy, "History, Medal of Honor Recipients," http://www.history.navy.mil/search.html?q=medal+of+honor (accessed 18 March 2015).

7. U.S. Navy, "History, Medal of Honor Recipients," http://www.history.navy.mil/search.html?q=medal+of+honor (accessed 18 March 2015).

8. Mark Mortensen, *George W. Hamilton, USMC: America's Greatest World War I Hero* (Jefferson, NC: McFarland, 2011), 131.

9. Ronald J. Brown, *A Few Good Men: A History of the Fighting Fifth Marines* (Novato, CA: Presidio Press, 2001), 68.

10. Clark, *Decorated Marines of the Fourth Brigade in World War I,* 96.

11. Ibid., 28.

12. Ibid., 178–179.

13. Elton E. Mackin, *Suddenly We Didn't Want to Die,* ed. G.B. Clark (Novato, CA: Presidio Press, 1993), 203.

14. Clark, *Decorated Marines,* 72.

15. Ibid., 50.

16. Brown, *A Few Good Men,* 64–68.

17. Mackin, *Suddenly We Didn't Want to Die,* 182.

18. Clark, *Decorated Marines,* 6.

19. Brown, *A Few Good Men,* 70.

20. Mortensen, *George W. Hamilton,* 143.

Chapter 9

1. American Battle Monuments Commission, *American Armies and Battlefields in Europe: A History, Guide and Reference Book* (Washington, DC: Government Printing Office, 1938), 304.

2. Raymond P. Rogers, *Memoirs as Told to His Daughters,* 5.

3. Mark Mortensen, *George W. Hamilton, USMC: America's Greatest World War I Hero* (Jefferson, NC: McFarland, 2011), 154.

4. Ibid., 160.

5. George B. Clark, *Decorated Marines of the Fourth Brigade in World War I* (Jefferson, NC: McFarland, 2007), 50.

6. Mortensen, *George W. Hamilton,* 165.

7. Ronald J. Brown, *A Few Good Men: A History of the Fighting Fifth Marines* (Novato, CA: Presidio Press, 2001), 74–75.

8. Peter F. Owen, *To the Limit of Endurance: A Battalion of Marines in the Great War* (College Station: Texas A&M University Press, 2007), 198–199.

9. Richard Rubin, *The Last of the Doughboys: The Forgotten Generation and Their Forgotten World War* (New York: Houghton Mifflin Harcourt, 2013), 183.

10. Elton E. Mackin, *Suddenly We Didn't Want to Die,* ed. G.B. Clark (Novato, CA: Presidio Press, 1993), 264.

11. James R. Scarbrough, *They Called Us Devil Dogs* (Scarbrough, 2005), 164.

12. Louis C. Linn, *At Belleau Wood with Rifle and Sketchpad* (Jefferson, NC: McFarland, 2012), 153.

13. Levi Hemrick, *Once a Marine* (Staunton: Clarion, 2014), 177.

14. Warren R., Jackson, *His Time in Hell, a Texas*

Marine in France: The World War I Memoir of Warren R. Jackson, ed. G.B. Clark (Novato, CA: Presidio Press, 2001), 211.

15. Carl Andrew Brannen, *Over There: A Marine in the Great War* (College Station: Texas A&M University Press, 1996), 56.

16. Charles Anthony Wood, *Clifton Bledsoe Cates 1893–1970: Register of His Personal Papers* (Washington, DC: Headquarters, U.S. Marine Corps, 1985), 5.

Chapter 10

1. Raymond P. Rogers, *Memoirs as Told to His Daughters,* 3. History does not record the exploits of the 5th Marines in Russia. Only a few comments on Marines are found in the writings of their service in the Russian intervention.

2. Title of a 1940s film and other works that described life between the wars.

3. Center of Military History, *United States Army in the World War, 1917–1919,* vol. 11: *American Occupation of Germany* (Honolulu: University Press of the Pacific, 2005), 209.

4. American Battle Monuments Commission, *American Armies and Battlefields in Europe: A History, Guide and Reference Book* (Washington, DC: Government Printing Office, 1938), 492–493.

5. George B. Clark, *The Second Infantry Division in World War I: A History of the American Expeditionary Force Regulars, 1917–1919* (Jefferson, NC: McFarland, 2007), 179.

6. Center of Military History, *American Occupation of Germany,* 15–16.

7. Ibid., 29.

8. Ibid., 28.

9. Ibid., 36.

10. John W. Thomason, Jr., *Fix Bayonets!* (Uckfield, East Sussex: Naval and Military Press, 2009), 236–245.

11. M. Eggr to C.F. Eggr, 15 February 1919.

12. Center of Military History, *American Occupation of Germany,* 210.

13. Ibid., 203.

14. Rogers, *Memoirs as Told to His Daughters,* 2.

15. Similarly, homes in the South after the U.S. Civil War could be seen with walls papered with Confederate money.

16. Center of Military History, *American Occupation of Germany,* 223.

17. Ibid., 123.

18. Ibid., 130.

19. Virginia Schomp, *Letters from the Battlefield, World War I* (New York: Benchmark Books, 2004), 76.

20. Ronald J. Brown, *A Few Good Men: A History of the Fighting Fifth Marines* (Novato, CA: Presidio Press, 2001), 78–79.

21. Edwin N. McClellan, *The United States Marine Corps in the World War* (Washington, DC: Headquarters, USMC, 1920), 57–58.

22. Ibid., 109.

23. Ibid., 13.

24. Ibid., 9.

25. Ibid., 61.

26. Carl J. Richard, *When the United States Invaded Russia* (New York: Rowman & Littlefield, 2013), 171.

Biographical Dictionary

1. Ronald J. Brown, *A Few Good Men: A History of the Fighting Fifth Marines* (Novato, CA: Presidio Press, 2001), 84; http://www.history.navy.mil/photos/awd/us-indiv/moh-10.htm.

2. Brig. Gen. Edwin Howard Simmons, USMC (Ret), and Col. Joseph H. Alexander, USMC (Ret), *Through the Wheat: The U.S. Marines in World War I* (Annapolis: Naval Institute Press, 2008), 71.

3. George B. Clark, *Decorated Marines of the Fourth Brigade in World War I* (Jefferson, NC: McFarland, 2007), 133.

4. U.S. Navy, "History, Medal of Honor Recipients," http://www.history.navy.mil/search.html?q=medal+of+honor (accessed 18 March 2015).

5. Ibid.

6. Clark, *Decorated Marines,* 159.

7. U.S. Navy, "History, Medal of Honor Recipients," http://www.history.navy.mil/search.html?q=medal+of+honor (accessed 18 March 2015).

8. Ibid.

9. Elton E. Mackin, *Suddenly We Didn't Want to Die,* ed. G.B. Clark (Novato, CA: Presidio Press, 1993), 12–13.

10. Alan Axelrod, *Miracle at Belleau Wood: The Birth of the Modern U.S. Marine Corps* (Guilford: Lyons Press, 2007), 34.

11. U.S. Navy, "History, Medal of Honor Recipients," http://www.history.navy.mil/search.html?q=medal+of+honor (accessed 18 March 2015).

12. E.B. Sledge, *With the Old Breed* (Novato, CA: Presidio Press, 2010).

13. Clark, *Decorated Marines,* 111.

Epilogue

1. Ronald J. Brown, *A Few Good Men: A History of the Fighting Fifth Marines* (Novato, CA: Presidio Press, 2001), 85.

2. Butler commanded the 13th Marine Regiment during World War I and was also the most decorated Marine in its history.

3. Brown, *A Few Good Men,* 86–87.

4. Robert N. Webb, *The Bonus March on Washington, D.C., May–June, 1932* (New York: Franklin Watts, 1969), 18.

5. Donald J. Lisio, *The President and Protest: Hoover, MacArthur and the Bonus Army* (New York: Fordham University Press, 1994), 49–50.

6. Paul Dickson and Thomas B. Allen, *The Bonus Army: An American Epic* (New York: Walter, 2004), 57–58.

7. Walter W. Waters, *B.E.F.: The Whole Story of the Bonus Army* (New York: John Day, 1933), 16.

8. John Henry Bartlett, *The Bonus March and the New Deal* (Chicago: M.A. Donohue, 1937), 14.

9. Martin L. Fausold, *The Presidency of Herbert C. Hoover* (Lawrence: University Press of Kansas, 1985), 161.

10. Jean Edwards Smith, *FDR* (New York: Random House, 2007), 284.

11. Her taunt would haunt her for years afterward and explains the antipathy of soldiers, veterans and their families toward her.

12. Waters, *B.E.F.,* 127.

13. Ibid., 177.

14. Smith, *FDR,* 28.

15. Felix Morrow, *The Bonus March* (New York: International, 1932), 10.

16. Dickinson and Allen, *The Bonus Army,* 53.

17. Ibid., 55.

18. Waters, *B.E.F.,* 188.

19. Ibid., 209.

20. Carlo D'Este, *Eisenhower: A Soldier's Life* (New York: Henry Holt, 2002), 220.

21. As always, when anything bad happened the reaction was "The Reds did it." See Waters, *B.E.F.,* 214.

22. Ibid., 226.

23. D'Este, *Eisenhower,* 221.

24. Dickson and Allen, *The Bonus Army,* 292.

25. D'Este, *Eisenhower,* 224.

26. Waters, *B.E.F.,* 223.

27. William Manchester, *American Caesar: Douglas MacArthur 1880–1964* (Boston: Little, Brown, 1978), 150. Eisenhower as president fired Lieutenant General Gavin for insubordination. It is apparent that the two did not see eye to eye on many things.

28. D'Este, *Eisenhower,* 221.

29. MacArthur's deputy, Mosely, wrote in his memoirs that he delivered Hoover's order to MacArthur, who was very much annoyed that his plans were being interfered with. See D'Este, *Eisenhower,* 222. There are several other versions of the delivery of Hoover's order, but all imply or state that MacArthur deliberately disobeyed the order.

30. Dickson and Allen, *The Bonus Army,* 194.

31. Smith, *FDR,* 284.

32. *Washington Post,* 4 August 1932, 6.

33. Some myths appeared, such as that of the boy who was bayoneted while trying to save his pet rabbit from the fire, but the truth was bad enough. Civilians were gassed and bayoneted, including some not involved in the Bonus Army. The whole affair was a national disaster.

34. John Henry Bartlett, *The Bonus March and the New Deal* (Chicago: M.A. Donohue, 1937), 70.

35. Smith, *FDR,* 285.

36. Manchester, *American Caesar,* 152.

37. Ibid., 149.

38. FDR criticized Hoover for not meeting with Bonus Army representatives. It appears that FDR learned from Hoover's mistakes. See Smith, *FDR,* 284.

39. Ibid., 260.

40. Webb, *The Bonus March on Washington,* 63.

41. Dickson and Allen, *The Bonus Army,* 276.

42. Ibid., 247.

43. Brown, *A Few Good Men,* 114.

44. Sledge, *With the Old Breed,* 277–278.

45. Michael A. Eggleston, *Exiting Vietnam: The Era of Vietnamization and American Withdrawal Revealed in First Hand Accounts* (Jefferson, NC: McFarland, 2014), 181.

Appendix A

1. David Bonk, *Château Thierry & Belleau Wood 1918: America's Baptism of Fire on the Marne* (New York: Osprey, 2007), 11; United Kingdom, "Learning Center, World War I," http://www.historylearningsite.co.uk/1918_world_war_one.htm (accessed 18 March 2015).

Appendix B

1. Some say it was named for the designer's wife, but if so, he never admitted naming it for his wife.

Appendix C

1. George B. Clark, *The American Expeditionary Force in World War I: A Statistical History, 1917–1919* (Jefferson, NC: McFarland, 2007) 69–70.

2. Edwin N. McClellan, *The United States Marine Corps in the World War* (Washington, DC: Headquarters, USMC, 1920), 29.

3. George B. Clark, *The Second Infantry Division in World War I: A History of the American Expeditionary Force Regulars, 1917–1919* (Jefferson, NC: McFarland, 2007), 202–205.

Bibliography

Primary Sources

Books

Barkley, John Lewis. *Scarlet Fields: The Combat Memoir of a World War I Medal of Honor Hero.* Lawrence: University Press of Kansas, 2012.

Blumenson, Martin. *The Patton Papers.* Boston: Houghton Mifflin, 1972.

Brannen, Carl Andrew. *Over There: A Marine in the Great War.* College Station: Texas A&M University Press, 1996.

Catlin, Albertus W. *"With the Help of God and a Few Marines": The Battles of Chateau Thierry and Belleau Wood.* Yardley: Westholme, 2013.

Evans, Frank E. *Daddy Pat of the Marines.* New York: Frederick A. Stokes, 1919.

Hemrick, Levi. *Once a Marine.* Staunton: Clarion, 2014.

Jackson, Warren R. *His Time in Hell, a Texas Marine in France: The WWI Memoir of Warren R. Jackson.* Edited by G.B. Clark. Novato, CA: Presidio Press, 2001.

Linn, Louis C. *At Belleau Wood with Rifle and Sketchpad.* Jefferson, NC: McFarland, 2012.

Ludendorff, Erich. *Ludendorff's Own Story, August 1914–November 1918.* 2 vols. New York: Harper & Brothers, 1919.

Mackin, Elton E. *Suddenly We Didn't Want to Die.* Edited by G.B. Clark. Novato, CA: Presidio Press, 1993.

Manley, Milford N. *The World War I Letters of Private Milford N. Manley.* Gardner: Dageforde, 1995.

March, William. *Company K.* Tuscaloosa: University of Alabama Press, 1933. William March was the pen name of James E. Campbell, 55th Company, 2nd Battalion, 5th Marine Regiment.

Paradis, Don V., and Peter F. Owen. *The World War I Memoirs of Don V. Paradis, Gunnery Sergeant, USMC.* 2010.

Pershing, John J. *My Experiences in the World War.* 2 vols. New York: Harper and Row, 1931.

Pickard, Dewey C. *My War: One Marine's Journey to Iwo Jima and Back Again.* 2012.

Rendinell, J.E., and George Pattullo. *One Man's War: The Diary of a Leatherneck.* New York: J.H. Sears, 1928.

Sledge, E.B. *With the Old Breed.* Novato, CA: Presidio Press, 2010.

Thomason, John W., Jr. *Fix Bayonets!* Uckfield, East Sussex: The Naval and Military Press, 2009.

Wise, Frederic, and Meigs O. Frost. *A Marine Tells It to You.* New York: J.H. Sears, 1929.

Articles

New York World-Telegram and Sun, 16 April 1951.
Washington Post, 29 July 1932.

Documents

Federal Bureau of Investigation. *Bonus Army.* Washington, DC: 1932.

Hamilton to Commandant Barnett, 19 November 1919, National Archives.

Unpublished Materials

Blair, Leo, to Luceile Hinkley, 28 June 1918.
 to Luceile Hinkley, 7 July 1918.
 to Luceile Hinkley, 22 July 1918.
 to Luceile Hinkley, 26 July 1918.
 to Luceile Hinkley, 3 August 1918.
 to Luceile Hinkley, 5 August 1918.
 to Luceile Hinkley, 19 August 1918.
 to Luceile Hinkley, 20 September 1918.
 to Luceile Hinkley, 12 October 1918.

Cleveland, Richard, to Helen Ericson, 12 August 1918.
 to Helen Ericson, 2 February 1919.

Collins, William N., to Mrs. Mary F. Collins, 9 January 1918.

Eggr, Matthew, Matt Eggr, to C.F. Eggr, 15 February 1919.

Davis, Roland E., to Ed Davis, 29 January 1919.
 to Miss Ruth Davis, 19 February 1919.

Elmer, William E., to Bro, 31 December 1917.
 to brother Farmer Ted, February 1918.
 to Brother Ted, 21 January 1918.
 to Farmer brother Ted, 8 January 1918.
 to Lillian M. Elmer, 31 September 1917.
 to Lilian M. Elmer, 23 November 1917.
 to Lilian M. Elmer, 24 November 1917.
 to Lilian M. Elmer, 14 December 1917.
 to Lilian M. Elmer, 23 December 1917.
 to Lilian M. Elmer, 31 December 1917.
 to Lilian M. Elmer, 8 January 1918.
 to Lilian M. Elmer, 14 January 1918.

to Lilian M. Elmer, 21 January 1918.
to Lilian M. Elmer, 28 January 1918.
to Lilian M. Elmer, February 1918.
to Lilian M. Elmer, 4 February 1918.
to Lilian M. Elmer, 14 February 1918.
to Lillian M. Elmer, 23 March 1918.
to Lillian M. Elmer, 14 April 1918.
to Lilian M. Elmer, 27 April 1918
to Mrs. Henry Tatge, 13 May 1918.
to Mrs. Henry Tatge, 4 June 1918.
to Mrs. Henry Tatge, 12 January 1919.
to Parents, Bros and Sisters, 14 November 1917.
Fay, William, to Mr. George Shipway, 25 April 1918.
to Mr. George Shipway, 19 July 1918.
to Mr. George Shipway, 10 August 1918.
to Mr. George Shipway, 14 August 1918.
to Mr. George Shipway, 30 September 1918.
to Mr. George Shipway, 20 October 1918.
to Mr. George Shipway, 27 November 1918.
to Mr. George Shipway, 8 December 1918.
to Mr. George Shipway, 17 December 1918.
to Mr. George Shipway, 4 January 1919.
5th Marine Regiment Roster, USMC Historical Division, Quantico, Virginia.
Gaggin, Verner S., to Mrs. Verner S. Gaggin, 18 October 1918.
to Mrs. Verner S. Gaggin, 19 October 1918.
to Mrs. Verner S. Gaggin, 21 October 1918.
to Mrs. Verner S. Gaggin, 24 October 1918.
to Mrs. Verner S. Gaggin, 7 December 1918.
Gardner, Paul, to Mr. and Mrs. Chas Gardener, 16 September 1918.
Hart, Gilbert. "Citizen Soldier I: World War I Recollections of Private James E. Hatcher, USMC."
Hatcher, Col James E., AUS (Ret.). "A Memoir of Service in WW I as a Private, USMC." Unpublished manuscript, n.d., Marine Corps Archives, Gray Research Center, Quantico, Virginia.
Illustrated Memoir of the World War, 1930.
Rogers, Raymond P. *Memoirs as Told to His Daughters.*
Smutz, Earl H., to Sister, 20 April 1919.
Tatge, Lillian M., to William Edward Elmer, 10 September 1918.
Wetzel, William, to Lillian M. Elmer, 7 November 1917.
to Lilian M. Elmer, 4 December 1917.
to Lillian M. Elmer, 27 December 1917.
to Lillian M. Elmer, 8 March 1918.
to Mr. and Mrs. Henry Tatge, 30 September 1918.
to Mr. and Mrs. Henry Tatge, 26 February 1919.
to Mr. and Mrs. Henry Tatge, 16 May 1918.
to Mr. and Mrs. Henry Tatge, 28 May 1918.
to Mr. and Mrs. Henry Tatge, 30 March 1919.
to Mr. Henry Tatge, 31 September 1917.
to Mr. Henry Tatge, 29 December 1918.

Secondary Sources

Books

Abt, John J. *Advocate and Activist: Memoirs of an American Communist Lawyer.* Chicago: Board of Trustees of the University of Illinois, 1993.

American Battle Monuments Commission. *American Armies and Battlefields in Europe: A History, Guide and Reference Book.* Washington, DC: Government Printing Office, 1938.

Asprey, Robert B. *At Belleau Wood.* Denton: University of North Texas Press, 1996.

Association of Graduates, United States Military Academy. *The Register of Graduates and Former Cadets of the United States Military, 2010.* West Point: Association of Graduates, 2010.

Axelrod, Alan. *Miracle at Belleau Wood: The Birth of the Modern U.S. Marine Corps.* Guilford, CT: Lyons Press, 2007.

Barry, John M. *The Great Influenza: The Story of the Deadliest Pandemic in History.* New York: Penguin Books, 2004.

Bartlett, John Henry. *The Bonus March and the New Deal.* Chicago: M.A. Donohue, 1937.

Berry, Henry. *Make the Kaiser Dance: Living Memoirs of the Doughboy.* New York: Arbor House, 1978.

Bettez, David J. *Kentucky Marine: Major General Logan Feland and the Making of the Modern USMC.* Lexington: University Press of Kentucky, 2014.

Blond, Georges. *The Marne.* Harrisburg, PA: Stackpole Books, 1962.

Bonk, David. *Château Thierry & Belleau Wood 1918: America's Baptism of Fire on the Marne.* New York: Osprey, 2007.

Brook-Shepherd, Gordon. *November 1918.* Boston: Little, Brown, 1981.

Brown, Ronald J. *A Few Good Men: A History of the Fighting Fifth Marines.* Novato, CA: Presidio Press, 2001.

Burns, Ross. *The WW I Album.* New York: Brompton Books, 1991.

Burrows, William E. *Richthofen.* New York: Brace & World, 1969.

Byerly, Carol R. *Fever of War: The Influenza Epidemic in the U.S. Army During World War I.* New York: New York University Press, 2005.

Camp, Dick. *The Devil Dogs at Belleau Wood: U.S. Marines in World War I.* Minneapolis: Zenith Press, 2008.

Capozzola, Christopher. *Uncle Sam Wants You: World War I and the Making of the Modern American Citizen.* Oxford: Oxford University Press, 2008.

Carnes, Mark C., and John A. Garraty. *American Destiny: Narrative of a Nation.* Vol. 2, *Since 1865.* New York: Penguin Academics, 2006.

Center of Military History. *United States Army in the World War, 1917–1919.* Honolulu: University Press of the Pacific, 2005.

_____. *United States Army in the World War, 1917–1919.* Vol. 11, *American Occupation of Germany.* Honolulu: University Press of the Pacific, 2005.

Chafe, William H. *The Rise and Fall of the American Century: The United States from 1890–2009.* New York: Oxford University Press, 2009.

Clark, George B. *The American Expeditionary Force in World War I: A Statistical History, 1917–1919.* Jefferson, NC: McFarland, 2013.

_____. *Decorated Marines of the Fourth Brigade in World War I.* Jefferson, NC: McFarland, 2007.

_____. *Devil Dogs Chronicle: Voices of the 4th Marine*

Brigade in World War I. Lawrence: University Press of Kansas, 2013.

_____. *Devil Dogs, Fighting Marines of World War I.* Novato, CA: Presidio Press, 1999.

_____ *The Second Infantry Division in World War I: A History of the American Expeditionary Force Regulars, 1917–1919.* Jefferson, NC: McFarland, 2007.

Cowing, Kemper Frey. *"Dear Folks at Home…": The Glorious Story of the United States Marines in France as Told by their Letters from the Battlefield.* New York: Houghton Mifflin, 1919.

Creation Films. *War Diaries, Letters from the Front.* Quebec: Madacy Entertainment, 2008.

Crosby, Alfred W. *America's Forgotten Pandemic: The Influenza of 1918.* New York: Cambridge University Press, 2003.

Cudahy, John. *Archangel the American War with Russia.* Chicago: A.C. McClurg, 1924.

Dallek, Robert. *Harry S. Truman.* New York: Henry Holt, 2008.

Daniels, Roger. *The Bonus March: An Episode of the Great Depression.* Westport, CT: Greenwood, 1971.

Davis, Arthur Kyle. *Virginia War Letters, Diaries, and Editorials.* Richmond: Executive Committee State Capitol, 1925.

D'Este, Carlo. *Eisenhower: A Soldier's Life.* New York: Henry Holt, 2002.

Dickson, Paul, and Thomas B. Allen. *The Bonus Army: An American Epic.* New York: Walter, 2004.

Eggleston, Michael A. *Exiting Vietnam: The Era of Vietnamization and American Withdrawal Revealed in First Hand Accounts.* Jefferson, NC: McFarland, 2014.

Evans, Martin. *Retreat, Hell! We Just Got Here!* Oxford: Osprey, 1998.

Fausold, Martin L. *The Presidency of Herbert C. Hoover.* Lawrence: University Press of Kansas, 1985.

Foner, Eric. *The New American History.* Philadelphia: Temple University Press, 1997.

Freidel, Frank. *Over There: The Story of America's First Great Overseas Crusade.* New York: Bramhall House, 1964.

Goodspeed, D.J. *The German Wars.* Boston: Houghton Mifflin, 1977.

Gutierrez, Edward A. *Doughboys on the Great War: How American Soldiers Viewed Their Military Experience.* Lawrence: University of Kansas Press, 2014.

Henry, Mark R., and Darko Pavlovic. *US Marine Corps in WW I 1917–1918.* Oxford: Osprey, 1999.

Hill, J. Wayne. *A Regiment like No Other: The 6th Marine Regiment at Belleau Wood.* Fort Leavenworth: U.S. Command and General Staff College, 2012.

Hirshson, Stanley P. *General Patton: A Soldier's Life.* New York: HarperCollins Books, 2002.

History and Museums Division. *A Brief History of the 6th Marines.* Washington, DC: Headquarters, U.S. Marine Corps, 1987.

Homsher, David C. *American Battlefields of WW I: Château-Thierry—Then and Now.* San Mateo: Battlefield Productions, 2006.

Johnson, Douglas V., II, and Rolfe L. Hillman, Jr. *Soissons 1918.* College Station: Texas A&M University Press, 1999.

Keegan, John. *The First World War.* New York: Vintage Books, 2000.

Kent, Susan Kingsley. *The Influenza Pandemic of 1918–1919: A Brief History of Documents.* Boulder: University of Colorado, 2013.

Kindall, Sylvian G. *American Soldiers in Siberia.* New York: Richard R. Smith, 1945.

Kolata, Gina. *Flu: The Story of the Great Influenza Pandemic of 1918 and the Search for the Virus That Caused It.* New York: Touchstone, 1999.

Langer, Adam. *My Father's Bonus March.* New York: Spiegel & Grau, 2009.

Lisio, Donald J. *The President and Protest: Hoover, MacArthur and the Bonus Army.* New York: Fordham University Press, 1994.

MacArthur, Douglas. *Reminiscences.* New York: McGraw-Hill, 1964.

Manchester, William. *American Caesar: Douglas MacArthur 1880–1964.* Boston: Little, Brown, 1978.

McClellan, Edwin N. *The United States Marine Corps in the World War.* Washington, DC: Headquarters, USMC, 1920.

McCullough, David. *Truman.* New York: Simon & Schuster, 1992.

Moore, Joel R. *The History of the American Expedition Fighting the Bolsheviki, Campaigning in North Russia 1918–1919.* Forgotten Books, 2012.

Morrow, Felix. *The Bonus March.* New York: International, 1932.

Mortensen, Mark. *George W. Hamilton, USMC: America's Greatest World War I Hero.* Jefferson, NC: McFarland, 2011.

Moskin, J. Robert. *The Story of the U.S. Marine Corps.* New York: Paddington Press, 1979.

Oates, Stephen B., and Charles J. Errico. *Portrait of America.* Vol. 2, *From Reconstruction to the Present.* Boston: Houghton Mifflin, 2007.

Owen Peter F. *To the Limit of Endurance: A Battalion of Marines in the Great War.* College Station: Texas A&M University Press, 2007.

Prost, Jay, and Antoine Winter. *The Great War in History.* New York: Cambridge University Press, 2005.

Remak, Joachim. *The First World War.* New York: John Wiley & Sons, 1971.

_____. *The Origins of World War I: 1871–1914.* Hinsdale, IL: Dryden Press, 1967.

Richard, Carl J. *When the United States Invaded Russia.* New York: Rowman & Littlefield, 2013.

Rickenbacker, Edward V. *Rickenbacher.* Engelwood Cliffs, NJ: Prentice-Hall, 1967.

Rubin, Richard. *The Last of the Doughboys: The Forgotten Generation and Their Forgotten World War.* New York: Houghton Mifflin Harcourt, 2013.

Scarbrough, James R. *They Called Us Devil Dogs.* Scarbrough, 2005.

Schomp, Virginia. *Letters from the Battlefield, WW I.* New York: Benchmark Books, 2004.

Sibley, Burton W. *History of the Third Battalion, Sixth Marine Regiment, U.S. Marines.* Hillsdale: Akers, Mac Ritchie & Hurburt, 1919.

Simmons, Brig. Gen. Edwin Howard, USMC (Ret), and Col. Joseph H. Alexander, USMC (Ret). *Through the*

Wheat: The U.S. Marines in World War I. Annapolis: Naval Institute Press, 2008.

Simpson, Colin. *The Lusitania.* Boston: Little, Brown, 1972.

Smith, Jean Edwards. *FDR.* New York: Random House, 2007.

Solzhenitsyn, Alexander. *August 1914.* New York: Farrar, Straus and Giroux, 1971.

Spielvogel, Jackson J. *Western Civilization.* Vol. 2. Belmont, CA: Thomson/Wadsworth, 2006.

Sullivan, Rebecca M. *Let Every Day Take Care of Itself: Letters to My Wife Stateside.* Nanosniche Books, 2008.

Terry, Charles. *Wilson's War: American in the First World War.* Np: CreateSpace, 2011.

Thomason, John W. *The United States Army Second Division Northwest of Chateau Thierry in World War I.* Edited by G.B. Clark. Jefferson, NC: McFarland, 2006.

Trotsky, Leon. *History of the Russian Revolution.* New York: Pathfinder, 1932.

Tuchman, Barbara W. *The Guns of August.* New York: Ballantine Books, 1962.

Turner, Martha Anne. *The World of John W. Thomason, USMC.* Austin: Eakin Press, 1984.

Vintage Library. *Massive Collection of WW1.* Vintage Library, 2010.

Waters, W.W. *B.E.F.: The Whole Story of the Bonus Army.* New York: John Day, 1933.

Webb, Robert N. *The Bonus March on Washington, D.C., May–June, 1932.* New York: Franklin Watts, 1969.

Willett, Robert L. *Russian Sideshow, America's Undeclared War.* Washington, DC: Potomac Books, 2003.

Winter, Jay, and Blaine Baggett. *The Great War and the Shaping of the 20th Century.* New York: Penguin Studio, 1996.

Wittner, Lawrence S. *MacArthur: Great Lives Observed.* Englewood Cliffs, NJ: Prentice-Hall, 1971.

Wood, Charles Anthony. *Clifton Bledsoe Cates 1893–1970: Register of His Personal Papers.* Washington, DC: Headquarters, U.S. Marine Corps, 1985.

Articles

Killigrew, John W. "The Army and the Bonus Incident." *Military Affairs* 26, no. 2 (Summer 1962).

Lisio, Donald J. "A Blunder Becomes Catastrophe: Hoover, the Legion, and the Bonus Army." *The Wisconsin Magazine of History* 51, no. 1 (Autumn 1967).

Merrow, Alexander. "Belleau Wood." *Marine Corps Gazette,* 8 November 2008.

"Newburgh Heritage." *Mid Hudson Times,* 10 July 2013.

Vivian, James F. and Jean H. "The Bonus March of 1932: The Role of General George Van Horn Mosely." *The Wisconsin Magazine of History* 51, no. 1 (Autumn 1967).

Washington Post, 4 August 1932.

Television Programs and Other Broadcast Sources

Dickson, Paul, Thomas B. Allen, and Robert Uth. *The March of the Bonus Army.* Directed by Robert Uth. Washington, DC: Public Broadcasting System, 2006.

Internet

Congressional Medal of Honor Society. "Archive." http://www.cmohs.org/recipient-archive.php (accessed 17 February 2015).

Historical Society of Washington, D.C. "Collections." http://www.dchistory.org/research/about-library-collections/ (accessed 18 March 2015).

Kansas State Historical Society. "James G. Harbord: A Kansas Portrait." www.kshs.org/kansapedia/james-g-harbord/12079 (accessed 17 March 2015).

U.S. Defense Department. "Medal of Honor Recipients." http://valor.defense.gov/Recipients/NavyMedalofHonorRecipients.aspx#p (accessed 17 February 2015).

U.S. Government. "Cates." http://www.arlingtoncemetery.net/cates.htm (accessed 18 March 2015).

U.S. Government. "Holcomb." http://www.arlingtoncemetery.net/tholcomb.htm (accessed 18 March 2015).

U.S. Marine Corps. "History." http://www.history.usmc.mil (accessed 17 February 2015).

U.S. Navy. "History." http://www.naval-history.net (accessed 30 January 2015).

U.S. 2nd Division Engineers. "5th Regiment." http://2nd-engineers.us/2nd-division/5thmarines.htm (accessed 18 March 2015).

Index

Numbers in *bold italics* indicate pages with photographs.